Diversity
IN Action

**Using Adventure Activities
to Explore Issues of Diversity
with Middle School
and High School Age Youth**

Sharon Chappelle & Lisa Bigman

with Francesca Hillyer

AND CONTRIBUTIONS FROM

Jo Ann Morris-Scott, IlaSahai Prouty, and Bart Crawford

A Project Adventure Publication

Copyright © 1998 by Project Adventure, Inc.

ISBN 0-536-01175-3

Printed in the United States of America

Foreword

Diversity in Action is a comprehensive, informative, and progressive book. As clinical psychologists, parents, authors, and lecturers, we are impressed with the innovative approaches, techniques, and exercises in this workbook. From childhood to later years, we never stop thinking about diversity and often that thinking involves being disturbed about our feelings toward other groups.

True, there are people who at some point in their lives become callous. They are firmly set in their attitudes and believe they're right, or they do not care if those attitudes are right—these people are satisfied to maintain an outlook that helps to maintain the status quo. Life is simpler that way, clear-cut, no gray areas.

But most of us experience inner turmoil because we sincerely want our attitudes, views, opinions, and actions to be healthy ones. Our moral gyroscope recognizes that it's better to be open to others whatever their differences. We want to live without fear and mistrust, and we want to learn from other cultures, ethnicity, and genders. We want to acquire a wide range of friends and experiences, to thrive in our occupations that place us in work environments side-by-side with people of many backgrounds.

We also want to raise children who will be emotionally balanced and will flourish in a 21st century society that will be diverse to an extent never before seen in American history. Later in life, we do not want to be left behind by changes; we want to understand and adapt to them so that we do not feel afraid and isolated.

It is precisely these admirable desires that create inner turmoil because as we pass through life our attitudes are evolving and being challenged. Perhaps the most disturbing recognition is that none of us can ever eliminate feelings of prejudice. They may ebb and flow, flare and recede, and passing from one stage of life to another we may believe we have conquered unwelcome feelings toward people different from ourselves—but prejudice is never extinguished.

That's okay. We must realize that only in a perfect world are troubling feelings nonexistent, and we live in a world that is certainly far from perfect. The best way to begin the healing process—and thus reduce prejudice—is to accept that we have these feelings. They will not go away by ignoring them. They will lurk within, suppressed, and then surprise us in embarrassing, unpleasant ways.

Of course, there are degrees of prejudice. In the "callous" category are people who refuse to accept that society is diverse or who go beyond that to active bigotry. Groups that consider one race superior to another, the skinhead movement, and perpetrators of bias crimes are just a few examples of callous people who are filled with a mixture of hate and fear.

Another category can be labeled "comfortable." These are people who believe that their feelings toward other groups are healthy, that they appreciate differences, and can interact with people from any background. We wonder if people in this category have genuinely found a high level of acceptance or are more capable of suppressing distressing feelings.

The third category we call "conflicted." Most of us reside in this category. Our goals and desire to be part of a more enlightened and enriching society do not quite match our feelings. We are disturbed when our daily experiences conflict with our ideals.

Almost every day, millions of us have an experience that conflicts with our honorable goals. Should we just accept that this will happen and hope we'll somehow push on? Well, that's one approach. But we can do more. It starts with maintaining a desire to resolve feelings of prejudice. At different stages in our lives the experiences will be different, but that desire can be a constant. The next step is to try to understand our feelings.

Unfortunately, there is no magical answer, no secret that once revealed will instantly transform us individually and then our society. If there were, there would be no need for this wonderful book. We believe that by offering examples that illustrate how they can be resolved, the minds and hearts of individuals can be changed for the better and the healing of a society in conflict will begin.

How do children acquire fear or any other unhealthy feeling toward other groups? The main influence is parents, who communicate their own attitudes in obvious or subtle ways. But there are other important influences too. Among them are teachers and the school environment as a whole; the media, especially television; and extended family members, especially grandparents or other older figures who came of age in a time when biased attitudes were more blatantly expressed and condoned.

During adolescence these influences change slightly yet are still powerful, and a new influence becomes extremely important. Young teenagers are profoundly affected by their peers. True, parents and teachers and the media still play a role (the latter influence may even intensify), but it is almost impossible for an adolescent to avoid acquiring the attitudes of the "group." Even if one disagrees with a group of friends, he or she is reluctant to oppose peers and risk being criticized and ostracized.

As parents, we have an enormous opportunity to positively influence our children. Many of us welcome this responsibility. We sincerely want to seize this opportunity and produce a generation more enlightened than our own. But even the most well-intentioned parent is startled to discover, usually at the most awkward moment, that their child has developed unhealthy feelings about people of other backgrounds. With some despair a parent thinks, "Where have I failed?"

You have not failed, at least consciously. But most of us harbor prejudice to varying degrees, and no matter how hard we try to combat, suppress or ignore our feelings, in subtle ways we communicate them to children. Parents face a double dilemma: dealing with our own feelings, and concern about what attitudes we are instilling in our children.

We feel strongly about this book because we believe that the diversity conflicts straining the fabric of our society won't go away all by themselves. Instead, they could increase as society inevitably becomes more diverse. In every community, occupation, school, and even family, the racial, sexual preference, and cultural make-up is becoming more diverse. Unfortunately, increases in "bias crimes" and heated debate between groups indicate that this diversity is causing divisiveness.

We realize that by itself a book will not heal the divisions in society, and that positive changes will not occur overnight. However, diversity has become a large preoccupation and many, many people are uncomfortable and unhappy with their feelings. In the normal flow of daily life, they aren't finding answers. We hope that every person who reads this book is positively influenced. Let's start with each individual, assisting them to first understand feeling—why they're there, where they came from, how others in a similar stage in life feel, and what to do to resolve those feelings. As the outlook of each person changes or becomes more open and accepting, there will be a cumulative impact on society.

As professional psychologists, we have counseled people of all races and ages, working with them to heal the wounds of prejudice and to resolve conflicting feelings. We have conducted numerous seminars and workshops in communities, with organizations, at workplaces, with children, and at schools and on college campuses. We are intimately aware of the questions people have and the admirable desire to take small steps toward a more harmonious society. *Diversity in Action* will provide you with tools and skills to challenge stereotypes and support you on the mission of celebrating diversity.

Derek S. Hopson, Ph.D. Licensed Clinical Psychologist

Darlene Powell Hopson, Ph.D. Licensed Clinical Psychologist,
Certified School Psychologist

Authors of:

Different and Wonderful: Raising Black Children in a Race-Conscious Society

Raising the Rainbow Generation: Teaching Your Children to be Successful in a Multicultural Society

Friends, Lovers and Soul Mates: A Guide to Better Relationships Between Black Men and Women

Juba This, Juba That: 100 African American Games for Children

The Power of Soul: Pathways to Psychological and Spiritual Growth for African Americans

Preface

Have you ever wanted to do something that seemed totally impossible? A project that you had no idea where or how to begin? Do you believe in destiny? We do, and the ways things just seemed to keep coming together for this book—the project we didn't know how to begin—has proved it to us.

Lisa and I have been paired as training partners for the A World of Difference program of the Anti-Defamation League of B'nai Brith for years. To look at us, you would think we are night and day—pardon the pun—and, while we probably thought so ourselves at first, we actually hit it off the very first time we did a training together.

As trainers, we deal primarily with facilitating and enhancing cooperative skills and problem solving techniques among groups challenged by the different facets of human diversity. This type of work requires an interesting blend of skill, know how, and experience. Getting the message across depends on all of these factors, in addition to personal style and presentation. Needless to say, it's not always smooth sailing, particularly in light of the fears and preconceptions so many of us hold close to our hearts.

The more we worked together, the more Lisa and I began to discover each other's strengths and weaknesses. We learned how to support, rescue, and validate each other. We knew instinctively how to handle the situation when one or the other of us became upset, emotional, or tearful. We drew together and confronted difficult participants who tried to sabotage our efforts, never letting each other down. Eventually, we even began finishing one another's sentences. Our relationship spread into our personal lives. Before long, we were calling each other to share the accomplishments of our children and to seek advice on how to respond to the numerous challenges they've faced over the years. Our bond was and remains strong.

A relationship like ours has been an invaluable asset to our diversity training. There is absolutely no way an individual or a group can drive a wedge between us. I remember one particular training session with approximately fifty social workers. Except for a handful of them, they were all of either African or Latino descent and proceeded to place Lisa in the category of a "white woman who knows absolutely nothing about us." I challenged them every step of the way, refusing to let them get away with dismissing her so easily. Another time, we were working with a group of sixty teachers of European descent. The tension was tangible, and most of them refused to acknowledge the validity of my experiences. When I left early, Lisa detected a sigh of relief. They were hoping that now that that "black woman" was gone, she could become "one of them, a white woman." Lisa confronted them clearly and directly, refusing to "let it go." We've never gone back to that school, but both of us feel the frustration of knowing that those teachers are responsible for the education of an entire school system of middle and high school aged children.

There have been so many times over the past four years that something would happen at one of our trainings and I would look at Lisa and say, "We have to write a book about this." At first, Lisa would look at me and say, "How are we going to do that?"

"I don't know, but we'll find a way," was always my reply. Eventually, we had both seen too much. Too many of the disturbing incidents, prejudicial views, comments and clearly discriminatory acts were happening among people in the educational systems of our country; the same ones who are responsible for our collective children. We began to say in unison, "We have to write a book."

As the idea took shape, we knew that we wanted to write a practical, hands on book, not something about the theory and history of discrimination or the different views surrounding the complex questions of human diversity. We wanted our readers to take away skills. The skills to give back to our children a sense of self-worth, value, pride, and acceptance of individual differences. We set ourselves a challenging goal, but from our point of view, that is the only kind worth pursuing.

Then the hand of destiny stepped in and put together the Anti-Defamation League with Project Adventure for a joint diversity training. We met Jim Grout and Bart Crawford and experienced first hand some of the advantages that adventure brings to an exploration of the issues surrounding diversity. The idea kept on simmering for another year, though, until we met up with Bart again and began sharing some of our future goals over the dinner table. I mentioned how much I wanted Lisa and I to write this book. Bart told us that Project Adventure's publishing department might be interested in our idea and set up a meeting for us to discuss the possibility. They accepted our proposal and there we were working with an internationally recognized organization with a proven track record in the prevention field. It seemed to good to be true.

Well, there was a hitch. To our dismay, we found out that we would have to participate in one of their workshops and experience a ropes course. I don't think I can even begin to describe our apprehension. It didn't ease up any when we received a letter describing some of the things we would need to do to prepare ourselves—increase the activity you are already doing. Already doing? What an assumption!

We did it, though, five days in Brattleboro, Vermont. It was an invaluable experience and we gained many first hand insights into how the different facets of diversity manifest themselves in adventure activities. As we walked through the woods on our first day, one of the members of our group shouted, "Look up there! They don't really expect us to go all the way up there." Well, we all looked, and saw the *Pamper Pole*, a small platform sitting on top of a pole about 65 to 70 feet up in the air. The silence that descended on our group was broken by a few nervous giggles.

The atmosphere was considerably changed five days later when we came back to the *Pamper Pole*. We were ready to challenge ourselves and we knew we could count on the support of every member of our group. While you won't be asking your groups to face the same kind of physical challenge represented by the *Pamper Pole*, you will be doing many of the same activities we did during the first four days of the workshop. Some of them seem silly—and they do get the group acting silly—some of them are simply high activity, and others challenge us to face up to many of our unconscious emotional processes and assumptions about others. What was important was that after four days, we were ready to do something we never thought we could possibly do in this lifetime. However much time you have with your groups, we hope this book will give you the chance to experience growth, learning and a strengthened ability to face the challenges of our diverse world with grace and trust. That is what Adventure learning is all about. You don't need to climb a 70 foot pole to see the results.

Our group did, however, and we watched as some of the men went first. Safely fitted with a harness and attached to a belay rope, they climbed the pole and swung out into mid-air to catch a trapeze. Some of them jumped, some of them didn't, and then we watched as our assumptions were blown into thin air. The women were ready to try it, too! (Neither of us admitted to each other until the workshop was over that we fully expected all of the men to do it, but none of the women.)

Lisa went first. While hugging the tree, she checked in with me first. "Sharon, are you down there?"

"Yes, I am," I answered, "and I'm not leaving."

"OK, I'm going to turn around now and get ready to jump."

After a final "Are you there, Sharon?" she did it. She actually jumped. When I saw her go, my heart dropped into my stomach, and I felt like I was her. Back on the ground, we hugged and laughed with tears in our eyes. I rejoiced for her, and she encouraged me to try.

Off I went. As I hugged the tree for support at the top, we both laughed about how we were the only ones that made the climb and ended up hugging the tree!

And then it was time to jump. I inched forward, checking in with Lisa every step of the way. "Lisa, are you there? Can you see my feet yet?"

"Keep coming. You can do it. I am right here," came her voice of encouragement. On the count of three, I went. My hands touched the trapeze lightly before I fell free and was slowly lowered back to the ground. My eyes searched immediately for my supporter, and she was there, hugging me as we laughed and cried at the same time.

This is what our book is about: learning how to take the risk to do something you've never imagined you were capable of, challenging yourself to change your views, stereotypes, and prejudicial thoughts, and creating an environment where you know that each and everyone of you will be there to support each other through your mutual growth and understanding. We hope this book will help all of you to keep encouraging each other, "You can do it. Keep going. I am here right now and always. Go ahead. Leap!"

We would like this book to be your guide on your personal journey through adventure and fun toward a world where we no longer use our differences as a wedge that divide us, toward a world where we celebrate our differences and similarities, creating bridges that will unite us through the future.

Happy journey.

—Sharon and Lisa

Acknowledgments

Acknowledgments are important. We don't give them as often as we should, nor do we receive them as much as we would like. Acknowledgments help us to contribute to one another. They are, we hope, lasting contributions. Together, and in that spirit, we would like to acknowledge the following people:

Marji Lipshez Shapiro, the friend who introduced us and brought Lisa into the field of diversity. Without you, we would never have written this book because we would never have met. Your trust, encouragement, ability to listen, probe, and challenge us with a loving heart have been a source of enormous support throughout.

Tom Zierk, thank you for being who you are; your integrity and warmth kept this project alive.

Francesca, there are no words. Thank you so much for your constant reassurance, wicked sense of humor, enthusiasm for this process, and for keeping everything straight. You were incredible.

Also, Jean Terry Walsh, your contributions to the chapter on physical and mental disabilities merit far more appreciation and recognition than this simple, heartfelt *thank you*.

To all our sister friends, thanks for the push, encouragement, and constant support.

Lastly, we would like to acknowledge all the individuals who have participated in the hundreds of trainings we have done over the years. You have contributed to our learning; you are the reason we have written this book. To all of you, we make the promise that we will always stand in the possibility of a future of unity and equality for all.

—Sharon Chappelle and Lisa Bigman

Lisa, thank you for believing in a dream, believing in me, and believing in yourself. Our dream is now a reality. You are so special to me. Much love and appreciation goes to my husband, Fred, and my two sons, Collin and Corey. Your patience, support and validation surrounded this process. Your willingness to allow me to spend so much time away from you was the biggest gift you ever could have given me. Thank you!

—Sharon

Sharon, thank you for challenging me to go beyond the limits I set for myself and for supporting me totally within that challenge. We had a great time. My love and appreciation to Jay, my husband, and my sons, Matthew and Grant, for your patience about going away late on vacations and my preoccupation that the book was taking too much time away from you. You supported me even though you weren't quite sure what I was up to!

—Lisa

Project Adventure and Diversity

We live in a world of perpetual motion, where people are often uncomfortable with the unfamiliar, where we are constantly challenged by the gap between process and outcome. I personally work and gravitate more toward the world of process, while living in a rather outcome oriented society. Discovery is an outcome of the process facilitated by the use of adventure.

Project Adventure's mission is to be the leading organization in helping others to use adventure education as a catalyst for personal and professional growth and change. Project Adventure and I have been exploring the issue of diversity for many years. It was in 1993 when my process began, for it was in March of that year that I attended my first diversity workshop held for internal staff by Project Adventure at the PA Covington, Georgia office. The past five years have been the start of an incredible personal and professional journey of self-discovery that has led to the development of Project Adventure's open enrollment diversity workshops.

The Project Adventure self-discovery diversity approach is multi-dimensional. Some workshops are aimed at understanding the nature of prejudice. For example, the PA workshop held for internal staff allows staff to understand the development of social identity, and how different groups may be targeted for prejudice by the nature of the system. The role of all participants in understanding how they may change the subtle systems that perpetuate our inability to value the diversity of all of us is addressed well. Other workshop designs may address the team functioning of diverse groups without addressing underlying systemic issues. At either end of the spectrum of diversity workshop designs, the Adventure processes addressed in this book can add tremendous value to the effect of the design.

By creating opportunities to experience diversity within a safe environment, workshop participants can learn first hand what diversity looks like, feels like, and sounds like. Our diversity/multicultual designs, developed over the past several years, allow participants to experience, as well as discuss, the ramifications of cultural differences and to become more aware of our many similarities. It enables insight to the behavior of self and others and lays fertile groundwork for guided discussions of diversity/multicultural issues. Adventure activities are tailored to promote understanding of the profound affects of bias on perception and therefore behavior.

Through games, problem solving initiatives, and activities, group members learn to develop trust, take risk, use divergent thinking in problem solving and develop leadership skills. More importantly, participants experience each other and the diversity of their group. These activities are carefully sequenced and group discussions are thoughtfully led. Through the cycle of doing and discussing, participants internalize key learnings. To complete the activities safely, group members must use communication skills; assume responsibility for themselves and others, and understand and appreciate diversity. This process is adventuresome, engaging and unique in the sense that every group approaches their experience differently, yet the outcomes demonstrate that all participants leave with a deeper understanding of themselves, each other, and their communities.

Some examples of the various ways in which our diversity work has played out in several settings are illustrated below. While they have been very different experiences, they are bound by the common thread of value and respect for differences.

Bristol, Connecticut

It is most appropriate that Bristol, Connecticut be listed here first. It was Bristol that boldly led us to a place we had not been by asking us to team up with the World of Difference, merge our curriculum and begin the first round of diversity trainings.

For the past seven years Project Adventure has been working with the community of Bristol as partners in developing adventure programming throughout the community and the school system. This process began when eight people from the schools and human service agencies of Bristol attended a Project Adventure Community Partnership Workshop in 1990. The energy, talent and tenacity of this group under the leadership of Joanne Galati and Eileen McNulty has built a spirit and force that has brought adventure programming to virtually every facet of life in the City of Bristol. Joined with the energies of Roland Chinatti and Ann Marie Mistretta, their efforts over the past seven years have led to Project Adventure naming Bristol's Pine Lake Challenge Course as our National Model Community Development site.

Throughout our relationship with the folks in Bristol, they have challenged us to expand and apply our adventure programs and innovations in new and creative ways. But no project has tested our creative skills as much as the exploration of diversity through adventure learning. Some four years ago, "The Interdistrict Leadership Project" (Creating Education that is Multicultural) workshop began. The impetus for this workshop was educators asking questions like, "How can we take our existing curriculum and make it Multicultural?" and "How can we create a safe environment where we can discuss challenging diversity issues?"

Our goal became to answer these two challenging questions while blending Adventure and Diversity to create a safe learning community for diverse populations. We began this process collaborating with the Anti Defamation League of B'nai Brith and came to meet Lisa Bigman and Sharon Chappelle. They were trainers for the Anti Defamation League's *A World of Difference* program. This work has also led to collaboration with Dr. Penny Lisi, Director of the Center for Multicultural Research and Education at Central Connecticut State University in New Britain, CT. What began as a single effort with twenty teachers from Bristol and New Britain, CT has led to some one hundred and fifty teachers being trained and approximately twenty four hundred students participating in one of twenty five different diversity curriculums. The Adventure/Diversity workshop is now recognized as one of the top training efforts in the state of Connecticut.

In many ways the efforts of Joanne, Eileen, Roland, and Ann Marie and many others in the City of Bristol created the foundation for this book to be written.

Japan

During a recent workshop in Japan, I witnessed in a particularly strong way how process leads to deeper understanding. The workshop was Adventure Programming, meaning the focus was to be around learning Adventure activities, along with the technical skills needed to facilitate a high and low challenge ropes course. The participants came from a variety of professional backgrounds, teachers psychologists, nurses and college students. There were seven women and three men attending the five-day training.

The group was doing a activity called *Prouty's Landing*. The participants have to get from one side of an area to another via a swinging rope. The particular metaphor for this activity was that there are insights and information that one can gain by changing the perspective from which you look at things. Sometimes this simply requires a change in position.

The group worked on the initial task and was then asked if they wanted an additional challenge. Without knowing what the challenge might be they agreed. The challenge was that all the male participants would be blindfolded during the activity. This meant that the women had to manage every aspect of this adventure for the entire group.

The participants did an outstanding job with this added challenge and then proceeded to have a rather powerful debrief. Men talked about never having been in the position to depend on women and feeling helpless as a result. Women talked about what it felt like to be in a leadership role and the confidence that came from that opportunity. They both talked about their fears associated with being in roles different than traditional cultural norms. This experience stands out as an example of adventure as the catalyst for a group of strangers to have a conversation through cultural and gender differences in a manner rarely available, if ever, in their day-to-day lives.

Manitoba, Canada

Manitoba was the site of another Adventure/Diversity experience that led to dialogue across the chasms created by history. The workshop was hosted by the Department of Northern Affairs, Canada. It was attended by members of the First Nation, Metis, French Canadians, and others that identified themselves as simply Canadians. The participants were recreation directors from various First Nation communities across Manitoba. This was the first time using the diversity/multicultural model with the intention of giving participants outside the United States an opportunity to discover issues that affected themselves, their clients, and colleagues.

The history of the relationship between the aboriginals of Canada and the European settlers is not unlike the history of the indigenous people of the US. Europeans coerced the native people of Canada out of land and ultimately their way of life. Assimilation was often brutal. The aboriginal people were denied the right to speak their own language, practice their own faith, and live their lives the way they had before white men came. The people of the First Nation are plagued to this day by the social problems that ensued from this treatment.

Problems do not exist just between the aboriginal people of this region and European Canadians. The Metis are children of mixed marriages, the offspring of indigenous mothers and European fathers. These children were neither First Nation nor European. They developed a unique culture, similar to but different from First nation. While the issues faced by the members of the First Nation are seen as federal problems, the issues faced by the Metis are not afforded the same status. This sets up an uncomfortable dynamic between Metis and First Nation members.

Many participants at this five-day workshop commented that this was the first time in their lives that they had ever engaged in a dialogue about diversity in a multicultural group. The participants reached out to one another across their differences to hear one another and be heard, some for the first time.

Detroit

This workshop was somewhat of a watershed experience in my own development as a diversity trainer. The workshop developed out of work done for the Multicultural Experience in Leadership Development (M.E.L.D.) at Wayne State

University in 1996 on diversity intervention. In 1997 the program chose to start their year off with a two-day workshop that focused on the participants' needs to address their own multicultural issues. Participants had trouble communicating through their own differences, making this program challenging for those involved. They took a pro-active stance and decided that at the start of this year they would hold a workshop to address multicultural issues and the role diversity plays, in their interaction as a group and for them individually.

The M.E.L.D. organization wanted Project Adventure to come in and set the foundation for a year long process to work on the groups' cross-cultural leadership and communication skills, which would assist them in creating a project that they would implement as a team and affect change in the greater Detroit area. During their time together, the group made incredible gains. By the end of the two days, participants were sharing back and forth about their cultural challenges. Using a "Circle of Hands," group behavior norms or guidelines were established, thereby addressing how the group members wanted to be treated and treat each other. This tool was used throughout the year as a way for the group to check in on their behavior.

Each of the scenarios mentioned above represent powerful examples of how adventure and diversity have been combined to create powerful and life changing experiences for people.

My hope is that this book will assist all of us as we find ourselves faced with the unfamiliar, and having to get comfortable with the uncomfortable. May we work tirelessly toward discovery, change and growth. Diversity is one of the final frontiers left to explore. It is a frontier far greater than the depths of all of outer space and the oceans combined, for it is the frontier that allows us to discover who we are as individuals and how we fit in society.

—Bart Crawford
1998

Contents

Chapter Eight

Section Three

Chapter Nine

Chapter Ten

Chapter Eleven

Introduction

Working through issues of human diversity can often be an unsettling experience. For some, *diversity*, in all its variety of forms represents a topic of little concern, somebody else's problem. For others, issues of diversity present an on-going struggle, a source of inner turmoil, a breeding ground for bitterness, resentment, and anger. For middle and high school age students, who are having enough trouble coping with all the physical and emotional changes occurring at this age, dealing with diversity can often be especially difficult. But it is also an opportune time to begin exploring the many facets of human differences—what are the obvious ways in which we are different? What are the subtle ones, those we easily overlook and rarely consider? And just as importantly, what are the ways in which we are all similar?

Exploring the notion of *difference* with youth is a challenging task. Those who work with youth, and for whom this book is designed, know very well how difficult it can be to get through to many of their students. Too often, in our eagerness to get down to work, we go right to the heart of things. We ask the difficult questions and find little forthcoming besides lots of unease and discomfort. The topics of diversity are difficult for individuals to explore and discuss openly and honestly in a group setting. For this reason, it's essential to take a step back, to first prepare the group for such a challenge.

One of the best methods for preparing individuals in a group setting to delve into topics of human differences is to start by creating a group environment that supports, encourages, nurtures, and challenges its members to be honest and open—with themselves and others. This type of group climate offers a safe place, both physically and emotionally, for the group to operate within. Individuals learn to trust that no matter what the topic or issue, their opinion will be respected, their ideas listened to, their experience accepted, and their individuality valued.

So how do we set about creating such a supportive environment? Since the early 1970's, the practice of adventure education has been implemented into countless arenas where people come together for some common interest and purpose. Schools, camps, corporate groups, mental health hospitals, community groups, after school programs, youth groups—even police departments and correctional facilities—have all adapted adventure education techniques to their own setting. In doing so, they have found that individuals within a group begin to open up a little more, to trust a little more, to challenge themselves a little more. All because they feel safe within their group setting, knowing that the group is there to both support them and be supported by their contributions.

The purpose of this activity guide is to help you, as someone who works with youth, begin to create such an environment for your group. Specifically, *Diversity in Action* offers guidelines for creating a safe and comfortable place for the participants in your program to explore and discuss issues of human diversity.

We have divided the book into three sections:

Section One—Background and Working Principles

Section Two—Creating Nurturing Communities

Section Three—Individual Identity

These three sections offer a progression of information intended to build your knowledge, understanding, and leadership skills during presentation of the topics and activities. The information in Section One provides critical background information that will assist you once you begin involving your group in the activities. Unless you are an experienced adventure facilitator, we strongly recommend that you read and carefully study the basic principles and facilitation tips presented. The activities presented in Sections Two and Three will merely offer entertaining recreation for your group if the processing and discussion skills are not in place and understood by you and your students.

Section One

The first section introduces Project Adventure and the theory and practice of adventure education. There are a number of basic operating principles that must be in place in order to create a safe learning community. One of these is the Full Value Contract, which asks participants to commit to certain rules for ensuring both the physical and emotional safety of each individual member of the group. Section One also introduces adventure activities, explores how and why they are so effective, and offers sequencing ideas to ensure that your group follows a progression of skill development. There is also a chapter that discusses how *facilitating* a group differs from simply *leading* a group. Adventure activities often ask the group leader to step back and be more of a facilitator—letting the group lead itself, solve problems on its own, and make its own decisions and mistakes. The facilitator of an adventure group offers guidance, support, and diligently monitors the feelings of the group, ready to step in if necessary.

You will want to refer back to these introductory chapters from time to time as your group progresses through Sections Two and Three. A lot of information about group dynamics, the leader's role, many helpful worksheet questions, and basic activities are included in Section One.

Section Two

Section Two, *Creating Nurturing Communities*, is designed to help you and your group develop a sense of community, team, and emotional and physical safety through the use of adventure activities. By first creating a learning community that supports all its members, you will be establishing a strong and caring foundation for working through the specific, diversity related topics presented in Section Three.

The chapters in Section Two cover such topics as: listening and communicating skills, how to validate the emotions that being different evoke in all of us—from stress, depression, and rage, to withdrawal—how to make allies who will stand by us and reinforce our sense of self, and learning how we define and create our group identities in society.

Section Two begins the activity chapters. Each chapter in this section and the next begin with some theoretical and background information to help your understanding of the subjects introduced. These portions end with a short summary, or concluding thoughts, and a list of some of the skills you will need to keep in mind as you and your group play your way through a set of activities.

We have also included vignettes that illustrate the issues raised in each chapter. The vignettes are followed by worksheet questions designed to help you, as the facilitator, reflect a little more deeply on the issues and topics you will be presenting. These vignettes and worksheets can also be shared with your group. You may want to use the vignettes as introductory readings for a day's activities, but spend some time on the worksheet questions on your own as well. It is more than likely that you will find many of your own beliefs challenged as you work through the activities with your groups, and the worksheets will help you identify some of these through the process of self-reflection.

As we began writing this book, we realized that each time we discover and digest new knowledge, we are presented with another challenge, another question that needs to be solved before we can move further along a continuum of growth. To help your groups track their progress, we have added a continuum to each of the activity chapters that presents the new knowledge and skills and some accompanying insights. Our goal is to provide a guide to help you acquire the necessary skills for examining broader issues of cultural diversity as well as the less evident complexities of individual difference.

In that light, here is the first continuum we think is important to understand when working with diversity topics:

Preference →Bias →Prejudice →Discrimination →Oppression

Bias and Preference, on one end of the continuum, are not necessarily harmful, and indeed are sometimes necessary to function in the world. Knowing what we prefer is a part of self-definition. It is one way that we distinguish ourselves as individuals. On a progression from Bias, Prejudice takes a step toward the other end of the spectrum in that it is a judgment, opinion, or attitude held in disregard of the facts, often formed before all the facts are known. Discrimination goes a step further; it is concrete, overt behavior based on prejudice and is measurable or demonstrated in some way. Oppression connotes actively keeping someone down through cruel or unjust use of power or authority.

The continuums presented in the activity chapters describe a range of behaviors and beliefs that form many of the barriers between people today. In this book we will be working toward a balance where we value individual beliefs and ideas while sending a clear message that prejudice, and particularly discrimination and oppression, are wrong.

Using the Activities

While each chapter comes with its own set of activities, most of the activities are interchangeable and can be used to work through almost any topic covered by this book. As you design your program, you may want to pick and choose activities, customizing them to your own needs.

To make this process easier for you, we have added a list of related topics to many of the activities. For example, as you go through the chapter on listening and communicating skills, you will see that each activity has a list such as group identity, racial identity, gender and sexual orientation, etc. that link it to other chapters in the book. How you process the activities, and what questions you ask your group, will determine the skills your group is acquiring. So, if you feel that one of the group problem solving activities in the listening and communicating chapter would be more appropriate for your work on racial identity, go ahead and incorporate it into your activity planning. Then, refer to the back of the activities section in the racial identity chapter for a list of general processing questions on racial identity.

Throughout the book, particularly in the activities chapters, we have tried to make note of the issues and challenges that may impede or assist your group through the learning process we present. Each chapter includes a brief review of the awareness your group will be moving toward and some of the skills you can expect them to pick up along the way. We have also noted issues that may require guidance from professionals with skills for dealing with more serious emotional issues such as Post-Traumatic Stress Disorder or childhood physical abuse. (See Caution to the Reader on page xxix)

Section Three

Section Three, *Discovering Our Identities*, continues the activity chapters and covers specific diversity related topics on individual identity, racial background, gender and sexual orientation, physical and mental abilities, and class background. This section provides a set of insights into the challenges that all of us face as we seek to establish our identity in a world of confusing signals—Who am I? How do I establish a positive self-image in the midst of so many conflicting messages about how I should behave, dress, act, or look in order to "fit in"?

The activities section of each chapter in Section Three addresses a range of issues—from creating common ground to stereotyping and other more complex issues centered around our search for personal identity. Depending on the amount of time allotted for your program or the specific goals you want to pursue with your group, you may want to work through each chapter chronologically or pick and choose the topics most relevant to you.

Be sure to work through the chapters in Section Two, however, before you begin with the issues presented in Section Three. Diversity is a challenging subject that often brings difficult emotional issues to light, particularly if you are using adventure learning techniques. We cannot stress enough the importance of establishing a safe and trust-filled environment before you begin to tackle some of the more complex topics covered in this section.

Conclusion

The conclusion, Chapter Fourteen, provides a look at prevention theory and how it applies to diversity work. We also present a list of ideas for ongoing activities that will help your school and community address issues of discrimination in positive and constructive ways. You may want to present these activity ideas as projects for individuals in your group or their parents to work on with local schools and community organizations on a long term basis. Many of the ideas we list have worked in communities across the country, helping to build understanding and resolve issues from the generation gap to youth violence and gang enrollment.

A Caution to the Reader

It is our hope that this book will become a useful resource for all professionals whose work with children, pre-teens, and teenagers has a primary focus on engaging them in positive, creative, and learning-filled experiences. Often times, these experiences provide alternatives to participation in harmful or negative behavior. This behavior includes, but is not limited to substance use and abuse, premature sexual involvement and unsafe sex, dropping out of school, gang activity, teen pregnancy, and criminal activity.

Discrimination and its fallout—from prejudice to oppression—isolate and alienate us from one another. They generate anger and depression in young people and create behavioral cycles that can become entrenched and difficult to interrupt. One of the goals of this workbook is to provide youth, and the professionals who work with them, with a safe environment and the tools to create experiences that will interrupt these cycles and teach our youth to value the differences that are an integral part of the human experience. Young people must be given the possibility to create environments where they can talk freely about the repercussions of prejudice and discrimination and acquire the skills for dealing constructively with these phenomena. Diversity work empowers people to make choices that acknowledge and value their differences. The more we know about one another, the less we have to fear.

Accepting that we are all different and learning how to cope with discriminatory behavior is also an immense challenge for many of us. Over the years, we have seen the entire spectrum of emotions evoked in our workshops— from gales of laughter to the triggering of an episode of Post Traumatic Stress Disorder. Learning about one another through engaging in experiential activities can trigger the release of bottled up rage, memories of psychological or physical abuse, and any number of pent up emotions. You can never predict in advance exactly what emotions and memories will be brought to the surface for participants during the activities.

We therefore strongly recommend that only experienced facilitators work with the program ideas and activities presented in this book. If you have any doubts whatsoever about your abilities or how to handle what might come up during your program, don't hesitate to turn to your colleagues, specialized professionals—school psychologists, program directors, guidance counselors, religious leaders, seasoned diversity trainers, etc.—and others with more experience for assistance, advice or direct intervention. Project Adventure also offers a variety of workshops for facilitators who are searching to refine their skills or learn how to apply Adventure to their setting. Maybe your program has funds set aside for education and training programs or perhaps you'll simply want to refer to someone in your program who can help you develop your skills and intervene if any troubling episodes do occur. Our goal is not to scare everyone off from engaging in the activities presented in this workbook, but we do ask that you stay aware of the pitfalls you may come across during this work.

Background and Working Principles

This first section provides a basic understanding of adventure education, how it is different from other methods of learning, and why it can be such an effective tool in creating a caring and exciting learning community. The principles and practice presented here will provide you with the tools to begin working through the activity chapters that begin in Section Two. We cannot stress enough the importance of understanding these ideas and how to then implement them through the activities. Adventure learning is a powerful way to bring people together, to help individuals feel safe to explore difficult and sometimes uncomfortable topics, and to challenge us to examine some of our most deeply held beliefs. Simply using the activities with a group does not mean that any meaningful learning will take place.

Using such principles as the Full Value Contract and Challenge By Choice will help your group establish an environment in which all members feel safe and can present their ideas and feelings without fear of ridicule or being put down. Learning the operating principles that form the foundation of such an environment and how to effectively facilitate your group's learning will help you to begin using the activities presented in Sections Two and Three to their full potential.

1

Where
Adventure
Meets
Diversity

A rubber chicken flies through the air and lands in the grasp of Sheila, a 71-year-old retired office manager. She thanks the thrower, Jenna, a rather unretiring 16-year-old high school junior. Sheila in turn throws to Chuck, a local police detective, who tosses the chicken across the circle to 14-year-old Shaun. The chicken flies, eyes twinkle, and laughter fills the room. Not a typical beginning to an event billed as a night of dialogue and titled *The Teen Years: Then and Now*. But as the *Name Game* draws to a close, it is quickly followed by more active group games—*Pairs Tag, Quick Line Up,* and *Speed Rabbit.*

The audience is now enthralled. Jenna, the 16-year-old leader of the activities, begins a spirited round of *Have You Ever?* The questions fly—"Have you ever been in a rock band?" "Stayed out all night?" "Invented something?" "Eaten tofu?" "Been bungee jumping?" Her last question is a masterful introduction to the evening's main agenda: "Have you ever wished that teenagers and adults could communicate better?" Everyone moves! It's unanimous, the audience is now primed to talk. Jenna seizes the moment and introduces the topic for the evening. She speaks briefly about the need to communicate and bridge the generation gap between adults and young people. She explains the guidelines for the dialogue about to begin:

- Everyone's opinion is of equal value.
- Family members should not sit in the same small group.
- Listening is participating.
- Respect your differences.

The Adventure Approach

Putting together groups as diverse as this one can present challenges for both participants and group leaders. Each and every one of the participants carries pent-up feelings of mistrust, anger, resentment, prejudice, or simple difference. Preconceived notions about others can range from physical looks to manner of speaking. So how do you get people to feel comfortable and safe enough to begin exploring difficult and sensitive topics—like issues of diversity? How can you bring people together to a place where they can be open and honest but at the same time respectful to others, where they can really listen to others whom they may have been taught, subtly or not, to mistrust?

Plato said that you can learn more about a person during an hour of games than you can by conversing with him for a year. Adventure programs, with activities like *Have You Ever* leading the way, have a powerful effect on groups. Adventure activities can bring people together within an atmosphere of openness, honesty, respect, and trust. And they begin by simply asking a group to play and have some fun. This is the magic of adventure.

Over the years, adventure programs have been used with church groups, adjudicated youth, and police departments; in school classrooms, prisons, corporate boardrooms, PE classes, camps, and therapeutic settings. It is safe to say that adventure programs have been used in nearly every type of setting where groups of people come together. And for several years a number of practitioners have been using and refining adventure techniques for programs where diversity is the main issue.

Bringing together young people to discuss loaded issues where diversity is the crux is never easy. Too often we want to jump right into the heart of the subject. We ask, "How do you feel? What do you think about this person or that group?" But if I tell you how I really feel, how do I know you will accept what I say? How do I know I will not be laughed at, put down, or be attacked for my ideas and feelings—for who I am? How can I know that I can trust you and the group? How can I learn to get past my own prejudices?

In order to delve into issues of diversity, especially with youth, you must first develop an atmosphere within which people feel comfortable and safe, where they know they will be listened to and treated with respect, and where group members have agreed to abide by certain rules of behavior that above all value each individual and his or her unique experience.

An adventure approach can bring you to such a place. By following a sequence of adventure games and activities specifically attuned to youth groups working on issues of diversity, you can create a comfortable and safe environment where ideas and feelings are listened to and treated with respect, not ridiculed or put down. Where the experiences of each individual, no matter how different or

Breaking Down Barriers

On the first evening of a two-day retreat, a group of male students from the Cambridge Rindge Latin High School in Cambridge, Massachusetts, sat together in one room, chatting and laughing about the day's experiences. To most observers, the scene would not have been out of the ordinary, but these boys were from two rival groups that had been involved for several years in an ongoing feud.

The two groups, one composed primarily of Italian American White males and the other of students of Color, hadn't given school officials any cause for alarm until recently. At the beginning of the academic year, two boys, one from each group, bumped into one another in the hallway. It was a minor incident but generated enough animosity to escalate the conflict between the two groups and set them openly against each other. On several occasions, school security personnel had to separate the groups when verbal threats seemed about to cross the line into physical violence. The conflict eventually culminated in a street fight. Fortunately, apart from bloody noses and black eyes, none of the boys was injured.

Project Adventure had led a successful intervention between two rival groups of female students a year earlier, so once again school officials turned to them for help in resolving the conflict. After a few meetings with the school staff to gather more information about the problem, Project Adventure proposed a two-day retreat for the boys, who were less than enthusiastic about the idea. Some of them walked out of an orientation meeting, refusing to participate. After most of the boys eventually agreed to go, Project Adventure and school staff members co-facilitated a weekend of activities centered around a peaceful resolution of their conflict.

They started the first day off with some fast-paced ice-breaker activities to get the boys loosened up and provide opportunities for nonviolent physical contact. The students mixed freely during the games but split back into their rival groups whenever it was time to process an activity or get instructions for the next one. For the most part, they were reluctant to talk about their feelings. Most of them stayed silent throughout the morning.

After lunch, however, there was a perceptible shift in the atmosphere. The facilitators asked the boys to separate from their closest friends and divide themselves into two groups, but this time balanced according to race, age, class in school, and favorite sports. Instead of the expected resistance and conflict, the boys worked it out in a few minutes on their own. From then on, the group moved smoothly through *Trust Falls*, where participants take turns falling backwards from a four- or five-foot-high platform into the arms of the group; *Mine Field*, an activity where a "sighted" partner leads a blindfolded partner through an obstacle course with verbal instructions; the *Mentoring Process*, an activity where two people share how an important, positive role model has affected their lives; and finally *The Wall*, an activity that involves the whole group in trying to help each participant scale a 12-foot vertical wall.

The group stayed committed and focused during the activities, but all of them remained reluctant to speak up or share their feelings about what was happening and how they were cooperating. It was clearly still too risky for them to expose their feelings to one another. The facilitators felt it would be better not to push them beyond their limits. Without giving up entirely, they kept the questions and processing to a minimum.

By the end of the first day, no miracles had occurred, but the boys were talking to each other and chose to spend the evening together as one group. At the end of two days, new friendships had formed and the boys had learned to trust and respect one another. During a follow-up interview several months later, the school reported that there had been no incidents of tension between the two groups since the workshop.

Adapted from *Lookin' and Bumpin', Conflict Resolution at Cambridge Rindge Latin High School*, by Paul Marienthal.

difficult to relate to, are accepted, and where the young people in your group begin to look through preconceived notions to value each person as a unique individual.

The Adventure Approach to Learning

Learning how to trust, learning how to develop allies, learning how to become an effective ally, getting comfortable with the uncomfortable, learning to accept that "my way isn't always the best way," increased self-esteem—all of these qualities can be learned and experienced through the adventure approach. This workbook seeks to provide opportunities to examine issues of diversity through adventure. The activities are designed to empower young people, helping them acquire enough confidence to make change happen and deal openly and positively with cultural and individual diversity.

The most crucial pieces of building understanding are often overlooked. Communication, trust, and safety are words that are easily spoken but not so easily achieved. They are the rudiments of any solid program that values people, and they must be worked at daily.

Why and how does adventure work? Adventure's most unique feature is its ability to help all people, through active participation and experience, build an environment of shared trust and emotional safety. Adventure challenges all of us to keep our minds open and develop conditions that foster a "group" or "team" approach to learning. This is a powerful way to learn about diversity. What better forum for discussing sensitive and difficult issues? The first section of the workbook contains more information about the history and basic principles of adventure, guidelines for using the adventure approach, and some ideas on how to make adventure work in your setting.

Defining Diversity

Diversity is defined as the differences that exist among human beings. It has become a hot topic in the United States, surrounded by an enormous amount of controversy. Diversity, as we define it within this book, includes differences in race, ethnicity, country of origin, religion, sexual orientation, age, physical and mental ability, gender, class, and looks. Diversity also includes physical characteristics, mannerisms, facial expressions, styles of dress, language, communication styles, gestures, geographic location, work experience, lifestyles, learning styles, and personality. In essence, diversity is the sum of all those parts that make us who we are—different individuals with the common experience of being human and the unique experience of being ourselves.

Within the chapters of this book a number of terms will be defined and explored. These include, among others, ethnicity, culture, sexual orientation, race, and racism. Of course, not everyone defines these terms the same way. Our hope is that by providing our sense of the terms and the groups that they represent, we will encourage your own exploration and further your own understanding.

Defining Self

Self-definition is a primary concept in this book. Judgment based on few or incomplete facts is often a basis for discrimination. Creating an atmosphere where it is safe for youth to explore and define themselves, and learn to listen to others to understand how they are doing the same, is the central task of this book. Sometimes simply asking how another person identifies him- or herself can validate how they perceive themselves,

> # We Do Not Believe In Ourselves
> ### e. e. cummings
>
> We do not believe in ourselves until someone reveals that deep inside us something is valuable, worth listening to, worthy of our trust, sacred to our touch. Once we believe in ourselves we can risk curiosity, wonder, spontaneous delight or any experience that reveals the human spirit.

releasing tension and opening up avenues for discussion. It's essential to clarify with each group member the terms that they feel most at ease with. Political correctness is not the goal in our era of fast change at all levels of society. What's most important is to connect with other individuals in a way that meets everyone's need for recognition and understanding.

Specific terms of definition have been the cause of a sometimes shallow understanding of diversity, helping to create categories that limit us. In the following pages we have attempted to discuss these terms in a context of openness, acknowledging that their use can cut both ways. Terms can bring forth the pride of self-definition and greater understanding, but when the understanding is not pursued, they can add to the divisions already alive in our society. Our hope is that through the activities in this book, youth and the people who work with them can together become aware of this double-edged sword.

Project Adventure

Project Adventure began as an alternative approach to both classroom and physical education learning. Through experiential, hands-on methods, teachers used adventure to provide students with the opportunity to work together in a number of crucial areas: developing communication skills, fostering a trusting environment, working cooperatively, improving self-esteem, working toward challenging goals, and problem solving. These broad goals created a net that supported and continues to support learning for all students.

One of the keys to creating and maintaining a vital program, whether you are a teacher, after-school care provider, or PE instructor, is being able to address pressing issues in an inclusive, progress-oriented way. For a generation now, issues of diversity have been a backdrop to our educational settings. Many of us have struggled to find ways to address these issues in the learning environment.

Project Adventure promotes fun as a primary tool for learning. We believe that learning that is engaging and exciting and fun will ultimately go deeper and stay longer with all those who participate. Some still consider the idea that learning need not be "work" a radical idea, but it is part of the bedrock beneath adventure concepts. Having fun is part of moving forward and of healthy change.

With these goals in mind, it's not a far leap to imagine adventure as a medium for teaching people how to respect, foster, and work with diversity. Acknowledging the individual, creating a forum for everyone to have a voice, and building healthy communities where trust exists are needed to deal successfully with issues of diversity.

Adventure activities have been adapted to many settings since Project Adventure began spreading its ideas around in 1971. Thousands of teachers, healthcare professionals, PE instructors, corporate trainers, recreation specialists, and others have experienced adventure workshops and integrated adventure into their settings. Adventure is a marvelous tool for provoking and instilling positive change in almost any environment. On the following pages, we've included a short description of how the town of Brattleboro, Vermont, has used adventure to help meet its community development goals.

Brattleboro, Vermont

The experience of Brattleboro, Vermont is a wonderful example of how adventure can adapt itself to a variety of environments and goals, helping individuals and groups to cooperate, trust one another, and work together to create positive change. Adventure in Brattleboro began in 1987 as part of The Leadership Project (TLP), a teen drug and alcohol abuse prevention program. Funded by a federal grant, TLP was piloted in four New England communities with the goal of promoting healthier lifestyles and habits through cooperative youth–adult partnerships. The project was based on the conviction that substance abuse prevention efforts are the responsibility of the entire community. Community wellness depends on involving all community members in a long-term, cooperative endeavor to change the conditions contributing to teenage drug and alcohol use. TLP identified teens as positive agents for change and also as one of its most powerful resources.

TLP selected a local coordinator to begin working in Brattleboro's high school. Her first job was to recruit teams of students concerned about peer drug and alcohol use. The team, a group that included both "model students" and "troublemakers," invited teachers, parents, and adults from the community to join them in trying to create a drug-free community. The students organized and facilitated a series of Dialogue Nights, which brought adults and youth together to communicate on specific issues. Using adventure activities to create an atmosphere of trust and safety, Dialogue Nights helped diverse groups to better understand each other's often vastly different experiences, values, and concerns. In their efforts to raise awareness around issues of substance use, the students also organized softball games, carnival days, and a variety of other activities designed to involve as broad a spectrum of community members as possible.

Federal funding for TLP ran out in 1989, but the group had generated so much enthusiasm for their work and such a significant drop in drug and alcohol use among local youth that the program kept on going and is still alive today, thanks to local support and funding from the Brattleboro Union High School. In 1991, adventure made more inroads into the community when Project Adventure was awarded federal monies from the Center for Substance Abuse Prevention for the formation of the Community Prevention Partnership. Dedicated to drug and alcohol abuse prevention, the Community Prevention Partnership expanded TLP's original focus on youth to include all members of the community in an effort to change the environmental conditions that contribute to substance abuse. The Community Prevention Partnership's goal is ambitious. In essence, however, it's a grassroots organization that is using the principles that have guided Project Adventure and adventure programs from the start: bring people together, give them some fun in an environment that encourages them to value each other and feel valued themselves, and the positive connections between them begin to happen spontaneously.

> *Adventure has been a powerful tool for change in the Brattleboro community, and what's perhaps the most remarkable of all, is that everyone has had a lot of fun along the way.*

Project Adventure's work through the Community Prevention Partnership in Brattleboro has been so successful that human service organizations throughout the community are using adventure to bring people together to achieve a variety of goals. These goals have included bringing teens together for a day of fun at the local teen center, preventing gang infiltration of local neighborhoods, raising local awareness about AIDS, and helping individuals convicted of domestic violence through their court-ordered rehabilitation. The programs gathered so much enthusiasm that the Community Prevention Partnership was brought in to work with the local police on a training designed to restructure the department, create a new spirit of teamwork, and inaugurate a community policing program. Their work is still going strong and, through the Partnership–police cooperation, neighborhood watch committees are making their communities safer places for all, teen drug use is down, and citizens and police are working together to make Brattleboro a healthy community for individuals of all origins, physical and mental abilities, sexual orientations, and economic positions.

Adventure has been a powerful tool for change in the Brattleboro community. What's perhaps the most remarkable of all is that everyone has had a lot of fun along the way. Meeting challenge and instilling change doesn't have to be a laborious process, as many of Brattleboro's citizens have learned.

Concluding Thoughts

The success of adventure programs lies in a simple understanding of how people of all ages can be stimulated to open up and enjoy the process of learning—fun. Fun and laughter are essential elements of any adventure setting. The trust that ensues from shared enjoyment binds the most diverse groups together in acceptance and a willingness to engage in honest discussion of sensitive topics.

Adventure is about building trust. Trust that I will not be ridiculed for sharing my fears, hopes, opinions, and dreams with other individuals who are different from me. Trust that others will accept me for who I am at the same time as they challenge me to examine my own beliefs and values. Trust that all people are worthy, myself included. Trust is a powerful tool for engaging youth in a process of discovering that honoring human diversity enriches each and every one of us.

Suggested Reading:

Schoel, Jim et al. *Islands of Healing, A Guide to Adventure Based Counseling.* Hamilton, MA: Project Adventure, Inc. 1988

Henton, Mary. *Adventure In The Classroom, Using Adventure To Strengthen Learning and Build a Community of Life-Long Learners.* Hamilton, MA: Project Adventure, Inc. 1996

Hillyer, Francesca. *Community Policing in Vermont, Adventure and the Brattleboro Police Department.* Hamilton, MA: Project Adventure, Inc. 1997

2 Operating Principles

In New England, the part of the country where we live and work, most towns used to have an open, grassy area called the Commons that played an important role in the life of the community. The Commons were open to the use of all. Sheep were grazed there, town meetings were held there. It was a place where everyone in the community came together to celebrate and play, work out personal disputes, and solve community problems; a place where people could see and feel part of their town's group identity.

Feeling that we belong, that we are part of a group, is one of the essential needs of all human beings. Community identity, a sense of common purpose, and connection with others provide us with a sense of safety and connection to the physical world. The Commons was a place for individuals to meet and recognize themselves as part of a community with shared values, beliefs, and physical needs. The Commons was also a symbol of inclusion—everyone, regardless of their strengths or weaknesses, was encouraged to contribute to the growth of the community. When conflicts arose, and someone was feeling excluded or discriminated against, the Commons was a place where they could work it out.

The metaphor of the Commons is a powerful one. The Commons of Project Adventure is created by four tenets that are introduced and used by every group that comes together. These four tenets are:

- The Full Value Contract
- Challenge by Choice
- Goal Setting
- The Experiential Learning Cycle

In this chapter, these four basic principles are introduced and explored within the context of diversity. They are the four cornerstones of the Commons you will be building with your groups.

The Full Value Contract

As any group comes together, it creates its own behavioral rules for how members treat one another. Every group goes through this, but the process is usually subtle; an unspoken code of conduct evolves over time. A classroom has a set of rules, as does a playground at recess. Members of a gang abide by a code, and so do employees in an office.

The adventure approach to learning brings this group development process out into the open. We begin by asking group members to think about how they want to work together and treat each other. The result of this process is called a Full Value Contract.

The goal of any Full Value Contract is to create an atmosphere in which everyone in the group feels safe, both emotionally and physically, to explore difficult issues without fear of being ridiculed or put down; a place where all group members feel recognized and have a voice and a way to participate in the decisions made by the group. In a classroom or school-age program, the Full Value Contract can be an opportunity to shift peer pressures toward productive behaviors and away from destructive ones. Simply put, the Full Value Contract should remind all group members to fully value themselves, others, and the group process.

There are several ways to develop a Full Value Contract with your group, ranging from an open-ended dialogue, where the students develop their own contract, to more structured approaches. With young children, we have used the concrete reminders of PLAY HARD—PLAY FAIR—PLAY SAFE and asked for their interpretations. With high school students, we have sometimes begun with the contract, and asked them to elaborate on each point. With students participating in a court-referred rehabilitation program, we have handed them an actual contract which they must sign to participate in the program.

Regardless of your situation, any Full Value Contract should adhere to the following guidelines:

BE HERE—Beyond simply showing up, be ready to participate and to work with others.

BE SAFE—Respect physical and emotional safety at all times. Allow trust to develop.

SET GOALS—Participate with the intention to achieve, to carry tasks and goals through to completion.

SPEAK THE TRUTH—Face experiences honestly, take the risk of speaking up.

LET GO OF NEGATIVES—Strive to release yourself from negative dependencies and move on.

CARE FOR SELF AND OTHERS—Reach out into the world and take responsibility.

BE OPEN TO OUTCOMES—Be open to the possibilities for learning in any situation.

Developing Your Own FVC

No matter how you develop a contract with your group, the members need to know, understand, and own each piece for themselves. In addition, make every effort to keep the contract alive. Post it on the wall, refer to it, revise it, design activities that include it. A living contract can be one of your most effective tools in dealing with issues of diversity.

It's usually a good idea to start with the basic framework of a contract for the group to discuss. From there they can adapt the words or add elements as they continue working together. It's important not to force the evolution of the group. A balance needs to be struck between how you guide them and how they guide themselves. In the beginning, raise questions that will help them solidify and clarify their contract, but make every effort to use their words and their leadership.

The Being

One of the activities we use frequently to work with our groups on the Full Value Contract is called *The Being*. *The Being* is a large outline of a living entity or object that the group picks to symbolize itself. It could be a person, animal, garden, village Commons, city block, lake, or anything at all. Give the group an old sheet or large piece of newsprint or poster board and have them draw the outline of the object they have selected to represent them. If they've decided to use a person, ask someone to volunteer to lie down on the sheet or newsprint so that the group can trace the outline of their body. Once that's done, ask the group to brainstorm a list of the positive behaviors they want the group to maintain—listening, caring, supporting, cooperating, respecting opinions—and write them down inside the drawing. Then ask the group to think of behaviors that distract them or keep them from meeting these positive behavioral goals—ignoring new ideas, goofing off, devaluing—and write those down outside the drawing.

You can come back to *The Being* whenever you want, adding behaviors as they come up or simply referring to it and asking if everyone feels that the group's guidelines are being adhered to and respected.

> *The Full Value Contract is a constant reminder to the group that while they are here to learn to accept individuals, this does not mean that all behaviors are acceptable.*

As you present the Full Value Contract, encourage your group to discuss what each of these statements means to them. Don't hesitate to add points if toward the end you see something missing. You are a part of this group and can ask for certain agreements as well.

When using the Full Value Contract with a group where you will be overtly talking about issues of difference, bias, and prejudice, there may be certain points that will need attention. Ideally, these issues will be brought up by members of your group as they discover things together, but you may wish to introduce them yourself. What follows is a list of other possible points for the Full Value Contract. Keep in mind as you read that a group is continuously in process. The bare bones of an initial contract may be elaborated, or a group may discover that two points are really saying the same thing, and the meaning can be distilled.

- Ask, discuss, and validate everyone's levels of comfort with physical contact.

- Respect the views of others and foster a diversity of perspectives.

- Allow equal opportunities for all to participate.

- Be aware of devaluing self and/or others and make a conscious effort to change this behavior.

- Do not make remarks that you know are hurtful to yourself and others.

Have the group discuss their levels of comfort with physical contact. What is acceptable for one person may not be for another. For example, we both like to hug people. When we work with individuals for the first time, however, we always do a quick check-in. "I'm a hugger. How about you?" This allows everyone to stay within their comfort levels. When you begin doing activities with your group that involve a lot of physical contact, you may want to check in with everyone and have a discussion about what feels comfortable. "What's normal for you at home?" "Does your family do a lot of hugging?" "How do you show your friends you care about them?" Ask everyone to remember that not all people feel comfortable about holding hands or hugging, and have the group check in with each other as a matter of course. Also, you should inform yourself of your organization's policies concerning sexual harassment. It is your responsibility to stay within the guidelines.

The Full Value Contract is a constant reminder to the group that while they are here to learn to accept individuals, not all behaviors are acceptable; for instance, what if someone in the group is using inflammatory or profane language? Swearing may have become an acceptable way to speak in our society, but perhaps not everyone in the group is comfortable with it. Ask the group to discuss how they feel and what they would like to do about it. Bring the group back to the Full Value Contract whenever you think someone's language or behavior has stepped outside acceptable norms.

What if someone abruptly leaves the group? What does that say about their sense of trust and valuing of the other members of the group? Acknowledge to the group what has happened and share with them how you are going to communicate with the person who chose to leave. Try to find out why they left. Were members of the group acting cruel or intolerant? Or did the group discussion touch on subjects they felt uncomfortable with?

Keeping the FVC Alive

It's important that you keep coming back to the Full Value Contract over and over again as you work with your group. Use your discussion time to add to your contract, and as you encounter new situations, add the behaviors the group would like to encourage. You may even want to keep a separate list of unacceptable behaviors—name calling, confrontational behavior, pushing, shoving, you name it—posted as a reminder. The Full Value Contract is the group's way to ensure that everyone's physical and emotional safety are respected at all times.

Worksheet: The Full Value Contract

Sometimes it's helpful to do some writing to prepare for dealing with a group of individuals who are significantly different from each other. This worksheet can facilitate a discussion of how the group will work together, or it can be an opener for revisiting the contract and making sure it is more than phrases on the wall.

- How do you want or like to be treated?

- How do you want or like to treat others?

- What does it mean to respect someone?

- What's the best way to respect you?

- What will help you cooperate with the people in this group?

- What does it mean to be safe physically and emotionally?

- What does it mean to take risks physically and emotionally?

- What does it mean to be present in the group?

- What can you do or say to help this group work together?

- What can you do or say to hinder this group working together?

- What's the most challenging thing about trying to work with the people in this group?

- What are the rules here?

- What does it mean to tell the truth?

- What do you feel are the consequences of telling the truth?

- What's your biggest fear about being in this group?

- What about the group makes you feel the most comfortable?

Challenge by Choice

From the very beginning, the concept of Challenge by Choice has directed all Project Adventure programs. So important is this concept that virtually every Project Adventure workshop begins with an introduction to Challenge by Choice. It is a pretty basic concept that says each individual has the right to make his or her own decisions regarding the level of challenge they choose to accept. At the same time, it does not give participants freedom to wander off or do other things during an activity. That is not respecting the group process.

Your role as leader must be to find ways to offer understandable challenges that can be accepted by the group as it maintains its right to make choices. Challenge by Choice offers participants—

- A chance to try potentially difficult and/or frightening challenges in an atmosphere of support and caring

- The opportunity to "back off" when performance pressures or self-doubt become too strong, knowing an opportunity for a future attempt will always be available

- A chance to try difficult tasks, recognizing that the attempt is more significant than performance results

- Respect for their individual ideas and choices

The goal of Challenge by Choice is to create a norm where group members recognize their right to make choices about individual levels of participation as the group moves forward. This participation can range from being involved with a particular activity to taking part in a processing discussion.

Challenge by Choice is a way of creating personal, positive goals. Challenging oneself within an atmosphere of encouragement and support looks very different from being pressured or coerced by others. Middle school– and high school–aged youth are familiar enough with pressure. Pressure often comes from peers, but that's not the only source. Pressure can take many forms: pressure to succeed, pressure to fit in, pressure to stand out, pressure to be smart or witty or first or last.

Using Challenge by Choice allows the individuals in your group to chart their own path through the challenges before them, creating their own goals. It's important that you verbalize this concept and refer to it often, reminding everyone in the group that the expectation here is not that they will bow to any unspoken pressures from the group, but that they will make their own decisions about how far and how fast they push themselves. Challenge by Choice affirms a person's right to assess a situation, make a personal decision, and say, "I don't want to do this activity right now" or "I want to lead the singing at the rest home this week."

Here are some things to keep in mind when using the philosophy of Challenge by Choice with a group:

- ◼ Not everyone needs to do everything. Too often adventure leaders boast that every group member did a particularly difficult activity. That may be a good thing, but it misses the point of Challenge by Choice.

- ◼ Sequence the activities carefully (see Chapter 3). Proper activity selection goes a long way toward supporting the challenge once an activity is in progress. Intensity decisions are an important accompanying factor.

Creating A Group Commons

If your program has space at its disposal, consider creating a permanent Commons. If you don't have space, the following ideas may help you create a common—physical or emotional—space anywhere.

Decorate the area where you begin your activities with objects or images of importance to the group. They may be representations of their families and backgrounds, or photographs of the group itself and the things they've done together. Group members may bring in objects that have symbolic meaning, or they may attach symbolic meaning to everyday objects.

Coming Together

Ask the group to think of a way to remind everyone that they are coming together as they enter the Commons. This could be any type of activity that suits the group.

A straightforward check-in: "It's taken me (time) to get here because (this is where I've been)"

A warm-up or set of stretches that the group does together

A song or set of rhythmic steps in time

Journaling and sharing out

- Time used setting goals is time well spent when dealing with an activity's challenge level. When the participant is clear about what she wants to do, it's much easier for everyone. Remember, goal setting doesn't take place only during a briefing session, removed from an activity. A person may decide whether to do something during the session.

- Group pressure is very real and can be used in a positive way when participants are familiar with each other and aware of each other's goals. That's why it is important, when choosing your activities, to reserve the more intense ones until the group members are more comfortable with each other. Because of the trust that develops in adventure groups, members are much more likely to respond to positive group pressure. The agreement in the Full Value Contract to confront and be confronted comes into play here. As long as we're confronting in a positive manner, group pressure can and should be used. It is then defined as group support. You must be aware, however, that group pressure can quickly go beyond the bounds of caring into aggression and abuse.

- Trust, to repeat, is a great support of challenge. Certain challenges require a strong dose of it. If the trust isn't there, perhaps more lead-up is necessary. On the other hand, effective challenging can bring about trust. Sometimes you need to take a calculated risk by pushing ahead at a certain time, counting on the trust to emerge.

- Individualize when necessary. Certain participants just will not do what the others are doing. Take the heat off by finding something supportive for them to do.

- Regularly infuse a sense of fun and fantasy into what can easily become a too serious approach.

Challenge by Choice is designed to be a kind and flexible guideline. If one of the members of your group decides not to participate in an activity because they don't trust the group yet, they haven't lost their chance. If they evolve to a place where trust begins to flourish, or see that the activity is not as threatening as they thought at first, they are welcome to change their minds and try a greater challenge. The important point is that we set our own level of challenge and can change it at any time.

Mark Murray, an experienced Project Adventure trainer, tells a wonderful story that exemplifies the concept of Challenge by Choice.

"One story that comes to mind from the school based group I was leading was of an 11-year-old student, Kim. She was stuck at the periphery of the group, physically and emotionally. Although she was there at every session, she never participated actively. Initially the group confronted her about her unwillingness to participate, but as we started to discuss the idea of Challenge by Choice, the group's behaviors changed to acknowledgment and encouragement, truly respecting her choice.

"One day we began a problem-solving activity called *Minefield*. This is an Initiative done in pairs, where a sighted person leads a blindfolded person through an array of strategically placed props on the floor without either of them touching a prop or any other participant moving though the field at the same time. Kim quietly came over and asked if she could lead me through the *Minefield*. I mentioned this request to the group, since it generally wasn't the norm that I participate in Group Initiatives. They enthusiastically supported the idea.

"I remember the grip of responsibility that she applied to my hand as she slowly and safely brought me through the field. I sensed that the attention of the group was focused on our passage, and upon completion a cheer rattled around the gym. I took my blindfold off and looked at the huge smile on Kim's face. I reflected to her that she appeared very pleased with our accomplishment, and she nodded her head in agreement. Then she quickly shared that at home nobody trusted her to do anything on her own, especially her father. The group took a few minutes to debrief her com-ments and a few members shared some similar thoughts. Then they returned to *Minefield* with Kim being led through the field by another group member. Although for the remainder of the year she never brought this issue up again, from that point on, Kim slowly started to trust, connect, and work more actively as a participant in the group, knowing that it was her choice and the group's!"

"This is one incident where I felt that the individual was actively engaged with the group in a thinking manner. It was also a situation in which she was measuring her time and deciding on the appropriate moment to become physically engaged. As practitioners and facilitators, each of you will need to make your own judgments about group members and what they require from you to create a group environment where they can not only say but believe these words: 'What I did I own, because I made the decision to accept the challenge!'"

Goal Setting

Goal setting is an integral part of any adventure group process. It helps keep the flexibility of Challenge by Choice moving in a productive, forward motion. It also enhances the use of the Full Value Contract as a guideline for the group's behavioral goals. Setting and revising goals should be an ongoing process that reflects the progress of each individual and of the entire group.

Goals can be set on a number of levels. For example, your group's long-term goal is to learn and practice tolerance and acceptance in a diverse environment. On a personal level, this may mean that some of your participants will need to set their own goals of self-tolerance and self-acceptance before they can meet the overall group goals. Striving to attain long-term goals, however, can be a frustrating process. It does not happen overnight, and it may not be possible to achieve within the time and resource limitations of your program. The solution is to make your goals short term—specific, attainable, and measurable. Don't ask the group to focus on goals that will require them to alter their behavior radically overnight, but do ask them to set SMART goals:

Specific

One goal at a time, without an alternative. Research has shown that if you say you want to do one thing or another, you rarely get beyond the "or" and end up doing neither. For example, think of the person who says they are either going to give up smoking altogether or cut down to three cigarettes a day. When they light up the first cigarette of the day, they've already failed at one goal, so why bother trying to keep up appearances?

This doesn't mean that you can't change your goals, but if you do, state your new goal without an alternative. What if, for example, your group sets a goal to complete the *Spider's Web* in 45 minutes without ever touching the web strands? Two tries down the road, they may realize that it's going to take them at least an hour to reach their goal. This doesn't mean they've failed, it simply means that they have set too high a goal and it might be time for some revision. Ask them which is more important, completing the *Web* within 45 minutes or not touching the strands? Or perhaps they want to do both, but it will take an hour, and this becomes their new goal.

Measurable

Set goals that are measurable in time and quantity. The above is a perfect example of a group goal that can be measured. How does this apply to personal goals? Maybe Jamie is having difficulty presenting her ideas to the group during problem-solving activities. Simply stating that she wants to get better at speaking up isn't a measurable goal. Have her set a goal of trying to speak up during at least one problem-solving activity each session. When you process the activities, ask her whether or not she has reached her goal. Remember Challenge by Choice, though; she may not want to share her thoughts with the group.

Achievable

Reasonable or attainable. Have the group set goals that are within their given strengths and abilities. Unreachable goals create frustration; attainable goals encourage everyone to participate and act as positive motivation for setting new goals. You are asking them to reach the limits of their potential, not do the impossible. For instance, if your group can complete the *Spider's Web* in 45 minutes without touching any strands, don't change the goal to 25 minutes if, given their level of cooperation, you don't think it can be done. George might be having a difficult time trusting some of the other boys in the group. Doing a *Trust Fall* may be an inappropriate goal for him, but a *Trust Walk* with his eyes closed, not blindfolded, might give him enough trust to set a new goal for himself.

Relevant

Makes a positive difference in overall performance. The goals your group sets should be directed toward improving their performance. Group Initiatives and Social Responsibility activities often challenge the group and its individuals to plan well before they try things together. Have them set a goal of listening to each other's ideas and come up with a joint plan before they attempt to solve a problem or tackle an initiative.

Trackable

Progress can be monitored. It's important to keep the goals your group sets woven into the fabric of your activities. As the leader, it's your job to check in on, revise, and celebrate their goals. Measure their performance frequently. One of the most powerful tools we can provide for youth is a sense that they can achieve what they set their minds to.

Experiential Learning Cycle

A misunderstanding about adventure and experiential learning is that these types of learning simply involve people becoming physically active with the material. In fact, activity comprises only one phase of the four-stage Experiential Learning Cycle. Activity is a vital part of this process as it offers first-hand experience with the material and a place to become engaged with the topic. But it is only the beginning of the cycle. From there learners must process the experience in order to find the meaning of it, construct knowledge from it, and then apply the learning to new situations.

> *"I hear, and I forget.*
> *I see, and I remember.*
> *I do, and I understand."*
> — *Lao-tsu, Chinese Philosopher*

The Experiential Learning Cycle begins with activity, moves through reflection, then to generalizing and abstracting, and finally to transfer or application. This cyclical process repeats itself, as learning identified in the application phase applies itself to the next activity.

Activity

The activity begins the process and can be any one of a number of activities implemented for a variety of goals. It may be a game whose purpose is simply to get a group loosened up and having fun. It may be a Problem Solving Initiative that introduces a particular topic. Activities can demonstrate a concept or

raise questions. Regardless of the specifics, the primary goal of the activity is to initiate as many connections with the topic as possible. What affects how we look at others? How do your friends' opinions affect your own? How can we develop strategies to change negative behaviors?

The activity phase of the Experiential Learning Cycle allows students to engage the material according to their individual strengths. Instead of just one entrance, many doors open onto the topic at hand. Students can enter a front, side, or even back door into the subject. Having stepped into the lesson, they are poised to learn.

Reflection

"So, what just happened? What did we do?" The second phase of the cycle, reflection, is a time of questions. During this part of a lesson, students review what they have done. The focus is on facts:

- What happened?

- What behaviors were observed?

- Did the group solve the problem?

- Who did which jobs?

- Who actively helped?

- Were the rules followed?

Reflection on the *What?* of an activity is like reviewing post-game videotapes, where the players see their actions from different angles and form a more complete picture. Students compare what each of them saw during the activity and check to see if their individual perception fits with what others saw. The examination of different perspectives and different answers that occurs here is an early step in developing skills for critical thinking.

Generalizing

If the reflection phase of the cycle asks *What?* happened, then the generalization phase asks *So What?* This takes examination of the activity to a deeper level. It asks the group to think about the meaning of the factual information gleaned from the reflection questions. How is the group cooperating? Are some people doing more of the talking than others? How are you sharing responsibility for each other's safety? Generalization is a time for your group to begin to make connections between their ideas and experience; what did they learn during the activity and how will they apply that learning to the next challenges?

- How did it feel for you?
- How did you work together?
- How did you solve the problem?
- What do you think you did that helped the group or held the group back from completing the activity?

These are the types of questions you will be asking the group during the reflection phase. This phase helps the group move beyond the factual *what* that happened during the activity. This is the time for both the facilitator and the group to learn more about who brought what skills to the activity and who helped or hindered the group and how. Reflection is also a time for the group to validate and acknowledge each other's experiences and contributions.

Application

The application phase of the Experiential Learning Cycle occurs when the group applies its new knowledge to the next activity or to their daily lives. It is the time for *Now What?* questions. "Now that we know we need to cooperate more with each other, how are we going to do it?" "Now I know that if I speak up about my feelings, people will listen to me. How am I going to try to speak up more, not just in this group, but with my family and in school?" "How can I show people that I am listening to them and respect their feelings?" "Can I avoid getting into conflict with my peers if I show them that I am listening to them and accepting their feelings as real?" Now your group is ready to test their learnings in new situations and with each other.

As your work with your groups progresses, keep in mind that the Experiential Learning Cycle is constantly evolving. It is not a static process, and one cycle leads into the next. Each time they begin to apply their learnings to an activity, they will move back through activity, reflection, generalization, and application, setting new goals and gaining new understanding each time.

Three Levels of Use

You can use the cycle on three different levels—individual, group, and facilitator. As individuals, group members go through a process of goal setting, experiencing, processing, generalizing, and applying what they have learned to the next activity and to their life outside the group. The group goes through the same process of doing an activity, discovering what happened, gleaning learnings, testing out those learnings, and applying them to future experiences. As facilitator, I will have an individual experience and a group experience, and I will also have the task of helping the group to process as they move along.

The individual experiences and thoughts of each person contribute to the larger group cycle. The extent to which each person identifies with the larger group experience will have much to do with how unified they feel and how cohesively the group works. It is important to remember that we will all have individual experiences that contribute in some way to the group experience but do not wholly define it.

In your group, as you work with issues of diversity, tune yourself to this individual/group dynamic. Often, members of the group who are not part of the racial majority or representative culture (whether racial or behavioral) will feel, though they may not express it, a greater distance between their own views and those of the collective. As this schism develops, these students may mask their feelings in the same protective manner they customarily use. If you identify a situation like this developing, either seek ways to bring the issue to the table or design activities that will naturally address the dynamic through problem solving and increased communication.

As the facilitator, you are an integral member of the group. It is important to think of yourself this way. As your group completes an activity, notice how you participated in it. As they process, notice what comes up for you. Being in tune with each of these levels is a handful and may become additionally difficult as you tackle challenging issues. For that reason, do some self-exploration in advance of working with a group, and continue to check in with yourself. Knowing what opinions or situations push your buttons and how you react is valuable information that will help you work more closely with a group. We are all works in progress.

Worksheet: The Experiential Learning Cycle

It can be difficult to anticipate what issues or opinions within the group will feel too hot to handle. This worksheet is designed to help in the discovery process. In addition, keeping a journal about issues or current events as they arise is a process that can aid your awareness.

- Spend a few minutes creating a timeline of experiences, memories, and events that reflect your awareness of human differences.

- What are the issues, either in the news or in your personal life, that you have thought about or read about in the last six months?

- How do you react if someone accuses you of perpetuating a stereotype or engaging in discriminatory behavior?

- How do you respond to inflammatory language or behavior that makes you feel uncomfortable?

- How do you respond when your students refuse to comply with your requests? When the members of your group "get into your face"?

- How do you respond when someone in your group gets up and leaves the room?

- What are some of the stereotypes you see acted out in the groups you work with? How do they make you feel?

Concluding Thoughts

The tenets we've covered in this chapter—Challenge by Choice, the Full Value Contract, goal setting, and the Experiential Learning Cycle—all work together to create an atmosphere of openness, trust, communication, and progress toward group and individual goals.

These concepts ask us to be conscious of the ways we behave together. They hold the group together and form a metaphor for your Commons. In the following chapters of this section you'll find more information about creating this space. Using these concepts as a foundation while the activities progress will help to remind your group of why they are working together. Whatever the activities are that you do together, there are reasons for meeting: working on understanding ourselves and the differences between us, and learning to communicate with each other constructively.

Suggested Reading

Myss, Caroline Ph.D. *Anatomy of the Spirit: The Seven Stages of Power and Healing.* Harmony Books: 1996.

SMART goals adapted from Kenneth Blanchard's *Leadership and the One Minute Manager,* 1985.

3

Sequencing Adventure Activities

We have selected the activities in this book to help you lead your groups through the four basic elements of an adventure experience: fun, trust, communication, and cooperation. These four elements don't have to happen in that order, but it is essential that you provide your group with an environment where each one can materialize. Together, they provide an atmosphere where participants can share both their insecurities and accomplishments without fear of being laughed at or ostracized by the other members of the group.

We have set up the activities in each chapter in a recommended sequence to help guide you. Sequencing is an art. As the facilitator, you will need to remain sensitive to the group's progress. That may mean changing the plans you've set up for the day's work. Pay attention to the needs of your group and be flexible. Not all progress is linear. A group that has worked its way successfully through many challenges may show up the next day or week acting unresponsive, uninterested, apathetic, or nervous. If that's the case, don't rush through the Ice Breakers and De-Inhibitizers because you had planned to put them to work on some difficult initiatives or process a particularly troubling and challenging set of issues that came up during your last session. Take the time to assess what you can do to break the tension. Maybe the group needs a fun day of laughter, giggles, and lots of running around.

Conversely, your group may be brimming with trust, communication, cooperation, and fun. They may be ready to move on to some challenging Group Initiatives after a couple of quick Ice Breakers. Let them lead you and set the tone.

Following is a description of each type of activity and how each contributes to establishing a safe group environment that includes all four of the basic adventure elements.

Ice Breakers

Ice Breakers help the group warm up and get acquainted with one another. All of us, adults and children alike, feel intimidated by a group of people we don't know. Learning each other's name, finding out what basic things the individuals in the group do or don't have in common, or simply participating in a group gale of laughter all help to develop trust and communication. Even with groups whose members know each other, the depth of their mutual understanding may not be all that deep. And there may be individuals in your group who have negative past histories with each other that present problems to working together. Ice Breakers provide opportunities for your group members to get comfortable working and simply being with each other. The activities and games are fun oriented, nonthreatening, and geared toward success.

Features of Ice Breakers include:

- Fun is a major component.

- Group members can interact in a nonthreatening manner.

- Ice Breakers can be easily accomplished with a minimal amount of frustration, verbal interaction, and decision-making skills.

- Participation does not produce much frustration.

Examples: *Cross the Line, Have You Ever?, Peek-a-Who, Everybody's It, Funny Face, Tic Tac Toe, Hog Call.*

De-Inhibitizers

De-Inhibitizers are similar to Ice Breakers in that they help the group warm up, but they also add an element of goofiness and minor risk taking. Adolescents, in particular, may feel somewhat uptight or uncomfortable acting silly or making mistakes in front of each other. This is where you, as the facilitator, might need to give them a hand. If you aren't afraid to participate in the activities, showing them that it's OK to look a little silly, they'll probably follow your example. Remember Challenge by Choice, though. Invite everyone in the group to join, but don't force anyone who acts reluctant or shy. They'll probably join in later when they see what a good time everyone else is having.

Groups with expectations about having to deal with difficult or personal issues may also benefit from De-Inhibitizers. Loosen up. Assure everyone of an atmosphere of fun and playful caring.

De-Inhibitizers provide a forum for your participants to begin taking some risks (we all appear inept from time to time), improve their cooperation with each other, and have a whole lot of fun at the same time. They also give groups challenges that are attainable. Participants work together, feel good about their success, share in the accomplishments, and learn techniques that will give them the confidence to try more difficult problems and overcome greater risks.

De-Inhibitizers are fun activities that allow participants to view themselves as more capable and confident in front of others. They help create a cooperative, supportive atmosphere that encourages participation, increasing confidence for all members in the group.

Success and failure are less important than making a good effort. If you sense some discomfort, check in briefly with your group about how they felt acting silly.

Examples: *Feeling Relay, Chicka Boom, Group Juggling, Red Baron Stretch, Inch Worm, The Truth Is Stranger Than Fiction, What Makes the World Go Round.*

Trust Building

Trust-building activities give the group an opportunity to place their physical and emotional safety in the hands of others by trying a graduated series of activities that involve physical and often emotional risks.

Trust building is at the core of the work you will be doing with your groups and requires continual effort

> *It is vital to establish an atmosphere of safe, honest participation...*

and practice. Establishing trust is an important step to helping teenagers feel comfortable with the complex challenges of human diversity. Start building trust slowly. Because your group will be taking more physical and emotional risks with each other when doing these activities, fears may begin to surface. It is vital to establish an atmosphere of safe, honest participation, since once trust is broken, it is very difficult to rebuild. If you are working with a group that has little reason to trust, this may be one of your most important goals. Work with only the most basic trust activities until you gauge that your group is ready to go deeper.

Stay open and reassuring with your group. Your ability to communicate what to expect from the activity will make the participants feel included and safe. Explain beforehand how much physical contact may be required; make sure that all your participants feel comfortable with it. Remind the group of Challenge by Choice and the Full Value Contract. Give everyone a chance to opt out if they feel uncomfortable with what's being presented. If the activity requires a blindfold, tell the group before you begin. Many people are afraid of being blindfolded. You can always give them the option of doing the activity with their eyes closed.

Choose your metaphors carefully. When you process these activities, remember that they may provoke some strong feelings of discomfort, both emotional and physical. It's important for you to set a tone of caring and safety that will create an environment for open dialogue. Remember that you are a pivotal influence on the group's ability to trust one another.

Trust-building activities involve group interaction, both physical and emotional. Trust-building activities:

- Generally involve fun, but some fear as well.

- Require the cooperation of group members—everyone's safety, physical and emotional, should be the primary concern.

- Risk taking occurs at many levels in most activities.

- The development of trust occurs gradually within the group.

Trust activities are chosen with the intent of building trust; initially, choose basic trust activities. These can be performed repeatedly to reinforce the safety of group members.

> **Examples:** *Trust Circle, Trust Falls, Trust Leans, Levitation, Eye to Eye, Minefield, Come to Me, Trust Wave, Circle the Circle.*

Group Initiative and Problem Solving

Group initiative and problem-solving activities focus on ways to help your group work together, communicate, and solve problems. Group Initiatives are a great way to help participants understand that taking advantage of different learning styles and individual experience enhances the group's overall ability to meet challenges successfully and find solutions to the problems they face. They emphasize verbal, listening, and physical skills in the group decision-making process. Everyone can contribute a skill to the process. No one loses; it's the group that wins when they begin to listen and learn from each other. They develop communication and cooperation skills as they progress through a series of problem-solving activities.

- Physical activity, verbal interaction, and discussion are major components in the sharing of ideas and solving group initiatives.

- Frustration is sometimes a natural part of learning communication, cooperation, and negotiation skills.

- Leadership abilities and skills show themselves differently with different group members. Let them lead themselves during each activity.

- Activities demand that group members demonstrate an ability to listen, cooperate, and compromise.

- Most activities require at least five members.

Examples: *The Clock, Great American Egg Drop, Nitro Crossing, Stepping Stones with a Twist, The Almost Infinite Circle, Blind Polygon, Spider's Web, Object Retrieval, Jumping Jack Flash.*

Social Responsibility

Social responsibility activities build on the trust and safety you have helped your group create through the previous activities. These activities provide an opportunity for open discussion of the issues of prejudice, discrimination, and bias and how to build relationships. While you will have already touched on most of these subjects, communication may have concerned more personal questions of "What did it feel like for you?" and "How can the group learn to respond more to the needs of each individual?" Social responsibility activities open the context of the group's communication into the broader social implications of their behavior. How do their thoughts, actions, biases, and communicative abilities affect their interaction with peers, adults, family, and society? These activities also help the group develop its ability to assess and work effectively with the strengths and weaknesses of all individuals in the larger context of social interaction.

- Successful completion of the social responsibility activities is dependent on the group's ability to support and encourage each other's efforts.

- Activities tend to help participants learn the value of thinking and planning ahead, instead of reacting in an impulsive and random manner.

- These activities emphasize that participants in the group must communicate and cooperate verbally and physically.

- Activities help participants develop skills in assessing problems and formulating solutions.

Examples: *The Power Shuffle, Body of Feeling, The Lunch Room, Stereotyping, Sculpting Each Emotion, What's Your Sign?, Hot Potato, People Need People.*

Closing Activities

Closing activities can serve a variety of functions. We feel that it is important to bring closure to your group's activities, whether it be on a daily or weekly basis. Particularly when working with diversity issues, troubling emotions are often brought to the surface. It is important for the group to feel a sense of closure about the work they have engaged in. Closing activities are also useful for the following reasons:

- They help participants deal with unexpressed, unresolved, and difficult feelings.

- They allow the group members to give and receive support.

- They provide clarity and direction for the next session.

- They help participants evaluate group and individual progress.

There are many possibilities for bringing closure to a group. Your organization may have some traditional closing activities of its own that you can use, or you can select one from the end of each activities chapter.

Personal Journal Questions

Personal journals are an important part of any growth or learning process. Over the years, we've found that journals give groups the opportunity to reflect and create new plans of action.

Journals help changes, questions, and concerns become specific to one's own life. They provide a place for introspective thought and reflection based on initial and continuing issues, concerns, and questions.

They provide a place for thoughts that need not be expressed to others. They are often a place where a call to action occurs. Journals are also a private space to re-examine progress.

Remember, personal journals are above all personal and confidential. They should not be read by the leaders or anyone else! Participants should feel free to share any portions of their journals with the group, but only if they want to.

A Journal Worksheet

Here are some ideas for questions that you might want to ask the group to answer for themselves in their journals:

- What was easy and/or difficult in the group today?

- What came up for you today during the activities that brought up questions about how you are different from others in the group?

- What is one thing that you would have liked to say to the group but couldn't?

- Who made the biggest impression on you today and why?

- What made you uncomfortable today and why?

- Choose someone to write to and record what occurred and any concerns or fears you may have had.

- What did you learn today that would make a difference in your life and to the people you value?

Concluding Thoughts

Adventure activities come in all shapes and forms. But each type has a specific function. The success of any program using adventure activities depends largely upon the sequence in which the activities are presented to a group. How you make decisions around which type of activity to use in any given situation, and which particular activity you choose, depends on your ability to read and assess your group.

The next chapter outlines some of the ways that facilitating an adventure program differ from more traditional leadership and teaching roles. It also provides information on how most groups form and behave during the time its members spend together. The ability to assess the stage at which a group is functioning is a critical skill for the facilitator. Without it, you might present activities that become boring and meaningless if not challenging enough, or cause mistrust, discomfort, and an unwillingness to take risks if the activities presented are too challenging. Understanding the different activity types, their function, and how to continuously read your group's developmental stage allows you to select just the right activity to move your group in the direction you want them to go.

Suggested Reading:

Rohnke, Karl and Steve Butler. *QuickSilver: Adventure Games, Initiative Problems, Trust Activities, and a Guide to Effective Leadership,* Project Adventure, Inc., Hamilton, MA, 1996

Rohnke, Karl. *Cowstails and Cobras II: A Guide to Games, Initiatives, Ropes Courses and Adventure Curriculum,* Project Adventure, Inc., Hamilton, MA, 1989

Rohnke, Karl. *Silver Bullets: A Guide to Initiative Problems, Adventure Games and Trust Activities,* Project Adventure, Inc., Hamilton, MA, 1984

4

Facilitating an Adventure Program

Using adventure activities in group work differs from more traditional forms of leading and teaching in several ways. The leader/facilitator doesn't provide all the answers to the group; the participants primarily learn from each other. And adventure experiences intentionally contain a certain amount of spontaneous unpredictability—they are intentionally fun.

In more traditional models of teaching and leading, the instructor or group leader is seen as the definitive source of information. The leader passes knowledge on, and the participants learn it. The participants are viewed more as receivers of information than as learners. Facilitating a program using adventure techniques means that your teaching style may have to undergo some adaptations. The facilitator presents activities in a way that allows the group to develop its own abilities, with guidance from the leader when appropriate.

Facilitators using adventure take people out of their standard frame of reference and ask them to engage in new and different experiences. You're not playing volleyball, basketball, or football. You're not sitting and listening to someone lecture. Adventure activities ask people to hit a beach ball as many times as possible without allowing it to touch the ground. Adventure activities ask people to create an animal using their bodies. Adventure leaders encourage using the same skills— cooperation, teamwork, communication, trust, decision making, creative problem solving—that are taught more didactically in schools, seminars, and training programs. The educational outcomes may be similar, but the approach is purposefully different.

The Group Process

Group work is always a challenge. Day to day you never know just how your group will behave. Will they be antsy, unable to sit still? Will they be rowdy or belligerent? Will they be eager to get on with their learning and dive into the activities? Project Adventure uses some guidelines to understand, first of all, how groups typically function. All groups go through pretty much the same formation processes. Understanding how these processes work, evolve, and affect how your group behaves will help you analyze your group on a day-to-day basis.

One of the methods we use to assess a group's level of functioning, developed by B.W. Tuckman, describes the functioning and general behavior of a group as its members spend more and more time together. A group's development has four stages:

Forming—Representative of the first years of life, this stage is represented by orienting to the idea of a group, testing out the group, and being dependent on the group or the group leader to understand what is expected.

Storming—Similar to the "terrible twos," this stage involves conflict with other members and with the leader and resistance to the rules or the influence of other members.

Norming—In this stage, group members have tested the waters and found the environment safe for sharing their anger, sadness, fear, joy, and other emotions. This sense of cohesion allows for acceptance of one another and one another's views. The group becomes a place to try out new behavior. This is an essential stage in the maturation of groups.

> *Try some Ice Breakers and De-Inhibitizers to relax the tension and help them see the humor in their situation.*

Performing—Finally the group, as a mature being, is ready to deal with the tasks that members bring to it. Instead of being caught up with testing each other's commitment or confronting each other's behavior, members can work with issues as they present themselves.

The stage at which your group behaves will influence the way it responds to the activities. A group that is still in the process of forming may need de-inhibitizers and low challenge trust activities to help it develop a more trusting and communicative environment, while a performing group will be ready for more demanding activities that require a greater level of trust and cooperation. Groups move back and forth along the spectrum; a group that was at the performing level on a given day may go back to storming on the next. Try some Icebreakers and De-Inhibitizers to relax the tension and help them see the humor in their situation. If your group is performing, keep the challenges coming, invite risk taking (obviously within established physical safety guidelines), and keep laughing.

Pay attention to your group. Watch how they are behaving and listen to what they are saying. You may have to alter your plans to fit the group's state of mind on any given day. As you get started, while you are doing the first planned activities, do a quick assessment. Make sure you are picking the right activities by asking yourself the following set of questions from what Project Adventure has dubbed the GRABBS checklist:

G   Goals—How does the activity relate to the group and individual goals that have been set?

R   Readiness—This regards capabilities in skills and safety. Is the group ready to do the activity? Will they endanger themselves or other participants? Do they have the ability to attempt or complete the activity? Will you have to change the events to compensate for lack of readiness?

A   Affect—What is the feeling of the group? What kinds of sensations are they having? What is the level of empathy or caring in the group?

B   Behavior—How is the group acting? Are they resistive? Disruptive? Agreeable? Are they more self-involved or group-involved? Are there any interactions that are affecting the group, both positively and negatively? How cooperative are they?

B   Body—What kind of physical shape are they in? How tired are they? Are they fidgety or rowdy and needing to work off some pent-up energy? What does their body language tell you?

S   Stage—Which developmental stage has the group reached? Remember that groups move up and down the levels of functioning.

Some other basic questions you might want to ask in addition to the GRABBS checklist:

- What activities will focus the group on the issues they want to examine?

- Considering that goal, what type of activity is best to start off the day? End the day?

- How many activities, in other words how much time, will be necessary to bring the group together?

- Will you need to be ready to deal with resistance from some members of the group? How will you address this?

■ Will they respond better to active games and initiatives, or will you need to moderate the activity level due to ability, space restrictions, or weather conditions?

■ How much information do they need or want about you and the program?

■ What is your contingency plan if an activity that you had in mind doesn't seem to fit the group's progress and stated goals? Do you have at least three alternative activities in mind to meet this contingency?

A Note of Caution

When using adventure activities and techniques with young people to explore issues of diversity, you will probably run into some challenging moments. The work is rewarding and full of surprises, and will demand that you draw on your finest facilitation skills. Because of the possibility of getting into some volatile issues and opening up deep-seated feelings, we recommend that you have experience working with youth groups before you begin using the activities and presenting the topics in this book.

We have seen the full spectrum of human emotions evoked during our workshops. Coming to consciousness about our differences and the treatment we've received from others during our lives is an intense process for everyone. While we hope that you and your groups will share only positive, fun-filled learning moments with each other, be aware that the experience of diversity can be traumatic for some people. Expect the unexpected, and don't be surprised if you or any of the members of your groups find long-suppressed memories and experiences coming to the surface. Rely on your best judgment and choose activities and discussion topics with caution. Know your group. Try to understand where they might go with a particular topic.

If you have any doubts about your ability to lead a group through a diversity program, don't hesitate to seek advice from your colleagues and peers or take a course in advanced facilitation skills. Most schools and other organizations involved with youths have skilled psychologists, counselors, and guidance professionals available for crisis intervention, and many have funds available for continuing education. Project Adventure offers open-enrollment workshops for facilitators throughout the United States; many are specifically designed to teach professionals how to integrate adventure with diversity training. Or you might want to find an experienced diversity trainer in your area and invite them in to co-facilitate your program with you. We don't want to discourage you from embarking on a challenging, rewarding experience, but we do hope you will take this as an opportunity to expand your knowledge and develop new skills.

The Role of the Facilitator

As stated earlier in this chapter, your role is more of a facilitator than of a traditional leader or teacher. The essence of good facilitating should be support, encouragement, and feedback. If you do all the leading for the group, they won't have the chance to experience the situation for themselves. A good adventure facilitator works with the group as a kind of safety net—someone who helps out the group if it gets in over its head.

The goal of the adventure facilitator is to see that the following basic elements of an adventure experience develop:

- Trust

- Communication

- Cooperation

- Fun

- Safety

Trust

Trust is the safety key that opens the experiential door. It allows people to share pieces of themselves without fearing that they'll be laughed at or ignored. It creates opportunities for youth to meet new challenges, knowing that others are there to support them. It means giving something a try, perhaps not succeeding, but knowing that the group will support additional attempts without ridicule.

Trust starts with you as the facilitator. From the start, if you model openness, encouragement, sensitivity, and competence, your group will feel safe with you. They will also feel safe with others in the group and may open up to them. Your role is to create a blanket of trust so that the members of your group can learn to rely on each other. This is not always an easy goal for adolescents to achieve and may require constant monitoring by you. It is your role as the facilitator to ensure that no one in the group is hurt by the experience.

Be prepared for some or all of your participants to look askance when you dance the first round of *Chicka Boom*, embody a *King Frog,* or try to get someone to laugh with a *Funny Face*. They may feel embarrassed or uncomfortable for a while. But they will participate, and if you demonstrate by example that it's OK to look a little silly, they'll feel more willing to take an emotional or physical risk. Show them that you know what you're doing. Let them see your competence, yet don't be afraid to get right in there and participate. Let your group know that you too are willing to take some risks.

Remember, your group needs to trust you first.

Communication

Communication is linked closely with trust, and it is central to the issues of diversity you will be tackling with your group. The more closely your group is working together, the more they will need to communicate with each other to prevent problems from arising. Communication is what will allow the members of your group to share their viewpoints and learn from the experiences of others. It also fosters an environment where the members of your group will feel safe enough to talk openly about their feelings.

Like trust, communication begins with you, the facilitator. Set a tone, help establish goals, and provide the framework for each of the activities. Your ability to communicate what to expect from the experience is a crucial element in establishing an atmosphere where each of the participants feels included and safe. Remember, fostering a diversity of perspectives requires that everyone feels like they are an integral part of the group, and that they can be, speak, or act without fear of ridicule or exclusion.

Strive for simplicity.
Keep things moving.
Participate in the games.
Have fun!

Your style of communicating can be as influential as what you communicate. Humor and personal warmth are always more effective than a strict or labored approach. You're not forcing anyone to participate—remember Challenge by Choice—you're inviting the members of your group to join in the activities. This freedom results in a greater sense of involvement and often helps people feel more comfortable about taking on new challenges.

Try to use mixer type games early on to establish bonds between the members of your group. *Have You Ever?*, *It's Bean Great Hearing You*, and *Who Are You?* are examples of some fun ways to ask the members of your group to share a little about themselves. Hearing about other people, recognizing that there are similarities and differences, finding something in common with someone else—all of these contribute to a sense of belonging. Creating a sense of belonging is an essential first step towards fostering an atmosphere that promotes learning about diversity.

As the facilitator, your job is to open the lines of communication. How? Listen to what everyone in your group is saying. Show each of them that you value their comments and suggestions. Ask if anyone has questions once you have explained an activity. Be open to changing a rule or adapting the action if you think it will increase the chances for getting everyone involved. Try not to restrict what the group does—provide opportunities for them to decide for themselves what they want to do.

Embody the behaviors you want your group to learn. People "understand" as much or more about you by watching what you do and don't do than by listening to what you say. In certain circumstances, this may mean that you will have to spend some time examining your own beliefs and behaviors. Stay aware of how you are responding to each member of the group and try to remain impartial.

Cooperation

Adventure activities focus on people working and playing together. This is one of the main reasons we believe they are such a good vehicle for promoting an appreciation of diversity. Whatever the setting, the goal of adventure activities is to increase each participant's ability to work as part of a group, and to develop in each person a better appreciation of what they can contribute.

People sometimes have the impression that because adventure activities focus on cooperation, there is no competition in a program that uses adventure as the primary learning technique. Competition isn't inherently bad, but we feel that designating individuals as winners and losers isn't necessary, particularly if your goal is to teach inclusion. The win-at-all-costs mentality causes many students to feel that they are not skilled enough to compete with their more talented peers and that physical activity or intellectual challenges are something to be avoided.

Cooperation doesn't have to replace competition. But since there are so many opportunities for youth to compete and lose, why not offer them opportunities where everyone can compete and win? You can structure competition so that everyone feels good about their involvement. After a group has kept their balloons off the floor for five consecutive minutes in *Equally Frantic*, it doesn't matter if everyone hit the balloons an equal number of times. The whole group takes the credit for breaking a world record; even someone on the periphery of the action feels included in the group's success. This sense of accomplishment early in a program can profoundly influence a group's ability to work together later on doing more challenging initiative tasks like the *Spider's Web*. Activities like *Group Juggling*, *The Clock*, *Peek-A-Who*, *Feeling Relay*, *Human Ladder*, and *Warp Speed* provide attainable challenges for most groups. Everyone feels good about their success. They work together, share in the accomplishment, and learn techniques that allow them to attempt more difficult problems, overcoming greater risks. Your group will be sharing in the advantages, not the disadvantages, of their diverse talents.

Remember though, working together takes effort and is not always easy. It takes practice. Some youth, given the experiences of their childhood, may not like to do it. Give the group time and expect some rough spots. Be there to support them when necessary, but don't give away the solutions.

Successful teams, performers, and artists spend countless hours developing their skills before they can use them proficiently. Create opportunities for everyone. Provide challenges. Encourage creativity and praise effort, even when it doesn't produce a successful solution.

Fun

Leading groups through adventure activities is serious business. Don't let any-one tell you otherwise. What's serious about it is that you are trying to help people learn and grow. Learning and developing new skills are serious endeav-ors.

The unusual thing about adventure is that it's also fun. Fun, and play, are not supposed to be serious. To most adults, in fact, fun is considered frivolous—something with little long term value. Fun is associated with amusement, recre-ation, and merriment, not usually with education, at least not in the traditional sense.

But fun is central to the adventure experience. Fun is important because people are involved when they're enjoying themselves. People are motivated, their attention is more focused, their energies are higher. Fun can be an end in itself, but it's also a powerful tool for encouraging everyone to get involved and share their different talents.

When your group seems sluggish, nervous, uninterested, or unenthusiastic, opt for fun. Engage your students in activities that create action, laughter, and en-ergy—*Pairs Tag, Everybody's It, Funny Face, Transformer Tag, Peek-A-Who, Hog Call, Group Juggling, Balloon Trolleys*, and *Equally Frantic*. It never fails. These activities are guaranteed to produce intensity, uncontrolled silliness, and that flush of satisfaction that says, "Let's do that again!"

As you begin to weave adventure into your work with youth, keep in mind that a successful adventure experience requires the fun component. Whether you work in a school, camp, service agency, club, athletic group or after-school program, the fun component will be necessary if you use adventure to bring your group together. Fun is intertwined in every activity, to the extent that some might say our groups have too much fun. For us, however, keeping the fun quotient high is our way of ensuring that the quality of the program is also high.

Keep the fun going, enjoy, and watch the learning happen.

Safety

The group's physical and emotional safety are issues that you will need to ad-dress over and over again when doing the activities. Don't be afraid to establish appropriate boundaries and ground rules for the group. Emotional issues can and do commonly arise from group-based activities. Use the Full Value Con-tract to establish guidelines for appropriate behavior and involve the group members in enforcing them.

You will need to monitor the group's attention and concentration levels, par-ticularly during trust sequences or any activities that involve spotting skills or physical safety. Are some participants standing around chatting while someone is preparing to do a *Trust Fall?* Remind participants of their obligation to the group and ask them to come back to the task at hand. Let the group know that everyone has an obligation to keep the group focused. Ask individuals to speak up if they feel that the Full Value Contract is not being honored. Remember too that the group's ability to focus will be important when discussing difficult issues. Attend to emotional safety the same way you would to spotting physical challenges.

You may want to call a mini-meeting from time to time to discuss behavior and help the group establish new safety guidelines. If need be, take a piece of easel paper and draw a line down the middle. Ask the group to state the qualities they feel enhance their sense of safety—listening, respect, caring, attention, cooperation, asking for help, giving assistance—and write them down on one side of the paper. On the other side, write down the behaviors that the group feels are detracting from their sense of safety with one another—"dissing," name calling, taking sides, excluding, fighting. You can hang this paper up on the wall and ask the group to come back to it whenever they feel that they have modeled the positive behaviors or as a reminder that the safety guidelines they established are not being honored. Or add the positive behaviors your group would like to model to your Full Value Contract to keep it alive.

Attending to Behavior

Accepting individuals does not mean that all behaviors are acceptable. Demonstrating trust, openness, and honesty does not mean that all remarks are acceptable. Safety and trust assume a high level of caring for each other. If you model appropriate behavior, the group will follow. Safety means commitment, commitment to each individual's welfare, ideas, and opinions. Ask the group to commit and don't be afraid to intervene if you feel that someone's physical or emotional safety is being jeopardized by an individual's or the group's behavior.

There may be moments when individuals step outside the bounds of permissible behavior and you will be obliged to respond. Try to be as open as possible with your group and convey to them what you are feeling and what you think an appropriate response requires. For instance, if two members of the group are attacking each other personally or if one of them directs the attack at you, you will have to respond.

In the case of a personal attack, try to withdraw from the subjectivity of the situation and process what is going on in front of the whole group. Make some observations about how you feel, what options you are considering in response. Take a time out and reflect on what is happening to you physically. Be open with the group and share your reactions with them. It is important that you acknowledge the other person's feelings while maintaining your own physical and emotional safety. Sometimes, the best thing you can do is simply ask the person confronting you what they need from you or from the group right now in order to resolve the conflict. Ask yourself the same question. If your participants get involved in a conflict ask them to do the same. Stay open, and remember, the group is there to support each and every member. Give them and yourself a chance to use the support and trust you have been building together!

Checklist

Finally, here's a quick checklist that covers the qualities we feel a good facilitator should model:

- Self-discloses thoughts and feelings when appropriate
- Invites others to self-examination by confronting them directly
- Identifies individual and human relations issues
- Emphasizes the "here and now" events
- Becomes involved with the group interactions through empathy and caring
- Observes body language and draws accurate inferences from it
- Listens to and draws out others through questions
- Gives praise and words of encouragement to others
- Supplies useful information about the experience when appropriate
- Accepts individuals, but not all behavior
- Creates a climate of trust and safety through enforcing rules and norms

Processing the Adventure Experience

What is processing? Simply stated, it is the act of helping a group apply the lessons that emerge from the experience of an activity to their daily lives. Processing encompasses the reflection, generalization, and application phases of the Experiential Learning Cycle (Chapter 2). During processing, your group learns how to transfer insights gained during an activity back to the real world. Processing helps your group understand how to connect the consequences of their behaviors not just to the activities, but also to their interactions with family, peers, adults, and others they encounter in their day-to-day lives. How your participants act and feel within the group is a reflection of their daily experience. Processing provides them with an opportunity to sift through their emotions and habitual responses within a safe environment.

Processing should not be looked upon as a separate activity; rather, it is connected to the whole experience. When you are processing an activity, keep in mind all the skills we discussed in the last chapter. Try to keep the discussion open, honest, direct, and compassionate. Ask questions instead of leading the discussion. If you model these qualities, it's more than likely that the group will follow your lead. If you don't feel comfortable with a topic, the group will sense your embarrassment. Often, it's better to be up-front with the group. Let them know what about the discussion bothers you. If necessary, try to find a colleague or friend with more experience to ask for assistance with the discussion next time the group meets. Or use the worksheets we've provided in the activities chapters to do some self-reflection around the issues that are challenging you. They may give you some insights that you can apply to resolving your discomfort with the group. Try to keep in mind that all of the facilitating skills we discussed in the first part of this chapter should be part of your processing repertoire.

Bear in mind that it's common for people leading adventure activities to come away from an experience feeling that it all worked perfectly and everyone did everything, only to find a whole set of complications. Maybe it was the perspective of a student who didn't feel supported, or another who felt railroaded. It is not uncommon to miss these things. The processing time allows the group to come forward with their own perceptions and conflicts. It is much better for the group to have these issues emerge in a group talk session rather than in the hallway or in a one-on-one discussion with the leader. Talking things out in the group gives the participants the opportunity to gain strength and become a more integral part of the change process.

One way to approach processing is to view it as a problem-solving activity, keeping in mind the same elements:

- Everyone participates.

- The Full Value Contract is in effect.

- Safety and trust issues are paramount.

- The leader provides the structure for the activity but relies on the group to provide the solution.

- The experience is focused on achieving positive outcomes.

- The group focuses on issues it's able to handle.

- Group and individual issues are seen as problems to be solved.

- Leaders and participants are bonded by their experience.

- Emphasis is on the present experience.

- Processing takes place after every group experience or whenever necessary.

- Participants are the agents for their own change and gradually need to take more responsibility for their learning.

Does processing require that the facilitator be passive? There's nothing that says you can't participate. "Relying on the group to provide the solution" could be construed that way, but in the processing, especially in some difficult interpretive situations, you must step in. Sit back as long as the group members are providing ample interpretation and feedback. If they aren't, then say something. But don't jump in immediately! Often we are so excited about an insight we've developed that we can't stop ourselves from dropping the pearl. Give the group the opportunity to come up with it. When it's time for you to say something, try to work it out so that the group says it. Oftentimes a well-placed question can crack a deadlock and get the juices flowing better than a monologue. Remember, the group wants you to be the expert because experts are safe to be with. They have all the answers. The group doesn't have to think when experts are willing to step in. Much of the flattery directed towards you as their leader is the group's method of keeping you on top and keeping itself free from the burden of interpretation and responsibility. It is not that you shouldn't share your knowledge, but you need to get the participants to do the thinking as much as possible, to dig into their feelings, to build up their own collection of observations, and to provide an atmosphere that allows them to act on their thoughts.

Sequencing Processing

A group needs to get warmed up before it can get to the nub of an experience. It's just like playing warm-up games before doing problem solving. That's why it's important to sequence the discussion.

So often we go right to the heart of things. A lack of group response to initial questions from the facilitator can come more from uneasiness with the questioning than from inability to discuss what has happened. We've all been there—we know the students have experienced something. We saw it in their expressions, heard it in their exchanges. So why can't they talk about it? Often it is because we jumped right into the most difficult and abstract processing topic, that of evaluation and opinion. "How do you feel?"

A more effective way to get students talking is by using the sequence of questions first discussed in Chapter 2 and the Experiential Learning Cycle: *What?, So What?,* and *Now What?*

What?

Asking what happened helps us ease into the discussion by beginning with the facts. This is an easy place for students to start, because in any adventure activity there are plenty of facts, occurrences, and interactions to work with. A good way to start a discussion of *What?* facts is by using a *Go Around,* where everyone in the group contributes a descriptive sentence. The description can also be shortened to one word.

So What?

Active listening presupposes that we do something with what we hear. Starting with *What?* leads naturally into interpretation and the next level of questions, the *So What?* Because we've gotten the group to talk, it's much easier to move on to this. It's here that group members abstract and generalize what they're learning from the experience. You can now begin to get into more questions about the effects of the factual information gleaned from the *What?* questions.

You can use the above *What?* technique in the *So What?* by simply shifting from the descriptive to the interpretive. Use the *Go Around* as a way for participants to describe how they feel about the event. You can also ask each group member to come up with a one-word or short-sentence definition of a key term, such as spotting, discounting, helping, involvement, leadership, confronting. Perhaps some of those key terms will arise from the *Go Around*. You can then build on what they're already talking about. In addition, try *The Whip*—a short round robin or a positive, nonthreatening activity in which each person completes a short statement like "I'm glad that I…"

During the *So What?* phase, you can also ask the group to reflect on goals they've been working on. The question "Did we honor the Full Value Contract?" gets us into those group goals. It is a general, nonthreatening question, one that can be asked after every experience, and a safe place to start because you're not focusing on any individual behavior. It translates as "Did we treat each other well, or did we discount each other? Was there support, or devaluing? Did we stick to the rules we set up?" The group is seen as an entity that needs to be taken care of, much as we take care of an individual. The group members are both the agents of change and the persons to be changed. We can say, "Without a healthy and responsible group, we are greatly diminished."

> The group members are both the agents of change and the persons to be changed.

The Now What?

The *Now What?* is the process of taking lessons learned from the experience and transferring them to other situations. It is standard at the end of processing to ask a question like "What lessons did we learn by doing *Minefield* that we can use when we listen to others?" Taking the learning from one activity and carrying it over to the next activity or discussion helps the group connect what they have been doing to a larger picture. Often *you* will clearly see what can be carried over, but the group will not have the foggiest notion. It is important to help them make the connections.

The *Now What?* is a good place for students to talk about goal setting away from the group. Use the energy of the experience to start participants thinking about what they can do in other areas of their lives. For example, the spotting energy that a particular person exhibited during a *Trust Fall* could be suggested as a lesson that can be applied to being able to concentrate during an academic class, or the caring that is necessary to support a friend going through a difficult period.

Feedback

The purpose of feedback is to provide constructive information about how someone's behavior affects others and how others perceive their actions. Learning how to give appropriate feedback isn't easy; the best way to say something honestly and respectfully isn't always immediately obvious. An important point to remember, though, is that you should always try to stay focused on what happened and how you felt, not why you think someone did something.

Feedback is a two-way process. The best feedback is nonjudgmental and demonstrates respect for the person on the receiving end as well. For example, if one of your participants was fooling around and distracting the others during a trust-building activity like the *Trust Fall,* process what it felt like for everyone. Instead of letting the group engage in accusations like "Mary, you didn't even try to catch me when I fell because you were goofing off with John," ask the participant to tell the group how they felt. "Mary, I felt like you weren't there to hold me up when I was falling and I was a little scared. How did everyone else feel?" Feelings are universal; being scared is an emotion that Mary can share with everyone else in the group. Through shared emotions, the group can begin to find a place of common ground.

As the leader, your role is to help the participants gain an understanding of the significance of their actions and behaviors. You will be bringing clarity to the feedback process, pointing out alternative perspectives, and raising questions. But remember, try not to tell your group what happened. Instead, guide them through the stages of interpreting the experience for themselves. Provide a framework for the discussion, maintain perspective, and keep the group's focus on the learning opportunities that present themselves during the activities.

Some of the skills you will need in order to create a productive processing session will come naturally, and others you will gain through experience. Leading a group through the processing of the activities does not mean that you are responsible for controlling the outcome. Leading a processing session does mean, however, that you are responsible for keeping the group on track and helping them to communicate effectively, express appropriate feelings, listen to each other, and give praise and encouragement. A safe emotional climate will allow them to grow and reach their own conclusions. We have set out some general guidelines for you to follow and a list of sample questions that, in our experience, create a foundation for safe and productive feedback and processing. Ultimately, however, you will have to follow your own instincts in each situation you encounter.

Processing Guidelines

The specific questions you ask during a processing session will depend on the goals your group has established for itself as they go through each activity, but here are some general guidelines:

Ask open-ended questions instead of making statements. Good processing means that the group is sharing ideas and information, not giving advice to one another. "How was that for you?" "How did you feel?"

Try to keep your questions appropriate. Don't follow up if you sense that someone in the group is uncomfortable or might feel like you are prying.

Accept individuals and their feelings, but not all behavior. Enforcing the group's established rules will enhance the climate of emotional safety and trust.

Show that you are involved with the group. Be compassionate and understanding. Show that you are willing to listen.

Pay attention to what is not said as well as what is said. Body language may be telling you more than what the group is saying out loud. Are they shifting around, visibly acting uncomfortable? Ask them to share what is making them uncomfortable.

Challenge by Choice. Respect the need for privacy if someone appears unwilling to respond to a question. Don't force them to divulge their feelings.

Don't rely on one person to represent an entire group. See if anyone else wants to answer and add something new to the discussion. "What do other people feel?"

Disclose your own thoughts and feelings when appropriate. "I am confused. How do other people feel about this?"

Focus on giving praise and encouragement to the participants. Never attack the personal worth of a participant, compare one student to another, or lose your temper.

Be nonjudgmental. Focus feedback on behavior rather than on the person. Be specific about what the participant did during an activity instead of commenting on why you imagine they did something.

Use "I" statements—your own feelings. Ask the group to focus on their own feelings, too. "How did you feel?" "What is everyone feeling right now?" Keeping the group focused on its feelings will help you maintain an atmosphere of open communication. If you hear the group engaging in recriminations like "she or he did this or that to me," ask them to describe how it felt, not what was done.

Try to keep your group focused on one issue at a time. "We want to move on to that. Let's see what else there is on this topic."

Focus on exploring alternatives instead of finding answers or solutions. "What can we learn from that?" "Does anyone have anything to add?"

Adventure processing is an art, not a science. Knowing when and how to provide support and guidance, when and how to step back or step in without controlling the outcome, are challenges to all adventure leaders. If you hear yourself doing most of the talking, you may need to ask yourself if you are asking questions or giving information to the group. Is the group staying focused on the issues at hand, or are they straying from them, perhaps trying to avoid emotions that make them feel uncomfortable? You may need to help them refocus, bringing the group's attention back to their stated goals, pointing out the comments and questions that are relevant. Don't be afraid to make mistakes with your group; it's natural. Try to re-examine your own style on a regular basis, stay open, and admit your mistakes to the group, if necessary. The more open you are and the more you take responsibility for learning from the experiences that present themselves, the more your group will, too.

Concluding Thoughts

If you have never led an adventure experience before, you may be feeling as though this chapter has been a long and intimidating list of dos and don'ts for guiding your group through a perilous journey of learning trust, cooperation, and communication. Perhaps you forgot about the fun component, however. Keep the fun going, and the getting there will happen naturally as you and your group overcome one challenge after another.

None of us were born with all of the skills it takes to facilitate an adventure experience—we still learn something new each and every time we lead a group. To our minds, particularly when you are teaching youth to flourish among people of different skills, backgrounds, appearance, and abilities, keeping an open mind is the greatest asset you can bring to this work. Diversity work in the context of an adventure experience will challenge you to re-examine your own beliefs and values. But if you stay open, so will your group. The most important thing you can do for yourself and the group is to support and encourage everyone to grow and learn through the experience.

Expect conflict; it happens in all groups. Process it when it happens and know that it is a natural part of the evolution of any group. Above all, trust your instincts, have fun, and enjoy the experience of learning through doing.

Suggested Reading:

Kennedy, Eugene and Sara C. Charles, MD, *On Becoming a Counselor: A Basic Guide For Non-Professional Counselors,* The Continuum Publishing Co., New York, 1990.

Nadler, Reldan S. and John L. Luckner, *Processing The Adventure Experience: Theory & Practice,* Kendall/Hunt Publishing Co., Dubuque, IA, 1992.

Rohnke, Karl and Steve Butler. *QuickSilver: Adventure Games, Initiative Problems, Trust Activities, and a Guide to Effective Leadership,* Project Adventure, Inc., Hamilton, MA, 1996

Rohnke, Karl. *Cowstails and Cobras II: A Guide to Games, Initiatives, Ropes Courses and Adventure Curriculum,* Project Adventure, Inc., Hamilton, MA, 1989

Rohnke, Karl. *Silver Bullets: A Guide to Initiative Problems, Adventure Games and Trust Activities,* Project Adventure, Inc., Hamilton, MA, 1984

Creating Nurturing Communities

This section explores some of the challenges we face while trying to build nurturing communities. Simply knowing who we are is only the first step in establishing a society that values human diversity. It is vital that we learn to identify the emotions of discrimination, learn to listen and validate, become allies, and prevent the spread of negative, discriminatory behaviors.

Each of the chapters in this section addresses one of these challenges. We have provided some basic background information to each topic, but it is not our intention nor within the scope of this book to delve into the subjects to any depth. There are whole books written on each of these subjects, and a few of the ones we have found particularly helpful are listed within each chapter as suggested reading. If you want an in-depth look at the topics presented in these chapters, these books are a good place to start.

This section also begins the activity chapters. As stated in the introduction, many of these activities can be used to work through other issues presented in the book. We have listed other areas where you might find an activity particularly useful under the heading, *Diversity Skills,* in the directions for each activity.

As you begin to present the activities to your group, especially if you have not used adventure activities before, refer back to the information presented in Section One. Have you discussed and developed a Full Value Contract under which you group will operate? Do you fully understand the concept of Challenge By Choice? Have you read through the sequencing section to ensure that you start your group off with appropriate activities? Without these basic principles and concepts understood and in place, your group may have fun and enjoy the activities but will miss out on their true teaching potential.

The vignettes included in each chapter are intended to illustrate the specific chapter's topic. Reading these to your group at the beginning of a session can be a good way to introduce the subject. Use the Continuum, Awareness, and Group Skills Ideas as a guide to the progression your group will be following. At the end of each chapter, there is a list of general processing questions that can be used with most of the activities.

5

Listening and Communicating

Before the students in your group can begin to tackle some of the emotionally difficult issues of diversity, you must first build an atmosphere of positive communication. Positive communication involves an exchange of ideas and beliefs that encourages new learning. It allows individuals room to maintain their own perceptions while at the same time recognizing the experiences and beliefs that form the basis of other individuals' viewpoints. One of the first steps individuals can take toward positive communication is learning to be active listeners.

Active listening is a skill we acquire through practice and training. Many of us know intuitively when someone else isn't really listening to what we are saying, something that is often communicated through body language. Here are some of the primary signals we sense, see, and feel when someone isn't listening:

- Interrupting—the speaker isn't allowed to finish stating their opinions.

- Eye contact—there is little or no eye contact with the speaker, or if there is, it is confrontational—direct and unyielding.

- Body language—arms and legs crossed, shifting position, body turned away from the speaker or aggressive, bordering on physical threat.

- Emotions—angry, threatening, upset.

- Tone of voice—loud, harsh, angry.

- Rebuttal—the conversation isn't over until the speaker gives up or gives in and comes around to the listener's point of view.

On the other side of the coin, however, we also have to consider how we convey our ideas and opinions. It's one thing to speak reasonably and calmly, giving our listeners the freedom to reflect and respond, but there are times when communicating becomes an opportunity to vent, create conflict, or behave aggressively. Most listeners shut down in the face of anger. Who can listen actively if the speaker is mirroring the signals we attributed in the above list to an inflexible listener?

Essentially, an environment of positive listening and communicating requires that both speakers and listeners learn how to engage in open discussion that provides everyone with a chance to express their views and be heard. Achieving this goal doesn't mean that venting or angry discussion isn't permitted—sometimes it's important and helpful to let people air their emotions—but it should not be more than a phase on the way toward creating an atmosphere of peaceful dialogue and discussion. Here are some of the signs we look for to show us that others are actively listening to and communicating positively with each other:

- Engaged—we are engaged in the discussion, but allow the speaker to finish expressing their views.

- Eye contact—we make eye contact, expressing interest and showing we are involved with what is being said.

- Body language—arms and legs uncrossed, body faced toward the speaker, sitting or standing in a comfortable relaxed position.

- Emotions—calm, relaxed, and unperturbed.

- Tone of voice—calm, easy, unthreatening.

- Understanding—the conversation isn't a means to force our views on the speaker; we try to understand and validate other points of view; we attempt to put ourselves in the other person's position without becoming judgmental.

How Do We Learn to Listen?

In our experience, the best way to develop good listening and communicating skills is through learning how to give and receive feedback. This chapter reinforces some of the basic facilitating and processing skills presented in the first section. You may find some of the information repetitive, but remember that the purpose of this chapter is to transfer these skills to the group and reinforce them at the individual level.

This chapter deals specifically with the skills required for becoming an effective listener and communicator. This means learning how to give and receive positive feedback. The Full Value Contract is an essential tool for helping your group learn this skill. If you haven't begun to develop a contract with your group, we suggest that this is a good place to start. Ask your group to discuss how they know they are being listened to. What are some of the ways they would like to include everyone's views in their discussions? How do they think they can communicate their own views without discounting the opinions of the other participants when there is a disagreement?

Feedback

Disclosing how you are reacting to the way another person is behaving or what they are saying is called feedback. The purpose of feedback is to provide constructive information that helps individuals understand how their behavior affects others and how their actions are perceived, regardless of the intention. Giving good feedback requires that you communicate in a nonthreatening manner. This does not mean that hushed tones are required, but that respect must be paramount. This attitude alone will help the person or persons on the receiving end of the feedback achieve an open, nonjudgmental attitude of active listening.

> *A productive feedback cycle, like safety and trust, assumes that your group has established a high level of caring for each other.*

A productive feedback cycle, like safety and trust, assumes that your group has established a high level of caring for each other. What is the best way to communicate the impact that someone else's behavior has on you? How do you do it without posing a threat to the other person and encourage them to listen to your views? How do you listen to others in a way that acknowledges the validity of their feelings, in a way that reassures them that, while their experience may be unique, emotional responses are universal? Positive communication and active listening skills both require that the giver and receiver withhold judgment and open themselves up to exploring, discovering, and gaining insights about the subject under discussion.

The Feedback Exchange

We agree that all of this is useful information, but what are some concrete methods for applying these insights? Here's a list of tips on the ways your group can begin to give each other effective feedback:

Are they ready? Check that the person about to receive the feedback is willing to receive it. Some moments are not appropriate, and asking if you can give feedback will put both the giver and receiver on the same level. If someone isn't ready to hear what you're saying, it won't have much effect. "Do you feel like talking about what just happened?" or "I understand that you're very angry about what just happened. I'd like to share my feelings about it with you, but I don't know if this is the right time. Do you want to talk now?"

Focus on behavior. Be clear, concise, caring, and constructive, including positive as well as negative behaviors. For example, if the group feels that someone has been holding back, not talking or participating in the activities, and there is general frustration about it, adopt a tone that shows you value the person's input. "Sharon, you haven't been sharing much with the group today. I've really enjoyed and appreciated the contributions you've made so far, and I miss hearing from you. Is there anything I can do, or the rest of us can do to make you feel more comfortable about joining in with us in the activities and our discussions?" In other words, let her know that she is a valued member of the group and that the group is willing to listen to her and do what they can to make her feel part of the group.

Focus on what you can hear and see, not on the inferences you draw from the behavior. "You haven't given us your input yet," not "You seem withdrawn and angry at the group."

Phrase feedback as a description, not a judgment, of the other person's behavior. Again, stick with a positive, caring attitude instead of accusatory statements like "Sharon, your behavior is inappropriate" or "Your anger is affecting the group negatively."

Describe behavior in terms of "more or less," not "either/or." As in, "Maybe it would have been easier for the rest of us to understand what you were saying if you had talked more about how you felt instead of what you thought I was 'doing' to you."

Relate behavior to a specific situation, not to what they may or may not have done in an abstract situation. Ask the group to stay on track and talk about what happened, not what could have happened.

You are not giving advice. Telling someone what they should be doing doesn't allow them to find their own solutions, individually or as part of the group. Have the group adopt an attitude of willingness to share ideas and information. If you model this kind of attitude, the group will follow. Ask everyone to share. "Does anyone have any ideas about what we can do to make Sharon feel more comfortable? Sharon, what do you think?"

Focus on alternatives, not answers or solutions to their behavior. Have the group share some of the ways they cope with their emotions or conflict.

Focus on the value the feedback will have for the receiver, not on the value of release that it provides the person giving the feedback. Similarly, keep feedback at a level that is useful to the person receiving it, not on the amount the giver might like to provide. Too much feedback can become damaging. It is important that feedback doesn't become an opportunity for group members to vent their feelings.

Use "I" statements and remind the group, using their Full Value Contract, of their responsibility for each other's safety. Statements like "We feel that you shouldn't have said…" or "They all thought that…" put the receiver on the defensive. It's no longer a one-on-one exchange, and an individual will feel like the group has ganged up on them.

A Two-Way Exchange

The process of giving and receiving feedback is a complicated one. Figuring out the best way to say something to someone honestly and with respect is not always easy. In addition, hearing feedback is another skill that takes practice. Hearing what a person means to say sometimes requires patience, good will, and asking for clarification. Being open to the possibility of change doesn't hurt, either.

In preparing to receive feedback, keep in mind that feelings get expressed in different ways by different people. Some of this comes from our backgrounds, some from our temperaments, some from the situation at hand. Each of us is different. As you and your groups learn to communicate across your differences, here are some additional points to keep in mind:

- Don't assume sameness.

- Monitor and stay aware of your instincts. What is natural to you may not be natural to others.

- Familiar behaviors may have different meanings.

- Don't assume that what you said was understood the way you meant it.

- You don't have to like or accept different behaviors, but you could benefit from attempts to understand what motivates them.

- Most people behave rationally, you just have to find the rationale.

Peter Senge refers to four types of communication in his book, *The Fifth Discipline*. It is helpful to look at those four types of communication and how they each have their place on the communication spectrum, with both positive and negative uses. Some modes of communication may be better than others for giving and receiving feedback, but don't rule out the possibility that feedback will come in any of these categories. Recognizing this and helping group members to choose their words and their whole way of communication with consciousness will be essential to guiding your group though difficult waters. When the groundwork has been done, getting angry, afraid, sad, excited, or happy will be easier for everyone in your group.

1. **Raw Debate**—Sometimes called "venting" or "hashing it out," raw debate has to do with discussing to "win" and asserting one's own view, if not loudly, clearly over others'.

2. **Polite Discussion**—Without going too deeply into the issue, polite discussion keeps things from getting too personal or too specific.

3. **Skillful Discussion**—The goal of skillful discussion is to reach a final understanding and to bring the issue at hand to a close.

4. **Dialogue**—Seeking to discover new ground and exchanging ideas is the name of the game with dialogue.

Concluding Thoughts

Even with all these pointers, the truth is, feedback doesn't always come neatly packaged and at the appropriate moments.

We all have different value systems that are the product of our experience, culture, family, and social backgrounds. Learning how to coexist peacefully requires a basic understanding that each of us has the right to live by our acquired value systems, providing that they don't inflict pain or injury on others.

The Full Value Contract you and your group have created is a useful tool for working with the skills you will be teaching in this chapter. One of the core principles of the Full Value Contract is an agreement to respect different views, even if they are in disagreement with yours.

Suggested Reading

Cruden, Loren. *Compass of the Heart: Embodying Medicine Wheel Teachings.* Rochester, VT: Destiny Books, 1996. A guide to integrating body and spirit, to connecting with the web of life through Native American and other earth-oriented traditions.

Senge, Peter. *The Fifth Discipline: The Art and Practice of the Learning Organization.* New York: Doubleday/Currency, 1990. Senge's book draws on science, spiritual wisdom, psychology, and the cutting edge of management thought to show how businesses can overcome their "learning disabilities" and beat the odds of failure.

Schoel, Jim, Dick Prouty and Paul Radcliffe. *Islands of Healing: A Guide to Adventure Based Counseling.* Hamilton, MA: Project Adventure, Inc., 1988. A book that explains adventure theories and their practical applications — establishing trust, a sense of belonging and self-esteem, challenge.

Dana, Daniel. *Managing Differences: How to Build Better Relationships at Work and at Home.* Wolcott, CT: MTI Publications, 1988. A review of communication skills necessary for addressing interpersonal and organizational conflict.

Worksheet

Try to list some of the things that prevent you from really listening to others. Are you more concerned with what is happening to you? Do your own thoughts get in the way? _____

_____

_____

How do you know when you are really listening? How does your body language change? _____

_____

_____

How do you know when someone is really listening to you?

_____

_____

_____

Can you list some occasions when you haven't listened or just assumed you knew what someone was going to say before they said it? How do you think it made them feel? _____

_____

_____

How do you feel when you perceive that someone isn't really listening to you? How do you express your frustration? _____

_____

_____

_____

How difficult is it for you to receive feedback? Can you think of times that you took feedback as personal criticism? How did you react, and how do you think your reaction prevented you from learning more about yourself?

_____

_____

_____

Buying Rutabagas

I was in the produce section of the grocery store one morning when an old man standing next to me began complaining about vegetables. "No rutabagas," he muttered. He looked sidelong at me as I poked at a package of tofu. "They got no rutabagas. They're a very sweet vegetable when they're fresh," he stated. "They got hardly any old kinds of vegetables here."

I agreed that the selection was sparse, and tried to continue my shopping. The old man stood there looking distraught. "Bet you don't even know what a rutabaga looks like," he challenged. "Young people [I am in my forties] don't know about those kinds of foods. It's all disappearing."

I struggled with my aversion to engaging with strangers, and let it be overridden by the need of this old man to be heard. I faced him fully and met his eyes. He drew himself up and proceeded to discourse on heirloom fruits and vegetables, and how they are becoming lost to us because no one cares, and young people are not learning about them.

He tried to list those foods for me—it was like an invocation. He faltered; his face strained. "I can't remember," he said, his voice shaking. "It's in my head but my tongue can't get it out."

There is so much disconnection in our society: age stratification, sexual division, racial separation, class hierarchy. Humanness is communal. How can our humanity be healthy without interrelationships that honor inclusiveness? The old man in the store was so unused to being heard that his brain seized up in the face of complete attention.

Lives battered by disrespect and violence can be healed by communion that listens, that touches in kind ways, that acknowledges common ground amid diversity.

—*From* The Compass of the Heart *by Loren Cruden*

Sunday School

We attend a United Methodist Church. It was our choice to make this change for various reasons. One included the belief that the most "segregated hour" in this country is the hour we choose to worship. We wanted to somehow change this. There are several interesting items worth mentioning about the United Methodist denomination:

—The Methodist religion arose from a division in the Episcopal Church over slavery. The Episcopal were pro-slavery and the Methodists opposed it for ethical reasons.

—It is a highly diverse Protestant denomination with many churches in urban areas. The majority of its followers are people of color and many parishes have relatively equal members of African, European, Asian, and Latino descent. The largest UMCs are in Korea.

—It is viewed as a "liberal" church with supportive views of women as clergy and of homosexuals. It holds annual worship services from the Native American tradition and provides members of all descents with an enormous amount of support for their cultural beliefs.

Our experience with our church and its members was a positive one for the first four years. Until our son entered the third grade and, consequently, the third grade Sunday school class. One day after church the following happened: Colin shared his Sunday school lesson… "Today we had to pick someone who we thought was a role model for us. I picked Malcolm X!" he said with much excitement. He went on to explain in more detail. "Mr. Thorn said he [Malcolm X] was not a good role model because he didn't like white people. I told him he must not understand. Malcolm X wanted Black people to have equal rights and that I had watched the movie with you and we talked about him. He was not a bad man. And he is still my role model!"

Well, of course I was proud of Colin. Proud of his ability to stand up for his opinion and his ability to articulate it clearly. I was extremely angry with Mr. Thorn, however. How dare he choose to shoot down my son's selection of a role model. How dare he make such an assumption and a damaging one at that! Needless to say, my husband and I addressed the issue with the superintendent of the Sunday school. In addition, we supported, reinforced, and validated Colin's response. In essence saying: even an adult has no right to push their way of seeing things on anyone else. You have a right to challenge that stance of "My way is the BEST way!"

Continuum

Venting ➔Speaking ➔Communicating—Hearing ➔Listening

We all need to vent our feelings from time to time, and it's a healthy thing to do. But what if we get carried away and do all the talking? Sometimes it's better to slow down and start trying to hear what other people are saying. Or even better, listen to their point of view. Maybe we have something to learn from them.

Awareness

It's easy to think our values are the only acceptable values. Respecting that other people will have different values than our own is an essential part of learning to welcome and relish the richness of human diversity.

Step One: Become aware of other people's values, needs, concerns, issues.

Step Two: Let them know you can respect those values even when they differ from your own.

Group Skills

Valuing—It's worth taking the time to value all individuals' personal, cultural, ethical, and social values. Stop, ask questions, and learn to listen to the answers.

Learning to listen to new voices—Once we open our ears and our eyes to the views of others, we will encounter new perspectives, and that is not always easy.

Successful listening is active listening. Pay continued attention to raising the awareness of your group as to how and when they are listening (or not listening).

A few questions that will help youth to "listen to how they are listening" are:

- I wonder how well I listen?
- I wonder why my communications break down?
- I wonder how I get into conflicts with certain people? I like these people, mostly.
- I wonder what I can do to become a better listener?

Activities

This chapter presents the first section of activities. The goal is to help your group learn some of the skills we've discussed above as well as how to begin applying those skills in a caring and perceptive manner. Because the objective of the Ice Breakers and De-Inhibitizers is to get the groups loosened up, relaxed, and enjoying the time they work together, we haven't included a list of processing questions unless they apply to the activity. You might not want to spend much time processing these first activities except to ask from time to time how the group feels. Is everyone enjoying themselves? Does the group as a whole feel that everyone is participating in an appropriate manner? Not everyone will want to respond. Remember to remind yourself and the group of Challenge by Choice—all members of the group have the right to decide at what level they want to participate. Your role as facilitator is to make sure that participants are responding and adhering to the norms the group has established for itself.

As you familiarize yourself with the activities presented in this and the following chapters, you will begin to find your own ways of presenting them. But to get you started, we've provided some ways of framing each activity. These "openings" will help you and your group see how the lessons from the activity can be applied to the diversity topics introduced in the chapter. In some cases, you may want to start by reading the opening to the group. In others, you may want to mix it in with the directions or add it on to the end of your instructions for the activity.

Inch Worm

Activity Type:	De-Inhibitizer
Activity Level:	Moderate, requires some strength and coordination
Space:	Your usual meeting room or outdoor field
Time:	About 10 to 15 minutes or until the group gets bored
Group Size:	Pairs
Prerequisite:	Ability to have close physical contact
Props:	None

Opening

It's not always easy to get where you're trying to go when you've got a partner with you. Let's see how well you can work together.

Directions

Split the group up into pairs and have them sit on the ground facing their partners. Now, tell them to inch toward one another until they are close enough to sit on each other's feet. Big feet offer an advantage or at least a certain comfort factor. Once they've arrived, tell them to grasp each other's elbows or upper arms with their hands.

From here, they get to decide which direction they want to travel in. Sideways movement is pretty much out of the question, so they'll have to go backwards or forwards, depending on whose perspective you take. After deciding, the partner in whose direction they're headed lifts their derriere off the ground and moves 12 inches or so toward whatever goal they have in mind. Movement's slow, so you might want to tell them not to be too ambitious about setting their goals. The second partner now lifts off the ground and in a cooperative, bug-like movement duplicates the step above and moves toward his or her partner.

Diversity Skills

Building allies, group identities, gender and sexual orientation, racial identity, physical and mental ability

Processing

You may or may not want to process this activity, depending on how your group responds. Sometimes it's better just to let them get their giggles out. If you do process, however, frame your questions around how easy or difficult it was for them to work together. What made it easy? How did they find a way of cooperating?

Have You Ever?

...this is your chance to find out if you're alone or not!

Activity Type: Ice Breaker/De-Inhibitizer

Activity Level: Low-key

Space: Enough room to form a circle

Time: About 15 minutes, or keep it going if you see the connections happening.

Group Size: Anywhere from 5 on up

Prerequisite: Some familiarity with each other

Props: None

Opening

How many times have you thought that you're the only one who's ever done something or felt a certain way? Well, this is your chance to find out if you're alone or not!

Directions

Have the group get into a circle. Ask them to either raise their hands or walk to a new place in the circle if the answer to the *Have You Ever?* question is yes.

Give players a few seconds to get their hands up or to move. People will often wait for someone else to respond before they do.

Once they've gotten going, you may want to add the rule that the last person to reach their new place in the circle or raise their hand gets to ask the next question. Let them think up their own.

Some *Have You Ever?* Questions

❑ Walked out of a movie in the middle? What movie?

❑ Slept through a movie that you paid for?

❑ Gotten an autograph from a famous person? Who?

❑ Broken a bone in your body? What bone?

❑ Hiked a mountain?

❑ Been out of your time zone?

More *Have You Ever?* Questions

- ❏ Been out of your state?
- ❏ Been out of the country?
- ❏ Tripped in front of a large group of people?
- ❏ Danced with someone you didn't like?
- ❏ Seen the President in person? Where?
- ❏ Gotten your hair cut and were embarrassed to go to school because of it?
- ❏ Seen a live python or other dangerous snake?
- ❏ Climbed up the Statue of Liberty and/or the Empire State Building?
- ❏ Traveled across the country?
- ❏ Been on TV?
- ❏ Been to a rock concert? Where? What band did you see?
- ❏ Stuck bubble gum behind your ear to store it?
- ❏ Been to the ocean?
- ❏ Known anyone who can speak five languages? Four? Three?
- ❏ Broken a window on your house? How or with what?
- ❏ Watched Sesame Street after the age of ten?
- ❏ Known anyone who won the lottery?
- ❏ Gotten mixed up between the boys' and girls' bathrooms and gone into the wrong one?
- ❏ Laughed loudly at a movie theater when no one else did?
- ❏ Been the only person at a movie?
- ❏ Had your stomach growl in the middle of a quiet class? In church?
- ❏ Talked on the phone with one person for six hours straight?
- ❏ Started your parents' car when you were younger than 14?
- ❏ Not been able to find the door handle when you were trying to get out of a car?
- ❏ Opened the windows of a car when the air conditioning was on?
- ❏ Called a 900 number?
- ❏ Turned on a radio when the volume was turned up very loud?
- ❏ Begged for something for a long time, and then didn't like it when you got it? What was it?

More *Have You Ever?* Questions

❏ Walked into a glass door because you didn't see it?

❏ Gotten a gift that you really didn't like?

❏ Been within two miles of a nuclear power plant?

❏ Remembered a phone number but not whose it was?

❏ Called a friend, but thought you were calling another?

❏ Eaten a whole pizza by yourself? What size?

❏ Broken your nose?

❏ Had stitches? Where?

❏ Fallen asleep during a class? Fireworks? A test?

❏ Sneezed and hiccuped at the same time?

❏ Played *Have You Ever?* before today?

❏ Been in a parade?

❏ Eaten raw oysters?

❏ Broken an established school athletic record?

❏ Helped an animal give birth?

❏ Developed and printed your own black and white film?

❏ Swum 50 yards nonstop underwater?

❏ Flown in a glider?

❏ Eaten one of the following: tripe, cow's tongue, pig's knuckles, brain, or mountain oysters?

❏ Given blood?

❏ Read a complete book by kerosene or candlelight?

❏ Been a participant on a ropes course?

❏ Been in every state in the US (all 50)? Anyone been to 40? 30?

❏ Ridden in a Rolls Royce?

❏ Owned more than one cat at a time?

❏ Swallowed a raw egg straight from the shell?

❏ Tried hang-gliding?

❏ Had a dog lift its leg on you?

❏ Received a belt other than white in Karate or one of the other martial arts?

More *Have You Ever?* Questions

- ❏ Cut a lawn using a push mower (no engine)?
- ❏ Been in a crowd of more than 40,000 people?
- ❏ Been dumped on by a seagull or other bird?
- ❏ Been accused of having an accent?
- ❏ Started a fire without matches or a lighter?

Challenge Level

As your group warms up to each other and you begin to feel that they are communicating openly, you might want to come back to *Have You Ever?*, but this time have them ask more pointed questions. Here are some examples:

- ❏ Been the last one picked for a sports team?
- ❏ Been so embarrassed you wanted to cry in front of other people?
- ❏ Been called by a name that puts down your background?
- ❏ Been excluded from something because of the way you look?
- ❏ Been included because of the way you look?
- ❏ Been told you can't do something because you're too young?

Let the group think up their own questions.

Diversity Skills

This activity works for almost any group and under any circumstances. Have them think of questions that relate to any of the topics in this book and let them discover what they share with each other.

Processing

Have You Ever? is a wonderful game for finding out that we all have things in common. Most people generally find out that they weren't the only ones to go through an excruciatingly embarrassing moment. Then again, sometimes they realize they're the only ones that did something. Ask the group to discuss what it felt like to realize that other people have done some of the same things as them or what it felt like to be the only person.

Circle the Circle ■

Activity Type:	Warm Up/Trust Building
Activity Level:	Moderate
Space:	Any open space
Time:	About 15–20 minutes
Group Size:	Any manageable size
Prerequisite:	None
Props:	Two hula hoops and a watch

Opening

We're standing here holding hands and it's a little uncomfortable, but maintaining our connections with each other is very important. Your challenge is to stay connected as you pass an important piece of information (hula hoop) around the circle.

Directions

Get the group into a circle and ask them to hold hands. Place the hula hoop between two players so that their hands are through the center of the hula hoop. The object of this activity is to get the hula hoop all the way around the circle and back to where it started by somehow getting people through the hula hoop without breaking hands. Group members can help each other as long as they do not break hands with the people on either side of them.

■ Let the group try it once without timing them.

■ After the practice run, ask the group to discuss what problems they had and how they can solve them so the next try will go more smoothly.

■ Ask the group to establish a time goal for themselves. This is a good lesson in group goal setting. If the group that you are working with is large, you may need to decide on a group goal using the input that the group has given you. We usually try to find an average of the goals that are suggested. (For example, if we hear 30 seconds, one minute, and three minutes, we might suggest a minute and 30 seconds as a group goal.) In a smaller or more mature group you can let them establish a goal by themselves—a good group decision-making challenge. Either way, ask one last time if everyone understands and agrees with the goal.

- Try the game again and time it.

- If the goal is not met after this run, you may want to encourage them to try again using the same goal or setting a new goal. Either way, ask the group if they have any ideas of how they could improve upon the last time. If the group does meet their goal, you may want to ask them to set a new one and try again.

Options

After the group has had a few tries at *Circle the Circle* with one hula hoop, you can add a new challenge. Choose a starting person and put one hula hoop in this person's right hand and one in the left hand. People on either side of the starting person should grab his or her hands through the center of the hula hoop. On "Go," the two hula hoops (a rumor and a fact) need to go in opposite directions around the circle. Both hula hoops must go around the circle and end up in the same hands that they started in. (The hula hoops will need to cross each other twice in order to successfully complete this.) Remind the group—at no time can they break hands. This activity may be frustrating, but it always works out when people work together!

Diversity Skills

Validating feelings, building allies, group identities, individual identity, ability, goal setting, cooperation.

Processing

As you process this activity, have the group think about how they cooperated both while they were establishing their time goals and during the activity.

- Did you stay connected?

- How about when you didn't have any information to pass?

- Did you set a realistic time goal?

- What's important about goal setting?

Human Camera

Activity Type:	Trust Building
Activity Level:	Moderate
Space:	You can do this activity just about anywhere. If you do this inside, it's nice to have a few rooms that the group can move around in. Outside, anywhere will do.
Time:	About 20 minutes; 5 for each person as camera and another 10 or 15 to discuss what they saw.
Group Size:	Any size
Prerequisite:	Be sure that your participants trust each other enough to be led around with their eyes closed.
Props:	None except for some good views, close-ups, and distant landscapes

Opening

Your partner will be your camera. Instead of a camera lens, they will use their eyes to "record" the pictures you want to take.

Directions

Have the group split up into pairs. One partner will start as the camera and the other as the photographer. The photographer asks the camera to close his or her eyes and leads them to an interesting object that they want to photograph. Remind the group about safety! The photographer activates the camera "shutter" by pulling gently on their partner's earlobe or tapping one of their shoulders and the camera quickly opens and closes its eyes to take the picture. Tell each pair to take four or five pictures before switching roles.

Diversity Skills

This activity lends itself well to discussions about how each of us perceives the world differently. Two people who see the same thing often remember it differently. Try it when you feel the group needs to think more about the different perspectives we all bring to group situations.

Processing

This activity can be processed first by the two partners and later in the group. We like this activity because it helps to build trust between group members and also because it's a wonderful opportunity for them to open a discussion on how we all see the world differently. Ask them to discuss what image the photographer wanted to record and what the camera saw.

- How was the camera's image different from the photographer's?

- What stood out the most for the camera? For the photographer?

- Do our different perspectives influence how we see and react to the world around us?

- What colors your camera filter, and how focused are you?

Ballon Trolleys

Activity Type:	Trust Building
Activity Level:	Moderate to high
Space:	A good-sized room with open space or an outdoor field
Time:	15 to 30 minutes
Group Size:	The more the better
Prerequisite:	None
Props:	Balloons and everyday obstacles

Opening

There's a song that talks about the "ties that bind us." These balloons represent things that connect us and how fragile connections can be.

Directions

Blow up enough balloons so that you have one to fit between every two people if they stand in a single-file line. For example, if X is a person and O is a balloon, the line would look like this: XOXOXOXOXOX.

The challenge is to move the entire group across an area without allowing any of the balloons to hit the floor.

This activity sounds simple enough, but it's not all that easy to execute. Your group will find that they have to do a lot of work to keep the balloons off the ground. You can increase the difficulty by prohibiting people from hugging the players in front of them; in other words, they have to move simultaneously but without being linked together physically.

You can add challenges to the activity by having the group do the following whenever a balloon touches the ground:

- The entire group has to start again.

- The two people who dropped the balloon have to go to the front or end of the line and replace the balloon.

- The group has to figure out a way to pick up the balloon and reinsert it where it was without losing any other balloons.

- All of the above. Use whatever consequence that you think your group will enjoy and that will add challenge and fun to the activity.

- Putting some obstacles around the space for the group to navigate around will add some more enjoyment. Try having them: go over a wrestling mat rolled up on the floor, go under a table or balance beam, step through a large hula hoop, step over a small barrier of milk crates, etc.

Diversity Skills

Building allies, group identities, ability, cooperation

Processing

This is a great activity for helping the group think about the different ways we communicate and work together, both verbally and physically.

- How did you communicate with each other in ways that didn't use words?

- How were other people helpful?

- How did other people make it difficult for you to keep the balloons off the ground?

- Did you find yourself making assumptions about someone who dropped a balloon? What were they?

- What did the other members of the group say or do that encouraged you to trust and work as part of a team?

- Did anyone say or do anything that made you feel that you weren't part of the team?

- All of us, whether we want to be or not, are part of larger groups with invisible ties binding us together. How do you communicate and affirm your connection to other people?

- How did you, as a group, communicate with each other?

Trust Circle

Activity Type:	Trust Building
Activity Level:	Moderate
Space:	Enough room for the group to form a circle
Time:	About 20 minutes
Group Size:	8 or more
Prerequisite:	Be sure they are feeling comfortable with safe physical contact.
Props:	None

Opening

Many cultures, particularly Native American, use a circle as a symbol of how the sum of parts is stronger than the individual. Think about what kind of energy and commitment you need to give the group so that the circle stays intact and connected.

Directions

Ask your group to arrange itself in a circle with their bumpers up. (Bumpers up is a hands-up, palms-out position that participants assume to protect themselves as they move slowly amongst one another.) Tell them that each person will walk slowly from one side of the circle to the other side and that everyone is to do this simultaneously. Obviously, there will be some jostling near the center of the circle, but if everyone is aware of the mass group movement, the gentle shoulder bumps and contact should be no problem. The goal is for them to re-form their circle with everyone ending opposite from where they started.

Challenge Level

If everything goes well, ask them to close their eyes and make a sightless trip across the circle. Remind everyone of the ground rules and the importance of keeping the group's trust intact. Walking only!

Diversity Skills

Validating feelings, building allies, group identities, ability, gender and sexual orientation

Processing

This activity is a good, basic trust-building exercise that will work with almost any subject. You may want to come back to it whenever you feel that the group is struggling with creating a safe physical environment during some of the more challenging trust activities.

- How did you feel when you had your eyes open compared to when you had your eyes closed?

- Did you feel competitive in any way?

- Did you trust the group to keep you safe?

- What happens when you think you might be hurt? Do you play differently? Is the same true for sharing your feelings?

The Almost Infinite Circle ■

Activity Type: Group Initiative

Activity Level: Low

Space: Anywhere

Time: You might want to give the group as much time as necessary to find the solution.

Group Size: Pairs

Prerequisite: None

Props: One piece of 10-foot-long rope for each person in the group

Opening

Life can be like a Rubik's Cube. We keep repeating the same patterns over and over again; we never seem to get anywhere. How can a little cooperation help us see the patterns and break out?

Directions

This activity seems to have no solution, but it will get your group actively working together in pairs trying to find one.

Separate your group into pairs and give each person a length of rope. Have them tie the ends of the rope onto their wrists, crossing in the middle, so that the two people are intertwined. See the illustration for clarification on how to do this.

The goal is for the two intertwined people to separate from one another without untying the knots, cutting the rope or slipping the knotted portion over their hands.

Answer any and all questions and keep emphasizing that there really is a solution to the problem even though it may look like a knife is the only answer.

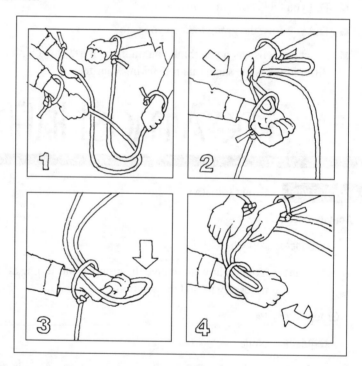

Solution: Try this out first with a friend:

- Form a loop in the center of your partner's rope.

- Pass the loop under either of your wrist loops so that the loop is pointed to your fingers.

- Pull the loop through with your other hand, open it wide enough to pass your hand through. Pass the loop over your hand and pull it down and back through the wrist loop. You're free, or you should be!

Diversity Skills

This is a fun activity for any group that likes a challenge and is learning how to work through problems with a little support from a friend. Building allies, group identities, individual identity, cooperation, communication.

Processing

- Were you able to solve this problem?

- What conversation was going on in your head when you heard the instructions for this activity?

- What were your thoughts—positive and negative—regarding your partner's abilities?

- How high was your level of frustration, and how did you respond to it?

- How does this kind of problem-solving activity reflect what you do when you are stuck in a real-life situation?

- What can you carry forward from this activity to the next?

Human Ladder

Activity Type:	Group Initiative
Activity Level:	Moderate to high. Some people may have difficulty climbing the ladder.
Space:	Any large open space will do. Make sure the floor is either carpeted or use gym mats. Grass is even better.
Time:	About 30 minutes. Make sure everyone who wants to has a chance to climb the ladder.
Group Size:	10 or more
Prerequisite:	Trust activities and spotting skills
Props:	6 to 10 smooth hardwood dowel rods about 3 feet long and 1 1/4 inch in diameter

Opening

Growing up and developing your own identity are a lot like climbing a ladder. Some people stay at your side, some are helping you up from behind, and others are giving you a hand from above. What are some of the things and people that give you support?

Directions

Have the group split into pairs and face each other in two lines. Each couple holds one rung of the ladder (a wooden dowel). The two lines form the ladder. The climber starts at one end of the ladder and climbs from one rung to another. As the climber passes by, the last pair to hold the rung can leave their position and move up to the far end. This will extend your ladder indefinitely.

> ### Safety Note
>
> The climbers should climb with hands on one rung and feet on another, thus distributing their weight evenly. People holding the rungs should feel comfortable holding the climber's weight. Extra support can be given to a holder by a spotter standing behind them.

Variation

You can change the direction of the ladder any time—make a right-angle turn or a circle. You can also add obstacles and change the height of the rungs.

Diversity Skills

This is one of those activities that can adapt itself to almost any subject. You can use it as an opener for processing cooperation, teamwork, physical differences, individual difference, gender issues, or any other subject that concerns you and the members of your group.

Processing

■ What did it feel like when you were climbing?

■ Did trusting the other people in the group make climbing easier?

■ Did you ever feel like you needed to go back a rung?

■ What happens to you in your life when you feel like you are faced with too many challenges and not enough support? How do you handle it?

How Do You Spell V-A-L-I-D-A-T-E?

Activity Type: Social Responsibility

Activity Level: Low

Space: Your usual meeting room

Time: Give the smaller groups 35 minutes to answer and discuss their answers to the questions. Process as a large group for about 15 minutes.

Group Size: 8–12

Prerequisite: Some time working together

Props: Easel paper and markers. Post the questions on a piece of paper where everyone can see them.

Opening

Have you ever had someone look straight through you while you were trying to talk to them or give them feedback about something? What does it feel like to have someone act as though you're not even there? Have you ever, intentionally or unintentionally, done that to other people?

Directions

Divide into groups of four or five people and hand each group sheets of easel paper and markers. Have the group answer the following questions on different sheets of paper.

V—Value—How do I show others that I value them?

A—Appreciation—What are some of the things—words and actions— that signify appreciation to me?

L—Listen—How do I know that someone has really listened to me and how do I listen to others?

I—Interpret—How do I interpret what other people think of me and how they listen to me?

D—Demonstrate—What are some of the ways I can demonstrate that I am really listening to other people?

A—Acceptance—How can I show other people that I accept them the way they are?

T—Touch—Whose lives do I touch and who touches my life with their words and actions?

E—Engrossed—When I am engrossed in a conversation, you know it because…

Diversity Skills

Validating feelings, building allies, group identities, individual identity

Processing

The processing should flow quite smoothly out of the questions when you bring the group together to discuss what happened in their smaller groups. Let them decide where they want to go.

What I Like About You Is...

Activity Type:	Social Responsibility
Activity Level:	Low
Space:	Your usual meeting room
Time:	About half an hour
Group Size:	Any
Prerequisite:	Your group will need a high level of trust. This activity should be used only after your group has been together for a while and is following their Full Value Contract, otherwise it could get out of hand and even harmful.
Props:	Make up a list with all the names of the participants and spaces after each for people to fill in specific feedback. The form should look something like this:

Name	First Impression	What I Learned About You	What I Like About You

Opening

A garden only grows when it gets enough sunshine, water, and weeding. Weeds choke it the same way negative feedback will choke us as we go about our lives. This is our chance to nurture each other the same way we'd like others to nurture us.

Directions

Review and demonstrate giving feedback. Explain that feedback means giving specific examples of how someone's behavior affects you. For example, "what I learned about Sharon was that she is a kind person. This was illustrated by her concern for me when I was sick and she took care of a training for me. What I like about Sharon is her straightforwardness. That reassures me that she will always be honest with me." Give the students 10–15 minutes to fill out their forms. Make sure that each person is getting feedback from someone else. Ask the students to choose someone they had the strongest reaction to (either positive or negative) during the first time they came together as a group. They need to have a backup person in mind in case their first choice was picked by someone else. Tell them they're going to:

- Share why they chose that person and their first impressions.

- Sit down in a circle directly across from their partner.

- Go around the circle and ask each person to share their impression of their partner. Keep on going until everyone has received feedback.

- You may have to be prepared to give feedback yourself if there's an odd number of participants.

Diversity Skills

This is another activity that can be adapted to any of the subjects in this book. Try relating the first impression to a specific topic—race, gender, class, ability, sexual orientation—and keep the discussion focussed on the topic you've selected.

Processing

- How did you feel when you heard your partner's first impressions of you?

- If you are a quiet and shy person, what was this activity like for you?

- How do you think our society perceives people who are quiet?

- If you are an outspoken and energetic person, what was this activity like for you?

- How do you think our society perceives people who are outspoken and energetic?

Closing Activities

■ Making the Connection

Stand in a circle with a ball of yarn (preferably in exciting colors). Hold on to the end of the string and toss it across the circle to another participant. Before tossing, share with the group a feeling about the day, an insight you gained, or something you learned. The person who catches the ball of yarn does the same thing before tossing it on to someone else. This eventually looks like a web connecting the group. This web may represent the support they give each other, or how we are all held together by the common bonds symbolized by the yarn. If one person drops their web corner because the group is not being supportive enough or because they are afraid, then the whole group is weakened.

■ Acknowledgment Mill

Give each person in the group a sheet of paper and ask them to jot down notes to themselves about three people who had an impact on them during the activities. When they're done, let them mill around and share their acknowledgments with those individuals. Before they go, ask them to stand in a circle and acknowledge the group.

■ Treasure Bag

Place an imaginary treasure bag inside a circle. Invite each member to put in the bag something they want to give the group to help it continue to grow: support, humor, friendship, nurturing, etc. When everyone has had a chance to put something in the bag, ask someone to volunteer to be "The Keeper of the Treasure Bag." That person gets to take the bag out of the circle and keep it, opening it up at the beginning of your next session or in the future when the group is encountering a challenging moment. Each time it is opened, ask the group if they have something new to add to the chest and invite someone new to volunteer as "the keeper."

Personal Journal Question

Challenge your students to truly listen to at least one person every day and let them know you heard them. Make an effort to write down what you've learned or gained from each experience.

Processing Questions

Here's a list of general questions you can ask whenever you want your participants to think about the ways they are communicating and listening to each other. You can use them with the activities in this chapter or any others you have selected from the book.

- ❏ Can anyone give an example of when you thought you communicated effectively with someone else in the group?

- ❏ How did you know that what you communicated was understood?

- ❏ Who didn't understand someone's attempt to communicate?

- ❏ What went wrong in the communication attempt?

- ❏ What could the communicator do differently next time to give a clearer message?

- ❏ What could the message receiver do differently next time to understand the message?

- ❏ Did you learn something about communication that will be helpful later? If so, what?

- ❏ Who made suggestions for completing the activity?

- ❏ Were all of these suggestions heard? Explain.

- ❏ Which suggestions were acted upon?

- ❏ Why were the other suggestions ignored?

- ❏ How did it feel to be heard when you made a suggestion?

- ❏ What interfered with your ability to listen to others?

- ❏ Did you prevent yourself from listening well? How?

- ❏ Did you listen in the same way today as you generally do? If not, what was different about today?

❏ Is it difficult for you to avoid judging others? Explain.

❏ Can you think of examples of when you judged others in the group today? When you didn't judge others?

❏ What were some advantages to you of not judging others?

❏ What were some advantages to others of your not judging them?

❏ How do judging and not judging others affect your ability to listen or communicate with others?

6

HOW DOES
It Feel to Be
Different?

Discrimination affects us all. It is not limited to racist, classist, or sexist attitudes, remarks, and behavior. Discrimination happens when we are singled out for comment or ridiculed for how we act, look, speak, move, or behave. Discrimination, in one form or another, happens to everyone, in varying degrees, at some point in their lives. The resulting emotions are powerful and long remembered.

An enormous amount of pain is associated with being the recipient of discrimination, and no one is immune to it. Remember being young and how it felt to be teased or picked on? Perhaps you felt it when you got your first pair of glasses and someone called you "buckeye" or "four eyes." Maybe you felt it when someone decided they didn't want to play with you because you weren't cool enough. It hurts when it happens, and the pain doesn't just disappear. Adults are a little more sophisticated in how they internalize these feelings, but we can all remember what it felt like, being young and on the outside of a group.

It is essential that adults working with young people understand the emotional effects and stages of discrimination. Our behaviors have an impact on both a student who is discriminated against and a student who is discriminating against others. As young people go through the process of discovering who they are, varying levels of emotion or anger can be generated through realizing how they have been and are treated by others.

As facilitators dealing with issues of diversity, we must work with students who feel they are discriminated against and validate the real emotions they feel. We must be careful not to dismiss or downplay these feelings. There can be a tendency to want to believe we are all similar when we are together in a group. This tendency can cause members of a group to dismiss how individuals are feeling—they are overreacting, or being too sensitive, or misinterpreting what they are hearing. Only by listening to and validating the very real feelings of each person will you help your students see each member as having their own place within the group.

> *In the middle of difficulty lies opportunity.*
>
> —Albert Einstein

Searching for individual identity within a peer group is very often an important part of development for adolescents. Expressions of individual identity abound in high school and middle school. They range from dress, friendship, music, and school activities, to body adornment (hair dye, tattooing, piercing), to gang membership, to teen pregnancy. Coupled with the developing awareness of one's self is the realization that we can sometimes change how we are perceived and ultimately treated by how we dress, how we behave, and who we talk to.

Being different evokes a range of emotions in all of us. Unless we know how to recognize and manage the symptoms, these emotions can control how we relate to others. Learning to accept that being different is all right can help us manage our emotions and turn them into positive forces for change.

Stress—The Effect of Discrimination

Generally speaking, stress is the most powerful effect of discrimination, and few of us are immune to it. Stress is defined as an individual's response to difficult, frustrating situations and can generate an enormous amount of anxiety and panic. If we don't learn how to work positively through stressful situations, stress can lead to:

Denial—denial that anything is wrong or that you may be thinking differently than you are acting

Rage—true, bona fide anger at the conditions and negative perceptions that surround you

Alienation—a gradual withdrawal from the support that surrounds you

Depression—the emotional and physical manifestation of hopelessness

Understand that stress, denial, rage, alienation, and depression are not "bad," per se. They are emotions that, once released, can act as powerful agents for change, renewed self-purpose and self-identity, and strength of character.

Stress is sometimes unavoidable. When we feel stress, the fight-or-flight mechanism is triggered in our brains, and our bodies are designed to respond. In the past, when humans were attacked by animals or invading armies, our response to the threat was physical. We either ran or stayed to fight. We physically metabolized the energy elicited by the stress of the situation.

Today, many of the challenges to our existence and beliefs—feeling like we don't fit in, that we are being singled out for ridicule, that no one else looks or acts like us, that we are alone, that we aren't as rich or beautiful as everyone else—aren't as obvious as an attacking animal. A physical response is not considered appropriate or necessary. So where does all the energy provoked by the perceived threat go? Eating disorders, high blood pressure, drug dependencies, teen pregnancies, alienation, and violent behavior are just a few of the effects that are becoming increasingly evident among youth as a physical response to present-day stress. No longer can we believe that children have no stress or that, if they do, it has little effect on them.

Take the example of Alisa, a second grader in Connecticut and the only child of color in her elementary school. Her teachers didn't make an effort to understand her, were unsympathetic, and would not discipline the children who taunted her. Alisa began falling behind in her schoolwork, but the school refused to acknowledge any connection between her school environment and her inability to keep up with the rest of her class. When her mother tried to point out some of the difficulties confronting Alisa at school and asked the administration to develop a more supportive atmosphere for her child, they accused her of being unfair and unyielding. Eventually, Alisa developed chronic nausea, insomnia, and school avoidance. These symptoms continued until her mother took action and found a sympathetic therapist who let Alisa express her feelings and develop ways of coping with the emotional stress she felt at school. Alisa ultimately changed schools because the environment stayed unchanging and unsupportive, and the administration would not acknowledge that the source of Alisa's physical distress was directly related to her school environment.

> *...It is not stress by itself—defined as the brain's perception of physical or psychological threat and the body's response to that threat—that is dangerous. It's the inability to cope with it that can play a major role in determining whether a person gets sick and whether that illness will be serious or even fatal.*
>
> —Judy Foreman, Boston Globe Staff

While we all respond differently to stressful situations, all of us are affected by name calling, disrespectful behavior, and hurtful remarks. Stress removes the innocence of young children. Although we may try to comfort ourselves with the saying "sticks and stones may break my bones, but names will never hurt me," names *can* be powerful weapons and they *do* hurt.

Some Points about Stress

■ Stress is not an objective, measurable phenomenon. Different situations cause stress for different people. Each individual's perception about what is hurtful is what is important.

■ Events are determined by the meaning assigned to them. Any event viewed as potentially harmful can trigger a stress reaction.

■ Most people feel threatened and experience the most stress when the things they consider most valuable—people, places, possessions, beliefs—are threatened.

■ Some people become accustomed to habitual stress, but don't always stop and take the time to label it or give it meaning.

■ It's important to identify the source of stress. Assessing belief systems—goals, values, faith, self-concept—helps determine what is under attack and why.

■ Certain situations *are* threatening—intruders, assaulters, the sight of a violent, angry group marching down the street—and merit a high-energy, very real fight-or-flight response.

Stress and the Stages of Crisis

■ Shock and denial—when the pain becomes overpowering, a person's system temporarily "blows out," leaving the person feeling numb.

■ Emotions erupt—emotions break out in tears or anger.

■ Anger—anger at lack of control, inequity, the pervasiveness of the problem, the unfairness of it all.

■ Illness—don't be surprised if physical illness occurs, our bodies often respond physically to crisis.

■ Panic—paranoia and the feeling of losing one's mind. What should I do? Who can I trust?

■ Guilt—guilt and the internalization of problems. Feeling responsible for negative treatment.

■ Depression and loneliness—feeling isolated, drifting further away from supporters.

■ Resistance—holding onto things instead of letting go and moving on.

■ Hope—against all odds somehow hope sneaks in and takes hold and grows.

■ Affirming reality—reconstructing one's life using new knowledge and strengths.

This sequence calls attention to the need to learn to use stress as a cue to action and positive change. It is important that we recognize the choices we have in each situation. We have a choice to speak or not, a choice to act or not, and each action has a consequence. Learning to stop reacting to events or situations and begin choosing actions that take us in a direction of positive change is a difficult thing to do.

The activities in this chapter were selected to help you create situations that parallel real life, where you and the group can look closely at moments of choice. One of the most important lessons you can leave with your students is that it is a skill in itself to recognize that each of us, through choices of how we react to discrimination, can make a difference for ourselves and others.

Standing Up for Ourselves and for Others

Waking up to our emotions can also be a transformational experience that results in renewed determination, clarity of purpose, and strength. In the chapter on physical and mental ability, one of the vignettes describes a young man with muscular dystrophy who speaks up in front of his classmates about how much pain and isolation their avoidance of him causes. How did this young man find the strength and understanding to verbalize the pain, anger, and blows to his self-esteem? Where does that ability come from? He tells about a friend of his who is also in a wheelchair and about how that friend listens, supports, accepts, and challenges him not to accept any rubbish.

As adults working with young people, we need to help them find their peer support systems as well as give them our unqualified support. This young man's talk could have backfired on him—it didn't—but he had the personal strength and courage to handle the potential firestorm. He accepts himself for who he is, and his message was heard and accepted.

Self-concept is a special collection of assumptions and beliefs about your limitations, your abilities, your appearance, your emotional resources, your place in the world, your potential, your worthiness.

—Donald A. Tubesing, "Kicking Your Stress Habits"

For individuals who want to fight discrimination and no longer accept stereotypes and prejudices, the first step is to listen to and validate other people's experiences. Too often when someone takes the risk and shares an experience of discrimination, we jump in with an experience of our own to illustrate how we have been a victim of discrimination also. This may be an attempt to commiserate and empathize, but it often comes across as a dismissal of the other person's feelings. Try to be an ally and ask how you can help the person instead of sharing your pain. Most of all, be willing to challenge what is being said or done in a positive, nonthreatening way. Be aware of your own discomfort and use it as information to question what is happening.

Recognize that no one escapes the effects of prejudice. We all can be victims of discrimination and we need to start now to fight the ignorance and the prejudices which exist. No one is immune.

> In Germany they first came for the Communists, and I didn't speak up because I wasn't a Communist. Then they came for the Jews and I didn't speak up because I wasn't a Jew. Then they came for the trade unionists, and I didn't speak up because I wasn't a trade unionist. Then they came for the Catholics, and I didn't speak up because I was a Protestant. Then they came for me— and by that time no one was left to speak up.
>
> —*Pastor Martin Niemoller*

Discrimination and Developmental Issues

Adult perceptions of the world and the way we deny, accept, or welcome diversity have an enormous influence on children. We are unquestionably their primary role models. A certain amount of self-reflection and analysis is a necessary part of understanding how your viewpoints and strategies for coping with diversity impair or enhance the skills of the youth in your group. How do you "color" your perceptions of the world according to the identity you acquired as a child?

As the saying goes, "If we don't love ourselves, we can't love someone else." One of our universal defense mechanisms is projection: projecting our own feelings onto others. Projection alleviates the pain of carrying a negative self-image, self-hatred, and other unbearable emotions. In some ways, we have already paid a high price for the constant invalidation of human worth our society perpetuates. It shows in the ever-increasing numbers of youth becoming involved with gangs. These children are establishing their own "families," families that support without question who they are and what they do—often without regard to race or ethnicity. The epidemic number of teen parents, the staggering numbers of youth who abuse alcohol and other drugs, the growing populations of teen runaways, teen throwaways, teens involved in violent behavior, teens who would rather die than let anyone know about their pain and suffering over questions about sexual orientation—all of these children are the victims of a sense of worthlessness and depression.

In 1969, Jane Elliott, a third-grade teacher, conducted a two-day lesson in discrimination, which has since become renowned, with her class in Riceville, Iowa. Martin Luther King had just been assassinated and the country was in turmoil regarding the issue of race. Ms. Elliott wanted the children of this all-white, Christian town to experience the injustice and sting of discrimination. She divided the class into two groups based upon eye color, something they had no control over. The students were given certain privileges and treated differently based upon whether their eyes were blue or brown. This social exercise was filmed as a documentary titled *A Class Divided*. When Ms. Elliott explained to the third graders how she was hating that day because her eyes are blue and she was therefore in the "out" group, she said, "There is a filthy, nasty word called discrimination. We are treating people a certain way because they are different from us. Is that fair? No! Nobody said that this was going to be a fair day."

It is such a simple and direct way to experience the effects of discrimination. Those children never forgot their lesson. Fourteen years later, the class reunited and explained the impact of what they had learned and how it influenced their ability to challenge prejudices held about differences. Most of all, they talked about the pain, anger, and lack of power they felt during those two days.

If you are not part of the majority racial or cultural group, you can feel a great deal of pressure. In the book *Voices of Diversity*, by Renee Blank and Sandra Slipp, an African American executive says, "I am constantly on display and nothing I do is seen as an individual trait: I feel as if I have to represent all black people." A worker with a disability says, "I'm often patronized, pitied, or treated like a child, but in fact I am proud that I'm independent."

In order for us to truly understand the impact of discrimination, we need to listen to people's stories. We need to "walk a mile in another person's shoes" to develop empathy, not sympathy. We all know how it feels to be hurt. This is the first step in overcoming barriers and developing communication.

Be careful, however, to understand the distinction between honoring and understanding others and mimicking their experiences. Using adventure activities, it can be tempting to think that having spent time in someone's shoes gives one the ability to say that one now knows what it's like. Being blindfolded during an activity or ignored as part of a three-hour role-play does have merit in developing empathy, but it does not give access to the complete experience of living one's life in these situations. When working with youth, encourage them to draw upon their own experiences, and to understand that while they may gain knowledge and understanding, they will not entirely gain access to these feelings, nor is that the goal.

As Jane Elliott says in *The Eye of the Beholder*, a video replay of her blue eyes and brown eyes experiment with a group of adults as part of a World of Difference video for the Anti-Defamation League, "I have some trouble with people saying, 'Why do people still feel that way? We've already told you that we accept you. Why do you still feel that way? It's your fault that you feel that way.'" Jane's answer is, "No, I don't think it's true. I think that history—and we have all kinds of experiences and history in this country—has proven to blacks and lots of other minority groups that we don't think of them as equals. And the people who do are the exceptions rather than the rule. And you never know if you are talking to an exception or the rule." The important lesson here is that we must become aware of how we respond to other people's experiences. It is not always easy to admit that all of us can and do discount what other people have experienced. But we all know pain, anger, and suffering—whatever their sources.

> *Happiness is not the absence of problems, but the ability to deal with them.*
>
> —H. Jackson Brown, Sr.

As youth begin to explore the difficult territory of the impact of discrimination, a looming question becomes *how can we possibly change behavioral patterns that are so deeply ingrained and constantly reinforced by our culture?* It is easy to become overwhelmed by feelings of hopelessness and despair. Don't! Don't let the same emotions that this chapter addresses ply you into inaction. As Margaret Mead once said, "Never doubt that a group of concerned citizens can change the world. Indeed, it is the only thing that ever has." Keep going. There are always new ways and new alternatives to fighting the hopelessness.

Concluding Thoughts

Look for the signs of stress and try to recognize the emotions. What is behind what people are saying or doing? What provokes reactions from the members of your group and what are those reactions? Try not to judge them as "wrong" or "bad."

Coping skills include identifying and releasing emotions. This is a frightening process for most adults, never mind teenagers. Listening to the truth in what they are saying will reassure youth that they are not alone in their struggle to speak out.

Help your participants identify their emotions. Ask them to work through the following three questions:

- Does the threat really exist? (It may, so go on to the next question.)

- Is the issue really important? (It may be and, if so, admit it!)

- Can I make a difference? (Maybe, maybe not. If so, help the individual develop positive, constructive responses. If not, help them find ways to develop new strategies and methods for reducing the physical and mental burden on themself.)

Stress is often a cue to positive action and change. Take the time to ask your students what things are stressful to them. Do they match your perceptions?

Your perceptions of what is stressful to teenagers may be different from theirs. A study published in the *Journal of Child Psychology and Psychiatry* (Vol. 28, No. 6) emphasized that what adults feel is stressful to children and what children feel is stressful can be miles apart. Some of the ten most stressful events for children, ranked by order of importance, were: losing a parent, going blind, being held back a grade, parents fighting, getting caught in a theft, being suspected of lying, a poor grade, being ridiculed in class.

Identify your own emotions. Are you acting on your own perceptions or are you responding to a true, outside stimulus? Check your level of denial. Do you refuse to be aware of what's going on because you might have to do something about it? Stop, look, and listen to the members of your group. Is someone reaching out to you for help?

Missing or misreading the signals is a fear for many who work with youth experiencing discrimination. When this happens, it's important to be direct and open about what happened and your desire to get better at reading the signals. Process these events with peers or other professionals, and use the experience as a learning opportunity for the future. The biggest mistake is to bury them without addressing them.

Suggested Reading

Tubesing, Donald A. *Kicking your Stress Habits: A Do-It-Yourself Guide*. Whole Person Associates, 1981. Everybody knows what stress is, but *Kicking Your Stress Habits* helps people do something about it. This workshop-in-a-book goes beyond lectures and statistics by encouraging readers to think, plan, and act for themselves.

Blank, Renee and Sandra Slipp. *Voices of Diversity; Real People Talk About Problems and Solutions in a Workplace Where Everyone is Not Alike*. New York: American Management Association, 1994. A collection of stories from people about their experiences in the workplace. How it feels to be different and some practical problem-solving approaches to the experience of diversity.

Dana, Daniel. *Managing Differences: How to Build Better Relationships at Work and Home*. Wolcott, CT: MTI Publications, 1988. A review of communication skills necessary for addressing interpersonal and organizational conflict.

Elliott, Jane. *Eye of the Beholder* and *A Class Divided*. Videos produced for A World of Difference, Washington, DC. The Anti Defamation League.

Worksheet

Identifying Discrimination

For this worksheet, choose a group to which you belong, that is important to you. Spend some time looking specifically at what stereotypes and discrimination look like for this group. Conversely, use this worksheet to examine what you understand about a group to which you do not belong.

What do you call this group? _____

Who is in this group? What kinds of people? _____

What are the terms used to identify this group (list both negative and positive)? _____

How would you describe the dress and behavior of the people in this group?

What music and food do they typically eat? _____

What kinds of words do they speak? Do they have an accent?

_____

How old are the majority of people in this group? _____

What are the stereotypes that people in this group believe?

_____

Do members of this group appear in the media (news, entertainment, advertising)? If so, how are they portrayed? _____

What kinds of jobs do the members of this group typically hold?

_____

What kind of education do they receive? _____

What is the best thing about the members of this group? What is the worst thing? _____

This worksheet is designed to reveal how a particular group is perceived. Consider what parts of that image come from fact, and what come from myth or fiction. How much of what you put down are stereotypes or generalizations? How much of these stereotypes do you believe are based in fact?

_____

Messages on TV

One afternoon when my oldest son was about six years old, he was watching the Nickelodeon channel on TV. I overheard the announcer urging the kids to call in and win a prize for a contest, and quickly told him, "Hurry up and call. You might win something." He rolled over and, without moving from his spot in front of the TV, said, "Mom, I can't call. There are no kids on the commercial that are black!" My heart sank. It was clear he had gotten the message that you had to be white in order to win the contest.

I asked him, "What should we do about that?" At first, he felt like he didn't have any options. As we discussed it further, he decided he wanted to "let the bosses of Nickelodeon know they should have all kinds of kids on their commercials so that all kids would know they have a chance to win." He dictated a letter to me, and we sent it off to Nickelodeon in New York City. We still hadn't heard anything from the station after three weeks so I called them up and insisted that he deserved a reply. He got one!

This Is Who I Am

Why would a child with light skin, straight blond hair, and green eyes describe herself as black? It sounds odd, but this is a true story. The bi-racial child of a friend of mine, who looks like the girl described, once checked the "Black/African American box on her paper work for seventh-grade homeroom. Her homeroom teacher was unamused and insisted that she change it... "immediately or go straight to the principal's office!" The principal was aware of the child's parentage and attempted to fix the misunderstanding—difficult to do once the child had already been punished and humiliated in front of her entire class for choosing to celebrate her racial background with pride. The situation was "resolved" with an apology from the teacher. The following year, that beautiful, bright young girl transferred to a private school.

Continuum

Coping ➜ Self-Awareness ➜ Self-Acceptance ➜ Positive Change

As we begin to develop an awareness of how our perceptions of the world affect our behaviors and, conversely, of how the perceptions of others condition our own behavior, we can begin to develop strategies for dealing effectively with stereotyping behaviors. We all need to develop new insights into what we can do to change ingrained patterns and create new options for managing the challenges of diversity.

Awareness

Stress and emotional disorder are the fallout of discrimination. It is as important to deal with these emotions as it is to dismantle discrimination itself. In some cases, dealing with the fallout is the only action that is appropriate, particularly if the source of the discrimination is beyond your control.

Group Skills

Recognition—Help the members of your group recognize their emotional responses to ridicule, negative perceptions of others, and outright discrimination.

Identification—Identify those responses. Help them improve their "physical barometers." What's happening physically? Has their jaw gone tight, is their stomach doing flip-flops, is their chest tight?

Response—TAKE SEVERAL DEEP BREATHS. Help them list their options. Should they respond, ignore, withdraw, attack, ally themselves with a perceived victim? Sit down and discuss what a valid response for them would be in a given situation and how they should act on it.

Reflection—Help them develop their own system of self-reflection. What will the consequences of their responses be?

Listening and hearing—Feelings are universal and everyone's pain is valid. Have them express how they feel when they hear about someone else's experience instead of trying to "one-up" the story with an experience of their own. Expressing how you feel about someone else's experience lets them know they were heard.

Affirmation—Teach by example. Affirm their feelings, and discuss their options with them so that they will learn to do this for each other. Help them develop their own self-affirmations for stressful situations.

Activities

Peek-A-Who

Activity Type:	Ice Breaker
Activity Level:	Low to moderate
Space:	Any space
Time:	15 to 20 minutes
Group Size:	Best with groups of 15 to 25 people
Prerequisite:	None
Props:	Group needs to know each other's names.

Opening

Don't you hate it when you see someone you know but can't think of
their name right off the bat? Let's try to see how well we really know
each other's names.

Directions

Divide the group in half. Have two people (you and another leader or
a volunteer) hold up the blanket. Put half of the group on one side of the
blanket and half on the other side. Make sure everyone is sitting two or
three feet back from the blanket, and be sure that nobody can see anyone
on the other side.

Each team chooses one person to go forward to the blanket. These players
should face the screen and be very close to it. Choosing this person
silently is best, but let the players discover this after they've blurted out,
"Hey, Zach, you go up there," a few times. It won't take them long to
figure out that this makes it pretty easy for the other team.

On the count of three, the people holding the blanket drop it to the ground
and the two chosen players, who are now facing each other nose to nose,
try to correctly name the person across from them. They can receive no
help from their teammates—it's one on one!

Whoever names their opponent first *wins* that person for their team and that person moves over to the winning side.

The first team to have everyone on it is the winning team. With larger groups this may never happen, so you may want to set a time limit at the beginning. When the time runs out, whichever team has the most people wins.

Some Things to Think About

Remind the group not to get too competitive—you're only trying to learn people's names and have some fun! It's the slightly competitive nature of this game that makes it fun. But be prepared to have people challenge your refereeing with statements like, "No, I said Barbi before she said my name!" In this case just reach into your pocket, fake like you pulled something out and pretend that you are watching a very small TV monitor. After a second or two tell the groups that after reviewing the super-dooper-slow-mo, you are sticking with your decision.

Challenge Level

You're in a crowded mall with your friends and see someone that you all know but you can't think of her name. The person's gone by the time you have a chance to tell your friends and now you have to describe what she looks like so your friends will know who she was.

For groups that know each other fairly well, an addition that is a bit more challenging for everyone goes like this: Have the two chosen people sit with their backs to the blanket. This time, when the blanket drops, they cannot see each other and the only way of guessing the other person's name is by using the information that their teammates provide (but they can't say the person's name!). My teammates might tell me that the person is a male, in twelfth grade, with a beard and a pierced ear. "That's Abe!"

This new rule challenges a group to use information other than just looks to identify each other. Something worth mentioning to the group is that you want them to use positive descriptions of each other. Remind the group of the Full Value Contract—respecting and valuing each other and no put-downs.

With a group that has people of different races, nationalities, physical abilities, or other diversity, this activity allows these differences to be viewed in a positive way, as part of who we are. This is why it is critical that you say positive things about the person. We can start feeling good about our racial, physical, and gender differences when we are allowed to use them as positive information about a person. For example, if we were playing with a group of colleagues, our team might say that the person that is across from me is Nepalese. I know that this must be Sanu. My group used information about who she is with full respect for the fact that her ethnic background is obviously an important part of who she is. To tell me it is someone with black hair, a female, and a diversity trainer also describes Jessica. The piece of information that helps me to know that it is Sanu and not Jessica is her heritage.

Diversity Skills

This is a great activity to use in the early stages when a group is getting to know one another because it helps them remember each other's names. Later, you may want to use the challenge level to help them understand just how much we judge people by their appearance and how that affects the way we treat them.

Processing

You may not need to do too much processing if you are simply using this game to help your participants get to know one another's names. If you use the challenge level, process around how the group described each other. Ask questions like:

- Does everyone feel that the descriptions were positive?

- What did it feel like to be described that way? Is that how you define yourself?

- Can you think of any other ways you'd like people to describe you?

- What thoughts of race, gender, ethnicity ran through your mind?

- Did you express those thoughts—if not, why not?

Who Are You?

Activity Type:	Ice Breaker
Activity Level:	Low
Space:	Your usual meeting room
Time:	About half an hour
Group Size:	6 or more
Prerequisite:	None
Props:	Pen and paper

Opening

Imagine that you could ask people you just met anything you wanted to know in order to learn something about them. What do you really want to know about other people when you first meet them? Don't lose that question!

Directions

Ask the group to brainstorm a list of ten or so questions that people would like to ask each other. You may want to monitor the choices to keep them appropriate.

Narrow the list down to two or three questions that people like best, then allow whatever length of time you want for mingling and conversing.

Provide pens and paper for recording the most interesting questions. If they want to ask more than two or three questions, do as many rounds as you have time for.

Consider striving for a balance of factual, personal (but not intrusive), humorous, and unusual questions to provide an air of adventure to the conversation.

- What is the funniest situation you have encountered during the last two months?
- What famous person, living or dead, would you most want to have dinner with?
- Who do you consider to be a personal hero/heroine?
- What is your favorite film of all time?
- Who is one of your favorite fictional characters?
- What's your most recent embarrassing moment?

Diversity Skills

Listening and communicating, building allies, group identities, or try it with any group that needs to get to know each other better. You can also develop questions about any of the topics in this book to provoke discussion around diversity concerns.

Processing

Processing flows naturally out of this activity. Have the group discuss what they learned about each other and why they decided to ask the questions they did.

Transformer Tag

Activity Type:	De-Inhibitizer/Warm Up
Activity Level:	Active
Space:	Outdoors
Time:	About 10 minutes or enough time for everyone to end up out of breath.
Group Size:	10–30
Prerequisite:	None
Props:	A coin if you decide to do the variation.

Opening

Before we transform the world, we have to transform ourselves. So, let's practice.

Directions

Demonstrate to the participants two body positions that won't affect their running. Typical choices are one hand on top of the head and one hand attached to the gluteus (right or left behind). Each person gets to decide which accepted body position is "right" at the start of the activity.

Give the group a minute or two to determine their game identity and indicate the start of the game by shouting "Declare" or any other suitable command. Players then immediately declare their identity by adopting one of the body positions.

The action involves one team—the heads, for instance—trying to tag and transform all the tails. If a head tags a tail, the tail becomes a head, and vice versa. Once transformed, the person tries to tag anyone of the opposing team. The game continues until one team successfully dominates the world! Then, rematch after rematch until the action loses its appeal.

Variation

Heads/Tails Tag requires a coin, preferably a large one (quarters work nicely). Identify the two body positions outlined above for the Heads and Tails. Once the group knows the two positions, the action starts as soon as the coin has been flipped in the air.

As the coin hovers above the group, everyone must declare as either a Head or a Tail. When the coin lands on the ground, people need to know which side is up. If it's Heads, Heads are it and try to tag all the Tails. Any Tail that is tagged is frozen. The action stops once all the Tails are immobilized. If Tails shows on the coin, the action is reversed.

This variation tends to be shorter, but the fun is in how people learn what side of the coin comes up. This moment of uncertainty adds a bit of a thrill to the game, especially if the coin rolls along the ground.

Diversity Skills

Listening and communicating, building allies, group identities, gender and sexual orientation

Processing

You probably won't need to spend a whole lot of time processing this activity, particularly if everyone needs time to catch their breath. So have some fun.

Draw a Place to Live

Activity Type:	Trust Building/Problem Solving
Activity Level:	Reflective
Space:	Your usual meeting room
Time:	About half an hour
Group Size:	8–14 in pairs
Prerequisite:	None
Props:	Sheets of paper and pens or markers

Opening

Our dreams and concerns have a big impact on the way we see the world, especially the place we live. What kind of place would you like to live in?

Directions

Ask everyone to stand and pick a partner, someone they perceive as different from themselves. Then, have each pair come up and take a piece of paper and a pen. Without talking to each other, both people in each pair put one hand on the pen, and together they draw a place to live. Notice that we have said "place," not a house or home. When the pairs have finished their drawings, ask them to process, in their pair, why they picked each other and how they communicated nonverbally about a place to live. If they're willing, they can share their experience afterwards with the whole group.

Diversity Skills

This is a great activity for helping your participants work together cooperatively and discuss the different ways individuals perceive the world. You can frame this activity around any aspect of diversity.

Processing:

You might want to let the group engage in a free discussion about their hopes and dreams, the similarities, differences and the fears we all have that our dreams won't be realized.

- How did you pick your partner?
- How did you communicate with each other?
- How did you find balance between your ideas?
- What was going on internally for you during the activity?
- Was there tension? Was it clear who led and who followed?

Two-Person Trust Lean

Activity Type:	Trust Building
Activity Level:	Moderate
Space:	Best outdoors on a grassy field, but any room with some open space will do.
Time:	About 35 minutes
Group Size:	6 or more
Prerequisite:	Make sure your group has built up a good deal of physical and emotional trust before you begin the *Trust Fall/Trust Lean* sequences. Read the preceding section on spotting skills and be sure you have gone over them carefully with the group. Remember, once trust is lost, it's a great deal harder to restore.
Props:	None

Opening

This activity represents the emotional trust we have in each other. The difference is that we'll be acting out our trust physically. It is the first step we'll be taking towards showing each other how much we care and support one another.

Directions

Before having the whole group do the activity, first ask a person to volunteer to be a "faller" and demonstrate for the group how to be a spotter. The faller should cross his arms across his chest so that his arms and elbows don't fly out. The falling person should also keep his knees and body straight. The spotter, you in this demonstration, stands a foot or so directly behind the faller and assumes the correct spotter's stance. After following the sequence of directions below, the faller leans back, beyond the point of losing his balance, and falls directly back. Start off with your hands just a few inches from the participant's back for the first few "falls," and catch the faller immediately after they begin "falling." Gradually increase the lean by allowing the faller to fall further with each attempt. Recognize, though, the point at which you or another smaller participant may have trouble supporting the weight of the faller.

The directions or calls are initiated by the faller and completed by the catcher. A typical sequence looks like this:

Faller: "Are you ready to catch?"

Catcher: "Ready to catch."

Faller: "I'm ready to fall."

Catcher: "Fall away."

If you think your group is ready, have them pair up and have each person in the group take turns being a "faller" and a "catcher." If you are at all unsure that your group is ready, have each pair demonstrate a proper fall and catch in front of the group before allowing them to begin as a group. Use this as an opportunity to make sure that everyone understands and follows the rules for correct spotting. As an extra safety precaution, you can have an extra person stand next to the catcher and perform back-up spotting.

Diversity Skills

Use this activity whenever you feel your group needs to work on basic issues of trust and respect. Frame your questions to reflect the subject you are working on and any difficulties they might be having with bridging their differences.

Processing:

- How did it feel to fall backwards into someone? To catch someone else?

- What was challenging about this activity for you?

- How did you perceive your ability to be a catcher?

- How did you feel about your partner's ability as a catcher?

Spotting Skills

When you really think about it, learning about diversity means building trusting and respectful relationships. Your group will be developing a large degree of trust and respect as it begins to cohere. Don't expect the trust to arise spontaneously. It needs to be nurtured over time. Expressing how we feel is a risk for all of us, adults and youth alike. We are all afraid that we'll be misunderstood or hurt if we open up to people we don't know well or trust completely.

Most of us hold our stereotypes close to our hearts, and you'll be asking the members of your group to interact in physically supportive ways with people they may perceive as very different from themselves. You may have to go slowly with your group. Do a quick evaluation using the GRABBS check list from Chapter 4. Do the participants seem ready to move on to the more difficult trust sequences? Is anyone holding back who might feel left out, too shy, or awkward about touching and holding other people? Assess your group carefully and follow your instincts.

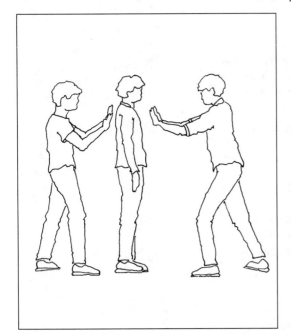

If you think your group is ready for some activities that involve a high level of physical trust, the place to start is with teaching spotting techniques. Spotting can best be described as one or more participants physically ready to support or actually supporting another participant doing an activity.

The *Trust Lean* activity is good for teaching the importance of good spotting skills. One person simply leans back beyond the point of losing their balance and is caught or supported by their partner. When describing this activity and how to spot, it is critical that students understand the importance of the spotter's role. There is no room for teasing or joking about not catching someone. Remind your students that the goal of the activity is to learn to trust others and to show others that they can trust you. Understanding the importance of spotting, along with a grasp of the real meaning and function of spotting, can prevent deterioration of the initially fragile feelings of trust.

Demonstrate and emphasize the relationship of good spotting to trust by showing the following physical aspects of spotting. Spend some time explaining the reason for each one. Practice with the group and give each participant the opportunity to demonstrate proper spotting.

- Stance: Balanced, centered, one leg slightly behind the other, knees flexed to absorb impact, hands up, palms out at about chest height with elbows bent.
- Focus: Eyes constantly on the participant who is about to fall.
- Absorbing force: "Give" with the body, moving or rolling in the direction of force.

Some Other Things to Remember

- Practice spotting in a controlled, contained context.
- Distinguish between spotting and assisting or helping.
- Actively promote the attitude that teasing and joking about not catching someone has no place in the activities you'll be doing.
- Supervise spotters closely, reminding them of proper techniques as needed.
- Rotate spotters so everyone has a chance to catch someone and get used to catching different-sized people. But this doesn't mean that you should let the smallest boy in the group catch the largest girl. Stay aware of who can appropriately spot whom.

Don't Touch Me

Activity Type:	Group Initiative
Activity Level:	Moderate
Space:	A large playing area; field or gym
Time:	15–30 minutes
Group Size:	8–30
Prerequisite:	None
Props:	Either a hula hoop or 6–8 foot length of rope; a stopwatch

Opening

What do the words "Don't touch me!" mean to you physically and emotionally?

Directions

There are a variety of ways to present this activity, so we'll present the different options along the way in these directions. Experiment with different groups to see which way you like to present it. Return to this activity and try it a different way whenever you want.

- Place the hula hoop or rope (shaped into a circle) in the center of your playing field or gym.

- Divide the group into an even number of smaller teams. You decide how you'd like to do it. For example, if you have twenty people you could have two groups of ten, ten groups of two, or four groups of five. Take your pick; any and all combinations work for this activity, as long as there is an even number of teams. Try to make each team have the same number of players, but if you have an odd number of people in the group, just make the teams as even as possible.

- Have each team go to a spot about 20 feet from the circle. Try to spread the teams out evenly around the circle. Each team must be lined up directly across from another team.

This activity is timed. On your command of "Go," the members of each team try to get to the same place as the team directly across from them. They will do this by passing through the circle in the middle. Each member must put at least one foot into the hula hoop or rope circle as they pass through the middle on the way to the other side. The time for the entire group will be the time it takes for the last person to get to his or her new spot.

> ## Safety Note
>
> You should encourage members to put bumpers up when they are going through the center: participants put their hands up, about a foot in front of their chests, palms facing out. Even in the heat of action, group members will be able to push off from someone in their path rather than possibly bumping heads.

Rules

1. Not only must each player touch a foot inside the circle, but for the entire time while they are passing through the circle, none of the participants can touch. Each touch results in a five-second time penalty. A ten-second time penalty will result if anyone kicks the circle (whether it be a hula hoop or rope), causing it to move or change shape.

2. Give the group some planning time before their first attempt. As in many activities, you can have a set planning time, like three minutes, or allow them to plan however fast or slow they'd like. Both bring up interesting discussions about how the planning time was used.

3. When planning is over, yell "Go" to begin the activity. Players cannot move in front of their designated spot until you've said "Go." You don't need to say this (because you want them to come up with the idea), but if someone should ask, once you have said "Go," any group member can move toward the center. Players don't have to wait behind their line until it is their turn to pass through the center.

4. After the last player has gotten to his or her new spot, stop your watch. This is the group's base time. Now check for penalties—touches of people or the circle. Ask the group if there were any touches. Let them judge themselves. Most groups will expect you to be the tough judge, but asking them to tell you will bring up issues of honesty and integrity—"Should I speak up when I know I touched Sue if I know that this is going to add five seconds to our time? The group might get mad at me. Maybe no one else saw it. Sue won't bring it up, will she?" Add up the time penalties, add them to the time it took them to complete the problem and you have the group's total time (and the current World Record!).

5. Give the group some more planning time before they have another go.

6. Depending on the group's mood, two, three, or four attempts should leave them smiling and feeling a sense of accomplishment.

Diversity Skills

Building allies, group identity, racial identity, gender and sexual orientation

Processing

- What did the group do that made you feel safe or unsafe, excluded or included?

- Where else in your life have you had those experiences?

- How well did your group cooperate during their planning session?

- How well did your plan work? If it didn't work, why do you think it didn't?

- If you didn't share the fact that you were touched or you touched someone to avoid getting a penalty, why not?

- Did you make any touches or see someone touching? Did you speak up about it?

- How does integrity or lack of it (in this case truth telling) show up in this group and in your life?

Sculpting Each Emotion

Activity Type:	Social Responsibility
Activity Level:	Moderate
Space:	Your usual meeting room
Time:	You'll need at least 45 minutes or more depending on the size of your group.
Group Size:	8–14
Prerequisite:	None
Props:	Only the participants and anything lying around the room that they want to use to make a "sculpture" of their emotions: paper clips, paper, pens, the stray rubber chicken, whatever.

Opening

Have you ever had someone say to you, "I can't believe you're feeling that way." We all know what it means and it makes most of us afraid to share our emotions with other people. But better than bury those feelings behind a mask, let's show others so they see and know!

Directions

Brainstorm as a large group the definitions of some emotions: rage, alienation, healing, depression, withdrawal, joy, and connection. Ask four volunteers to "sculpt" one of these emotions. They can use other people or props and their own bodies to express the emotion in their sculpture. Depression, for instance, could be portrayed by someone lying on the floor in a fetal position and covered with pieces of paper that list the causes of depression—poor grades, dissing, appearance.

If the group chooses anger, they may decide to stand with one hand on their hips, the fingers of the other pointing at one another, and their faces contorted in an expression of anger. Let the rest of the group identify the emotion that is being expressed and then have the entire group discuss practical solutions for resolving the emotion. The object of this activity is to help your group get in touch with their emotions and then examine alternative responses and possible ways the group can support them. For depression, some of the solutions might be to take a walk every day, start seeing a counselor, or begin keeping a journal.

Diversity Skills

You can use this activity any time you feel that your group is beginning to identify and work through emotional issues and may need some help identifying new responses or positive coping skills.

Processing:

■ What was difficult for you to see or feel during this activity?

■ How did you feel as you saw the different emotions being "sculpted"?

■ How does this relate to how you deal with these emotions?

Creative Problem Solving through Role Playing   Replay

Activity Type:	Group Initiative
Activity Level:	Moderate
Space:	Your usual meeting room
Time:	30 minutes
Group Size:	10–14
Prerequisite:	For this activity it's critical that your group has learned how to communicate their feelings openly and without fear of ridicule. Make sure that they are able to give and receive feedback and support in a kind and perceptive manner.
Props:	Note cards or paper and pencils

Opening

Our minds are like video machines. We keep replaying problem situations until we wish we could just push the stop button.

Directions

Split your group into a few small groups of four or five people. Have each person take a few minutes to think of a situation where they needed help and someone tried to help by prescribing a course of action they felt instinctively was not in their best interest. Ask them to jot down some notes about what happened and share the situation in their small group.

Let each person do a role play with their group and come up with new ways to tell the person in an assertive manner that their feelings were invalidated and that they are not comfortable with the solution.

Diversity Skills

Listening and communicating, building allies, group identity, self-affirmation, risk taking, listening without judgment.

Processing:

■ How did it feel to identify that type of situation?

■ What did you learn about yourself through your sharing?

■ How did you feel validated by your group—or not validated?

■ What were your key learnings?

What's Your Sign?

Activity Type:	Group Initiative
Activity Level:	Moderate
Space:	Your usual meeting room
Time:	No less than two hours, and you could let it go overnight and come back to it next time.
Group Size:	15 or more
Prerequisite:	None
Props:	Index cards—See the next page for the information to write on one side of the cards. You will need a fairly even number of cards in each group with the letters A, B, C, D, or E on the opposite side from the information.

Opening

A lot of times we don't get all the information we need because we think someone won't have it or because we're afraid to ask. This creates a void of resources. Let's try to fill it up.

Directions

Split your group into five smaller groups and hand each person an index card. Explain to them that the first goal of this activity is to identify people from their same group. To get them started, have them go around asking each other, "What's your zodiac sign?" The next question is "What kind of Leo (or Cancer, or Aquarius, etc.) are you?" Each person should reply according to the group listed on their card: "I'm a C kind of Leo," for example. Tell them to assemble in their small A, B, C, D, or E groups once they've identified the other members.

Now tell them that this is a competition. Each card has a secret word or words written on it that, put together with the word or words from the other groups, will create a sentence. Their goal is to find out what secret word the other groups are holding and be the first ones to solve the sentence. There's a catch, though. Each card also has information about how they're expected to treat people from the other groups. This information is held secret by each group. Give them five minutes to figure out how they're going to approach each of the other groups to ask for the words and then let them mingle and try to solve the puzzle.

Index Card Information

A Group

You have important information to share with the group that will help the group achieve their goal.

Secret Word: *Diversity*

How you treat others:

B group – You are gentle and kind to them in a patronizing way, but you know that they can't really help.

C group – You are in competition with them. They think they have the right answers but they don't. Besides, you don't really trust them.

D group – You need their physical strength, but you really dislike them because they pick on you. Besides, they're really stupid.

E group – You really want to be part of their group, but you know that you won't fit in. Besides, they're all snobs.

B Group

You have important information to share with the group that will help the group achieve their goal.

Secret Word: *Is*

How you treat others:

A group – You are gentle and kind to them in a patronizing way, but you know that they can't really help.

C group – You are in competition with them. They think they have the right answers but they don't. Besides, you don't really trust them.

D group – You need their physical strength, but you really dislike them because they pick on you. Besides, they're really stupid.

E group – You really want to be part of their group, but you know that you won't fit in. Besides, they're all snobs.

Index Card Information (continued)

C Group

You have important information to share with the group that will help the group achieve their goal.

Secret Word: *The*

How you treat others

A group – You are in competition with them. They think they have the right answers but they don't. Besides, you don't really trust them.

B group – You are gentle and kind to them in a patronizing way, but you know that they can't really help.

D group – You need their physical strength, but you really dislike them because they pick on you. Besides, they are stupid.

E group – You really want to be part of their group, but you know that you won't fit in. Besides, they're all snobs.

D Group

You have important information to share with the group that will help the group achieve their goal.

Secret Word: *Strength*

How you treat others:

A group – You need their physical strength, but you really dislike them because they pick on you. Besides, they're really stupid.

B group – You are gentle and kind to them in a patronizing way, but you know that they can't really help.

C group – You are in competition with them. They think they have the right answers but they don't. Besides, you don't really trust them.

E group – You really want to be part of their group, but you know that you won't fit in. Besides, they're all snobs.

Index Card Information (continued)

E Group

You have important information to share with the group that will help the group achieve their goal.

Secret Word: *Of Life*

How you treat others:

A group – You really want to be part of their group, but you know that you won't fit in. Besides, they're all snobs.

B group – You are gentle and kind to them in a patronizing way, but you know that they can't really help.

C group – You are in competition with them. They think they have the right answers but they don't. Besides, you don't really trust them.

D group – You need their physical strength, but you really dislike them because they pick on you. Besides, they're really stupid.

Categories

As the group's leader, you are the only one who knows what the letters signify.

Computer Nerd	—	A
Special Education Student	—	B
Gifted	—	C
Sports Jock	—	D
Popular (the IN group)	—	E

The secret words add up to the saying "Diversity is the strength of life."

Diversity Skills

This activity works well for any group learning about the importance of including others and respecting one another despite our differences.

Processing

If the group has been together a long time, it's interesting to process how long they took to share or not share information. For example:

- You've known each other a long time; why didn't you share information immediately?

- Why didn't you question the way you were supposed to treat different groups?

- How did you feel about approaching friends that way?

- How were you treated by others who were not in your group?

- How were you treated by those in your group when you first approached them?

- How did you make decisions on who to ask for information?

- Who were you willing to share with?

- How did this activity make you feel?

- How does this parallel what happens in school for you?

Tip: If you don't have time to make up all the cards, meet with each of the groups separately and verbally give them the information and secret word.

Closing Activities

You Fill Me Up

Give the group one full and one empty pitcher of water. As each person pours water from the full pitcher to the empty one, ask them to state what they add to the group and what they want the other participants to take away with them.

Passing the Magic

Take a wand and pass it around the group. Invite the participant holding the wand to share something—a feeling regarding what happened in the group that day; what they learned from the group; what they are willing to give to the group; i.e., humor, support, leadership, risk-taking, etc.; something they were unable to share before; or what they have gained from the group.

Letter to Yourself

Give each person a sheet of paper and ask them to take a few minutes to write a letter to themselves. You can use this letter for a variety of purposes. Some of the questions you might ask are:

- What felt risky for you today in the group and where do you think you need to start taking more risks in your life?

- What did you learn today? What else do you still need to learn from the group?

- What question did you want to ask of the group or of an individual member but chose not to today? What held you back from asking that question?

- How are you feeling right now in the group and what do you want from this group?

These are only a few examples of the questions you can ask your group. Create your own questions based on the activities and your goals for the group that day. After they have completed the letter, have them seal it and give it to you. Save the letters as an opener for the next time to bring them back to the place where they were. In a circle, ask if anyone wants to share anything before leaving.

Personal Journal Question

Write what you plan to do the next time someone discriminates against you or someone else.

Processing Questions

- ❏ Can you name a feeling you had at any point during the activity (mad, glad, sad, or scared)? Where in your body did you feel it most?

- ❏ Is that feeling a common one in your life?

- ❏ Did you express that feeling to others? If not, what did you do with the feeling?

- ❏ Do you usually express feelings or suppress them?

- ❏ Would you like to feel differently in a similar situation? If so, how would you like to feel?

- ❏ How do you imagine others felt toward you at various times during the activity? Were these feelings expressed?

- ❏ What types of feelings are easiest to express? Most difficult?

- ❏ Do you find it difficult to be aware of some feelings at times? If so, which ones?

- ❏ Are some feelings not appropriate to express to the group at times? If so, which ones?

- ❏ Does expressing appropriate feelings help or hinder completing the initiative?

- ❏ Is it difficult for you to avoid judging others? Explain.

- ❏ Can you think of examples of when you judged others in the group today? When you didn't judge others?

- ❏ What were some advantages to you of not judging others?

- ❏ What were some advantages to others of your not judging them?

- ❏ How do judging and not judging others affect the completion of the activity?

- ❏ Were some behaviors of others easy not to judge and other behaviors difficult?

❑ How are you different from some of the others in the group?

❑ How do these differences strengthen the group as a whole?

❑ What would this group be like if there were very few differences in people? How would you feel if this were so?

❑ How are you like some of the others in the group?

❑ Were these commonalities a help to the group in completing their task? Explain.

❑ Were these commonalities a hindrance to the group in completing their task? Explain.

❑ Do you think you have other things in common with some of the group members that you haven't found yet?

❑ How did this setting help you discover how you are similar to others?

❑ What have you learned about trust, respect, acceptance, and cooperation as they relate to differences?

7
Building
Allies

Once your group has embarked on the process of learning how to really listen to others, to communicate effectively and honestly, and to validate each other's personal experiences and beliefs, the next step is to learn how to work together as allies. Being an ally goes beyond merely "tolerating" differences, or understanding someone's point of view. Taking the extra step to be an ally means connecting and committing to supporting someone, often in challenging situations.

What Are Allies?

The Random House College Dictionary defines an ally as "1. A person or thing that is united with another, as by treaty. 2. A person who collaborates or associates with another." The purpose of this chapter is to help your group begin to understand what it means to be an ally. Your challenge, as the facilitator, will be to establish an association among the members of your group and to show them what it means to unite with others in ways that transcend perceived similarities and dissimilarities.

For example: Two members of a commonly associated group of students at a high school—students who play sports, for instance—may not be allies nor have any intention of becoming allies. Or perhaps most of the members of your group are Asian, male, and 16 years old. This does not automatically create the necessary association that defines true allies. Then again, you may find that something gels between the most outspoken member of your group and the least active participant—they become allies through an unspoken agreement or understanding.

True allies have common goals that go beyond the borders of ethnicity, sexual orientation, body size, physical ability, personal interests, and all the other combinations of individual difference. During war time, nations with completely different cultures and political structures unite as allies against a common enemy. In our work, we try to create allies who unite to battle the stereotypes that keep us apart and fearful of one another. Allies celebrate the right of each individual group member to be unique and to be valued, and the worth of each individual's contribution to the whole.

One of your roles will be to help students see and accept their individual strengths and weaknesses. Adventure activities have a unique ability to do this in a manner that is fun and nonthreatening. All students in your group will have things they are good at, which add to the group. Once students begin to recognize their strengths in the group, they will likely begin to transfer these to situations outside the group—to family, classroom, church, etc. It is important that you model the acceptance you will be expecting from your group. Show them that you are willing to be an ally, that you believe in the power of the group to stick together and support each individual member.

> The shadow side of perceiving difference is a divisive sense of otherness that projects fear. This fear goes by many names: racism, sexism, species arrogance, bigotry, selfishness, hatred, miserliness, jealousy, control, alienation, ridicule, revenge, scapegoating, demonization, and so on.
>
> When differences are not divorced from connectedness, they are instead seen as diversity—aspects of each person's uniqueness that enrich wholeness and begin to describe manifest potential...
>
> This experience would not be possible, however, without the context of life's web. Singularity is relative to multiplicity. Without a group, individuality is meaningless.
>
> —*From* The Compass of the Heart *by Loren Cruden*

Lessons from Geese

Fact 1:   As each goose flaps its wings, it creates an uplift for the birds that follow. By flying in a V formation, the whole flock adds 71% greater flying range than if each bird flew alone.

Lesson: People who share a common direction and sense of community can get where they are going more quickly and easily because they are traveling on the thrust of one another.

Fact 2:   When a goose falls out of formation, it suddenly feels the drag and resistance of flying alone. It quickly moves back into formation to take advantage of the lifting power of the bird immediately in front of it.

Lesson: If we have as much sense as a goose, we will stay in formation with those headed where we want to go. We are willing to accept their help and give our help to others.

Fact 3: When the lead goose tires, it rotates back into the formation and another goose flies to the point position.

Lesson: It pays to take turns doing the hard tasks and sharing leadership. As with geese, people are interdependent on each other's skills, capabilities, and unique arrangements of gifts, talents, or resources.

Fact 4: The geese flying in formation honk to encourage those up front to keep up their speed.

Lesson: We need to make sure our honking is encouraging. In groups where there is encouragement, production is much greater. The power of encouragement (to stand by one's heart or core values and encourage the heart and core of others) is the quality of honking that we seek.

Fact 5: When a goose gets sick, wounded, or shot down, two geese drop out of formation and follow it down to help and protect it. They stay with it until it dies or is able to fly again. Then, they launch out with another formation or catch up with the flock.

Lesson: If we have as much sense as geese, we will stand by each other in difficult times as well as when we are strong.

—From a speech by Angeles Arrien, based on work by Milton Olsen.

How to Be an Ally: Some Dos and Don'ts

Asking for What You Need

Two trainers were preparing for a corporate diversity training. As Sandy and Leslie were working on the easels in front of the room, the president of the company came into the room. He walked right past Sandy, who is African American, and went over to Leslie, who is white, and introduced himself. He shook hands with Leslie and said, "You must be the trainer for the session." He completely ignored Sandy. Leslie introduced Sandy as her training partner and he shook hands with her. As he walked away, Leslie said to Sandy with a look of amazement and understanding, "It happened!" What Leslie meant was that Sandy had been ignored, overlooked, invalidated as a possible trainer because of her race. Leslie's awareness of these issues had been raised enough where she finally noticed this unconscious slight by the president. Sandy said, "Yes, it did and it happens all the time." Leslie felt very uncomfortable and said, "Now, what do I do?" She felt like she should do something, but didn't know what. By confronting the president, she ran the risk of offending a client. Do nothing, and he would continue the behavior. Sandy said, "You're doing what needs to be done right now. You have acknowledged to me that it happens. That is all that I need right now."

Taking this story as an example, here are some steps you can take to show your allies that you are taking a stand.

Share what you observe, as Leslie did with Sandy. Even if the situation makes you uncomfortable, acknowledge what you saw. If you are uneasy, say so. "I'm not quite sure how to respond to what just happened. It's not that I didn't see it. It's just that I am scared to confront the principal, my teacher, whomever." Silence can easily be misinterpreted as acceptance. The worst thing you can do is look away or refuse to discuss what just happened because you're afraid. Try not to change the subject or laugh it off as though nothing happened.

Caution

When facilitating groups exploring diversity issues, there may be times when you will be caught between your desire to help someone out in a difficult situation and the need to maintain confidentiality. While it's important that both you and your group engage each other's trust—and this means that what happens during your meetings stays with the group—some situations may warrant talking to an outside professional. If you or any members of the group have the slightest reason to believe that someone may be at risk of causing physical harm to themselves or others, it is your responsibility to take action. It is better to be wrong if you believe that one of your group is at risk.

Check in and ask what you can do. In the above example, it was enough for Sandy to have Leslie acknowledge the problem. She didn't need her to go any further. By asking what you can do for someone, you are giving them your unqualified support—you are being an ally. This person will be far more comfortable asking you for help if they need it.

Respect the requests of others. Remember that whatever you think about the situation and what *you* think needs to be done, it is essential to respect the other person's wishes. If someone asks you to leave it alone and not do anything, they probably have very legitimate reasons that you know nothing about. Once the question has been asked, hold yourself to what you have been asked to do.

Make yourself available to help. Once you've asked what you can do, it's important that you follow up on your offer. But be realistic about it and know your own limits. What are you willing to do and what will the impact of your actions be? In Leslie and Sandy's case, Leslie felt trapped because confronting the president could have lost them a client. Fortunately, Sandy did not need her to take action. Again, don't stay silent. It's important to discuss just how much you feel you can do without jeopardizing your own sense of emotional and physical safety.

Problem solve. Get your group involved in discussing what their options might be and what kinds of action are appropriate for different situations. What kind of resources are available to your students and their allies? Can they go to a teacher, administrators, parents, peer mediators? Make a list of the options, what they can do and the perceived consequences of any actions they take.

Thoughts on Being an Effective Ally

■ Within and between groups, we are all different. That should be both understood and celebrated.

■ We all are capable of being effective allies for people from groups other than our own.

■ You are critical in fighting for your own and other people's freedom from oppression.

■ Apparent rejection of your offer(s) to be an ally to another group frequently stems from larger social issues, and not your specific offer.

■ Allow for and be patient about differences in communication styles between your own and other groups.

■ Understand that people are the experts on their own life experiences. This doesn't mean you can't understand their experiences or use your own to find solutions, but they know their own environment and experiences better than you.

■ Whenever possible, actively ask and seek understanding of oppression experienced by members of other groups.

■ Appreciate and, when appropriate, help people take pride in the history of their own group.

■ In your quest for better understanding, allow for and learn from disagreements. Do not allow this process to prevent or inhibit you from being an effective ally. Remember, your intent and the outcome you receive don't always match.

■ Language and behaviors that are comfortable for you are often cultural. Understand that what may be comfortable for you may make people from different groups uncomfortable.

Concluding Thoughts

The important point to all this is that we can be allies for each other in spite of our differences. Becoming allies moves us beyond description and recognition of discrimination and empathizing with its victims. Taking action in support of others, and being supported in return, is essential to the process of making positive changes within a diverse community.

Suggested Reading

Cruden, Loren. *Compass of the Heart: Embodying Medicine Wheel Teachings.* Rochester, VT: Destiny Books, 1996. A guide to integrating body and spirit, to connecting with the web of life through Native American and other earth-oriented traditions.

Rusk, Tom and Patrick D. Miller. *Power of Ethical Persuasion: From Conflict to Partnership at Work and in Private Life.* Cassette, Penguin Audiobooks, 1993. This practical program revolutionizes our dead-end communication patterns and motivates people to treat each other with greater respect, caring, and fairness.

Haycock, Katie. *Improving Student Achievement Through Partnership.* AAHE Publications, 1992

Worksheet

What's important about my allies: _____

_____

_____

The most important thing about having an ally (or friend) is: _____

_____

_____

The ways I know (have known) that a person is really supportive of me are:

_____

_____

_____

The people who are currently my most trusted allies are (at work or school, at home, in my family, in my community, in my circle of friends):

_____

_____

_____

When I want to support someone I will: _____

_____

_____

I find it difficult to support others because I: _____

_____

_____

Possible strategies for supporting that person are: _____

_____

_____

Michael

Michael is a gay man with cerebral palsy who works for the Victory Program, an HIV/AIDS and addiction awareness training and educational program that also provides housing and rehabilitative services in the greater Boston area. A year ago, Michael attended a five-day Project Adventure Diversity workshop. He tells the following story about his experiences in how to forge alliances and why it has become a major part of his personal growth process.

"In retrospect, I think it began with a recognition of my heterophobia—my fears of being with straight men—and a new willingness to work through those fears during the time I spent at the Project Adventure workshop. One of the workshop participants, John, personified everything I had always feared about 'gay-bashing' homophobic men. He was a straight, white, educated, upper-middle-class jock, and I felt a surge of negativity just looking at him on the first day of the workshop. By midweek, once an atmosphere of trust and safety had been established within the group, I realized that John might not be everything I had imagined and felt confident enough to confront him with my fears.

"During one of the activities where we split into smaller groups, I told John what I was feeling and about the conflict I was having between my past experiences with straight men and my experience of him as an individual. Just verbalizing my fears gave me an enormous sense of relief, but there was more to it than that. John was visibly hurt by what I was saying, and I think that shook me up more than anything else. Gay men have many of the same stereotypes about men as women do, that is, straight men don't have feelings or don't allow themselves to show their feelings. But here was John openly showing me just how much it can hurt to be told that someone has negative perceptions of them. Our conversation opened a door for both of us and we began communicating freely about homophobic and heterophobic stereotypes and all the misconceptions that grow up around people with different sexual orientations.

"This was the beginning of a wonderful and very tough process for me. Before the workshop, I had been in danger of closing myself off to straight men, of staying too bitter to listen, to see, to understand them as people. After the workshop, I couldn't leave it at one straight guy, and I began taking chances with other men who fit my stereotype of 'gay bashers.' Two of these men are colleagues of mine who I approached immediately after the workshop with my new desire to open up and communicate. For almost a year now, we've talked almost every day about subjects ranging from media perceptions of gays and straights to intimate discussions about sex and sexuality. All of us have learned an immense amount about each other, and while we may not be coming from the same place, we listen to each other and we defend each other's views if they are attacked.

"Then, a couple of months ago, I went back to another Project Adventure workshop for diversity trainers and, again, one of the members of the group, David, fit all my negative stereotypes about straight men. David is a proactive person, and when I told him about my experiences over the past eight months, he was very open and willing to engage in conversations on how we could take the learning further, taking it beyond personal experience and incorporating it into future trainings and workshops. David also gave me an opportunity to symbolically apply and solidify my new outlook during one of the ropes course activities we did together.

"I had asked David to be my partner for the *Wild Woosey. The Wild Woosey* is a set of cables about two feet off the ground that begin at the same point and slowly spread out into a V shape over about a 20-foot length. Each person stands on one cable and, leaning into each other, they try to walk together as far down the separate cables as they can without collapsing into each other and the space that gradually opens up between them. There's a point in this exercise when you really have to connect—physically, emotionally, and mentally—with the other person in order to build up enough mutual confidence and strength to keep going. There was a specific moment when David and I were about to lose it, and he told me to look into his eyes so that we could get steadier. I felt myself pulling back automatically from him when he said, 'Look into my eyes.' But then I said to myself, 'Stop it. Go for it. He means what he's saying.' I did go for it and looked into David's eyes and we completed the length of the *Wild Woosey*.

"Why do I feel like this experience was real and valid? Most likely because I find myself attempting to help others learn how to look at things from a different perspective on a daily basis. Not long ago, I was in Provincetown with a group of men who were talking about how 'stupid' straight jocks are, and I just had to interject and tell them about my experiences over the past year. While I was telling them their stereotype wasn't true, I was laughing inside, thinking to myself, 'Here you are defending straight jocks to a group of gay men.' But you know, it felt good and it felt right. I also know in my heart that in Connecticut, John is not allowing gay men to be put down, that my two colleagues are doing it daily and that David, too, is doing the same thing where he is. I know they can't ignore the problem any more and that makes these people my allies. They're covering my back. The work we're doing will spread from us to others and, soon enough, I hope, everyone will be defending our right to be different."

Continuum

Individual ➜Partners ➜Allies ➜Community

Once your group discovers and accepts that each of them feels and thinks differently, that each individual wants to be accepted and supported by others, they need to learn how they can both offer and accept help from others. This kind of sharing is what true community is all about.

Awareness

Allies don't have to look alike or believe in the same things, but they do need to share some basic understandings and common goals. Being an ally implies partnership and mutual respect. It can't be done alone.

Group Skills

Asking and checking in—Checking in with other people and asking what they need is one of the simplest and most effective ways to show your support. Silence can be misinterpreted as acceptance, so speak up about what you just saw.

Helping others—Being available to help others when they ask for it. What can you do and how?

Identifying the problem—Figuring out exactly what the challenge is and how to solve it.

Taking action—Once you've listed your options, it's important to act on them together.

Activities

Hog Call

Activity Type:	Ice Breaker
Activity Level:	Moderate
Space:	The best place to do this activity is an open field or gym.
Time:	15 to 30 minutes, depending on how much time you devote to processing
Group Size:	The more people, the more chaos. Anywhere from 20 to 40, but if you have fewer, don't let it stop you from trying!
Prerequisite:	Since this activity requires that participants close their eyes, be sure they are comfortable with this. Players also must understand the bumpers up position (See page 76) and keep their hands up in front of them at all times. Before you even get started, give them a firm warning that NO RUNNING is allowed. If there are any obstacles such as large trees in your playing area, make sure that you and your coleaders are spotting during this activity.
Props:	None

Opening

Rumor has it that pig farmers call their pigs home yelling, "Soooooooie!" This game is modeled after the pig farmer's call. How do you find what's your's in the middle of a chaotic world?

Directions

Your group needs to partner up. Have the group get into two lines facing one another. Once this has been done, have the players reach one hand out to the person across from them in order to form pairs. If there is an odd number of people, one small group can be made up of three players.

Each pair needs to come up with two words (three for the group of three, if you have one) that they can associate with. For example: Left and Right, Peanut Butter and Jelly, Big Toe and Little Toe, Black and White, Top and Bottom, Coca and Cola, etc. Each person in the pair takes one of the two words.

Send one line of people to one end of the field or gym and the other line to the other end. This means the pairs will now be split up and standing on opposite sides of the playing area. If any two members of the pairs are lined up directly across from each other, you may want to have one line "scramble up" before proceeding with the directions.

Have all players close their eyes and assume their best bumpers up stance. On your command of "Go," the lines begin walking toward one another as players yell their partner's word, while at the same time listening for their partner, who is calling out their other word. The players continue calling their partners' words until they find each other. When they do find each other, they can open their eyes and watch the others who are still struggling to find their partners.

Diversity Skills

This activity adapts itself to almost any type of goal setting for learning about the different subjects presented in this workbook. See Processing, below, for more information.

Processing

Hog Call is a wonderful way to get people to share goals and learn about their differences and similarities. It is especially good to partner up people who on the surface have little in common. You might have the pairs sit down for ten minutes after they have found one another and discuss their goals for the day (or workshop, etc.). After the ten minutes are up, have all of the pairs come back together as a large group and ask them to introduce their partners and their goals. At the end of a program, *Hog Call* can be used in a similar way, except have the pairs talk about their highlight of the day, what they got out of it, or whatever else would help to wrap up your session.

Tic-Tac-Toe ■

Activity Type:	De-Inhibitizer
Activity Level:	Low
Space:	Enough for the group to sit in a circle on the ground
Time	15–20 minutes (unless you play the marathon version)
Group Size:	8–10 or so
Prerequisite:	Some good natured play
Props:	None

Opening

It takes concentration and confidence to learn how to respond quickly. Let's practice.

Directions

Sit in a circle, legs crossed.

This game involves three hand signals (with sounds) from the ancient executioners handbook.

1. Tic!

Hand (either) under chin. Smile (peaceful bliss). Fingers will point either to the person on the left or the person on the right. The person pointed to responds with:

2. Tac!

Hand (either) swings over the top of head. Furrowed brow. (As in "So this is how it is!") Fingers will point either to the person on the left or the person on the right. The person pointed to responds with:

3. Toe!

Both hands point forward. This is the classic frontal sword chop. Sound out as loud as possible, pointing clearly at someone across the circle. That person continues with Tic!

The sequence is always Tic! Tac! Toe!

And so on, until someone makes the wrong cry or motion, or waits too long to respond. This is the group's signal to bang fists on the ground (politely but vigorously) letting that person know that they must cross over to the other side (slide out of the circle).

Play continues on, while those out of the game become hecklers, hoping to confuse someone else and thus lure them over to the 'other side'. No touching is allowed by hecklers.

The game ends when there are only two participants left, surrounded by a group of hecklers. At this point it might be a good idea to have a parade, or a game of tag that involves no heavy duty thinking.

Slow and thoughtful presentation of the rules with ample practice time helps to build confidence in the players, and insures that each participant has time to master the mystical qualities of these rules, thereby reducing the chance of being eliminated the first time the hand of fate is pointed in his or her direction. In addition it is important to honor the role of the heckler by modeling some effective techniques, pointing out that this role affects the length of the game and is a vital strand in the web of *Tic Tac Toe*.

Variation—this results in expanding the activity. *Marathon Tic Tac Toe* begins with a volunteer heckler. When someone in the circle is eliminated, he or she changes places with the heckler, so that there is only one person at a time in this role. *Marathon Tic Tac Toe* tests the attention of the group, and is not the best way to initially present the activity.

Because *Tic Tac Toe* engages the entire group, no member is ever intentionally eliminated, and there is generally a sustained level of energy and humor that moves the game along at a rather rapid pace. The only area that may cause a delay is when a participant tries to cover a mistake and refuses to accept the consequence of elimination. This is generally managed quite well by peer group pressure when the group decisively yells, "You're out of the game!" If resistance continues, however, the most effective approach is to ignore the behavior and carry on. If it happens again, take a moment to check the member's perception of what just transpired. If necessary, clarify the rules and begin again.

Finally, there have been times when hecklers have gone beyond the bounds of reasonable and proper behavior to capture the attention of the group. Again, knowledge of the group will dictate whether to set limits in the beginning. Fun, speed and enthusiasm are the necessary ingredients which will bring a new meaning to the terms *Tic Tac Toe!*

Diversity Skills

Tic Tac Toe is an activity that seems to fit anywhere and anytime. Whether a group has been scattered and needs something to pull it together, or they have been in a long discussion on a serious issue and need a laugh, *Tic Tac Toe* fits nicely. As a game of concentration, it is a nice change from more physical and active games.

Processing

In processing the activity, be as dramatic and serious as possible in order to capture the group's interest. This also encourages their playful, theatrical involvement.

- What did it feel like to get eliminated?

- Did you find it hard to admit that you made a mistake and had to leave the circle? Why?

- What was it like to be a heckler? Did you feel excluded from the group?

- How important was the heckler's role?

- Was it hard not to get distracted?

- Can you think of any ways that people distract you from what you've set out to do in your life? How do you handle the distractions?

Everybody Up

Activity Type:	De-Inhibitizer
Activity Level:	Moderate
Space:	Any place will do, but make sure the floor is not made out of cement! Also, move any objects like desks or chairs to avoid bumped heads.
Time:	15 minutes
Group Size:	Anywhere from 2 on up
Prerequisite:	None
Props:	None

Opening

Everyone always says that two is better than one. Let's see how it's done. The object here is to help everyone in your group stand up, and help yourself as well.

Directions

Have the participants pair up and then sit down facing one another with the toes of their shoes pressed together. Now have them reach out and grab their partner's hands. By pulling hard against each other, the pairs gently but firmly pull themselves up to a standing position.

After they've done it in pairs, introduce groups of three and four, even five. Can they work together to get *Everybody Up?*

Diversity Skills

This activity is great for challenging people to think about some of the stereotypes they have about people who are different from them physically. It's good for validating feelings, group identity, gender and sexual orientation, physical and mental ability.

Processing

After a few people have been able to do it, have everyone switch partners to have male-female pairs or pairs of people of different sizes get a chance to work together. If they've succeeded once, they should also be able to do it with different partners.

- ■ What was hard about this activity? What was easy?

- ■ Was this problem exactly as it seemed? Are there other situations that are like that?

- ■ What have you learned in this activity that you will carry to the next?

Caution

While the directions seem simple, this activity is not so easy to do. Remind the group of their Full Value Contract, especially the part to play safe. Rough pulling can be painful and diminish feelings of trust the group may be developing. Encourage people to keep trying and to think about what they can do to increase their chances of succeeding. As in some of the other activities, strength is less important than using a well-thought-out strategy.

Make a Sandwich

Activity Type:	Trust Building
Activity Level:	Low
Space:	Your usual meeting room
Time:	30 minutes
Group Size:	4 or more
Prerequisite:	Clean hands. Most of the time, people want to eat the sandwich they make.
Props:	Enough bread, peanut butter, jelly, plates, and knives for each person in the group. Blindfolds. If you don't want to have too much mess to clean up, cover a large table with a plastic cloth beforehand.

Opening

Who do you trust to make your food the way you like it? How do you tell others what you want?

Directions

Ask the group to pair up. One person in each pair starts off blindfolded with the sandwich-making equipment in front of them. The object is for the blindfolded partner to make a peanut butter and jelly sandwich via their partner's verbal instruction. No touching is allowed. If they make a hole in the sandwich, they have to start all over again.

Diversity Skills

Listening and communicating, validating feelings, group identities, gender and sexual orientation, or use this activity any time you want the group to think more about the ways we cooperate and share with one another.

Processing

- How did it feel to be blindfolded?
- What did your partner do that showed trust?
- How did you communicate with each other?
- What are some of the foods you eat with your family?

- What's important about how they're made?

- Have you ever tried to share these foods and how they're made with others? (This could lead in to organizing a diversity dinner. Have your participants and their families come to a pot-luck dinner—each family brings their favorite specialty.)

■ Come to Me

Activity Type:	Trust Building
Activity Level:	Moderate
Space:	Your usual meeting room
Time:	20–30 minutes
Group Size:	Any
Prerequisite:	This is a blindfolded activity, and as with any trust or sightless activity, knowing your group and judging what they are ready for is important.
Props:	Enough blindfolds for half the group

Opening

Let's try to see how we define our personal space parameters and understand what experiences influence them.

Directions

Split the group into pairs. One partner wears a blindfold, or simply closes his or her eyes; the other partner remains sighted and begins the game by standing approximately 10–15 feet away. As soon as the blindfolded players declare themselves ready, the sighted partners begin to walk towards their sightless partners until that person holds up her hands (palms out, of course) and says, "Stop!"

Variation

A slightly different focus to the activity changes the dynamic, making this into more of a game. When the sighted players approach their partners, the intent is to be as quiet as possible and to get as close as possible before the sightless player stops them. Circling around behind partners, standing still, and other strategies enliven this variation as the sightless players attempt to determine where their partners are. Depending on the styles of the players and the safety level of the group, this version may cause more or less nervousness for the participants.

People generally respond well to this variation, both as a trust builder and just for the fun of trying to sneak up on the other person. But you may want to outline what types of sneaking are appropriate, and identify any behaviors that are inappropriate (no tickling or making fun of the sightless people, for example) to help keep the environment within your established safety levels.

Diversity Skills

You can try this activity at just about any time in your group's development. As a trust activity, it is a revealing exercise to explore one's comfort level as another person enters your personal space and mentally measure what level of discomfort is experienced by that person's approach. Some people enjoy allowing a partner to get close enough to touch; others stop them at a distance of several feet. It can produce some lively discussion about why the sightless person said, "Stop." It may also raise questions about how comfortable they are in close proximity to people who are not like them.

Processing

- How close do you let people get to you before it affects your comfort zone?

- What kinds of risks do you feel like you're taking when you let people get close?

- How does your family express their feelings physically? Are they comfortable with touching and being close together?

- Does your culture give you signals about touching and being close? What are they?

Object Retrieval

Activity Type:	Group Initiative
Activity Level:	Moderate
Space:	Outdoor field or gym
Time:	45 minutes to an hour
Group Size:	10 or more
Prerequisite:	None

Props

A bicycle inner tube cut in half (slice off the valve area). Four sections of rope, 20 feet long. One section of 40-foot-long rope. A #10 tin can or bucket.

Opening

Inside the bucket is a special serum that, once injected into a few people, will bring world peace to all of us via its special ability to spread through your sneezing. The only problem is, there's just enough to create world peace, but the scientists don't have the formula to make another batch. It's your job to retrieve the serum without spilling a drop so that the world will know peace. There's another catch to this: the only tools you have to achieve your goals are the ones I'm giving you now.

Directions

Outline a 30-foot-diameter circular area with your long rope. Place the tin can, one third filled with water, in the middle of the circle.

Give the group the rest of the props and brief them on their mission along with the following stipulations:

- Any and as many knots as desired can be tied in the ropes or rubber sections.

- The ropes and inner tubes cannot be cut.

- No one may enter or make contact within the area outlined by the circumference rope. If ground contact is made, they have to begin again from the start.

- If any of the water is spilled, even a drop, they go back to the beginning again.

Diversity Skills

Group identity, racial identity, gender and sexual orientation, or any time you want the group to challenge their cooperative skills.

Processing

- How did the group pick a solution?

- Did anyone emerge as a leader?

- Did you play the role of ally to anyone? How?

- What was your initial reaction to the problem?

- What did each of you do to attain peace? (*Go Around*)

- What were the things you could have done?

- What are the things in life that we can each do to create peace?

Jumping Jack Flash

Activity Type:	Group Initiative
Activity Level:	High
Space:	Enough room to swing a 20-foot jump rope
Time:	30 minutes
Group Size:	Any
Prerequisite:	None
Props:	A rope about 20 feet long, for jumping over

Opening

Just because you're part of a group doesn't mean you lose your own identity. How can you be yourself, but still do your part to help the group achieve its goals?

Directions

The performance objective of this activity is easy for an individual, but often frustrating for a group. You and a co-leader or volunteer should stand 10' to 15' apart and swing the rope in a wide arc. As part of the criteria for success, everyone must jump one at a time through the spinning rope so that the rope never turns without someone being in there to take a jump; i.e., a player cannot just run through, a jump must be taken. If the rope makes a turn without someone completing a jump, everyone must begin again, even those who have successfully made it through.

Diversity Skills

This activity adapts itself well to working across differences because the problem is essentially one of effective leadership, planning, and implementation. It's also a valuable teaching aid, because when the group finally decides to work together, the efficiency and sense of flow provide more hands-on learning about teamwork than you can verbalize.

Processing

- How did you decide to organize yourselves so everyone would go through?

- Who knew how to jump rope in this group?

- How did you learn it? Did you teach it here? How?

- Was jumping the rope threatening to anyone?

- What could have been done to make things easier?

- How did individuals fit into the group as part of the whole? How does this fit in with working together as allies?

Speak Out

Activity Type:	Social Responsibility
Activity Level:	Low
Space:	Your usual meeting room
Time:	30 minutes
Group Size:	Any
Prerequisite:	None

Opening

When I was 16 and had just got my driver's license, my dad made me change each tire on the car for four nights in a row. Before I did it the first time, I told him I already knew how to change a tire. He told me that thinking you know how to do something and practicing how to do it are two different things. This is a chance for you to practice "speaking out" what you think.

Directions

Have participants pair up and share an experience where they felt different or left out. Have them answer the following questions:

One of the things I don't want to have happen again is...

And what I need from you and other people is...

Example: "One of the things I don't want to have happen again is for someone to act as though I do not exist and I am not there."

"What I need from you and other people is for you to ask me if I need help."

Diversity Skills

This activity will help your group develop their ability to ask others for the support or help they need in appropriate ways.

Processing

Have the group pair up and talk about what they just shared.

- What was it like for you to share what you don't want to happen again?
- What barriers are there to asking for what you need?
- What do you need in your relationships with people that will encourage you to ask for help?

People Need People

Activity Type:	Social Responsibility
Activity Level:	Moderate
Space:	Any
Time:	15 minutes
Group Size:	12 or more
Prerequisite:	None
Props:	Name tags with part of a phrase or saying that you have been working with as a group. For example, you could use parts of the Full Value Contract, or group goals such as:

- Be ready to participate.
- Be safe physically and emotionally.
- Set goals and work toward them.
- Speak the truth.
- Let go of negatives.
- Care for self and others.

Opening

On your name tag there is a phrase which is part of our Full Value Contract. Please introduce yourself to others in the room and try to find the people in your group with name tags that will complete your phrase.

Directions

Have them mill around the room and try to put the sayings together. Afterward, unscramble the phrases as a large group, if necessary.

Diversity Skills

Listening and communicating, group identities, individual identity, or whenever you feel the group needs to reinforce the tenets of their Full Value Contract.

Processing

- How did you get information?
- What was confusing in this activity?
- What did you like best about this activity?
- Finally, what are the points of the Full Value Contract again?

One Step at a Time

Activity Type:	Social Responsibility
Activity Level:	Low
Space:	None
Time:	Until your next meeting. This is an overnight, written assignment.
Group Size:	Any
Prerequisite:	None
Props:	None

Opening

A lot of video games depend on how well you can work out a strategy to get where you want to go. Think of this like a game and work on how you want to surround yourself with allies who are going in the same direction as you are.

Directions

Give each participant the following written assignment to work on overnight:

"Describe a real situation where you felt very different and needed allies to give you support. Write HOW you would approach a potential ally to ask for what you need and describe WHAT you would have asked for."

The next time you meet, have the group share their answers with a partner. Ask them to choose someone they don't know well or wouldn't normally pick. Part of the challenge is for them to share information with someone they might not feel all that comfortable with or trust.

The partner responds to the HOW and WHAT by stating:

"That sounds good because… and what I would add is…"

After they share the information, have them role play HOW they would ask for support and WHAT they would ask for now that they've gotten feedback from their partners.

To finish, have them share:

"I chose you as a partner because…"

Diversity Skills

While this activity is primarily geared towards building allies, you can modify the assignment and adapt it to more specific situations. For example, "Describe a real situation where you felt very different because of your race, gender, ability, etc. and needed allies to give you support." It is a good tool for helping your group learn to listen with compassion and increase their awareness of the impact of discrimination.

Processing

- What was hard for you in this activity?

- What was easy for you in this activity?

- What have you learned?

- How can you apply this learning outside of this group?

- When you chose a partner did you pick someone who was safe or risky? Why?

- What did it feel like to have someone make suggestions about the way you handle your interaction with others?

- Were you able to hear what your partner suggested?

- Did someone suggest something that was useful?

Map of My Allies

Activity Type:	Social Responsibility
Activity Level:	Low-key
Space:	A place for writing
Time:	15–20 minutes
Group Size:	8–12
Prerequisite:	A day of working together on ally-building skills
Props:	Paper and pencils or markers

Opening

We've spent some time together figuring out what an ally is and how to be an effective one. For the next few minutes, let's create maps that show who our allies are, or who we want them to be.

Directions

Have each person in the group plot a diagram of their allies in relationship to themselves. It may be helpful to use a grid, timeline, or concentric circle format. Have them start by putting themselves on the page, then add their closest allies, continuing on to the people who aren't their allies yet, but who they would eventually like to have as a part of their network. Ask them to think about why they included their closest allies and strategies for bringing potential allies closer to them.

Diversity Skills

This activity is primarily designed to help your group think more about who their allies are, what they want their allies to be like, and ways to become effective allies.

Processing

- What was hard for you in this activity?

- What was easy for you in this activity?

- What have you learned?

- How can you apply this learning outside of this group?

- When you chose a partner did you pick someone who was safe or risky? Why?

- What was it like to have someone make suggestions to your approach?

- Were you able to hear what your partner suggested?

- Did someone suggest something that was useful?

Have each person share their thoughts if they wish, and talk about how best to support current allies and develop future ones.

Closing Activities

■ I Am Who I Am

Have each person finish the sentence:

"I am who I say I am, and I am committed to…"

Ask them to identify their commitments to being an ally in the fight against discrimination and prejudice.

■ Fist to Palm

Have participants pair up and face each other. Have one partner reach out his arm with the palm open and up. Tell the other partner to place her fist in her partner's palm. Then say to the group, "Try to open your partner's fist." Process what happens. Now have them repeat the exercise, but this time, say, "Open your partner's fist." Process what happens.

The first time, most people react as though it's some kind of competition. You used the word "try." The second time, more participants will probably cooperate because you made an assumption and said, "Open your partner's fist." Discuss what happens with positive statements regarding cooperation and the assumptions we make in life.

■ Plus/Delta

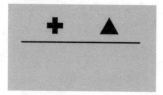

Plus/Delta (Positive Change) Chart

Draw a line across the top of a piece of easel paper. On the left side place a plus sign, and on the right side place a delta sign. On the left side of the easel paper, ask the group to list the plus or positive things about the group and its activities today. On the right side, have them list the delta or the changes they would have made in the group for the day or the changes they want for the next time. Review both lists and determine how to address the changes next time.

Personal Journal Question

What did I get from this group that I didn't realize I needed?

Processing Questions

❏ Who didn't understand someone's attempt to communicate?

❏ What went wrong in the communication attempt?

❏ What could the communicator do differently next time to give a clearer message?

❏ What could the message receiver do differently next time to understand the message?

❏ Did you learn something about communication that will be helpful later? If so, what?

❏ Do you usually express feelings or suppress them?

❏ How do you imagine others felt toward you at various times during the activity? Were these feelings expressed?

❏ Are some feelings not appropriate to express to the group at times? If so, which ones?

❏ Can you think of specific examples of when the group cooperated in completing the activity? Explain.

❏ How did it feel to cooperate?

❏ Do you cooperate in most things you do?

❏ How did you learn to cooperate?

❏ What are the rewards of cooperating?

❏ How did cooperative behavior lead to successfully completing the activity?

❏ How can you cooperate in other areas of your life?

❏ Did you think anyone was blocking the group from cooperating? Explain.

❏ Can you give examples of when you trusted someone in the group?

❏ Is it easier to trust some people than others? Explain.

❏ Can you think of examples when trusting someone wasn't a good idea?

❏ How do you increase your level of trust for someone?

❏ On a scale of 1 to 10, rate how much trust you have in the group as a whole. Can you explain your rating?

❏ What did you do today that deserves the trust of others?

❏ How does the amount of fear you feel affect your trust of others?

❏ How are you different from some of the others in the group?

❏ How do these differences strengthen the group as a whole?

❏ What would this group be like if there were very few differences between people? How would you feel if this were so?

❏ How are you like some of the others in the group?

❏ Were these commonalities a hindrance to the group in completing their task? Explain.

❏ Do you think you have other things in common with some of the group members that you haven't found yet?

❏ How did this setting help you discover how you are similar to others?

❏ What did it feel like to ask for help from someone you used to think of as the member of a group that wouldn't help or support you?

❏ What have you learned about trust, respect, acceptance, and cooperation as it relates to differences?

❏ What was the most difficult part of this activity as it relates to how you deal with people who are different from you?

❏ What was the easiest part of this activity as it relates to how you deal with people who are different from you?

❏ Did this activity challenge any of your beliefs?

❏ What are your feelings now?

❏ Do you think there are more commonalities or differences between _____ and _____?

8

Group Identities

Research shows that our brains have a natural tendency to search for meaning. One of the ways we do this is through "patterning." We create internal maps based on our experiences that help us find our place in the world, search for meaning, and create order out of chaos.

This is reflected in the way we begin to notice things once a point of reference is available. For example, because of a conversation with my friend Michael about how much he likes light blue Ford trucks, I may begin to notice them everywhere. This is probably not because there are suddenly more blue trucks around, but because my brain has a context for these trucks and a place to file them.

Creating Categories

As children we begin to create categories that help us to navigate through the world. Our attempts to make sense of things take a number of forms. Our language development occurs simultaneously with the development of our understanding of our environment. For example, when a child begins to sort out things with her siblings, she may begin to talk about things possessively. "This is mine, and that is yours." Beyond figuring out what is 'mine,' the child begins to assign meaning to just exactly what owning something means. Mine means it's mine to play with whenever I want, and perhaps it's mine to share with a friend who comes over, or mine to put in my room when I am done.

The category of "mine" and the meaning attached to it become something that children rely on to help make sense of the world. Remember being young and thinking something was yours, or wanting it to be? It is confusing and upsetting to discover that simply calling it mine doesn't necessarily make it so.

Figuring out what I like, who my friends are, how big or tall I am; all of these are part of a continual process of self-definition. Children actively create categories and place themselves and others into them. By middle school and high school, many of these categories are solidly formed.

For adults, the results of this process is a variety of identifying categories—the way we dress, who we associate with, how we vote, the subtle or not so subtle messages we give our children. In broad strokes it colors the way census information is collected by the government.

Newspapers categorize information to help us decipher the news by placing it into sections, including the front page, the editorial section, and the living section. The assumptions made about categories can go unnoticed. The paper has made decisions about what deserves to be on the front page and decisions about how we live, and has placed all the opinions on the Op/Ed page. Reading further into each section, we notice opinions in every area, and articles that might be front page news to us are placed in the last section.

We also tend to place people into categories based on what we assume about different styles of clothing. A woman wearing comfortable white shoes and an all-white outfit goes in one category, while another wearing shorts and sneakers and carrying a backpack goes in another. A man wearing a dark suit and fancy shoes and carrying an umbrella fits a different category from one wearing a cap on his head and a worn jumpsuit with his name on the pocket.

The US Census pulls together many types of categories and lumps them into one document to help the government know who its citizens are. Unfortunately, by creating the categories, it also reflects the perspective of the people asking the questions. Based on their reference points, we are asked to place ourselves in categories according to our gender, income, political party, race, etc.

Since 1977, the official categories of race and ethnicity have been White, Black, American Indian/Eskimo, Asian/Pacific Islander, Hispanic, and Other. The Office of Management and Budget, because of pressure from many areas, has been holding hearings to add additional classifications (Hawaiian, six different kinds of Latino, Multiracial, Middle Eastern, Arab American, Creole, Germanic, and Others). But this appears to be a patch on the larger problem of assigning designations for institutional purposes. Designations that unavoidably slight groups outside the majority of people or outside the creators of the census.

The census reflects what we each are asked to do daily throughout our lives. The process of defining ourselves with others in similar groups is central to how we understand ourselves and others. The official debate is still under review, but some of us have opted for our own definitions. On a recent Oprah Winfrey show, Tiger Woods told the audience how as a child he had created a new word, *Cablinasian*, to define his identity, because he felt limited by the "black," African American category of administrative forms. Cablinasian stands for Caucasian, Black, Indian (Native American), and Asian. What is important about this is not the word itself, but the fact that he is proud of his multiracial heritage and prefers to self-identify.

The Groups We Belong To

The activities in this chapter describe a process for discovering what groups are important to the teenagers you'll be working with.

This chapter briefly discusses eight broad, group categories, including race, ethnicity, religion, gender, sexual orientation, age, physical and mental ability, and class. For more in-depth resources, please refer to Appendix IV for a list of community resources and publications to help you gain more information about particular areas.

This is not a comprehensive list of group breakdowns, and there may be others that are important to your group. The activities presented in this workbook are designed to be adapted to the issues most important to your group. If religion is one of your concerns, for example, frame the activities around how your group feels regarding religious differences and similarities.

Race

The concept of race has been a common way of categorizing people since the 18th century. A race is defined as a group of people sharing common, outwardly visible characteristics including skin color, hair type and quantity, and facial, body, and head features (Grolier Electronic Publishing Co., 1995).

Oftentimes, characteristics ascribed to different races are broad generalizations, because the original concept is based on genetic transmission of characteristics. Some members of a certain race will have all the characteristics, most will have at least one.

To many people, the concept of race is no longer useful, and is even considered harmful because it has historically been at the heart of oppression and prejudice. The superiority of one race over another has long been debated, theorized on, and fought over.

In the United States, the race issue has been synonymous with the oppression of blacks by whites. The reality is that racism takes many forms and is pervasive in our culture. Some say it is the primary cause of violence today. The colors of our skin are given extreme importance and are often used as a starting point for prejudice and racism.

Ethnicity

We have not let go of our impulse to categorize by outward appearance, but the concept of ethnicity, inclusive of some outward characteristics and still relying on generalizations, is more commonly used today as a way of distinguishing people. Ethnicity encompasses a broad definition of culture, including ancestry, religion, and national origin, as well as one's values, customs, and language. For example, many whites may feel that they are Italian, French, Irish, Scottish, Polish, etc. Many blacks identify with Jamaican, Haitian, African, or Cape Verdean cultures. Asians may feel allegiance to their Japanese, Korean, Chinese, or Filipino heritage.

Many people prefer to identify themselves via their ethnic origin as opposed to their race. This is perhaps due in large part to the difference between "old" and "new" immigrants. In the 1800s, when most immigrants to this country came from Europe, becoming an American essentially meant dropping one's ethnicity. Language was usually the first to go. Many people we have worked with over the years have shared memories of their parents or grandparents telling them they were not allowed to speak Italian, Polish, French, or Welsh at home. English became their official language. Today, we are told something different. Becoming an American does not have to happen at the expense of your language, customs, or culture. You can maintain these, be proud of them, and still be an American.

Religion

Religion is a topic that has generated an enormous amount of controversy over the centuries. Religion both unites and divides us. Virtually all religions preach love, but hatred easily becomes the reality when profound and deeply held beliefs clash. Religion can be one of the most difficult aspects of diversity to deal with and deserves far lengthier treatment than could be covered in one chapter of this workbook. (At the end of this chapter there is a list of resources on the subject of religious diversity if you and your group want to learn more about religious beliefs and their divisive effects on our society.)

As a facilitator, you will have some challenging moments as you attempt to foster these values within your group, especially when confronted with hostile or intolerant remarks.

Who and how we worship is greatly determined by our cultural and ethnic background. Honoring the traditions of all religions and defending each individual's right of personal choice are goals of religious tolerance. We must learn to embrace everyone and their beliefs in an inclusive, respectful way. But how can we teach these skills to the youth we work with when religion relies so heavily on sectarian beliefs for its transmission from one generation to the next?

We have found a great source of support and information in the literature and youth educators of the Unitarian Universalist Association. This liberal religious association of congregations is bound together to engage participants of all ages in developing, articulating, and living a comprehensive religious philosophy that addresses significant life issues as well as discovering their Unitarian Universalist faith, sources, and potential as an evolving religion in the world community of diverse faiths. Their pamphlet, *Spiral Journey, Unitarian Universalist Religious Education for the Twenty-First Century*, is a wonderful affirmation of our own beliefs and commitment "to nurturing the free mind and open heart in children, youth, and adults." The pamphlet goes on further to explain what the Unitarian Universalists teach their children and the nature of religious education:

"What do we teach our children? A short answer would be:

> to respect themselves and others
>
> to love in ever-widening circles of human community
>
> to search for their own truth in the company of other seekers
>
> to seek liberty, peace, and justice in our world
>
> to engage their whole selves—mind and body, heart, and soul—in creating a meaningful life journey."

As a facilitator, you will have some challenging moments as you attempt to foster these values within your group, especially when confronted with hostile or intolerant remarks. And they do happen. Many children have been taught to believe that Hindus worship false Gods, Christians are infidels, Unitarian Universalists have no creed, the Jews killed Christ, Africans are pagans, you name it. These are only a few examples of statements we have heard over the years.

So what do you do? Again, we turn to our Unitarian Universalist friends for support. They generously contributed a handout they use in their classes that shows the professed beliefs of different religions. The similarities are striking:

God Concepts and the Golden Rules

Judaism

God is righteous. What is hateful to you do not to others.

Christianity

God is love. All things whatsoever you would that others should do to you, do ye so to them.

Buddhism

(Buddhism has no God concept.) Hurt not others in ways that you yourself would find hurtful.

Islam

God is mighty and omnipotent. No one of you is a believer until you desire for another that which you desire for yourself.

Confucianism

God is permanence, law, order. Do not unto others which you would not have them do unto you.

Hinduism

God is essence, the only reality. Do not unto others that which would cause you pain if done unto you.

Zoroastrianism

God is good. Have good thoughts. Do good deeds. Speak good words.

Jainism

God is pure soul. Regard all creatures as you regard your own self.

Taoism

God is the first cause. Regard your neighbor's gain as your own gain; and regard your neighbor's loss as your own loss.

Sikhism

God is wisdom and love. Everybody asketh for happiness; nobody asketh for misery.

Shintoism

The Gods are the spirits of nature, and the righteous, pure and just—living or dead. Find fault with yourself rather than with others.

These *Golden Rules* are an important lesson in understanding that all religions teach us to "do unto others as you would have others do unto you." They are an excellent starting point for any discussion on religious tolerance. You may even want to incorporate the *Golden Rules* into your group's Full Value Contract as you work through questions of religion. If you are confronted by an angry statement from one of your participants, try bringing up the *Golden Rule* of their own tradition. You will be demonstrating your respect for their religion as well as reminding them that their own tradition does not condone intolerance or anger toward others. You will also be fostering an atmosphere of respectful inclusiveness that will bring your group that much closer to valuing, supporting, and embracing individual difference and the freedom of personal choice.

Gender and Sexual Orientation

Gender is an inescapable facet of our identity. From day one, we dress differently, are spoken to differently, and are expected to respond differently to the experiences of life. Many of the stereotypes we hold about gender are unconscious. We simply expect men and women to react in a certain way based on what we have been told or what we see. It's important for youth to recognize these assumptions and understand that while men and women are different, they are both worthy of being accorded equal treatment.

Issues of sexual orientation create enormous discomfort for youth and adults alike. Many of us feel that it is easier to avoid our feelings about the rights of gay, lesbian, bisexual, and transgender youth than to engage in open discussion. One of the central premises of this book is that all youth have the right to define themselves and to be treated with a respect that recognizes this right. It is important to remain aware that our adult biases perpetuate many of the stereotypes that youth assign to different sexual orientations. As you work with your groups around this issue, remember that it is not our role to sit in judgment, but that we are responsible for teaching our youth to honor and celebrate differences.

Age

Age, the eternally shifting part of our identity, is another piece around which we form biases. Our preconceptions and assumptions about a person's abilities and constraints are influenced by age. Two of the most common groupings are the young and the elderly.

We often judge the elderly based on little or no personal experience, but rather through the stereotypes created by our culture. We judge the young believing that since we have all been there, we know what being a teen is like. It is all too easy to make generalizations about individuals and their likes, dislikes, capabilities, and beliefs. The challenge is to see the person behind the category.

Physical and Mental Ability

Differences in physical and mental ability have long been the basis for bias and discrimination. We fear what we do not understand, and people with disabilities are rarely understood for who they are and what they contribute. For some people, it is "not polite to ask." Others are simply not sure how to communicate with people with disabilities and whether they should. In addition, people with disabilities have historically been kept separate either by lack of access or by intention.

We have devoted an entire chapter to this topic (see Chapter 12), which explores in greater depth how adventure activities can be an arena for exploring how people with different mental and physical abilities can work together, and how challenges can be structured to be universally accessible.

Appearance

We all make quick judgments based on the way people look. First impressions can become our reality unless we pause to look closer. If my first impression of you, by a gesture you make, the way you speak, a shirt you wear, or maybe the way you lean against a store counter, is that you are a felon (or a member of Congress, or a police officer, or a journalist), this is the image of you that will stay in my mind until I am forced to examine it consciously.

The game of categorizing and making assumptions by looks can be a dangerous one because many of our first impressions turn out to be incorrect. But there is also a gray area here. Many of the things we perceive at first glance turn out to be correct after further verification. The fact is, lazy viewers of the world can get along pretty well relying on first impressions. The challenge is to become conscious of how we filter what we see, knowing when and how our impressions form so that we can reexamine them before they become something we "know."

Class

Many experts working with diversity issues today believe that one's class— privilege or the lack of it—is the defining issue that runs through all categories of difference. It's an intriguing question. We wonder which came first: does discrimination determine your earning power and social status or do your earning power and social status determine how you are treated by society?

Chapter 13 discusses some of the prevalent theories about class and social status and how they define the way we perceive and are perceived by others. This topic ties very closely into the work you will be doing with your groups on identifying and becoming aware of the assumptions we make. Appearance, gender, race, ethnicity, physical and mental ability—all of these determine our habitual responses. The purpose here is to identify those responses, delve into where they come from, and through this, develop skills for changing them.

These Factors Combined

These groups, and the particular qualities and histories surrounding each of them, make up the historical context of bias, prejudice, discrimination, and oppression in the US. Consider how the history of racism and of sexism work to create a significant historical context for interracial dating and marriage, or how the history of religion in government has influenced our laws and views of gays, lesbians, and bisexuals.

Institutionalized oppression refers to the existence of deeply ingrained patterns and ways of thinking in our society that are discriminatory and oppressive. These patterns are often woven together across groups and social status.

Concluding Thoughts

Some of the messages young people hear about their social group orientation and membership are confusing because they haven't yet completed their own identity process. They are uncertain of where they fit in and how they want to be identified. Some of the things young people may hear are: "you don't fit in," "one choice is better than another," "deny a part of who you are in order to avoid problems." Take some time to understand and value where the members of your group are on the spectrum of identity development.

The "bubble factor" describes the stereotypes or assumptions we make about people based on what we see and/or what we think we know. It's like in the comics, where you have a bubble over your head with words in it that everyone can see. Hopefully, your awareness level is high enough that you can recognize those initial thoughts/ assumptions/ stereotypes when they happen to you. As you see or recognize your group members making some of these assumptions, take advantage of teachable moments. Call attention to the assumptions about categories and the way we change categories as we develop.

Most of us naturally judge others through the filters—experiences, education, family influences, socialization, etc.—that form the basis of our assumptions. Unless we allow experiences or ideas that contradict those assumptions to get through, our assumptions become part of our assumed reality. The end result is often one of biased or discriminatory thoughts or behavior. The activities in this workbook will help you and your group create opportunities for new experiences and ideas to "filter" through, changing many of the assumptions and patterns that lead to discriminatory behavior.

Suggested Reading:

In this chapter, we have included sources for further reading on subjects of religious diversity. Please refer to the Appendix and the chapters on specific areas of diversity for other subjects covered by this chapter.

Hoertdoerfer, Patricia, and Judith Frediani. Sp*iral Journey Unitarian Universalist Religious Education for the Twenty-First Century*. Boston: Unitarian Universalist Association, 1995. A brief guide to the UUA curriculum for children, youth, and adults with an introduction to Unitarian beliefs and the goals of Unitarian religious education.

Gooding, Margaret K. *Growing Up*. Boston: Unitarian Universalist Association, 1988. A Unitarian Universalist religious education text. Source of "God Concepts and the Golden Rules."

Reed, Christine, and Patricia Hoertdoerfer. *Neighboring Faiths*. Boston: Unitarian Universalist Association, 1997. Engages junior high school students in actively exploring their relationships to a variety of world religions.

Gray, Robin F. and José A. Ballester y Marquez. *Race to Justice: A Racial Justice and Diversity Program for Junior High*. Boston: Unitarian Universalist Association, 1995. Helps twelve- to fourteen-year-olds understand and fight racism and celebrate racial, ethnic, cultural and familial diversity.

Frediani, Judith and Jacqui James. Editors. *Weaving the Fabric of Diversity*. Boston: Unitarian Universalist Association, 1996. An anti-bias, pro-diversity program for Unitarians Universalists to examine their own experiences, values, and congregations with the goal of creating more welcoming and diverse religious communities.

Worksheet

What experiences formed your own identity? _____

_____

How did you learn about social group identities? Did you worry about fitting in or were you given the freedom to self-identify and make your own decisions around your group identity? _____

_____

How does being "in the box"—thinking based on categorical assumptions— limit your relationships with others? _____

_____

What are some of the advantages and skills you have learned from your identi- fication with a social group? _____

_____

What are some of the assumptions you make about the categories people fit in? Have they changed as you developed personally and professionally? How?

_____

_____

What happens when incorrect assumptions are made about people? Do they impact how people are treated and respected? Have you had any personal expe- rience of this? _____

_____

What if an individual is not clear about their own group identity? What is identity development? _____

_____

What if you appear to be part of a group you do not identify with? _____

_____

Kristen

Kristen, Sharon's biracial stepdaughter, recently embarked on her emancipation from her Connecticut home, family, and high school friends and left to attend college at Loyola, in Baltimore, Maryland. Her first few days were like any other freshman's—getting to know the lay of the land, buying books, adapting to life with diverse roommates, and worrying whether she had made the right decision about college. After a week, she called up crying and said she needed to talk to somebody. Once she calmed down, she told us about the incident that had disturbed her so much.

She was on the way to the cafeteria with her roommates, an African American and a biracial Bahamian, when two individuals from the black student organization walked up to the three of them. They stood in front of Kristen, ignoring her, and spoke exclusively to her roommates about attending the next meeting of their organization. Kristen was hurt, but even more so, she was angry and she didn't know what to do about it. "I can't believe they did that to me. Who do they think they are? They don't know anything about me except how I look. So they assume I'm white. I mean, regardless, you shouldn't treat anyone like that."

I asked her what she thought she ought to do about it and what would make her feel okay—not great, but okay. Kristen answered, "I have a mind to show up at that meeting and tell them just what they did." We rehearsed what she wanted to say over the phone and a week later Kristen went to the meeting. She stood up in front of everyone and shared her experience of having people judge her and make assumptions about her without ever taking the time to get to know her. She declared her identity as an African American woman who loves both her African American father and Euro-American mother. She described what it was like to grow up in a white community and the pain of watching how people's attitudes toward her changed as she went from middle school to high school. She told them how when she was depressed about not getting invited to parties and out on dates, she had decided that for emotional, political, social, and "real" survival she had to identify herself as an African American woman. Speaking up was a big step for Kristen, and it relieved much of the paralysis and silence that had been bottled up inside her by other people's misconceptions of her identity.

All Little Girls Are Princesses

Recently, a remake of the Shirley Temple movie *The Little Princess,* came out on video, and we watched it with our children. In one of the scenes, Sara, the princess, is locked up in an attic room with Becky, a West Indian child maid, because there is no more money left from her missing father to pay for her room and board. The other wealthy white girls sneak up to Sara's room one night to hear her tell wonderful stories about princesses. At one point, she has all the little girls so captivated by her story that they scream out in terror when she describes a monster.

The headmistress hears the tumult and banishes Sara and Becky to their rooms with no food for a day. Before she locks the door behind her, she can't resist making a sarcastic and disparaging remark about princesses to Sara. She tops it off with the comment, "And you're not a princess!" But Sara, who was brought up to believe that all girls, pretty or not, are princesses, stands up straight and screams back, "All girls are princesses! Didn't your father ever tell you that?" There is a visible shift in power, both physically and emotionally—the camera actually makes Sara look like she's growing taller— as the conflict between the pride of self-esteem and the pain of having none is played out. The headmistress storms off, slamming the door behind her. Out in the hallway, the camera shows us her saddened and tearful face. The hurt of years of invalidation and self-hatred came washing out with those tears.

Continuum

Boxed In →Exploring the Box →Moving Out of the Box →Knowing Who You Are

When you begin to explore how your assumptions of group identities are guided by "in the box thinking," you can begin to move "out of the box" and into looking beyond initial assumptions at others. It is a process of moving from the box to a wider understanding of your own social group orientation and membership and what it brings you. It is learning to identify the messages—both positive and negative—that make you what you are.

Awareness

People can become very angry about labels and categories and will state that they just see people as people. Yet all of us categorize people and make assumptions about the social group that they belong to—be it socioeconomic, gender, racial, sexual orientation, physical or mental ability, etc. One way we can learn to improve our relationships is through recognizing how and why we stereotype people who seem different from us.

What happens when incorrect assumptions are made about people? Does it impact how they are treated and respected?

Group Skills

The basic skill your group is beginning to acquire and that you will be reinforcing is how to validate, as opposed to invalidate, each other's experience—listening, learning from, and interacting positively with each other.

Many of these activities promote self-discovery and getting in touch physically with emotions. Ask the group what they are feeling as different issues surface. What emotions are they experiencing? Have them do a barometer check. Sometimes this means getting in touch with what is happening to them physically. Ask them to identify those feelings. Are their jaws clenched, did their stomach start doing flips, did someone get a tight feeling in their chest? Most of the time, this will help them identify what they're feeling so that they can express it clearly for other people in the group. Talk to them about how important it is to take a deep breath, relax, and begin expressing themselves from there.

Encourage your group to develop out of the box thinking and viewing skills. Lazy viewers and in the box thinkers never challenge their individual perceptions or learn how their impressions form in the first place. Give the group a chance to explore their own boxes—discuss where their assumptions come from and whether or not they are valid.

Activities

Chicka Boom

Activity Type:	Ice Breaker/De-Inhibitizer
Activity Level:	Moderate
Space:	Enough room to form a circle
Time:	About 20 minutes
Group Size:	Works for just about any size group over 10, but the bigger the better
Prerequisite:	None
Props:	None

Opening

Try introducing *Chicka Boom* with the following story that most of our groups have enjoyed:

Years ago there was an old storyteller named Chicka Boom, who would travel from village to village in his country. He was a wonderful old man who wove tales of fantasy and myth, constructing games from his imagination. His one joy in life was children. He loved children and would spend endless hours playing games with them. When it was time for the storyteller to move on, he decided to leave the village children the present of a game before he left. The game, named after the storyteller, is still played today by children everywhere.

Directions

Gather the group in a circle in a big open space. The leader stands in the center and asks everyone to join in the song and dance by following his or her actions and words. After one verse everyone should know the words and steps.

The leader begins the song and dance.

Song:	"Go up…Chicka Boom, Chicka Boom, Chicka Boom."
Dance:	Hands pointing up towards the sky, going up and down with the beat. The feet also move, so that opposite foot and hand are moving at the same time.
Song:	"Go down… Chicka Boom, Chicka Boom, Chicka Boom."
Dance:	Hands now pointing down, continuing motion with the feet.
Song:	"To the right… Chicka Boom, Chicka Boom, Chicka Boom."
Dance:	Hands pointing to the right, feet still moving up and down, taking small steps to the right.
Song:	"To the left… Chicka Boom, Chicka Boom, Chicka Boom."
Dance:	Hands pointing to the left, feet moving up and down, now taking small steps to the left.
Song:	"Now you know where it's at, it's a little of this and a little of that. So, come on in and get down."

At this point turn around and pick someone to join you in the middle. Both you and the player you picked now lead the group in another round of the song and dance. At the end of this next verse, pick two more people (one for each of you), and the four of you now lead it, then pick four more. Keep going until everyone is in the middle. Once everyone is in the middle, do one last verse. Yahooooooooo!

Diversity Skills

If you do *Chicka Boom* with some rhythm and dancing, it's an activity that will get your group moving and dancing together at any time during your sessions. Try it at the start of your day, when things are getting too serious, or even as a stylish closing to the day.

Processing

There's not a lot to process with this activity, so go ahead and enjoy it.

Group Juggling

Activity Type:	De-Inhibitizer with some Problem Solving
Activity Level:	Moderate
Space:	A nice-sized open area with no breakables around. Outside is best if the weather permits.
Time:	15 to 20 minutes
Group Size:	5 or more
Prerequisite:	None
Props:	Several fleece balls, rubber deck rings, or other small, soft objects; paper, pens, and Scotch tape

Opening

You're starting your first day of school and each of you has a million things to do. Each of the balls we will be juggling represents one of those things.

Directions

Have the group come up with a list of all the things they have to do on the first day of school—buy books, find their new homeroom, sign up for sports, find their lockers, find out whether their best friend is still in the same homeroom, etc. Write each one down on a piece of paper and tape it to one of the balls or rings.

Ask them to form a circle. It's best if you join the circle the first time around and be the starter, just to get things going.

The first part of the activity involves establishing a pattern where one object will be passed around the circle so that each group member gets it once, and it ends up back with you, the leader. Start the pattern by throwing the ball to someone else in the circle. They, in turn, toss the ball to someone else. No one can toss to someone right beside them; it must go at least two people away. An easy way for the group to remember who has gotten the object and who hasn't is to have everyone start with their hands out in front of them. As the players receive the object they put their hands down.

Everyone needs to remember who they got the object from and who they threw it to. You will be the final person to receive the object. Check in at this point to be sure that everyone in the circle has gotten the ball once. It should have started and finished with you. Once the pattern is established, they are ready to move on.

Begin by throwing the object to the same person you threw to in the first round and repeat the same pattern. As soon as that person has passed the ball on to the next player, add another object then another, and another, and another. Continuing with the same pattern, the group will be juggling several objects at once. As soon as an object has gotten all the way through the pattern and back to you, keep the game going by again throwing it to the next person in the order.

Many objects will go sailing by players and get dropped or collide in midair—just keep adding more. The group may want to decide what to do when someone drops one. Will they all stop and regroup? Give them several tries at it. Luck is a big factor here, but there are also strategies to get better that involve problem solving.

You can have the group try to set their own goal, like how many objects they think they can juggle at one time. Most groups will guess on the high side because it's generally a puzzle to figure out how many objects are actually moving at one time. Add some sort of penalty seconds for each ball dropped, or count the number of rounds without a drop.

If things get too chaotic, yell, "Stop!" (Maybe someone in the group will do so on their own.) See what happens between attempts. Does the group stop to plan or change things or just start right in again?

Diversity Skills

Group Juggling can be adapted to any subject in this book. You can write labels on the balls that reinforce specific issues. For example, if your group is working on listening and communicating skills, have them write out all the things that prevent them from listening or help them to listen well and tape them to the balls. Or, if you are working on validating feelings, have them write down their emotions and try juggling those. For the later chapters, pick a subject and have them write down their ideas about what race, gender, ability, or class issues separate us. Use your imagination, and *Group Juggling* could become one your group's favorite activities.

Processing

How you process this activity will depend on the subject your group is juggling.

- How did the group help or hinder you from juggling all the things you had to do?

- Did you find a way to get support and help from the other people in the group? How? Did you have to ask or did people cooperate naturally?

- What did the group do to successfully juggle all those jobs together with everyone else?

- What did the group do that wasn't successful?
- Did you notice yourself categorizing people during the activity?
- What categories could arise from this?

Funny Face

Activity Type: Ice Breaker

Activity Level: Moderate

Space: Your usual meeting room

Time: 10 to 15 minutes

Group Size: At least 5 or 6

Prerequisite: None

Props: None

Opening

Babies, small children, and puppies bring out the silliness and playfulness in all of us. We're not afraid to make funny faces just to make them laugh. With our peers, it seems like we're always holding back and trying to "look good." So coaxing someone to smile is serious business!

Directions

Split your large group into smaller circles, say 5–7 people per silly set. The rules state that after the GO signal everyone in the circle tries to make the other members smile. If you slip and show the slightest smile you are eliminated and can then step back to watch the experts do their thing. A participant isn't allowed to touch another player, and all eyes must stay open, otherwise, anything goes.

Diversity Skills

This activity is a great Ice Breaker for almost any group. Try it whenever you feel like your group could use a good dose of acting silly.

Processing

Let the group enjoy themselves, but if they want to, try some discussion about how it felt to let go of appearances and act silly around their peers.

Three-Person Trust Lean

Activity Type:	Trust Building
Activity Level:	Moderate
Space:	A grassy field is best, but any open space will do.
Time:	About 30 minutes
Group Size:	6 or more
Prerequisite:	Good spotting skills and the *Two-Person Trust Lean* described in Chapter 6
Props:	None

Opening

In the real world, you're not always dealing with people on a one-to-one basis. Think about how you are trusting two different people at once. Does it feel the same way? Who's taking care of what part of you?

Directions

Same as the *Two-Person Trust Lean*, but by adding a second spotter in front of the falling person you can create a backward and forward falling motion. Have fallers go through the same set of commands and then let themselves be gently rocked back and forth between the two catchers. Add a couple of spotters on the outside.

Diversity Skills

This is a basic trust-building activity. As far as we're concerned, there's always room for trust to grow. Come back to this activity whenever you feel that trust has become an issue with your group or needs to be viewed from a different angle.

Processing

When you review spotting and trust sequences with your group, think about what you noticed in the group as they moved through learning how to trust each other physically. Many of the fears and discomfort we all feel regarding issues of diversity are expressed in our body language. Were people holding back? Did anyone seem particularly uncomfortable? Think of ways to discuss this with the group and relate to their experiences outside the group.

- How did this feel different from the Two-Person Trust Lean? How would you compare the two activities?

- What challenged you most this time?

TrustWave ■

Activity Type:	Trust Building
Activity Level:	Moderate to high
Space:	A large indoor space or outdoor field
Time:	About half an hour
Group Size:	10 or more
Prerequisite:	This activity seems incredibly simple, but the challenge level is deceptively high. It requires a high degree of alertness from all the participants. If you have doubts about your group's ability to perform their roles diligently, either don't try the activity or allow walking only for the first round or until everyone seems comfortable with the task.
Props:	None

Opening

Sometimes it looks like all the doors are closed to us and everything is going against us. But once you gather some momentum, you'd be surprised by what can happen and how those barriers just disappear.

Directions

Divide your group equally in two and form two straight lines with each participant standing opposite someone from the other line. The lines should be just far enough apart so that when the participant's arms are fully extended, at shoulder height and in front of them, their hands reach to approximately the wrist of the person opposite. These two lines are the spotters.

The goal is for one player, the runner, to start about ten yards from the group and walk, or slowly jog, between the two lines of people. The players in the lines have their arms raised at shoulder height straight out in front of them, effectively forming a barrier to the approaching runner. Just before the runner reaches them, the spotters raise their arms up over their heads to allow the runner to pass and lower them as soon as the runner has gone by.

Ask runners to attempt to maintain the same speed throughout their runs. Slowing down is not a problem, but speeding up obviously can be.

Allow all participants an opportunity to be a runner, but remember Challenge by Choice. Some members in your group will be willing to go early on, while others will want to watch how the group is attending to the runner's safety.

Safety Factors

Needless to say, the spotting lines must be extremely careful or the runner will get hit in the face or head. Spotters need to carefully watch the runners and judge their speed. Spotters should lift their arms with sufficient time to ensure that the runner is not hit. It is critical that you closely monitor the group and be sure they are fully attentive to each runner's safety. If they are not, or begin to goof around and lose focus, end the activity immediately.

Allowing a ten-yard space before the runner enters the line helps people gauge the speed and judge when to lift their arms.

Don't allow players to start only 2 or 3 feet away.

It is appropriate to set a series of commands to indicate a runner is starting, much as with a *Trust Fall*. The runner should ask the spotting line, "Ready?" and wait for a reply before starting.

If there are more than 10 people in the spotting lines, be sure that the spotters are all focused on the front of the line and the runner before starting. When runners have been hit, it has often been because people in the middle or the end of the line did not see the runner coming or did not react quickly enough.

Diversity Skills

Again, this is a basic trust-building activity that you can come back to whenever your group needs to work on trusting one another.

Processing

- What, if anything, held you back or pushed you forward?

- Were you confident that the group would make way for you?

- Did you feel comfortable running or was it threatening?

- Was it hard to pull up your arms in time for the runner to get through?

- How did it feel to make it the whole way down the line?

- In this activity, you are taking a risk by entering another group of people. Have you ever done anything like this in school—that is, entered another group? How would you describe that experience?

Bridge It ■

Activity Type: Group Initiative

Activity Level: Low

Space: Two separate rooms

Time: 1 hour or more

Group Size: 10 or more

Prerequisite: None

Props: One set of the following for each group:

> 4—Styrofoam cups
>
> 8—8" small-diameter sticks (ask the participants to gather them first)
>
> 1—roll of masking tape
>
> 1—small box of Legos or Tinker Toys
>
> 1—paper and pencil
>
> 1—set of terminology

And the following for both groups:

> 2—tables
>
> 1—sheet or blanket
>
> 1—chair for each person

Opening

We all know that words have different meanings depending on what country or even what part of a country you come from.

Two countries are separated by a body of water but want to establish a trade and cultural relationship. The river is plagued by bad weather and almost constant fog. The two countries have a common language but the dialects differ considerably.

Directions

A good way to start this activity is by dividing your group in half in an inventive way. Rip two full-page pictures out of a magazine and cut them into jigsaw-like pieces so that the total number of pieces equals the total number of people. Throw all the pieces at random into a container and ask each person in the group to pull out one piece. After everybody's taken a piece, ask them to pool their pieces and make the pictures. The group splits down the middle according to who belongs to which picture.

Place the tables next to one another. Hang the sheet or blanket vertically over the point where the two tables meet. (You can also prop up a piece of cardboard or poster board. Just as long as the participants can't see around whatever you use.) Put an equal number of chairs on each side of the divider. One group is side A, the other is side B.

Place all the props for each group on the separate tables.

The terminology change papers should read something like this:

> **Side A—** the word top means bottom; side means under; and a laugh means high.

> **Side B—** The word tape means wide; sticking out your tongue means how many; and crisscross means parallel.

Explain to both groups that the purpose of this exercise is for each separate group to build a bridge toward the other group, to meet at the divider, so the bridges connect and look as much alike as possible. Do not offer any guidelines except to say that only the props on the table can be used. In order to establish a necessary dialogue between groups, three five-minute meetings have been arranged (be very strict on the timing) at a common site (use another room). As the members adjourn to the meeting room, remind them that they must not look on the other side of the sheet; offer blindfolds if necessary.

Only one member from each group may talk at each meeting, and these two individuals sit facing one another, separate from the other people in the room. No comments from the group are allowed during this time.

The timing of the planning and building sessions should look like this:

- Each group is shown their building area and props and given 7 minutes to talk over ideas for building their portion of the bridge (among themselves, *not* with the other group) and to begin construction if they choose to.

- First five-minute meeting of the chosen group representatives in a separate room. A new representative should be chosen each time.

- Seven-minute separate group discussion and building time back at the construction site

- Second five-minute representative meeting

- Five-minute discussion and building time

- Third five-minute representative meeting

- 10-minute race to get the work completed

Now comes the unveiling and a period of time set aside for debriefing the process, levels of accomplishment, and comparison of approaches.

Diversity Skills

Bridge It is a great activity for provoking reflection about the dynamics of communicating across our differences. Try it whenever you want the group to think about how we are all constantly building bridges to narrow the gap between individuals.

Processing

■ What were some of the biggest misunderstandings between the two groups? How did they happen? Was it only because of the different dialects?

■ Did you ever feel as though you understood each other? What did it feel like?

■ What kinds of connections did you make with each other? Were they only verbal?

■ How did your assumptions about the meanings of words influence your ability to communicate with the other group?

■ What do you think could be done to improve communication between two groups who have different languages and values?

■ Do you find yourself making assumptions like ones you made here about other groups in school? What are some of the assumptions? Why do you make them? How can we avoid making incorrect assumptions?

Blind Polygon

Activity Type:	Problem Solving
Activity Level:	Moderate
Space:	A big room or outdoor space
Time:	20 minutes
Group Size:	5 or more
Prerequisite:	This is a blindfolded activity, so be sure that all the members of your group feel comfortable with wearing one.
Props:	A rope that is long enough for each member of the group to hold on to with plenty of elbow room between participants.

Opening

There's an old saying that God gave us "two eyes and a mouth for a reason." Think about what it means not to have your eyes anymore and how it changes the way you perceive things.

Directions

Blindfold all of the members of the group. If there are no blindfolds around or if people don't want to use a blindfold, ask them to close their eyes.

Place the rope on the ground near the group members' feet and instruct them to find it.

Explain to the group that the object of the activity will be first to find the rope and then to form it into different shapes. All group members must be holding the rope and therefore are part of the solution. They can talk to each other.

Tell the group that the first shape they have to make is a square.

Ask the group to let you know when they feel that a square has been formed. If they go on for a while, ask them if they think they have a square yet. When greeted with a "no," let them continue, even if they are in a square! If the group thinks that they have made a square, have them take off their blindfolds or open their eyes. After looking at their "square," give them time (one minute) to discuss a plan for how they will work out the next shape you give them. Other shapes you can use are triangle, circle, or rectangle.

If you can't find a rope lying around, you can also do this activity by asking the group to hold hands and form the shapes.

One solution that some groups use is to move people around. This is perfectly acceptable but don't mention it to them. If they ask if it's legal you can tell them yes, but let them get creative rather than giving them helpful hints.

Diversity Skills

Try *Blind Polygon* whenever you want your group to think more about the ways we communicate with each other—listening and communicating, validating feelings, building allies, individual identity.

Processing

- A lot of communication issues usually come up with this activity. Depending on what happened in your particular group, a few typical questions might be:

- When was communication a problem? Why (were too many people speaking all at once)?

- Were any people or ideas not listened to? Why? How might that have hurt the group in trying to solve the problem?

- When did it get better? What changed to make it better?

- How important do you think eye contact is to the way we communicate with one another?

- Who were some of the leaders during the activity? What did they do that might be considered leadership?

- Did what happened during this activity look anything like what happens in other groups (class, student council, sports team, counseling group, etc.)?

Stereotype Skits

Activity Type:	Social Responsibility
Activity Level:	Low
Space:	It's best if you have a few separate rooms for this activity so the different teams can work out their skits separately.
Time:	About 45 minutes
Group Size:	Large enough to have 2 or 3 teams of 4 or 5 people each
Prerequisite:	None
Props:	The available furniture and anything lying around the room if they want to use it.

Opening

We are all identified by others as belonging to various groups or cliques. Let's see if we can cut out some daily occurrences that remind us of how we get categorized.

Directions

Divide the group into teams of four or five people and ask them to think up a skit about something typical they've encountered in school that shows how much we make assumptions about what clique other students belong to. It might be a class with a teacher who only calls on the boys, gym class when the captains get to pick who they want on their team, or finding a table to sit at in the cafeteria. (You might want to help the group out by giving them a few suggestions: a typical day in math class, working in the science lab, a girl trying to sign up for the football team, taking out a book from the library.) The purpose of this activity is to show how we all make assumptions about what groups people belong to—nerds, Valley girls, jocks, class clowns, brains, etc.

Diversity Skills

The skits we've generated from this activity usually provoke gales of laughter, but it's also a great way to show exactly how we stereotype people and fit them into different groups because of the way they act or look.

Processing

- What were you thinking about the actors in the skits? Did you fit them into roles like jock, nerd, class clown, teacher's pet?

- How were you treated during the activity? What did it feel like to be treated that way?

- Have you looked at people that you didn't know well and treated them according to stereotypes—or thought about them in that way?

- Can you think of one thing you want to change now that you've participated in this activity?

The Lunch Room

Activity Type:	Social Responsibility
Activity Level:	Low
Space:	A good-size room
Time:	40 minutes
Group Size:	5 or more
Prerequisite:	None
Props:	None

Opening

I'm going to ask you to get comfortable, relax, and close your eyes. Think about how lunch time is often the time of day when you connect with your friends and know that you're with people who think and feel the same way you do. Doesn't it feel good to know that they understand you without having to explain yourself?

Directions

Ask the group to sit in a circle and get comfortable. Have them close their eyes, focus on their breathing, and feel their muscles start to relax. If you see that some of them still feel uncomfortable, repeat the directions out loud in a soft, low voice once their eyes are closed. In the same tone of voice, read the following guided fantasy to them:

Go back to your childhood and think about when you were in kindergarten. Think of the person you shared your innermost thoughts and secrets with. What was it about that person that made you feel special and let you know that you could trust him or her? What did that person look like, say, and do? Where did you like to play with your friend? What made you feel safe and happy in that place?

Now think about when you were nine years old and in the third or fourth grade. Who was your best friend then, and what games did you play together on the playground? Did you spend time together outside school? What was it about that person that made you feel you could trust them? What did that person look like, say, and do?

Now you're getting ready to go to middle school for the first time. You're a little nervous and don't quite know what to expect. On the first day of school, it feels like everyone is different from you and you don't quite fit in. It's a large school and you don't know many kids in your classes. Lunch time comes and you breath a sigh of relief. You've been on your best behavior all morning and need a break. You need some time just to be yourself. You're waiting in line and suddenly you see your best friend sitting down at a table. Thank goodness, now you have someone to sit with and talk to about how hard it is to be around all these new faces and people who look different. What does your best friend look like and how do you feel when you are with them? What does your body feel like physically? How do you know you can relax?

Oh no! The lunch line has taken longer than you thought and your friend is gone. Everyone is staring at you and wondering why you don't have any friends and you're not sitting down. You feel so different, isolated, and alienated. No one calls you over. All of a sudden, someone you know slightly through your best friend waves. You breathe a sigh of relief. They look like your best friend and they are smiling. Somehow you connect when your eyes meet and you feel like you are not alone. You sit down and feel welcomed.

Diversity Skills

This activity will help your group understand why we feel the most comfortable with the people who support us and nurture our identity, particularly at lunch time. During our diversity trainings, people often ask us why all the black kids or why all the Latino kids sit together at lunch time. This question is always posed as a "color" problem. We reply with a question, "Why do all the athletes or computer club or cheerleaders or chess club members always sit together?" Lunch time is a time to relax and be ourselves without unnecessary explanations or justifications. Hopefully, it's a time to be understood by our peers and the group we feel the most comfortable with.

Processing

■ What stood out for you as you did this activity?

■ What feelings did you have?

■ Where were those feelings in your body?

■ What did you learn about yourself?

Pieces of the Pie

Activity Type:	Social Responsibility
Activity Level:	Low
Space:	Your usual meeting room
Time:	30 to 45 minutes
Group Size:	5 or more
Prerequisite:	None
Props:	Pie-shaped pieces of paper in different colors for different categories

Opening

Remember what it was like when you were little and used to argue with your brother, sister, or friend about who had the biggest piece of pie? How did you know which piece was the biggest, and therefore better, in your mind?

Directions

Create pie-shaped pieces of paper that represent different aspects of a person's self-identity and how much power that person has. You will need enough pieces for each participant to be able to take several. It's best to have enough pieces in each category for each participant to take one. Whoever has a majority or power position gets a blue piece of pie. For minority use another color like white.

Put the pieces of pie on the table and ask each participant to select the pieces that describe them. After they have completed their selection, have them place their pieces together to form a pie. Tell the students what the blue and white mean. "Traditionally in our society we have had groups who are in power and groups who are not in power. This is an opportunity to visually examine how much power you have." Have them share their pies in groups of 4 and discuss what they mean to them. What do they notice?

	BLUE	WHITE
Gender	Male	Female
Race	White	Person of color
Age	Older than 15	Younger than 15
Sexual Orientation	Heterosexual (Remember, some individuals might not feel comfortable revealing this information.)	Homosexual
Physical Abilities	Physically able	Physically challenged
Socioeconomic Level	Middle class or higher	Blue collar or working poor
Honor Roll	On Honor Roll	Not on Honor Roll
Sports	Good athlete	Not such a good athlete
Computer Skills	Great	Poor
Appearance	Considered nice-looking	Not considered nice-looking
Language	English primary language	English is secondary language
Group identity	Part of the "in" group	Not part of the "in" group
Religion	Christian	Non-Christian

Challenge Level

You might want to try reversing the balance of power once the group has done the activity once. White means you hold the power instead of blue. Try engaging them in a discussion about different cultures and how they perceive power differently from ours. In some countries, being fat is desirable because it means you are wealthy. Not all cultures are Christian dominated. How would it feel to be a minority Christian in an Islamic or Buddhist culture or an English speaker in China? Power is relative to the dominant culture. This is a good way for your group to discern how the culture we live in sends us messages all the time about what is "good" or "bad."

Diversity Skills

Pieces of the Pie can be tailored to fit almost subject. Have your group brainstorm different situations they come across when it's obvious who has the power and who doesn't and then make the activity specific to the discussion. It's also a good way to help teenagers determine the amount of power—perceived and real—they have in the world according to how the world identifies them.

Processing

■ How did you feel when you put your pie together and saw how much power you do or don't have?

■ What did you learn from your discussion with each other?

■ What options do groups that don't traditionally have power in our society have for getting ahead or living peacefully in our society?

Closing Activities

Start and Stop

Ask each member in turn to answer the following questions:

What are you going to start doing with this group next time to contribute to the whole?

Can you think of something that distracts from the group's harmony that you are going to stop doing next time?

Are We Done Yet!

Ask the group to form a tight circle, shoulders touching shoulders. As they move around in a clockwise direction, ask them to chant "*Chicka Boom, Chicka Boom, Chicka Boom,* are we done yet?" Stop and ask a participant to share whatever they want. Then start moving again and repeat the refrain. Stop, move again, stop, move until everyone who wants to share something has had a turn.

Personal Journal Question

What has been the most important thing you have learned about yourself and your identity within this group and the social group you identify with most?

Processing Questions

- ❏ How do you imagine others felt toward you at various times during the activity? Were these feelings expressed?

- ❏ Is it difficult for you to avoid judging others? Explain.

- ❏ Can you think of examples of when you judged others in the group today? When you didn't judge others?

- ❏ What were some advantages you gained by not judging others?

- ❏ What were some advantages others gained by your not judging them?

- ❏ How do judging and not judging others affect the completion of the activity?

- ❏ Were some behaviors of others easy not to judge and other behaviors difficult?

- ❏ How were group decisions made in completing the activity?

- ❏ Were you satisfied with the ways decisions were made? Explain.

- ❏ Did the group arrive at any decisions through group consensus? (Some didn't get their first choice, but they could live with the decision.)

- ❏ Were some decisions made by one or several individuals?

- ❏ Did everyone in the group express an opinion when a choice was available?
  If not, why not?

- ❏ What is the best way for this group to make decisions? Explain.

- ❏ Do you respond in similar ways in other groups?

- ❏ What did you like about how the group made decisions? What didn't you like?

- ❏ Can you give examples of when you trusted someone in the group?

- ❏ Is it easier to trust some people than others? Explain.

- ❏ How are you different from some of the others in the group?

❏ How do these differences strengthen the group as a whole?

❏ What would this group be like if there were very few differences in people? How would you feel if this were so?

❏ How are you like some of the others in the group?

❏ Were these commonalities a help to the group in completing their task? Explain.

❏ Were these commonalities a hindrance to the group in completing their task? Explain.

❏ Do you think you have other things in common with some of the group members that you haven't found yet?

❏ How did this setting help you discover how you are similar to others?

❏ What have you learned about trust, respect, acceptance, and cooperation as they relate to differences?

❏ Did you find yourself responding to any stereotypes? What were they? How do you think you might respond to the same situation in the future?

❏ What has changed for you as a result of participating in this activity? How do you think you'll perceive people who are different from you—blacks, whites, gays or whomever is appropriate—as a result?

❏ How does this activity relate to the real-life experiences you are faced with at home, in school, in your neighborhood?

❏ What was the most difficult part of this activity as it relates to how you deal with people who are different from you?

❏ What was the easiest part of this activity as it relates to how you deal with people who are different from you?

❏ Did this activity challenge any of your beliefs?

❏ What are your feelings now?

❏ As a result of this activity, what are some of the things you think or feel that we all have in common?

Discovering Our Identities

During adolescence, all of us search for ways to define ourselves, to create a unique identity that sets us apart from the rest of the crowd and from our parents. At the same time, we fervently hope for acknowledgment and acceptance from our peers. All of us grow up with certain assumptions about the *right* way to behave. Some of these assumptions are valid and form the bedrock of our moral and ethical character. Others are more difficult to interpret. Thin is better, blond is better, athletic is better, grunge is better, my God is better, rich is better. The list is infinite.

In our opinion, it is essential that we give our youth the ability to filter these messages consciously and with awareness. The process of becoming aware and conscious includes learning to value our own strengths and abilities. We have said it before, and we will say it again before the end of this book: self-esteem is one of the most precious gifts we can give to our youth. Through self-esteem we gain a true sense of who we are in the face of confusing and conflicting signals about what is right or wrong, better or worse, true or false. The knowledge we acquire through self-esteem helps us perceive others more clearly and value them not for what we have been told they are, but for who they truly are.

This section addresses some of the messages we receive about our identities and the identities of others. The activities in this section are geared to teaching a set of skills for learning about individual identities. Learning is discovery, and we believe that discovering what we like about ourselves and others is a fun and exciting process. Enjoy your travels; many treasures are waiting to be discovered.

9

Individual
Identity

Have you ever stood in front of a mirror and looked intently at yourself? Sometimes the experience feels surreal, and you wonder, "Is that really me? It doesn't look like me. Who is me, anyway?"

The experience of being me, of being unique and different from everyone else, influences how we perceive others. And the reverse is also true—what others see and how they categorize me influence their initial perceptions and response to me. What are the things that make each person a unique me? What are the things that we have control over and what are the things that we are stuck with? This chapter briefly looks at how we can become more aware of how we form our perceptions and learn to look at ourselves and others as unique persons, honoring all the quirks and joys of our individual identities.

Exploring the Box—
Who Am I, Anyway?

In their book, *Workforce America! Managing Employee Diversity as a Vital Resource*, Marilyn Loden and Judy B. Rosener describe primary and secondary dimensions that identify individual differences. Primary dimensions are those that are the very essence of our individuality: gender, race, ethnicity, physical and mental ability, age, and sexual orientation. Primary dimensions are also defined as those we cannot change without resorting to surgical intervention.

Secondary dimensions are those things we can change: socioeconomic status, religious beliefs, where we live, marital status, parental status, sports interests, hobbies, values, and many others. Defining these differences as secondary dimensions is not intended to diminish their importance. What is important is to differentiate them from the primary dimensions we cannot change and that initially influence the way we are treated, and the way we treat others. Age, for example, has an instantaneous influence because it is something we observe immediately. A child is unlikely to treat an adult the same way he treats his contemporaries until that adult, through his behavior or explicit permission, indicates that he's happy to play the same way as a child.

We have a wide range of options regarding our secondary dimensions. These characteristics can be more subtle, and we can have a great deal of control over them. But secondary dimensions are often the cause of concerns and issues of diversity. Secondary dimensions often present a source of discomfort, influencing attitudes toward people who seem to be different because of what they wear, what they believe, and how they behave.

Development of Self

One of the most influential ways we acquire our sense of self is through our parents. What they say or imply, and the way they act about primary and secondary characteristics have a huge impact on our own attitudes. Peers, media, and authority figures like teachers add to the messages youth get as they develop their identities and position themselves in the world.

Middle school in particular is a difficult time for children developmentally. It is a time of great insecurity, often expressed in cruel behavior towards others. This behavior sometimes continues through high school but is usually better disguised as the rules become clearer about how we should behave towards people who are different from ourselves—who are richer or poorer, who play soccer instead of football, who don't go to church or temple, whose parents aren't married or who don't have steady jobs. By the time teenagers get to high school, many of their attitudes are formed. The challenge is to give youth opportunities to explore what they now believe and methods to consciously develop what they would like to believe.

Another way we acquire that sense of self is through our own internal processes, how we synthesize and evaluate the input we receive from peers, adults, the media, and society in general. Some values and judgments we internalize and make our own, others we disregard, and still others we may overtly deny but cannot quite totally disregard. An example of the latter happens with generalizations like "all blondes are airheads." What if a young girl is blonde like her mother and everyone says how much she looks and acts like her mother? While she may not admit that she believes the statement about blondes, every time she does something wrong or feels stupid, the mantra about "airheads" comes back to haunt her. This kind of internalized judgment, if it goes unrecognized, may hold her back in school or influence her career choices as she goes through young adulthood.

Weight, usually considered a secondary characteristic, is a challenging issue throughout our lives. American society gives us clear signals that if we are overweight, we are second-class citizens. Fat children have fewer friends, they are called on less in class, they are the last to be chosen for team sports, people stare when they are eating or out buying clothes. Overweight individuals may find it harder to find jobs. It can be a very painful existence.

A while back, we attended a weekend self-improvement seminar and met a woman, Katlin, who works as a school administrator. We noticed that she walked with a pronounced limp. We couldn't see a brace because she wore long skirts, so we assumed that she must have cerebral palsy or had polio as a child. Throughout the weekend she was outgoing, warm, and even funny. At the last session, she stood up and asked if she could speak with the group.

> "I want to share something with you guys that I have never talked about in public," she said. "All during middle school and high school I was Miss Popular. I had lots of friends, participated in tons of activities and was captain of the cheerleading squad. One day during practice, I felt a severe pain in my leg. The pain persisted and my parents took me to several doctors over a period of time. One of them I'll never forget. He said, 'Look, you sprained it or tore a ligament. That's all. So stop whining about it!' Well, I tried to grin and bear it, you know, trying to accept that I must be imagining this awful pain and thinking that I should be able to deal with it.

> "Several months later, I couldn't take it anymore. My parents took me to a specialist, and very shortly after I was diagnosed with cancer. We were told they were going to have to amputate my right leg immediately. From that moment on, I have never felt like a whole human being again until now. I had internalized so much of the negativity and stereotypes associated with being a woman and disabled. All this even though I have a wonderful husband, great kids, and a job I love. I hadn't figured out how to be whole until now. Now, I realize that it's simple. It means letting go of the past, accepting that it happened with no judgments, and knowing that I create all of the possibilities in my life from this day forward!"

Much of what happened to Katlin over the years had to do with some of these internalized messages:

Athletic people should endure pain.

Healthy means having all parts of your body.

Happy means having all parts of your body.

Doctors are always right.

Any of our primary or secondary characteristics can affect our sense of self. This example shows that how we react and the messages we send regarding the characteristics that make up someone's identity can have a powerful impact.

How do all these factors work from a developmental point of view? As infants we really have no clue. We are hanging out, trying to get our needs met. We know we are hungry, tired, or wet, and we cry, looking for a response from our parents. Studies have proven that infants do have a sense of who they are in relation to their parents. Shortly after birth, infants respond to the voices of both parents, suggesting that the relationships between parents and their children start in utero. In the book *The Secret Life of the Unborn Child*, the authors tell the following story. A man was with his mother when he began humming a particular tune. His mom looked up, somewhat startled, and asked him how he knew that tune. He replied that he didn't know, saying, "It's just a tune I've always had in my head." It turns out that when his mother was pregnant with him, she spent hours playing the violin, and the tune he was humming was one of her favorites, something she had played over and over.

Stages of Development

As children begin to mature, it's important for the adults who nurture them to be aware of their stages of development and help them learn to accept and relish the richness of human diversity. We have broadly mapped out some of these stages from the perspective of individual identity formation as follows: (Note: these stages represent broad age groupings and are intended as reference points only.)

2 to 4 years old

At this stage, children are concerned primarily with testing their independence and finding out where they begin and end in relation to their parents. Peers begin to enter the picture on a more frequent basis and social skills begin to improve.

Children, exposed more often to their peers, begin to notice that the world is full of people of all different sizes, shapes, colors, and sexes. Parents, teachers, and day-care workers or nannies should work together to reinforce and develop the child's self-esteem and sense of self-worth. Providing children with toys, materials, and books that reflect the full spectrum of human diversity—race, age, gender, size, physical and mental abilities—will send the message that all people are human and worthy of love and friendship.

4 to 10 years old

Children continue to test the boundaries of their independence, pushing them as far as they will go. They begin to acquire a further sense of sexuality—"I'm a boy, you're a girl." Peers and their values become more important and the world gets larger and less frightening.

At this age, children may already have a clear understanding of who they are and how their background affects them and their position in the world. Children test language through name calling, and test friendship through complex social games. Some children can become acutely aware of the cruel world.

It's essential to teach our children that they can respond constructively to criticism of all types. As parents and friends, our goal should be to enhance their feelings of self-worth, self-esteem, and self-confidence and to help them acquire decision-making and conflict-resolution skills. This workbook seeks to provide us with the skills to acknowledge and validate the pain, brainstorm options for coping, support our children in their decisions, share our own feelings of pain, anger, or disgust, and intervene in positive ways, ways that help make all of us accountable for our children's growth and actions.

10 to 19 years old

Children begin to flex their muscles at this stage; they are getting, setting, and solidifying their identity. "I am me! Adults just don't understand my feelings, concerns, and issues." Finding their own sense of self is paramount, and emotions are intensified for youth during this period.

> *Support and validation are the most effective tools we have for teaching our children to take pride in who they are.*

This is a difficult age, and sometimes it's a real challenge to work with youth on questions of identity. Difficult, but necessary. During this stage of development, popularity, fitting in, and dating seem to take precedence over life itself. Parents must learn to accept that when kids adopt a form of dress or a way of talking, walking, or whatever, this is their way of saying, "Look, I fit in with everyone else." It's a form of pride, a statement of identification with their peers. Rather than turn away in disgust when we see our children acting out their new identities, we should acknowledge and validate their process of growth. Support and validation are the most effective tools we have for teaching our children to take pride in who they are.

Concluding Thoughts

Secondary dimensions of individual identity, the ones we can change, are normally the focal point of a young adult's concerns about "fitting in." One of the greatest challenges for adults who work with young people is to help them acquire the confidence to accept that who they are—individuals with both qualities and shortcomings—is enough. Rich or poor, blonde or brunette, heterosexual or homosexual, Christian or Shamanistic, we all have something to contribute to and gain from our communities.

As you work with your group, try to become aware of the messages you might be sending about how someone's appearance or actions affect you. Examine your own beliefs and reflect on some of your own biases. Do you believe that "all blondes are airheads"? While your own beliefs may not be this obvious or seem so silly, we all have fixed ideas about other people and how they should look or act. Are any of your beliefs influencing the members of your group? Are you subtly sending messages that one person's opinion is better than another's?

Teenagers are constantly trying on new ways of behaving, dressing, and feeling. They are consciously trying to fit in with their peers while looking for their own sense of self-identity in a world that sends out many confusing messages. Show them as best you can that you accept them for what they are as they are.

Suggested Reading

Loden, Marilyn and Judy B. Rosener. *Workforce America! Managing Employee Diversity as a Vital Resource*. New York: Irwin Professional Publishing, 1991. Excellent analysis and explanation of what diversity is and means to all of us and how to manage for positive results.

Verny, Thomas MD. and John Kelly, *Secret life of the Unborn Child*. Delta Books, 1981. This book deals with the cognition and awareness one has while in utero.

Edelman, Marian Wright. *The Measure of Our Success. A Letter to my Children & Yours*. New York: Harper Collins Publishers, 1992. A wonderful evaluation of our country's view and treatment of all our children. The book, written in letter format to Edelman's sons, is about the 25 lessons of life.

Worksheet

What messages did you receive about your identity when you were growing up?

_____

_____

What, if any, different messages did you get from your family and peers?

_____

_____

How do other people describe you? _____

_____

Do their descriptions differ from the way you describe yourself? How?

_____

_____

What do you think are some of the most important aspects of who you are?

_____

_____

Do you think others can see them, or do they have to get to know you before they discover them? _____

_____

How important is your identity to your self-definition? Why? _____

_____

Are you named after someone? If so, what does your name say about who you are and how others expect you to be? _____

_____

Do you have a nickname? If so, what does it say about you? _____

_____

Have you or anyone in your family ever had their name changed? Was it because of immigration or for religious reasons? How has the name change affected you or your family? _____

_____

My New York, Your New York

In history class, talking about how cities grow, everyone got onto the subject of the biggest city in the US—New York. "I've been there," Elaine said. "It's a beautiful place. The best part about it are the places to eat all kinds of food." She had everyone's attention now. "And the museums. I love the museums."

"What did you see there?" asked Tim.

"Well, I remember that everything was gigantic, and wide sidewalks with stores all along and lots of people, all looking different. New York is a great place! I'd live there in a second."

"I was there last summer too," put in Brenda. "But it's not like you say. Are you sure it was New York?"

"Yes. It's like that."

"I don't remember such a nice place. I didn't see any museums."

"It is like I say."

"My family must live in a different part of New York. It's dirty there and scary. My grandma sent me to the store and there were bars over everything. It didn't even look open. Lots of buildings all alike, lots of people, like you say, but it wasn't exactly a picnic. I think my parents moved away because it was so violent. One of my aunts was killed there, and my cousin went to jail. My mom said it was because of the city. I wouldn't trade living here for there."

"I don't think New York is like that at all. New York is a great place."

What's It Like to Be Overweight?

Alex is a 14-year-old female who lives with her parents and younger brother Nathan. She was born premature, coming in at under two pounds. Because she survived, she became her parent's "miracle baby." Her Dad, Kevin, is of average height and weight. Nathan is described as pudgy. Terri, her mom, is overweight. Her clothing size varies from a size 18 to a size 24.

Terri knows that she is overweight but tends to minimize and at times glorify the fact. "What can I say? I love to eat. And anyway, Kevin loves all of me!" One day Alex came home and said some boys had been teasing her, calling her "rotundo butt" and other equally nasty names. Her mom's reaction was to interpret their nastiness in the following way: "Honey, they just like you. They see that body of yours and they like it. They're just trying to tell you that."

A year or so ago, Alex came to the attention of school officials. She had threatened suicide when one of her teachers confronted her with an incomplete assignment. Her reaction was not only extreme, it was a serious call for help. Her parents were called in, and while they seemed concerned about the problem, they never followed through with the suggested counseling.

Alex and her mom remain overweight, despite the numerous attempts of their close friends to get them involved in a nutrition and exercise program. She has internalized a view that her body is desirable and sexy, but still wonders why she doesn't have a boyfriend yet.

Continuum

Trying to fit in ➜ Noticing the Differences ➜ Figuring Out How to Negotiate the Differences ➜ Celebrating and Valuing Human Difference

Individuality—let's honor and celebrate our uniqueness and learn to recognize how people that are different from us are constantly enriching our lives. Each of us is unique. Our personalities, physical characteristics, challenges, minds, and backgrounds all contribute to who we are. If we pretend that we all have similar problems and strengths, we will neglect important elements of other people's essence.

Awareness

We all have something to contribute to the lives of others and we all have something to learn from others. Intellectually, most of us understand this, but when confronted with people who don't look like or, more subtly, don't act or think like us, anger, confusion, alienation, isolation, and violence are all possible outcomes, especially for a young adult dealing with his or her own problems of asserting independence and identity. The challenge for youths is to learn to welcome, listen to, and accept each other, secure enough in their own personal growth and the conviction that sameness is not necessarily best.

Group Skills

Accepting—All of us are different, that's what makes us alike. Children often think that they are the only ones who have difficulties, problems, or a particular disadvantage. The objective of the activities in this chapter is to create common ground for the group to learn things about each other, to find out that each one of us feels isolated or alone at times, and that this is part of the human experience.

Trust—Adventure activities are the best forum we have found so far to help bring individuals together in an open, trusting atmosphere. Trusting others is the first step for dealing with old wounds and learning to let go.

Communication—Your group will begin to learn how to open up to each other and communicate constructively. Feelings are universal. Everyone has them, and everyone can identify with them. Ask your group to first verbalize what they are feeling instead of jumping straight into discussing what happened or "what someone else in the group did to them." Learning to express how they felt when something happened may open a chord of recognition in the other group members. How many times have we thought, "Oh yeah, I remember when I felt like that and it hurts."

Letting go and living forward—As Katlin said, becoming whole means "letting go of the past, accepting what happened with no judgments, and knowing that I create all of the possibilities in my life from this day forward!"

Activities

■ Truth Is Stranger Than Fiction

Activity Type:	Ice Breaker
Activity Level:	Low
Space:	Your usual meeting room
Time:	Anywhere from 15 minutes to an hour, depending on the ingenuity of your participants
Group Size:	8–10
Prerequisite:	None
Props:	None

Opening

Have you ever spent a lot of time dreaming up a fantasy world full of imagined facts and, occasionally, some real things that happened to you? What about the wildest, craziest things you've ever done but never dared to tell anyone about? Here's a chance to share your stories with the group.

Directions

Tell the players they each get to share three stories about themselves. Two stories are true; one is a lie. The group then tries to determine which stories are which.

Short Version

If you want the game to move quickly, allow a short period (30 seconds) for questions and then everyone votes on the stories they think are true. After the vote, the storyteller reveals the truth. As soon as the truth is told (amidst comments of "You gotta be kidding?" and "You did that?"), a new person can share three stories.

Long Version

Once the stories are related, allow some time for questioning the story-teller. The aim is to ask pertinent questions in order to find out whether the tellers have enough information to back up their stories. People normally enjoy the questioning, and beleaguered tellers sometimes feel as though they are involved in the Inquisition. After a specified time (2–5 minutes) or when no more questions remain, the group votes on the stories and the teller tells all.

Once the truth is revealed, there may be a desire to delve into the story in more detail. Allow time for this; it's where the action's at.

You will find that people inadvertently almost always tell their true stories first, then finish up with some wild tall tale. Just human nature, we suppose; i.e., feeling the need to be initially honest.

The only drawback you may encounter is that novice storytellers feel they have to come up with outlandish stories in order to be part of the game. Occasionally, people have felt awkward because their stories didn't display as much pizzazz as those of other players. As the leader, be ready to start the story sequence with some tales of your own, or announce the game and then give people 5–10 minutes to think of some stories before play begins.

Diversity Skills

Listening and communicating, building allies, group identities, or any time you want the group to work on their listening skills.

Processing

- Sometimes the truth is difficult to believe. How do you hear and validate other people's experiences?

- What were some of the things that really happened that you just couldn't possibly believe?

- How did you guess that the stories were true or untrue? What gave it away for you?

- Did you notice how someone's body language changed while they were telling their stories?

- How did you know you were really listening to the stories?

Copy Cat, Copy Cat

Activity Type: De-Inhibitizer

Activity Level: Low-key to moderate

Space: Any open space

Time: About 15 minutes

Group Size: This activity is most fun with a group of 10 or more.

Prerequisite: None

Props: None

Opening

It's probably been a long time since any of you played Follow the Leader. This time all of you get a chance to be leaders and followers.

Directions

Ask the group to form a circle. Tell the participants they each have to pick someone in the circle to be their leader but not to tell anyone who their leader is. Explain that the object of the activity is for them to mirror the pose their leader is in. Whenever their leader moves, they have to do the same thing. Ask them to try to watch their leaders without staring directly at them. That way, the leaders won't know who's following them.

Before you give your cue to start, make sure everyone has selected a leader and have them close their eyes and get into a comfortable position. When they open their eyes on your cue, the fun begins!

Most of the time, after several patterns of movement go around the circle, everyone ends up in the same pose.

Diversity Skills

This activity lends itself to helping participants become more aware of how they unconsciously follow or lead other people in their daily lives.

Processing

Whether or not you want to process this activity is up to you, but here are some questions you might want to try out on your group.

- ■ How easy was it for you to follow your leader without staring at them?

- Could you figure out who was following whom?

- Did you ever feel left out or uncertain?

- What did it feel like to try to conform to someone else's movements?

- Do you ever feel the same way at school? Are there consequences if you don't conform?

Equally Frantic

Activity Type:	De-Inhibitizer/Problem Solving
Activity Level:	High
Space:	Indoors in an area with nothing to trip over or run into
Time:	About 15 to 20 minutes
Group Size:	10+ The more you have, the more frantic they'll be.
Prerequisite:	None
Props:	At least one blown-up balloon for each participant, indelible markers, and a stopwatch

Opening

What are some of the things we need to keep in mind as we learn to treat individuals fairly and with respect?

Directions

Give everyone in the group a blown-up balloon. Have each person label their balloon with something that to them represents fair and respectful treatment. As they proceed through the activity, remind them that this is what they want to be practicing.

When you say GO! everyone hits their balloon up into the air. The goal is for the group to keep all of the balloons up in the air by hitting them with their hands or heads (no feet, someone might get kicked). Since it's a group activity, let them know that they don't have to hit their own balloon, but all the balloons have to be hit, not held.

When you give the GO! signal, start your stopwatch. Now all the group has to do is keep all the balloons in the air. There's a catch to this, however. Every 15 seconds or so, add another balloon to the game. The group must keep the new balloon from hitting the floor just like all the others.

If a balloon does hit the floor, it is called a "berserk", and you signal its presence to the group at the top of your lungs with a loud scream of "AAAAAHHHHH!!!"

If that same balloon stays on the floor for five seconds without being picked up, it becomes a "hectic", and you scream again. Every five seconds it stays on the floor, it becomes another hectic. This means you get to scream again.

After six screams, whether they are for berserks or hectics, the group becomes frantic and the game ends. Stop the watch and let the group know what their current world record is.

Give the group a minute or two to strategize for the next try and then get them started on an attempt to break their previous world record. This is where the problem-solving part comes in. The group may decide they need to arrange themselves in a certain way or give people certain jobs like receiving all incoming balloons. Lots of good ideas will emerge during this planning session. Some will help, some may not, so give the group a few chances to plan and try new ideas.

Diversity Skills

Listening and communicating, validating feelings, building allies, group identities or any other subject you choose. You can vary this activity according to how you ask the participants to label their balloons.

Processing

- How did you label your balloon?—Do a "go around." Did you see any of these things happening during this activity? Be specific with your example.

- Did you do a good job of keeping things in balance? Keeping things fair?

- What could you have done better?

- What kinds of things make you "berserk" or "hectic"?

- What can we do to keep our own activities and lives from getting too frantic?

Circle of Friends

Activity Type:	Trust Building
Activity Level:	Moderate
Space:	Enough room to form a tight circle
Time:	About 20 minutes
Group Size:	10 to 15 people
Prerequisite:	Spotting skills and *Trust Leans*—group comfort with touching.
Props:	None

Opening

Imagine yourself circled by warmth, love, safety, and concern. Let's all try to create that feeling.

Directions

Ask the group to stand shoulder-to-shoulder in a tight circle with one person—the faller—in the center. The first time around, you might want to be the faller if no one else volunteers. The faller gets into position— arms crossed over chest, legs straight, knees locked—and begins to lean slowly in any direction to the point of losing his balance (like the *Trust Lean* in Chapter 6). Before the faller leans too far out of plumb, the people in the circle redirect the faller toward another point of the circle. Have the catchers *gently* keep the faller moving around the circle in any direction, always maintaining physical contact with them. This fall-catch-redirect sequence continues in a gentle fashion until it becomes obvious that the faller is relaxing (but remaining rigid) and that the catchers have gained confidence in their ability to work together in handling the weight of the faller when he comes their way. Change people in the center until everyone who wants to has an opportunity to be the faller.

Diversity Skills

Like all trust-building activities, you can use this whenever you want your group to develop a feeling of physical and emotional safety with one another. *Circle of Friends* could also be a great activity to try when your group is working through questions of gender and sexual orientation, physical and mental ability, or racial identity to help them get used to being close to people who look different. But be certain your group can comfortably deal with these issues.

Processing

- What did it feel like to be the faller?
- What challenged the faller the most?
- What was it like for the catchers?
- How did you communicate with each other?
- What thoughts ran through your mind regarding your abilities and safety?

The Nuclear Fence

Activity Type:	Group Initiative/Problem Solving
Activity Level:	High
Space:	You can do this activity outdoors or in a gym if you can set up the three support poles.
Time:	30–45 minutes
Group Size:	8–12
Prerequisite:	Trust activities, spotting
Props:	A long length of 3/16" bungee cord tied between two trees or poles at about 2 1/2' from the ground.

Opening

This rope represents a barrier between you and other people. You've learned a lot together and now it's time to share it, but you've got a barrier to cross first. What are some of the things this barrier could represent in real life? (close-minded adults, lack of respect, hostile environment, etc.)

Directions

Have the group stand on one side of the bungee cord and ask them to cross from one side of the cord to the other without touching the cord. The group must travel en masse — that is, there must be a constant physical connection between all participants. If this connection breaks down at any time, the group must start over again. If anyone touches the cord or breaks the "force field" under the cord, the same consequences apply.

Diversity Skills

Focus on the challenges and difficulties they have with learning to take a stand for themselves in their daily lives. How hard is it to fit in?

How do they feel when they are ridiculed for being different? How do they respond when their peers make fun of people outside their group? Do they participate, stand quietly by without interfering, or stand up for the person taking the verbal abuse? What happens when they do stand up for someone? Do their friends support them?

Safety Cautions

Do not let your group members throw anyone over the rope. Injury will result. No diving. Don't let the last person perform a head-first dive into a shoulder roll. Encourage spotting.

Processing

- How did you solve or try to solve the problem? How did you come up with ideas?

- Did you feel that the group was listening to you and that you could really express yourself? Why or why not?

- If you could, what was it about the group dynamic that made you feel as though you had a right to express yourself?

- If you couldn't, what held you back?

- How does this apply to what happens to you in school and other places?

The Clock

Activity Type:	Group Initiative
Activity Level:	Moderate to high
Space:	Any open space
Time:	About 30 minutes
Group Size:	Ten or more
Prerequisite:	None
Props:	None

Opening

Have any of you ever thought, "If I can just get through this day and make it until school is over. Or until next year when I'll have my driver's license, then I can truly start living my life and be happy." Well, life is happening now, not later. So try to focus on what's stopping you from being fully present in your life today! The *Clock* is ticking! Let's see how fast we can do this activity.

Directions

Ask the group to hold hands and form a large circle. Indicate to the circled group that you would like them to rotate clockwise 360 degrees in one direction and then return 360 degrees back to the start. The goal is to see how quickly the group can complete the double rotation. The attempt is timed but time is stopped if contact is broken anywhere in the circle and they must start over. Group cooperation is obviously essential. A good time for 30–35 people is anything under 30 seconds. In establishing a time goal, assign about one second per player, subtracting an additional second for every ten participants.

Place markers (like sweatshirts) inside the circle at both six o'clock and twelve o'clock positions (three o'clock and nine o'clock too, if you're compulsive) so that the group has boundaries to rotate around and reference points for starting and finishing.

Challenge Level

If you want to increase the difficulty of this moving problem, ask the group to begin and end in a seated position on the ground. The clock stops when the last person sits back down.

If the group breaks contact in three consecutive attempts, stop the activity for that day and suggest coming back to it at another time. This gives the group something to look forward to and encourages conversation about what they were doing wrong and how to improve the next time.

Diversity Skills

Listening and communicating, building allies, or any time you want your group to work on cooperation skills and solving a problem together as a team.

Processing

- Why did the group have so much trouble retaining a connected grip?

- What could have been done to keep the group together as they attempted the rotation?

- Is it important to have fast people in the group?

- Would it have been more efficient to exclude the slower members? More satisfying?

Great American Egg Drop

Activity Type:	Group Initiative
Activity Level:	Low
Space:	Anywhere
Time:	About an hour
Group Size:	At least 10–12 so you can split them up into smaller groups.
Prerequisite:	None
Props:	20 straws, 30 inches of tape, and 1 egg per group. You'll also want a garbage bag, paper towels, and a trash can for cleanup. You can also try using different amounts of tape or substitute paper clips and rubber bands for tape.

Opening

Between W.W. I and W.W. II, the American Air Force was tackling the problem of airlifting food to people in starving countries. The Air Force had a particularly difficult time with eggs and couldn't figure out how to drop them from a plane without breaking them. If you are successful at this, the Air Force would be happy for your input, as they still haven't quite got it. (Nobody at the Air Force would respond when we tried to question them, so this may not be true.)

Directions

Split your group into teams of four to six people. After you've given each group their materials, ask them to construct the safest vehicle for their egg to travel in when dropped from a height of about six feet. The objective is to keep the egg from breaking when it lands. The egg must be inside the vehicle somehow (the straws cannot be lying on the floor and the egg dropped onto them). Give the groups 30 to 40 minutes to develop their egg-saving vehicles.

Ask each group to develop a name and a commercial for their product at the same time they are building their vehicle. Encourage them to develop something that lets everyone else know why their product is the best, most protective, most efficient egg protector on the market. Groups will present their commercials just before dropping their eggs.

After 30 to 40 minutes have everyone get back together in a large group. See which group would like to be the first to present their commercial and drop their egg. Each group should have a representative stand on a chair and drop the egg from a height of about six feet. You can also just have them reach up as high as they can and drop their vehicle from there. Sneaky groups will have their shortest person do it, while not-so-sneaky groups may have their tallest, which obviously makes the heights different but, hey, let them figure that one out.

If any eggs survive the first test, increase the height to eight feet. If any of them survive the second round, increase the height some more, and so on. The egg that makes it to the highest drop without breaking is the winner. You can make the activity less competitive by allowing only one or two rounds and declaring any eggs that don't ooze the winners.

Diversity Skills

You can use this activity to develop just about any theme with your group. Depending on the length of time your group has been together, you might want to try one or more of the topics presented in the processing section.

Processing

Who did what? How did you divide yourselves up to do the construction and write the commercial? Did you decide who did what based on who wanted to do what or who might be best at each task? Were some people left out of the process? Did the people writing the commercial get left out of the building of the vehicle?

Planning—Was there a common plan that everyone was committed to? Did you plan first or just start building? If there was no plan, would one have helped? Would it have saved time in the long run to have taken the time to hear suggestions from people and then develop a plan, as opposed to just doing, doing, doing? Did the group spend too much time planning and run out of time to complete the construction?

Leadership—Who took charge and why? Did leadership change as the group went through the planning and building stages? Did anyone help to keep the group together and keep everyone involved?

Diversity—Did you make assumptions about people's skills and abilities? Did anyone do something differently than was expected? Was anybody in the group pigeonholed and expected to assume a certain role? How does this play out in school relationships? Do some kids in school have a certain reputation that we expect them to act according to? Does everyone always live up to their reputations?

The Power Shuffle

Activity Type: Social Responsibility

Activity Level: Low

Space: Enough room to form a circle

Time: About 30 minutes

Group Size: About 10

Prerequisite: This is a disclosure/sharing activity. Choose the questions you'll use based on what you know about your groups ability to share.

Props: The *Power Shuffle* category sheet (see directions)

Opening

Some of us have more power than others out in the world, but power isn't something you can hang on to forever. We all float in and out of power positions on a daily and sometimes hourly basis.

Directions

Have the participants form a circle and ask them a series of questions from the following list. Ask them to indicate their membership in a group by joining the others who identify with the groups in another circle inside the circle. Remember, though, Challenge by Choice. Remind the group that they only have to step in if they feel comfortable about indicating their membership in one of the groups. Tell them to snap their fingers if the question doesn't apply to them personally, but does apply to someone they know, family, friends, neighbors, peers, etc. Reform the circle after each question.

Questions

Age

Are you 15 or younger?

Ten or younger?

Do you think of yourself as old or feel old?

Do you think of yourself as young or feel young?

Do you like your present age?

Age (continued)

Have you ever felt disregarded, hurt, or harmed by someone older than you?

Have you ever felt disregarded, hurt, or harmed by someone younger than you?

Gender

Are you female?

Male?

If you're female, can you think of any male or masculine parts of your personality?

If you're male, can you think of any female or feminine parts of your personality?

If you're a girl, have you ever wished you were a boy?

If you're a boy, have you ever wished you were a girl?

Do you want to have children?

Do you plan not to have any children?

Race

Are you a human being?

Are you Asian American or part Asian American?

Are you African American or part African American?

Are you Native American or part Native American?

Are you Hispanic or Latino/a or part Hispanic or Latino/a?

Are you white or part white?

Are you biracial or multiracial?

Are you not sure what race you are?

Do you believe that different racial groups don't exist?

Are you a US citizen?

Are you an immigrant to the US?

Are you a first-generation American?

Is your first language something other than English?

Are you multilingual?

If you're white, have you ever wished you were black, Asian, Latino, or Native American?

If you're black, Asian, Latino, or Native American, have you ever wished you were white?

Class

Have you and your family always had enough to live on?

Do you and your family not have enough to get by on?

Have you ever worried about having enough to eat in a day?

Have you ever been homeless?

Has your family ever received public assistance?

Have you ever had anyone serving you—nannies, housekeepers, or servants?

Does your family assume you will go to college?

Sexual Orientation

Do you know anyone or are you close to anyone who is hetero-sexual?

Do you know anyone or are you close to anyone who is lesbian, gay, or bisexual?

Religion

Do you participate in an organized religion?

Are you being raised as a Jew?

Are you being raised as a Muslim?

Are you being raised as a Buddhist?

Are you being raised as a Christian?

Are you being raised as something different?

Do you think God exists?

Do you think God doesn't exist?

Ability

Have you ever had a temporary disability like a broken leg or arm or a bad back?

Have you ever felt depressed?

Have you ever used a cane, crutches, or a wheelchair?

Do you wear a hearing aid, eyeglasses, or contact lenses?

Are you afraid when someone different from you gets close?

Do you feel curious and want to know more about people who are different from you?

Family

Are you the oldest child in your family?

The youngest?

In the middle?

Do you have two parents at home?

Do you have only one parent taking care of you?

Is your father taking care of you?

Are your parents divorced?

Do both of your parents come from the same racial background?

Different racial backgrounds?

Diversity Skills

The category sheet covers just about every subject in this book and we encourage you to try them all with your group. You can do them all at once or focus on specific categories, adding some questions of your own, as you work through the chapters.

Processing

■ Is it easier to identify with some categories more than others? If so, why?

■ What does this make you realize about how we respond to people who are different than us?

■ What does this make you realize about how we gravitate to and like some people and why sometimes we feel repelled by or don't like others?

■ What does this teach us about how we value or don't value the differences in people?

The Messages We Hear about Who We Are

Activity Type: Social Responsibility

Activity Level: Low

Space: Your usual meeting room

Time: One hour

Group Size: 5 or more

Prerequisite: None

Props: Index cards and pencils

Opening

What do you do about those little voices in your head that constantly remind you how much better your life would be if something about you were different? How do those voices stop us from achieving our goals?

Directions

Hand out five index cards and have each person write out the top five messages, one on each card, they have always heard or thought they heard from parents, teachers, friends, society at large, etc. Examples of such messages are—"You're really smart," "You would be so pretty if you could lose some weight," "You're not a good ballplayer," "You're just average," etc.

Collect all the cards and divide the group into smaller groups of four. Ask everyone to come up and draw one card at random. (Keep the remaining cards for the next activity.) When each participant has taken a card have them discuss the following questions in their small groups:

- Have you ever had this experience?

- How did it or does it make you feel?

- What are some of the implied messages?

- What are some of the behaviors one might assume if you're receiving this message?

- What are some of the limitations or opportunities around these messages? (Have them write down the answers to this question to share with the larger group.)

Diversity Skills

Group identities, validating feelings, self-affirmation

Processing

■ What did you learn about yourself?

■ What helped you to share with your small group?

■ What held you back from fully sharing with your small group?

■ What understanding did these messages give you about the messages that you and your peers receive from society at large?

■ The Payoffs and Costs Game

Activity Type:	Social Responsibility
Activity Level:	Low
Space:	Your usual meeting room
Time:	45 to 60 minutes
Group Size:	5 or more
Prerequisite:	*The Messages We Hear about Who We Are*
Props:	Play money, the index cards from *Messages*, and pencils

Opening

If you know anything about hockey, you know that there's a penalty box. When a player does something that looks good, the crowd roars and the player gets to bask in their approval. But if the move was illegal, he's out of the game and has to go in the penalty box. Can you think of behavior that puts you in the penalty box?

Directions

Hand out the remaining messages from the previous activity, *The Messages We Hear about Who We Are*, giving at least two cards to each participant. You can hand the cards out randomly or put them in a hat and have each person pull out two. Ask the group to read the messages they picked and write down the payoffs and costs of each of their messages. Examples of

this would be: "You would be so pretty if you would lose weight."
Payoff is: Don't have to take responsibility for being involved in my
social life. Cost is: Am unhappy because I don't have a social life.
"You're so smart." Payoff is: Get good grades in school and the teachers
like you. Cost is: Not all your classmates feel comfortable around you.
Some of them think you're a nerd and others are competitive. "You don't
listen when I'm talking to you." Payoff is: Get to ignore what's going on
around you and live in your daydreams. Cost is: Your parents start to nag
constantly.

Give each participant $20 of play money. Have them pair up and share
the payoffs and costs of each of their messages. Everyone gets to negotiate what they think the value of each payoff and cost is worth relative to
what their partner got. Give them time to discuss how the messages limit
the opportunities we have in life.

Diversity Skills

Group identities, validating feelings

Processing

- What did you learn about the messages you discussed?

- How did money change the game for you? What was its impact on
  the game for the group?

- What does what you've learned about the impact of the messages
  mean for you in this group? With other people in your life.

Closing Activity

Two Strokes and a Wish

Sharing something about ourselves with other people sometimes feels like taking an emotional risk. When we do share, it's often because we hope that others will validate how we feel. The truth is, validation first needs to come from ourselves.

Share two positive things about yourself and one wish you have for yourself based on what happened today in the group.

Personal Journal Question

What did you share with the group today about yourself that you couldn't have before?

Processing Questions

❑ How do you imagine others felt toward you at various times during the activities? Were these feelings expressed?

❑ Is it difficult for you to avoid judging others? Explain.

❑ Can you think of examples of when you judged others in the group today? When you didn't judge others?

❑ What were some advantages to you of not judging others?

❑ What were some advantages to others of your not judging them?

❑ How do judging and not judging others affect the completion of the activity?

❑ Were some behaviors of others easy not to judge and other behaviors difficult?

❑ Did everyone in the group express an opinion when a choice was available? If not, why not?

❑ What is the best way for this group to make decisions? Explain.

❑ Do you respond in similar ways in other groups?

❑ What did you like about how the group made decisions? What didn't you like?

❑ Can you give examples of when you trusted someone in the group?

❑ Is it easier to trust some people than others? Explain.

❑ Can you think of examples when trusting someone wasn't a good idea?

❑ How do you increase your level of trust for someone?

❑ On a scale of 1 to 10, rate how much trust you have in the group as a whole. Can you explain your rating?

❑ What did you do today that deserves the trust of others?

❑ How does the amount of fear you feel affect your trust of others?

❑ How are you different from some of the others in the group?

❏ How do these differences strengthen the group as a whole?

❏ What would this group be like if there were very few differences in people? How would you feel if this were so?

❏ How are you like some of the others in the group?

❏ Were these commonalities a help to the group in completing their task? Explain.

❏ Were these commonalities a hindrance to the group in completing their task? Explain.

❏ Do you think you have other things in common with some of the group members that you haven't found yet?

❏ How did this setting help you discover how you are similar to others?

❏ What have you learned about trust, respect, acceptance, and cooperation as they relate to differences?

❏ Did you find yourself responding to any stereotypes? What were they? How do you think you might respond to the same situation in the future?

❏ What has changed for you as a result of participating in this activity? How do you think you'll perceive people who are different from you—blacks, whites, gays, or whoever is appropriate—as a result?

❏ How does this activity relate to the real-life experiences you are faced with at home, in school, in your neighborhood?

❏ Was any kind of discrimination going on this activity? If so, what?

❏ What was the most difficult part of this activity as it relates to how you deal with people who are different from you?

❏ What was the easiest part of this activity as it relates to how you deal with people who are different from you?

❏ Did this activity challenge any of your beliefs?

❏ What are your feelings now?

❏ Is there anything in this activity you would do differently now and why?

❏ As a result of this activity, what are some of the things you think or feel that we all have in common?

❏ Do you think there are more commonalities or differences between _____ and _____?

10

Racial
Identity

The awareness of difference begins with our first perceptions of others. Before we open our mouths to speak, we have already perceived the color difference, an awareness that affects both verbal and non-verbal communication. The history of racism in the United States and how the color of our skins affects our daily interactions are issues that must be dealt with as we work with young people on issues of diversity.

Race enters into people's minds through history, personal experience, and the media. The race issue has been such an important topic in the area of diversity that it is often the easiest to talk about. Because of this, exploring diversity through race and racism is often a good way to open the door to discussions about other, more subtle issues that divide us.

Racial issues have been so central to our understanding of diversity that much research has been done in this area. Recently the concept of race has been debated as a result of the proposed addition of a multiracial category to the US Census. The current categories for race designation are White, Black, American Indian and Alaska Native, Asian and Pacific Islander, Hispanic or Spanish.

Among advocates of adding a multiracial category to the US Census are those who do not fit into the present categories and want to be more accurately described. Those against adding a multiracial designation have several reasons. Some feel the categories are already too numerous; some feel that people should designate themselves according to what runs most in their blood; some feel that the darkest race should be the deciding factor; some feel that racial categories only perpetuate a concept that divides us; some feel that if the approximately 2.5–10 million people who are multiracial remove themselves from other categories, the gains made toward fair representation for these groups will dissolve.

This deeply institutionalized issue demonstrates how our culture asks us to know and state who or what we are. Census categories are important on several levels, providing a way for broader definitions and sometimes good or bad actions to take place. The very fact that many people of color resist the multiracial category because they feel the steps the government has taken to ensure equal treatment for Native Americans, African Americans, and others will be washed away shows how many complex issues are involved.

Origins of Racial Classification

Today most anthropologists believe that race is not based on sound biological evidence but is a social and political construct founded on a desire to make the world more understandable and more ordered, with a clear power structure. In spite of this, we cannot deny that social and political constructs have a strong influence on how we learn about our racial identity and thus view the world. In a 1997 *Boston Globe* article headlined "In Shift, Many Anthropologists See Race as a Social Construct," David L. Chandler states that "every person belongs to a racial group from which he or she derives a psychological, emotional, and behavioral filter through which the self, others, and the world are seen."

Language and the Meanings Assigned to Color

One of the ways to illustrate how deeply our culture carries biases about skin color is to look at the language we use when discussing race. White, black, red, and yellow have been commonly used terms with meanings that permeate our understanding of color and of race.

It is fascinating to observe the extent to which Western, Anglo Saxon culture is permeated by the belief that white is *good*—pure, virginal, and innocent like angelfood cake and Obi-Wan Kenobi. Black represents *bad*—dark, evil, ominous, and ugly like devil's food cake and Darth Vader.

Color Definitions

Black—from the Latin to burn. Very dark color; heavy, serious; of or relating to the Negro race; the absence of light; thoroughly sinister or evil, connected with the supernatural, esp. the devil; grim, grotesque or distorted humor.

black art, blackball, black book, black death, black eye, blackjack, black magic, blackmail, black out, Black Monday

Brown—of dark or tanned complexion; any of a group of colors between red and yellow in hue; of medium to low lightness, and of moderate to low saturation; a brown skinned person.

brown bag, brownie point, brown nose, brown sugar

Dark—devoid of light, wholly or partially black; arising from or showing evil traits or desires; evil, dismal, sad; lacking knowledge or culture; not clear to the understanding; not fair, swarthy, secret; possessing depth and richness; murky, gloomy.

Dark Ages, in the dark, dark horse, Darkest Africa

Light—from the Greek for white. Something that makes vision possible, brightness, sight; spiritual illumination, inner light, truth; something that enlightens or informs, a set of principles, standards or opinions; a note-worthy person in a particular place or field; not dark, intense or swarthy in color; to set fire to, animate, illuminate; having little weight, not heavy, of little importance, trivial; capable of moving swiftly or nimbly on one's feet; frivolous, changeable, cheerful; mild flavor, easily digested.

light fingered, light footed, light headed, lightweight, enlighten, lighten up

Red—flushed esp. with anger or embarrassment; ruddy, florid; inciting or endorsing radical social or political change esp. by force; communist; failing to show a profit.

red alert, red cap, red cent, red coat, red-eye, red-handed, red herring, red Indian, red man, red-neck, red skin, red head, red tide

Tan—to convert to leather or some similar substance; to make skin tan esp. through exposure to sun; thrash or whip, a sound spanking; a variable color averaging a light yellowish brown.

White—free from color; being a member of a group or race characterized by reduced pigmentation and distinguished from persons belonging to groups marked by black, brown, yellow or red skin coloration; free from spot or blemish; free from moral impurity, innocent; not intended to cause harm, favorable; fortunate, notable, ardent, passionate.

white collar, white elephant, white face, white heat, white hope, white list, white out, white wash, whitey

Yellow—becoming yellowish through age, disease, or discoloration; having a yellow or light brown color of skin; featuring sensational or scandalous items or ordinary news sensationally distorted; mean, cowardly.

yellow journalism, yellow dog, yellow fever, yellow peril

Whether or not we choose to acknowledge it, we all perceive color differences. Children ask questions about differences until adults begin to suppress their remarks. At a certain point in their development, we let them know that it is "wrong" or "impolite" to acknowledge any differences out loud. The differences children notice are primarily but not always racial. Have you ever told a child not to stare at someone who is physically or mentally challenged? What about when they begin to notice that not all of us have the same sexual orientation, that some people dress differently?

Passing Down Our Understanding of Race

Diversity is more than race, however central that concept is in our consciousness today. Cultural, ethnic, class, and even individual background are proving to offer more in-depth ways of looking at diversity. They also provide us with an escape from the roots of a racist society that are bound up in our language. Moving toward an awareness that the system we operate within is profoundly discriminatory is crucial to creating a trusting environment where youth can build connections with one another.

The words we use, the clothes we wear, who we have lunch with, the movies we choose to see, the programs we watch on TV, all contribute to how we collaboratively build and pass on our understanding of race. Perhaps the most subtle way we pass on our understanding of race to the youth we work with is in the way we define ourselves. Our own self-definition, and how we see ourselves in relation to others, is like a template for influencing others. Sometimes the most persuasive argument for a point of view is the one that states, "I wasn't aware there was another way to look at it."

Teachable Moments

From a very early age we begin to receive messages from family and friends about our place in the world. As we begin to coo, cry, yell, or scream, we are sending and receiving signals that tell us how important we are, how much we are loved, what we want, and what others need to do to comfort us. If visitors from another planet, unbeknownst to us, came to visit the millions of nurseries in our country, they would probably see the same funny, warm, loving, and validating scenario occurring in nearly every household. They would walk—or fly—away thinking, "Hey, Americans sure do start out the same, no matter who they are or what color they are."

The same visitors, coming back two to four years later, would most likely pick up on an entirely different set of cues being sent and received both inside and outside the family. It is at about the ages of three and four that children in a multi-racial society begin to ask questions about physical differences. Their observations and assumptions may not be as sophisticated as those the students in your group might make or that we make as adults, but the wondering begins early: "Mommy, is that lady dirty?" and "How come I'm chocolate and he's vanilla?" and assertions like "I am not black, I'm beige."

These instances represent unique and valuable learning opportunities, teachable moments, and you never know when one will come along. To take advantage of teachable moments is to act when the time is right, responding to events and questions as they arise, pausing in the middle of an activity to examine what was said or done. Taking advantage of teachable moments goes beyond the abstraction of language and ideas; it means you are using concrete examples to explain otherwise complex notions. Examining what has been said or assumed immediately is a powerful way of teaching youth about assumptions and differences. It is right up front, requiring genuine response and discussion.

For example, if a child makes a prejudicial remark or repeats something they heard at school, stop and ask them, "What do you think that means?" Young children often repeat things they hear without realizing the implications. Take a few minutes to explain the true meaning of prejudicial language, making it clear why it is hurtful and not appropriate. Or try stopping in the middle of reading a children's book with only white children depicted and ask children if they see anything wrong with the pictures. Point out to them what is wrong. "All the people in these pictures have white skin. That's not the way things really are, is it?" Have children use crayons to shade some of the people in the drawings so the book will reflect the world we live in.

How can we as adults respond appropriately when we see a teachable moment? Whatever the response, it is crucial to remember two goals: The first is to foster their own positive self-image and love of self. The second is to give them the tools for seeing others as they are, in an optimistic light, however different they may look or seem. With middle and high school aged youth, the assumptions may not be so obvious, the examples not so clear, and the lessons of positive self-image and love of self not so easily learned. The goal of many of the activities in this book is to create teachable moments to help you and your groups pause and examine biases as they surface.

Racial Identity as Part of Individual Identity

In his book *The Influence of Race and Racial Identity in Psychotherapy*, Robert T. Carter states, "As an individual grows up as a citizen of the United States, he or she also learns that each citizen belongs to a racial group. The challenge for each individual is to incorporate race into his or her personal identity." Because we live in a racially diverse society, where race is a distinctive aspect of our culture, our children are inevitably influenced by the meanings we assign to their racial groups.

All people, regardless of their ethnic or cultural background, grow up as part of a racial group. We usually define what racial group another person belongs to according to skin color, but that is not always an accurate gauge of how individuals identify themselves. The vignette in Chapter Eight about Kristen, who was treated as white by her fellow black college students, is an example of how dangerous it can be for us to categorize people based on looks alone.

Many people are baffled by the question of what determines racial identity. Racial identity is composed of far more than the color of one's skin. It is multifaceted and amorphous. It is governed by "one's early social experience, history and politics, conscious input and labeling, and the genetic accident that dictates external appearance" (*The Color Complex*). Our racial identity is a state of mind, an acceptance of one's past, present, and future; it also affects our values, understanding of our culture, how we relate to others, and how they relate to us.

Children of Color

All children receive verbal and nonverbal messages about their identity. Racial identity is an integral part of our individual identity, and our skin color often affects how we are perceived by others who do or don't belong to our racial group. As a result, the messages we get are often linked to our skin color—from light to dark. There are several reasons for the messages that get communicated. In some families, it is a way of preparing children for the way they will be treated by society. For others, it is because adults want to help them seal in a sense of pride, a sense that they belong to something greater than themselves or their family. Depending on the circumstances, these messages can reinforce a healthy sense of self or contribute to emotional conflicts as the child matures.

Parents who confront racial issues early on may initially upset the child, but these lessons can become a source of positive thinking about racial identity and a greater acceptance of human diversity.

Many children do not receive these messages from their families, but from friends, media, school, and their communities. "One's identity as it relates to race is affected by the manner in which race is denied, avoided, or discussed in the family or other socializing institutions; e.g., school. For example, a white male raised in a predominantly white environment with no mention of race is implicitly taught that he is superior to visibly racial/ethnic people. A black person whose family minimizes or denies the significance of race may hold similar beliefs. Consider the situation of a light-skinned Latino living in a racially mixed community, whose family teaches only about ethnicity; e.g., Mexican, Cuban, or Puerto Rican and not race. This person might be the object of envy and hostility because of their color and distinctive physical features and might be confronted with racial remarks.

These examples show how the context of one's family influences the development of characteristics—racial and nonracial—that constitute personal identity" (*The Influence of Race and Racial Identity*).

Most experts believe that parents and caregivers play an essential role in helping children form a positive racial identity. Parents who avoid talking about race with their children or who deny that race is an issue transmit less understanding about race and racial differences and may not be communicating a strong sense of racial identity. Parents who confront racial issues early on may initially upset the child, but these lessons can become a source of positive thinking about racial identity and a greater acceptance of human diversity.

Stages of Identity Development

In the last chapter, we discussed the different stages of individual identity development that children pass through on their way to adulthood. Here, we will look at those stages again from the perspective of racial identity formation for children of color.

Children of Color: 2–4 years old

Children begin to notice that the world is full of people of different colors. It is at about this age that children begin to make remarks like "I want to be the same color as everyone else." Generally, but not always, this type of statement comes from children who find themselves to be the only child of color in their daily environment.

As we mentioned in the previous chapter, it's important that parents work closely with their children's primary caregivers to instill positive racial identity. It's also essential that the toys and books children are exposed to depict all kinds of people.

Children of Color: 4–10 years old

Children have already gained a good understanding of how their racial background impacts their place in the world. Some have heard stories about their ancestors and the impact racism had on them. Through knowing their past histories, these children gain a greater understanding of their cultural and ethnic traditions as well as their racial identities.

Optimistically, the assertion would be that the world is safe for people of all colors. Because we live in a society where racism is an issue, however, parents' fears often transmit the message to their children that they must be very, very careful. As for all children, this is the age when they are most likely to be exposed to name calling and words they hardly know the meaning of: nigger, spic, faggot, gook. Their newfound maturity also brings a greater understanding of the subtleties and covert operation of racism in our society.

It is essential to teach children of color that they have options. If we don't, we will be contributing to the negative cycle of blame, anger, and a sense of victimization. While not everyone succumbs to feelings of victimization, children who feel that they have no options are certainly more susceptible to the increased anger, rage, humiliation, sadness, and depression that plague so many people in today's society.

Pre-Teens/Teens of Color: 10–19 years

Again, this is a difficult age, and sometimes it is a real challenge to work with children at this age on questions of racial identity. Difficult, but necessary.

How teens of color respond to and assimilate the problems of race depends largely on the following:

Geographical location—North, South, Midwest, and West

Physical environment—inner city, suburbs, neighborhood, countryside

Racial diversity—does everyone look like them or does no one look like them?

Family and significant adults—how do they feel about their identities, where do they fit into society, how do they cope?

Peers—are they open or closed to diversity, cruel or accepting?

Many of these problems are intensified for children who grow up isolated from other children of their own race. Do they sound like who they are? Are they "black enough," "Latino enough," "white enough," "Asian enough"? Can they fit in with groups of other kids? Why don't they feel comfortable around them? Is it wrong if they'd rather play hockey than basketball? Why is hockey a "white" sport and basketball a "black" sport? These children are affected by and may even begin to believe some of the stereotypes that abound about their own race and cultural background. It is difficult enough for parents to instill a sense of self-worth in their children without the burden of institutionalized racism and hatred. It is even more difficult when these families are isolated.

White Racial Identity

Many people believe that race is not an issue for whites, and whites tend to identify more with a specific ethnic background—Polish, Italian, German, Lithuanian, etc.—than a white racial identity. Developing a positive racial identity is just as important for whites, however, as it is for members of other racial groups. In *Black and White Racial Identity: Theory, Research and Practice*, J. E. Helms writes that "the evolution of a positive white racial identity consists of two processes, the abandonment of racism and the development of a nonracist white identity."

Helms goes on to note that for many of us, whites and people of color, the sense of white superiority is so prevalent that it works as a racial norm in our society, on an individual, institutional, and cultural level. "Most whites do not recognize their race until, or unless, they have to confront the 'idea' or the physical reality of blacks and other visible ethnic groups in their life space."

We'd like to share the following story with you as an example of what many white Americans grow up to believe and some of the feelings youth may experience as they move toward acquiring a positive sense of white racial identity:

> As a white, Anglo-Saxon, Protestant female growing up in rural East Tennessee, I never thought about my racial identity. It was like living in a house with electricity—I always expected the power to be on because I lived there. Occasionally, there were power failures, but they were always fixed quickly enough and certainly had nothing to do with me. Why would race be an issue—I was white, and it certainly wasn't a problem for me.
>
> I think that my experience is very typical of how many white people in this country feel about their racial identity. It is a non-issue because, as a member of the white majority group in the United States, you are accorded many privileges that you simply take for granted. I have not experienced the unspoken and spoken barriers of race. And there has been a passive acceptance on my part of the status quo.
>
> It wasn't until I became a part of a religious minority that I even became aware of the subtleties of discrimination, and how angry and uncomfortable that made me feel. I converted to Judaism when I married at 25. Not long after, I heard my first anti-Semitic remark. I say "first" because it wasn't until then that I had developed a sense of what it is like to be "different" in our society. My awareness had shifted. I know the remark wasn't directed at me personally because the speaker didn't think that I was Jewish. Regardless, it was very threatening to my feelings of security.
>
> It makes me very angry that people think remarks like that should not be taken seriously and that people who do take them seriously are overreacting. There is a real history for minority groups in this country to feel threatened and valid reason to react.

For whites, it is not always easy to listen to a different perspective and make an honest effort to understand the experiences of people of color. There are several reasons for this. One is that whites have no frame of reference for understanding the experiences of people of color. Two, they don't want to hear or validate discriminatory experiences because they may feel guilty for belonging to the racial category of "discriminators" and/or feel angry because they feel they have not personally displayed discriminatory behavior—*Don't blame me.*

Third, if whites do hear and validate the experiences, then they will need to address the very difficult question of responsibility and what individuals can do to change or heal injustices. Many people feel overwhelmed about what to do when they begin to see how prejudice and discrimination affect us all. Some feel that they lack the skills to address these issues and affect positive change. There is also great resistance to change because of concern about losing power, fear of being rejected by members of their own group, and for some, a righteous sense that for whatever the reason, racism is legitimate and justified.

As whites become aware of their white racial identity and heritage, it's important to remember that not all whites defend racism, and that simply being white does not define an individual as an "oppressor." While the overwhelmingly white bias of our society is responsible for the inherited patterns of racist behaviors, not all individuals are to blame for this. If we all work together to change our institutions and cultural beliefs and respond to individual incidents of racist behavior, we will be taking steps toward erasing inequality.

As adults who work with youth, our goal is to help them gain a new understanding of white racial identity, one that does not oppress, idealize, romanticize, or deprecate people of color on the basis of race. It is our responsibility to help them nurture positive individual and racial identities that will give them the courage and enthusiasm to explore connections with all people, regardless of color, ethnic origins, gender, sexual orientation, physical and mental ability, class, looks, or any other perceived differences.

Multiracial Identity

The issue of race is getting more convoluted as mixed marriages increase in significant numbers. Multiracial children can feel isolated, alienated, and confused as they sort through how they are going to define themselves, particularly if their parents send mixed messages. They may also be exposed to derogatory comments and name-calling. Names do hurt, and sometimes they hurt for a lifetime. "Hi yellah," "whitey," "half breed," and "red bone" can cause irreparable psychological damage if adults do not intervene. Many multiracial children are exposed quite early in their development to a sense that they do not belong, and sometimes their parents don't have a clue about what their children are feeling. Denial is a defense mechanism that operates for all parents who don't want to see their children in pain. If parents are ill equipped to deal with the questions and conflicts their children are facing, however, the problem will perpetuate itself, and the children will be ill equipped to cope with how society views and treats them.

Again, this illustrates the importance of being open with children about race, responding to questions, and teaching them to value all the parts of their racial identity and heritage. In *The Influence of Race and Racial Identity in*

Psychotherapy, Carter argues that in order to gain a biracial or multiracial identity, children must be taught to accept all aspects of their racial heritage. Denying one or another will undermine the process of acquiring a bi- or multiracial identity. For example, if a child who looks white rejects their black, Native American, Hispanic, or Asian identity they have to "become" white and give up any part of their identity that is not white. This can create enormous conflict as they begin to navigate the world around them. How do they explain the appearance of family members and relatives who do not look white? Developing a multiracial identity is a challenging task for children in our society, particularly when skin color is so often the basis for assigning people to a racial category.

Carter concludes that it is possible for children to develop a bi- or multiracial identity if they are taught to value and identify themselves first as a person of color. "Take black and white as an example. When one has first developed a positive black identity and uses the black identity as a foundation, it allows incorporation of the white aspect of identity. Only then can a person be truly biracial, identifying with both racial groups. One can be positive, internalized, and biracial, and not have to compromise any part of oneself. The person would also have a psychological home where he or she is accepted—maybe not on all terms and with everyone, but enough to be…grounded in a biracial identity."

> *When kids begin to dress, walk, and act in certain ways, it may be a form of pride, a statement of identification with their culture....These are their ways of establishing an identity and making a statement on how they want to fit into society.*

Ultimately, self-definition is the name of the game. Race terms are so woven into the fabric of how we as adults understand ourselves that, as the world continues to become more multiracial, we will need to listen to the cues that children give us about the meanings these terms have for them. If terms of race refer to some combination of culture, skin tone, looks, and class, including some things we choose and some that are given to us, the use of race terms to identify individuals is not going to disappear overnight. But if we approach it openly and with caring, the exploration of what these terms mean and how we classify others and ourselves can be a starting point for discussing with youth how they see themselves in relationship to one another.

When kids begin to dress, walk, and act in certain ways, it may be a form of pride, a statement of identification with their culture. In the '60s, an Afro and a dashiki meant you were a militant. Today, we see youth continuing to express who they are through their clothes and self-adornment—baggy pants, gigundo shirts, designer name brands, kerchiefs, too-small shirts and polyester from the '70s, body piercing and tattoos. These are their ways of establishing an identity and making a statement on how they want to fit into society. We who work with youth cannot ignore their messages.

Concluding Thoughts

Racial identity is the sum of many parts, not simply the color of one's skin. Remember, it's not always easy to be politically correct these days—terms are in constant evolution. It's often better to ask someone how they identify themselves instead of making assumptions based on their color or behavior.

Talk about race with children. Share your feelings and encourage them to express their's. This is one of the most important ways for children to develop a strong sense of self. By the age of two or three, children are already asking questions about racial differences. While they may not see or understand all the nuances of skin color and racial identification, they do know the difference between white and black and are curious about it. Nurture their curiosity and explain the difference in terms they can understand when they make statements like "Krissy is white, and we are black." Answer their questions in an open manner and encourage them to keep seeking new ways to define themselves.

Try to keep your emotional biases out of discussions with your group and keep dialogue open-ended and informational. Talking about race is a wonderful learning opportunity. It discourages stereotyping and reduces fear; in short, it humanizes.

Stop! Look! Listen! Talk! When you hear or see youth expressing prejudicial thoughts or engaging in discriminatory acts directed at themselves or others, stop immediately and address the issue. It is often what we don't say that fosters negative thoughts and behavior.

Support and validate children. Drs. Darlene and Derek Hopson, authors of *Raising the Rainbow Generation*, have pointed out that low levels of self-esteem make children particularly vulnerable to prejudicial attitudes. They list the following as indicators that children may be having trouble establishing their sense of self-worth:

Disrespect

Self-defeating behavior

Feelings of inadequacy

Withdrawal

Trouble at school

Self-deprecating remarks

Bragging

Poor or inadequate social skills

If you notice that a child has some of these difficulties, move quickly to help correct them. The best way to do this is to show your unequivocal support, letting the child know that you care for them for who they are and what they do, regardless of their mistakes. Try to make sure that you praise more often than you scold and correct. If you realize that you are using the "three f's"—fussing, fighting, and feuding—too much, take the time to correct yourself. We found something that works well with our children. You may want to try it with your own or at the end of your day's session with your group. At least once a day, usually when it's time to say goodnight, we tell them all the things we like about them or what they've done during the day that was wonderful and positive. Things like: "Thank you for cleaning the counters off without being asked." "Thank you for reading your brother's favorite book to him; it gave me a chance to fix dinner." They love it. Who wouldn't? Remember to praise more often than you criticize. Try to spend individual time with children. Take a few minutes before class, before the game, in the hallway; you don't have to give up your day to give them a special moment. You'll get to know them in a new way if you nurture positive relationships, and the benefits last a lifetime.

Watch for and take advantage of teachable moments. Respond to questions as they arise. Stay aware of your own assumptions about race, the way the youth in your group dress, and human diversity in general as you engage them in discussion. What are some of your assumptions about color that may or may not be in the list we've included in this chapter?

Provide positive role models and positive expressions of people of color in books and programs. All children have the right to see people who look like them in a positive light. Make sure children are aware of the many positive contributions people of color have brought to our lives. If you are a teacher or a youth group leader, select reading materials that reflect a broad range of cultures and nationalities.

Suggested Reading

Carter, Robert T. *The Influence of Race and Racial Identity in Psychotherapy.* New York: Wiley & Sons, 1995. An in-depth look at the development of racial identity for all racial groups from the perspective of a practicing clinical psychologist.

Helms, Janet E. (Editor). *Black and White Racial Identity: Theory, Research, and Practice (Contributions in Afro-American and African Studies, No 129).* Westport, CT: Greenwood Publishing Group, 1990. This book presents the major theories of black and white racial identity. Original research addresses the relationship of racial identity to other personality characteristics such as value orientations, decision-making styles and counseling process variables.

Hopson, Darlene Powell, Derek Hopson and Thomas Clavin. *Praising the Rainbow Generation; Teaching your Children to be Successful in a Multiracial Society.* Fireside Books, 1993.

Rosemond, John. *"Raising Unbiased Children, Stopping Prejudice Before it Starts"* Better Homes and Gardens, July 1990

Russell, K., M. Wilson, and R. Hall. *Color Complex: The Politics of Skin Color Among African Americans*. Orlando: Harcourt Brace Jovanovich Publishers, 1992. Demonstrates an "insightful examination of color prejudices... and how deeply white racism continues to intrude on black psyche and behavior."

Hacker, Andrew. *Two Nations: Black and White, Separate, Hostile. Unequal*. New York: Charles Scribner and Sons, 1992. Reviews the author's understanding of the role and meaning of the major two races in America today. Discusses how our nation is moving towards two societies, black and white, separate and unequal.

Dickens, Floyd, Jr., and Jacqueline Dickens. *The Black Manager: Making It in the Corporate World*. New York: AMACOM, American Management Association, 1982. This book is the culmination of a lengthy study about how successful black managers coped, survived, and made it in the white corporate world.

Terkel, Studs. *Race: How Blacks and Whites Think and Feel About the American Obsession*. New York: The New Press, 1992. A collection of essays that reflect how blacks and whites feel about race in America today.

Worksheet

What is your racial, religious, or ethnic background? What can you share about it that evokes a sense of pride? _____

_____

What is a stereotype of your racial, religious, or ethnic background that really makes you angry? _____

_____

When was the first time you consciously noticed a racial, religious, or ethnic difference in someone else? How did you feel about that experience?

_____

_____

Can you think of a prejudice that was a part of your upbringing?

_____

_____

Do you feel comfortable talking about problems of racism? What if you are a member of a group that is perceived of as racist? _____

_____

What are some of your own experiences of discrimination? Were you discriminated against or did you do the discriminating?

_____

_____

How do the participants in your group feel about their own race?

_____

_____

What are some of the norms they have been exposed to in their families, neighborhoods, schools?

_____

_____

Has anyone in your family or ethnic group ever made you think—directly or indirectly—that looking white is better than looking Latino, Asian, Native American? What about the participants in your Group? _____

_____

Toy Store Dolls

Last year, my two sons were given some gift certificates for Christmas. A few weeks after the holiday, I took them to a large toy store chain. The boys were itching to use the certificates, and as usual they were totally overwhelmed by the selection. I knew I was destined to be there forever, so I sent them off hunting on their own and began wandering the aisles. I stopped at the doll section to check out what was available, and what I saw made me feel terrific. African American, Asian, Latina, Native American, and, of course, European dolls were all sitting there on the shelves. I certainly didn't have that kind of a selection as a child.

As I was standing there, feeling great and taking it all in, a little girl of European descent came down the aisle with her mother. The girl, about four years old, grabbed a black doll and said, "I want this one." Her mom answered in a whisper, saying, "No, not that one. Get this one," and picked up a white doll. The little girl, upset, shouted loudly, "But I want the black one! She looks like my friend." The mother grabbed the black doll out of her child's hand, put it back on the shelf, took up the white one, and announced to her daughter, "It's this one or none at all!" During this confrontation, the mother refused to look in my direction. I had an overwhelming urge to walk over to her and attempt to explain the zillion, far-reaching implications of what she did, but I was frozen to the spot, paralyzed by anger, grief, and astonishment.

Later, in the car, I told my boys about the scene I had witnessed and tried to explain to them why what she had done was wrong. If that woman had approved of her daughter's choice instead of showing her obvious dismay and disgust, she would have sent a message to her child that, no matter what, she supports her daughter's decisions, and that it's all right to have friends of a different color. Instead, she instilled a value judgment that black dolls are bad. Sooner or later, this message will become "your choice of a friend is bad."

Shannon

We have a very close friend who is Cape Verdean Portuguese. For political and social reasons, she identifies herself as black. Jackie has been married to John, a white Anglo-Saxon Protestant, for 25 years. They have three bright and beautiful daughters. We have been close friends with them for 24 of those 25 years.

When their oldest girl, Shannon, was three years old, Jackie told us the following story: Shannon was going to nursery school at a local Protestant church, and one day the class went on a field trip accompanied by some of the parents. The wee, sweet children—all of whom happened to be white—started calling Shannon black and teasing her about it. Jackie said to us, "I was getting upset, scared, worried, and I didn't know what to do. The funny thing was that Shannon wasn't upset at all. She just turned around, looked at the other kids, and announced, 'I am not black, I am beige.' And there was no further discussion!" What made Shannon so resilient in this situation? We honestly don't know for sure, but we do know that she had always received the same loud and clear message from her parents: they loved her for who she was, black, white, beige, and all. Categorically and with no exceptions.

Continuum

Color Blindness →Color Awareness

There are two sides to this issue. For whites, it's sometimes a matter of recognizing that being a person of color carries with it a unique history and special experiences in this country. If a white person walks into a room and says to an African American: "I see you as just another person, not white and not black," they are not only denying who the person is and what their experiences are, they are also indirectly denying that racism exists. They may also not even be aware of that denial until a teachable moment happens and someone takes advantage of it. Each of us wants others to validate our feelings, to understand that while every individual's experience is unique, feelings belong to all of us.

What about African Americans? Our society continuously sends up reminders about their skin color. Color blindness isn't a behavioral option, but denial is. Sharon, an African American, says, "I've never been color blind. But there were times in my life when I wanted to be color blind because it was easier. It was much easier than acknowledging the problems. At the beginning of my career, I just acted 'as if,' hoping that would make the problem go away."

Our friend Bart calls this the "D Train." "The denial train. I'm black, but there are things I need to get done personally and professionally. If I let all the baggage weigh me down, then I'm just not going to get stuff done. It's not blindness, it's denial."

Awareness

The color issue does exist. It's real and we can only go beyond it by acknowledging its existence.

If you act as though, or believe, that you don't see someone's color, perhaps you're not allowing yourself to see the full person. If we pretend that we're all human, that we all have the same problems, we might be neglecting an important aspect of someone else's life. Shouldn't we think about the impact our skin color has on the way other people treat us?

Group Skills

Self-definition—How we define ourselves far outweighs the perceptions others have of us. Who am I? What skills do I have to contribute to the groups I am a part of?

Validating others—Understanding ourselves is the first step. Listening and learning from others is the next. Everyone's feelings are valid and no one experiences them more or less than anyone else. How do the other people in the group define themselves?

Team playing—We're all different, but that doesn't mean better or worse. Together we're a lot stronger than we are on our own.

Conflict resolution—None of us agrees with everything that everyone else does. Many of us also feel uncomfortable when we challenge other people's opinions. Conflict is a normal part of our existence. What is important is that we learn to recognize our feelings, process them openly, and try to work peaceably through our disagreements.

Activities

■ Cross the Line

Activity Type:	De-Inhibitizer
Activity Level:	Moderate to high
Space:	A large open room or grassy field
Time:	About 15 minutes
Group Size:	More than 5 or 6
Prerequisite:	None
Props:	Masking tape or a rope to make a line; tape player and music (optional)

Opening

What we think about ourselves and who other people think we are often keeps us in a "box." Let's get out of our boxes and try to experience things differently than we ever have before.

Directions

Put your line down in a straight line about 20–25 feet away from the group and tell them that the line represents the threshold of looking at things differently. Ask the participants to cross the line one by one, and in a different way than the person before them. For example, if the first person skips, the next person could hop. Once all participants have crossed, ask them to return, only this time with a partner. Increase the group size by twos until the entire group crosses simultaneously. Ask the groups to synchronize their movements while they cross.

Option

You can play diverse ethnic music—Peruvian, Middle Eastern, polka, rap, country western, jazz, rock and roll—or music in a different language—Spanish, Hebrew, etc.—and use it as an opportunity to see how we feel and listen to music differently.

Diversity Skills

Cross the Line encourages groups to develop out-of-the-box thinking skills. Participants must make a consciously effort to move differently each time they *Cross the Line*.

Processing

- How did you decide you would cross the line—as an individual, as part of a pair, part of a group of four, etc.?

- Did the group accomplish their goal of doing things differently?

- What were some of your feelings and reactions to the music?

- How can we use music to learn about different cultures?

Pairs Tag ■

Activity Type:	De-Inhibitizer/Trust Building
Activity Level:	Moderate to high
Space:	A large, open indoor or outdoor space
Time:	About 10 minutes
Group Size:	6 or more
Prerequisite:	None

Opening

Do you have a favorite song that you hum a lot or that you identify with? Let's see how well you know that tune.

Directions

Have everyone pick a partner that they see as different from themselves in some way, then ask each pair to pick a song or tune they will use as a signal. Go around in a circle and ask each pair to demonstrate their song. Explain to the players that they will be playing tag with just their partners. Ask each pair to choose one player as "it." The "its" chase their own partners at a fast walk (no running). When the players who are "it" tag their partners, the "taggees" have to spin around twice while singing or humming their tune. Then they are "it" and get to go after the partner who just tagged them.

Diversity Skills

This activity is a great opportunity for your students to practice physical safety and working cooperatively with people who look different from themselves.

Processing Questions

■ How did you pick your partner? Why?

■ How did you decide on the tune you would sing?

■ What did you notice?

Levitation

Activity Type:	Trust Building
Activity Level:	Moderate
Space:	A room or outdoor space
Time:	45 minutes; if time permits, let everyone try who wants to.
Group Size:	Enough people to lift one member of the group safely over their heads.
Prerequisite:	Spotting skills, *Trust Leans*, and *Circle of Friends*
Props:	None

Opening

Feeling trust, warmth, and safety lifts up everyone's spirits and helps us see what's possible. Let's go for it.

Directions

Ask someone to volunteer to be a faller. Have them stand inside the circle formed by the rest of the group with their eyes closed. Have everyone place their hands on the faller's body, and ask them to get ready to raise the faller over their heads. Make sure to remind the group that the faller's physical safety is literally in their hands, and check that all of the body parts, particularly the head and shoulders, have enough people both lifting and spotting. The faller issues the commands, and when she's sure that the spotters are ready to spot, falls gently back into the waiting arms. The group should first get the faller's body parallel to the ground and then slowly raise it above their heads. Have them gently rock the person back and forth, and then slowly lower the levitated participant to the ground. At this point they can take their hands away. The "faller" should maintain a stiff and flat position throughout.

Diversity Skills

Levitation is an activity that involves quite a bit of physical contact and attention to taking care of one another. Such close contact and intensity works toward building allies across perceived difference and begins a process of looking at and accepting group identities, individual identity, gender and sexual orientation, physical and mental ability, class, etc..

Processing

■ Did you know how high off the ground you were?

■ What were your concerns?

■ How did you arrive at a level of trust?

■ Did any diversity issues come up?

Spider Web ■

Activity Type:	Group Initiative/Trust Building
Activity Level:	Moderately physical
Space:	Enough room to set up a *Spider's Web*; a soft floor
Time:	This activity can take anywhere from 45 minutes to a couple of hours. It really depends on how quickly your group gets frustrated and how much determination they have to achieve the goal you out for them.
Group Size:	6–12
Prerequisite:	*Trust Lean, Circle of Friends, Levitation* are helpful lead-ins. The group will be passing people in the air through the *Web,* so it's critical that they have learned to take care of each other physically and have good spotting skills.
Props:	A portable *Spider's Web,* available from Project Adventure, or you can fabricate your own.

Opening

This side of the web is the world as we know it today. Over on the other side, however, there's a world that's free of discrimination, anger, injustice, and dissing. Your goal is to get everyone in the group over to the other side so we can all be part of a free and just world. Because everyone creates their own world in a different way, you can only go through each hole once and then it's closed off to the group. Beware, each hole represents a possible solution, but if you touch the web around it, you'll destroy its potential for solving the problems of the world.

Building Your Own Web

Find two trees that stand about 10' apart from each other or plant two vertical support posts about 10' feet tall the same distance apart. Place 6 anchor points in these trees of posts—any type of substantial eye screw will work. Place these anchors at 7', 4', and 1' above ground level on each support.

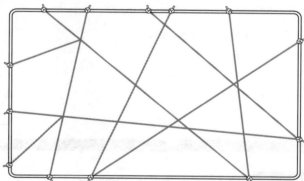

Start by tying one end of a nylon cord—our experts say that parachute cord works best—to any one of the anchor points and run the free end through the other anchors in sequence to make a rectangular frame. Be sure to take a turn around each anchor and pull the cord tight. Also tie a bunch of loops—figure eight or butterfly knots—in the framing cord while you're stringing it up. These loops will serve as the anchor points for the web strands.

Using the loop and anchors, construct a web arrangement. You can continue using the parachute cord or use small diameter bungee cord. Make sure you have enough holes for each member of the group to go through (double up if you need to), and make sure the size of the holes you create vary enough for people of all shapes and sizes to fit through without touching the cord.

You can also tie four or five bells anywhere on the web to alert you if someone passing through the web touches one of the strands.

Directions

The goal of the *Spider's Web* is to move every member of the group through it without touching the web material. If someone does touch, they have to start again, even if they have gotten through an opening.

The activity is more challenging if you stipulate that a web opening can be passed through only once. Each time someone goes through or fails in an attempt, that hole is closed off. But this only works if there are enough openings for each member of the group plus a few extras.

Diversity Skills

Agility and flexibility are issues that may be touched on during this activity, particularly in connection to weight, size, and height. Be mindful of the possibility that there may be some joking around this, and try to keep the group aware of their commitment to the Full Value Contract. At the same time, this is a wonderful activity for provoking discussion around how the group would like to make the world a better place for all of us, how each of us have a place, and some of the concrete ways your students can make these goals a reality at least within the context of the group.

Processing

This activity lends itself to discussion about whether or not the group successfully completes the challenge and what helped them succeed or caused them to fail. Here are some basic processing ideas, but you'll probably find yourself coming up with plenty as the group gets caught up in attempting to solve the activity.

- How did the group find a solution? Was everyone talking at once or did a leader or leaders emerge?

- Did you feel comfortable discussing your ideas with the group?

- Did anyone feel that the group wasn't listening to them? What did it feel like to be ignored? Why did you feel this way?

- How difficult was it to come up with a solution that worked for everyone?

- Did you feel uncomfortable when the rest of the group was passing you through the holes? Why?

- How do you think the group should have done the activity?

- Can you think of any problems in your lives where it's difficult or easy for a group to come up with a solution that works for all those involved?

- Do you think it's easier to plan when one person does the leading or talking or when everyone puts their heads together and listens to all the options? Why?

Racial Autobiography

Activity Type:	Trust Building
Activity Level:	Low
Space:	Your normal meeting place
Time:	About half an hour, or you can choose to do this activity as a homework assignment.
Group Size:	Any size
Prerequisite:	None
Props:	Pen and paper

Opening

If you're like me, you probably don't think about what it means to have electricity in your house. It's just there. But what if it starts going on and off all the time? It will probably then become something you think about all the time. Some of us don't have to think about what it means to be different from everyone else. This is a chance for us all to become more aware of where we come from.

Directions

Ask each person to write at least one paragraph on the following subjects:

What I knew about race when I was _____ (toddler, child, pre-teen, teenager, young adult).

A memory that I have involving race is when _____.

What I notice about race now is _____.

If you do this as a homework assignment, encourage participants to research the topic by talking to their family members and friends. Students don't have to share what they wrote with the group unless they want to do so with a partner. What is important is that they identify their feelings and write them down on paper.

Diversity Skills

Racial Autobiography, as we've set it up here, is specific to questions of racial identity. You can also frame the questions to reflect other aspects of individual identity, such as gender and sexual orientation, class, physical and mental ability, group identities, religion, and so on.

Processing

- How did you feel when you first heard the assignment?

- What feelings emerged for you?

- Where did you have difficulties?

- What was easy about the assignment?

- What did you learn?

- How did it feel to share what you wrote with a partner?

- What are you feeling right now?

Key Punch

Activity Type:	Group Initiative
Activity Level:	Moderate to high
Space:	A gym or playing field with at least 15' by 30' of open space
Time:	45 minutes to an hour
Group Size:	10 to 15 or more
Prerequisite:	None
Props:	Thirty gym markers numbered from one to thirty with a permanent marker. Enough rope to make a 15' x 30' rectangle on the gym floor or field. If you don't have, or can't afford 30 gym spots, use circular flexible plastic container caps, like those covering a tennis ball can. Don't forget to number the caps.

Opening

A militant group of nihilistic hackers have injected a very virulent virus into the government's Socially Serious Program. You represent the government's best chance to create a computer de-bugging program that will expel the virus and save billions of dollars.

To achieve their goal, this highly trained group of viral professionals must physically touch all 30 gym spots in numbered sequence as quickly as possible.

All limbered up? Let's banish that virus!

Directions

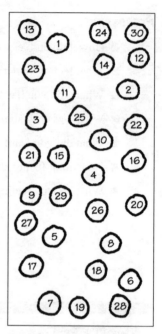

Don't be put off by the length of this description! *Key Punch* is easy to present and is more difficult to do than it seems.

Make a 15' by 30' rectangle with the rope and place the numbered spot markers (starting with #1), orienting them as illustrated.

The plan is to have all even numbers on one side of the rectangle and all odd numbers on the other side. Also zigzag the numbers up and down the rectangle. As you place the numbers, try to arrange them so that your odd/even and zigzag planning is not obvious. (Note that numbers 1 and 30 are located at the end of the rectangle farthest away from the starting line.)

When placing the spots, put them more than one step inside the boundary. This added distance forces the people touching the keypads to step inside the boundary, not just reach over the edge.

Thirty feet from the end of the gym-spotted rectangle, put down a length of tape or rope to designate a starting line and to mark the planning area.

Rules and Considerations

The entire group must begin and finish behind the start line. The stop-watch starts when the first person steps over the line and stops when the last person crosses back over the line.

Only one person can be on the keyboard at a time. That is, only one participant can be inside the boundary rope. If two people are inside the rope simultaneously, a glitch occurs and a penalty time is added to the score.

If any number is touched out of sequence (for example, 3 then 5), this infraction causes the computer to crash and a penalty time is added to the score.

Any part of the body may be used to touch each numbered gym spot in sequence.

The team cannot walk back to the computer area between attempts in order to study the number setup. All planning must occur behind the line where the group starts each round. Any time the group or a player crosses this line, it is considered an attempt.

Tell the group that they have 30 minutes or five attempts, whichever comes first. If they use five attempts in 18 minutes, they're done; if they try only three times in 30 minutes, they're done.

Penalties

Something suitably devastating is appropriate so that the group will want to avoid errors. Ten seconds per infraction seems to have a reasonable effect; besides, it's easy to add the penalty seconds and then adjust the time.

Diversity Skills

This is a great activity for helping your group develop cooperative problem-solving skills on just about any topic.

Processing

- How well did you work together as a group?
- What were some of your challenges?
- What issues emerged for the group?

Key Punch Phase II

Activity Type:	Group Initiative
Activity Level:	Moderate to high
Space:	Same as for *Key Punch*
Time:	1 1/2 hours
Group Size:	10 to 15 people
Prerequisite:	Read the directions carefully and don't try this one unless you are sure that your group is ready for some challenging questions on racial identity and discrimination in our society.
Props:	Same as for *Key Punch*, with the addition of a wristband for each participant. Use equal numbers of three different colored wristbands.

Opening

You can open this activity the same way you did the last one or think up your own fantasy challenge!

Directions

Add the following twist to put a diversity spin on this activity:

Have each participant put on a wrist band (distribute the colors randomly).

Give the group a few minutes to plan. Then announce that anyone wearing a blue wristband cannot participate.

Let them plan a few more minutes. Now tell them that anyone wearing a red wristband cannot participate. Ask them to sit out with the blue group.

Give the remaining green group two more minutes to plan and have them attempt the activity.

Ask the green group if they want to invite the other groups back in, but tell them that they can only choose one. See what happens.

Tell them you made a mistake and both groups can be included.

Diversity Skills

Phase II of this activity is specific to the work you will be doing with your group on racial identity—awareness of the impact of active oppression, risk taking, self-affirmation, listening without judgment.

Processing

■ How did it feel to be the superior group—green—and be allowed to play when the others couldn't?

■ How did it feel to be in one of the groups that was discriminated against and couldn't participate?

■ What could the green group have done to include the other two groups? Why did they or didn't they include the others?

■ How did you feel about participating or not participating in this activity?

■ How did you work together or not work together to address the problems that came up during this exercise?

■ Have any of you ever felt excluded from a group and not allowed to join in? If so, could you share what it felt like to you at the time?

■ How does this activity relate to the problems of injustice, power, discrimination, and prejudice in our society?

The Diversity Spectrum

Activity Type: Social Responsibility

Activity Level: Low

Space: Your regular meeting room

Time: 30 to 45 minutes

Group Size: Five or more

Prerequisite: None

Props: Blackboard or easel paper, Post-its, chalk or a felt marker

Opening

Think for a minute about how other people identify you. What do you think stands out the most about our identities?

Directions

Draw two circles or squares, one inside the other, on the blackboard or piece of easel paper. Using Post-its, list one of these components on each piece—race, age, gender, ethnicity, sexual orientation, and physical/mental ability. Stick these to the inner circle or square. These are your primary dimensions of diversity.

Ask the group to brainstorm a list of what they feel are the secondary dimensions of diversity. Explain to them that the outer circle includes the things we like or don't like, the things we can change about ourselves, and the personal tastes that make us different from others. Some of these could be: religion, where you live, sports you play, musical interests, the group you hang out with, dating status, socioeconomic level, etc. Have them choose what is important in their lives and what they feel influences how they see the world and how the world sees them.

When the group is done, ask them to stand in a circle and have each person, one at a time, select a Post-it from the outer square, describing what it means to them. Ask participants to be specific, if possible, and give examples. Let two or more people talk about the same component if they want, but try to cover all the ideas they came up with for the spectrum.

When everyone has said all they want to about the outer circle, ask them to pick one of the six primary dimensions in the middle and have them describe what it means to them.

Diversity Skills

The *Diversity Spectrum* is a great activity for encouraging your group to speak about the process of developing a strong, healthy personal identity.

Processing

- How did you decide what you were going to speak about?

- Did anyone say something that sparked an idea in you and encouraged you to speak out? What was it?

- Were you surprised by any information that was shared?

- How did you feel physically while sharing? Where in your body did you feel it?

- How were you validated by the group while sharing?

Stereotyping

Activity Type:	Social Responsibility
Activity Level:	Low
Space:	Your usual meeting room
Time:	An hour and a half
Group Size:	Any size
Prerequisite:	Don't try this activity unless you feel your group is talking openly about racial issues and has developed a high level of emotional trust.
Props:	Sheets of paper with the name of a racial group written on the top, pens

Opening

All groups have stereotypes that have been handed down through the ages. How do you think those stereotypes hurt or help the self-image of the people who belong to those groups?

Directions

Give each participant a sheet of paper with one of the following racial categories written at the top: African American, Caucasian, Hispanic, Asian, Native American. Ask them to list all the stereotypes they can think of about that group on their piece of paper.

When they have finished writing their lists, put the students into homogenous racial groups of four or fewer students and have them each share and discuss what they came up with. Allow about 30 minutes for this portion of the activity.

Then, put together each of the small, homogenous groups. You'll end up with two or more large groups, depending on the racial breakdown of your students. Ask each student to read two stereotypes out loud to the other groups. No one is allowed to speak until everyone has read from their list.

If the racial breakdown of your group is uneven or you have only one or two students to represent a particular group, use the categories below to generate questions.

Generate a discussion around the questions that appear in the processing section of this activity.

Phase II

Expand the categories to include some of the following groups.

Religion: Catholic, Jewish, Protestant, Buddhist, Islamic

Ethnicity: Polish, Italian, English, Jamaican, Haitian, Cuban, Puerto Rican, Chinese, Korean, Indian

Gender and Sexual Orientation: Male, female, lesbian, homosexual, bisexual

Geographical: West Coast, East Coast, Southerner, Midwesterner

Process in a similar manner.

Diversity Skills

This activity can be adapted to any of the topics in this workbook according to the categories you select.

Processing

- Were you comfortable doing this activity? Were you more comfortable by yourself or in a small group? Would you have been less comfortable if your small group was more diverse? Why or why not?

- Why do you think stereotypes are so difficult to discuss? What can we gain from discussing stereotypes?

- What was it like to write down the stereotypes?

- Were you uncomfortable listing the stereotypes??

- How easy was it to think up the stereotypes?

- What do you think can be done to fight the stereotypes?

Just Because

Activity Type:	Social Responsibility
Activity Level:	Low
Space:	Your usual meeting room
Time:	An hour and a half
Group Size:	Enough to divide into three groups of 4 or 5
Prerequisite:	This activity asks that the members of your group put themselves into a racial category. Not everyone will feel comfortable with this. Make sure that everyone feels comfortable in one of the categories, and if this isn't the case, process the feeling immediately with the group.
Props:	Index cards and pencils

Opening

How do you deal with the assumptions that others make about who you are? What are some of the ways you can deal with them in a positive as opposed to a resentful manner?

Directions

Divide into three groups. Ask the participants to select their own group.

Group I: People of color; African American, Asian, Hispanic, Native American

Group II: White, Caucasian, European

Group III: Mixed racial heritage

If there is only one student with a particular heritage, it is the leader's responsibility to participate in this activity with this student. You need to be prepared to help with the group's interactions. It is probably best to have two leaders for this activity so that no one feels left out.

Ask the participants to complete the following statement with the members of their group. Tell them they will be sharing their answers with the larger group.

Just because I'm (self-identified racial group), don't assume that_____ .

Give the small groups enough time to discuss the feelings this statement generates for them. When everyone is ready, ask each person from the small groups to stand up facing the other two groups and complete the sentence. The other groups do not respond during the first round of this activity. Ask them to just sit and listen to what others have to say. If necessary, let the groups have more than one turn at completing the sentence.

When each group has had a chance to share their answers, process what happened when they were in the smaller groups and when they shared their thoughts with the larger group.

Diversity Skills

Racial identity

Processing

■ How did you feel when you were asked to identify with a racial group?

■ What was it like being with people like you and sharing information?

■ What was your first thought when you realized that you were going to be sharing information with the larger group?

■ How did you feel when you had to just listen and couldn't ask for clarification on the information the others were presenting?

■ Did you notice anything special about your body language?

Just Because, Part II

Directions

Have everyone go back into their racial groups and make up a list of all the questions they wanted to ask but couldn't during the first part of the activity. Give everyone a chance to share their questions and listen to the answers. Again, remember Challenge by Choice. Go over the ground rules for asking questions with the group. Not everyone may feel comfortable with certain questions.

Processing

■ How did you feel about asking questions?

■ How did you feel about being asked a question?

■ What did you need from this group in order to go through this process?

Closing Activities

Key Words

Get a big piece of easel paper and some felt pens and ask the members of the group to brainstorm key words that describe their experiences for this session.

Start and Stop

Give each participant two small sheets of paper with the following statements at the top of each page: "One thing I am going to start doing in my life" and "One thing that I am going to stop doing in my life." Ask them to write their responses, relating them directly to what they have learned from the group activities that day. When they've all had a chance to write down their replies, ask them to form a circle and place a garbage can in the middle. Invite each participant to read what they are going to start doing and then tell them to toss what they are going to stop doing into the garbage can without reading it out loud. Next time you meet, have them review how they did with their commitment to start doing and stop doing.

Play a Song!

Play a song that has a meaning for the group. Have everyone just sit in a circle and listen. Ask them to bring in songs that have a special meaning for them.

Personal Journal Questions

What was the most painful thing for you to share today about your racial identity? What did you share that made you the most proud?

Processing Questions

- ❏ Is it difficult for you to avoid judging others? Explain.

- ❏ Can you think of examples of when you judged others in the group today? When you didn't judge others?

- ❏ What were some advantages to you of not judging others?

- ❏ What were some advantages to others of your not judging them?

- ❏ How does judging and not judging others affect the completion of the activity?

- ❏ Were some behaviors of others easy not to judge and other behaviors difficult?

- ❏ Did the group arrive at any decisions through group consensus (some didn't get their first choice, but they could live with the decision)?

- ❏ Were some decisions made by one or several individuals?

- ❏ Did everyone in the group express an opinion when a choice was available? If not, why not?

- ❏ What is the best way for this group to make decisions? Explain.

- ❏ Do you respond in similar ways in other groups?

- ❏ What did you like about how the group made decisions? What didn't you like?

- ❏ What have you learned about trust, respect, acceptance, and cooperation as they relate to differences?

- ❏ Did you find yourself responding to any stereotypes? What were they? How do you think you might respond to the same situation in the future?

❏ What has changed for you as a result of participating in this activity? How do you think you'll perceive people who are different from you (blacks, whites, gays, or whoever is appropriate) as a result?

❏ How does this activity relate to the real-life experiences you are faced with at home, in school, in your neighborhood?

❏ What did it feel like to ask for help from someone you used to think of as a member of a group that wouldn't help or support you?

❏ Was there any kind of discrimination going on this activity? If so, what?

❏ What was the most difficult part of this activity as it relates to how you deal with people who are different from you?

❏ What was the easiest part of this activity as it relates to how you deal with people who are different from you?

❏ Did this activity challenge any of your beliefs?

❏ What are your feelings now?

❏ Is there anything in this activity you would do differently and why?

❏ As a result of this activity, what are some of the things you think or feel that we all have in common?

❏ Do you think there are more commonalties or differences between _____ and _____?

❏ What will you remember most about having participated in this activity?

11

Gender and Sexual Orientation

From our earliest moments, gender influences the way we are treated. Regardless of gender, all children need support, care, and encouragement. We have become more aware of the effects on children of treating boys and girls differently, yet this unequal treatment is still pervasive in schools, churches, government, and in our homes. Most of this inequality is not based on research but is rooted in our history and our cultural backgrounds.

The struggle to create equal footing for women and men is being waged both privately and publicly. The atmosphere today is perhaps the most aware and equal ever, but the scales still tip back and forth, trying to establish a balance between the ideal of total equality and the traditions that place men and women in very different roles.

As soon as we begin to differentiate ourselves from the people around us and begin to absorb the unconscious examples of our parents, friends, and teachers we learn what it means to be a girl or a boy. What we learn may come to us as unconsciously as what we eat, how we dress (at least early on), and what our ambitions are. The meanings that lie deep within the terms boy, girl, man, and woman are powerful undercurrents in our interactions with others. The way children play with one another is practice for real-life situations later on.

Two principal theories—nature and nurture—have dominated most discussions concerning the development of gender identity. Proponents of the nature theory argue that our gender roles and personalities are determined by our biology or reproductive functions. Women naturally tend to become tender and loving mothers while men develop into aggressive hunters and dominant leaders. Nature theorists contend that we are happiest when fulfilling the roles that nature has determined for us. Defenders of the nurture theory argue that influences from our environment—parents, peers, teachers, and other role models—have a greater influence on the development of our gender identities. Our culture pressures men to conform to masculine stereotypes and women to female ones. Both of these theories are plausible; men and women are different physiologically and we do respond consciously and unconsciously to others according to stereotyped preconceptions.

Adventure activities can provide a way for many of these unconsciously developed, deeply rooted understandings to come to the surface, particularly during the processing stage. Have your groups examine some of the stereotypes that prevail in our language and media about how boys versus girls are supposed to behave. You may want to brainstorm a list of "typical" male and female behaviors and ask your group to reflect on how these preconceptions affect the way they interact with each other during the activities.

Sexism in the United States

The equal rights movement of the 1970s brought sexism to the forefront of our consciousness. We continue to uncover and attempt to eradicate the subtle ways that sexist behavior persists in our society. For the most part, sexist behavior has become something most often perpetrated by the insidious "they"—the Bad Guys. The challenge for people working with youth today is to call attention not only to the obvious behaviors that perpetuate stereotypes and denigrate women and girls, but also to the images in the media that influence us and to the indirect ways we continue to participate in sexist views even as we work to remove them.

We are all familiar with the research showing that the self-esteem of girls plummets as they reach the age of ten or eleven; that in school, vocal boys are called on more frequently than girls. These findings are useful, but we still need new tools for creating an environment that treats young boys and girls equally.

If eliminating sexism is truly our goal, we have three important tasks before us: first, to discover ways of working with youth that will effectively combat the stereotypes of men and women in our culture; second, to look within ourselves and become aware of how we perpetuate sexist views in our thoughts and behavior (seeing the problem as "out there," instead of "in here"); and third, to promote open environments that are supportive of youth as individuals, as boys and girls who are different and equal.

Adventure activities work well as a means of breaking down the stereotypes and internalized sexism that we have consciously or unconsciously passed on to our youth. Many of these stereotypes become entrenched because of different physical, emotional, and mental characteristics. As your students test themselves physically, the activities will help them gradually become aware of real physical abilities versus the stereotypes they hold.

All of us can fall unwittingly back into these assumptions. In the preface, we told the story of how both of us had assumed that only the men would do one of the high elements on the ropes course during our Project Adventure workshop. We proved ourselves wrong! Emotionally, adventure activities tend to bring laughter, smiles, tears, hugs, and frustration to men and women alike. Mentally, each and every one of the members of your group will have the chance to test their problem-solving and cooperative skills and see the results. As you process the activities and your group begins to cohere, they will naturally come around to talking together about some of the assumptions they have made.

Preferential Treatment/Unequal Treatment

Through our own participation in our sons' school communities and environments, we've found that some of the following conditions still exist. The list is by no means exhaustive, and some of the points may not hold true in your own community. We are offering this list to get you started on thinking of some of the ways that you see boys and girls treated unequally. We hope it will help increase your own awareness of some of the unconscious assumptions we all make about gender differences.

Boys still tend to excel over girls in the areas of math and science.

In classroom settings, teachers still tend to call on boys more than on girls.

Far less money—and this translates into fewer scholarships—is put into college scholarships for girls in sports than for boys in sports.

By the age of 11, many girls begin to question and stifle their zest for learning.

As we did our own informal market study, we found that the number of computer and electronic games on store shelves that are geared toward girls is still limited. This is important because, besides being fun, these games teach the computer skills the next generation will need for professional advancement.

Boys are still discouraged from participating in artistic activities but are encouraged to take part in any type of sport.

Toy companies, too, seem to discourage the notion that little boys should like, want, and play with dolls. Dolls for boys are called "action figures." We wonder, is this a subtle message that males cannot and should not be nurturing figures for children?

Sexual Orientation

When exploring the subject of sexual orientation with teenagers, the concept of self-definition cannot be stressed enough. It is not for us as facilitators to judge and label the youth that we work with. It is for them to define themselves. Adventure activities are designed to create trust and a structure that will foster open discussion. It would be inappropriate to ask everyone in your group to share their sexual orientation or to create other opportunities that risk outing someone who is not prepared to reveal their sexual orientation, whatever it may be. If you sense that personal information may be discussed, it may be appropriate to add confidentiality to the Full Value Contract.

On the other hand, if one of your participants suddenly shares that they are questioning their sexual orientation, your reaction or lack of reaction will guide the group through the most appropriate responses. It is important that you pause and validate their feelings instead of continuing on as though nothing has been said. Guide the conversation appropriately, stating the obvious, if necessary. "You're feeling comfortable enough to share this with the whole group. What can the group do for you now and how are the others in the group feeling about this?" Stay open and reassuring so that the group will feel comfortable continuing the discussion and processing their feelings openly.

Gay, Lesbian, Bisexual, and Heterosexual Youth

Just when we feel we are making progress on sexism and how it relates to youth, homophobia comes into the picture.

Recently there has been a debate in our public schools about the right of gay, lesbian, and bisexual students to meet in clubs or organizations sponsored by the schools. The feeling is that as responsible adults we should not be "promoting" this type of "abnormal behavior." This thought could not be further from the truth. This workbook is centered around the concept that all youth have the right to define themselves, to be treated with respect, and to be acknowledged for who they are as individuals.

As we discuss certain types of discrimination more in depth, it is essential that we look more closely at this basic concept. Much as many of us would prefer not to examine the assumptions we make about gay, lesbian, and bisexual youth and adults, an exploration of how this concept of self-definition looks in specific situations is critical to learning how to treat our youth as individuals. Here are some thoughts to keep in mind when working with gay, lesbian, and bisexual youth.

Emerging Identity

It is important when working with gay, lesbian, and bisexual youth to remain aware that their sexual identity is in the process of developing. Awareness of their sexual identity and "difference" may have been with them since early in life, but awareness of same-sex attraction commonly develops later, between the ages of eight and fourteen (*Being Homosexual*). Theories about the development of homosexual identity are complex and varied. We do not feel that it is within the scope of this book to cover them in depth. If you would like to do more reading on this subject, please refer to the back of this chapter and Appendix IV for a list of resources. The good news is that there are more resources available today than ever before. Gay, lesbian, and bisexual youth, and those who are wondering about their identity, are growing up with the possibility of a more open environment than has ever existed in our society.

One persistent problem for these youth is that the adults who deal with them are often rooted in biases that are nearly impossible to escape. We each help to create the closet that keeps youth from talking openly about their feelings.

For this reason it is important that you spend time identifying and working through your own feelings, and then go on to examine how you are going to deal with these subjects with your group. The activities we have selected for this book are designed to create an environment where differences, self-definition, and open, honest, and caring discussion of the issues that make up our identities will happen. Responsible facilitation of these activities requires compassion, sensitivity, and an understanding of youth in a variety of life situations. We have included a number of worksheet questions on sexual bias and gay, lesbian, and transgender issues and strongly suggest that you think about these questions on your own before working through these topics with your group.

Transgender Youth

Transgender is an umbrella term used to describe transsexuals, cross-dressers (transvestites), intersexed people (hermaphrodites), and others whose sexual identity does not fit into definitions of "normal" males and females.

A transsexual is someone who feels that their physical gender, or anatomy, does not correspond with their emotional and psychological gender identity. A transsexual can be either male or female. Generally transsexuals try to resolve their anatomical/identity conflict through a sex-change operation, but hormonal methods, either estrogen or androgen therapy, are a viable alternative for some. The term transsexual refers to "both pre- and post-operative men and women, though once surgery is completed the new identity of male or female is preferred" (*Grolier Multimedia Encyclopedia*).

Transvestites, or cross-dressers, are usually males who "experience sexual satisfaction from dressing in clothing generally worn by the opposite sex. Most transvestites are heterosexual and are not interested in changing, by way of sex reassignment surgical procedures, into the opposite sex…. Apart from their cross-dressing, which may be only occasional, transvestites tend to be conventional in their sexual habits and often marry" (*Grolier Multimedia Encyclopedia*).

Hermaphrodites "may have either one ovary and one testis or gonads containing a combination of ovarian and testicular components. The genitals may be female or male or some combination of both, and some hermaphrodites are capable of having sexual intercourse with either sex" (*Grolier Multimedia Encyclopedia*). Babies born with this condition are sometimes surgically altered to either male or female depending, usually, on how easy the medical procedure will be. Difficulties arise, however, when the gender that was selected for medical reasons, and hence becomes the way the child is environmentally raised, does not fit the child's own internal gender identification.

While certain aspects of blurred gender lines have become more mainstream in recent decades, others have not. While you may not have to deal directly with these subjects in your groups, it's important that you work through your own assumptions on the questions of transgender youth. Try to keep your information factual instead of based on the images we receive via the media. While the increased visibility of transgender individuals has spurred some positive images, the media still tends to prefer exposing us to negative ones.

Transgender youth will be struggling with their own set of identity issues as they arrive at their own identity. Knowing that clear gender boundaries exist can be a source of comfort for group members who are taking risks and exploring new territory. Try to stay aware that comments about stereotypical gender behavior may be their way of staying in an emotionally and psychologically safe place. Peer pressure will tend toward clarity of category, where boundaries (of all types) are marked.

Concluding Thoughts

Become aware of how you use language and what your assumptions are about gender characteristics.

Notice and speak out when you see that you or someone else in the group has made an assumption, spoken or not, about how someone's gender will detract from or add to an activity.

Acknowledge that males and females are different physically, but encourage discussion about whether our emotional differences are caused by our socialization or by physical differences.

Encourage discussion about how and why gender differences and identity may make us more or less self-confident during activities and in our lives.

Sex has traditionally been a subject that we all feel more or less uncomfortable talking about. Sexual orientation is even more of a taboo subject. It is our responsibility to be open with our youth and convey the message that talking about sexual orientation—specifically gay, lesbian, and bisexual—does not encourage sexual experimentation, but instead helps us learn more about who we are becoming and who we know ourselves to be.

Creating a positive environment for gay, lesbian, and bisexual youth can be a daunting task, especially if we are not used to the concept. What follows is a list of concrete actions that can make the difference between an environment that is hostile or indifferent and one that is caring and supportive:

- Use inclusive, non-homophobic language: partner, lover, significant other in place of (or in addition to) girlfriend, boyfriend, wife, husband; sexual orientation in place of sexual preference. Use the words gay, lesbian, and bisexual. Don't dismiss this language as politically correct.

- Respond to homophobic behavior in yourself and the youth you work with. Tolerate no jokes, comments, actions, or behaviors that are anti-gay.

- Emphasize the positive aspects of homosexuality. Include gay, lesbian, and bisexual resources in your collection.

- Don't assume everyone is heterosexual.

- Don't assume you are reading the signals correctly. Become aware of and free yourself from gender stereotypes, and lesbian and gay stereotypes.

- Take the risk of talking with youth about homosexuality and heterosexuality.

- Take the risk of discussing gay, lesbian, and bisexual issues with colleagues.

- Discuss the benefits of allowing people to be open about their sexual orientation and the drawbacks of closed environments that do not encourage "outing."

Suggested Reading

Goldberg. *Shunning 'He' and 'She',* They Fight for Respect." New York Times, September 8, 1996.

Isay, Richard, MD. *Being Homosexual: Gay Men and Their Development.* Northvale, NJ: Jacob Aronson, Inc., 1995.

Baker-Miller, J. *Toward a New Psychology of Women.* Boston: Beacon Press, 1986. Author redefines women's experience and its social/political reflection.

Cheeseboro, James W. *Gay Speak: Gay Male and Lesbian Communications.* Pilgrim Press, 1981.

Gilligan, Carol. *In a Different Voice: Psychological Theory and Women's Development.* Cambridge: Harvard University Press, 1993. "The most insightful book on women, men and the differences between them."

Marcus, Eric. *Is It A Choice? Answers to 300 of the Most Frequently Asked Questions about Gays and Lesbians.* New York: Harper Collins Publishers, 1993.

Parr, Susan. *Homophobia; A Weapon of Sexism,* Little Rock, Ark: Susan Parr, The Women's Project, 1988. A little book about the effect of homophobia and sexism in personal/organizational lives.

Pipher, Mary. *Reviving Ophelia: Saving the Selves of Adolescent Girls.* New York: G.P. Putnam and Sons, 1994.

Schaef, Anne Wilson. *Women's Reality: An Emerging Female System in a White Male Society.* San Francisco: Harper & Row, 1981. A surprising look at gender discrimination issues.

Robinson-Harris, Tracy, and Ritch C. Savin-Williams. *Beyond Pink and Blue: Exploring Stereotypes of Sexuality and Gender.* Boston: Unitarian Universalist Association, 1994. This book invites thirteen to fifteen year olds to examine their cultural understandings of sexuality and gender roles, and the operation of gender stereotypes and prejudice on their lives.

Worksheet

Gender Identity and Sexism

Can you list some of the assumptions you hold about male and female abilities in sports, the arts, sciences, literature, business, and other fields of human endeavor? _____

_____

What are some of the ways the media perpetuate stereotypical images of males and females? _____

_____

How has your gender affected your professional life? Has it made you more or less self-confident about seeking promotions and getting ahead? _____

_____

Can you think of different ways that language affects the values we give to male and female characteristics? _____

_____

Do you feel that an important dream or goal went unfulfilled because your parents did not offer you proper guidance or direction or seemed not to care during adolescence? Do you feel that you would be doing something very different if they had given you more encouragement? _____

_____

Was power evenly divided between your parents, or was your father "the ruler of the roost"? How did you feel about the division of power in your household?

_____

_____

If you come from a family with siblings, were the males favored over the females? Were you raised to believe that girls were less capable or deserving than boys? _____

_____

If you could do it all over again, what would you change about your adolescence? _____

_____

Worksheet
(Continued)

Sexual Orientation

How do you feel about other people's sexual orientation, particularly gay, lesbian, bisexual, or transsexual? _____

_____

Do you feel prepared to answer questions about these issues and process them if they come up in the group? _____

_____

How would you deal with the subject of sexual orientation and process it in a group setting? _____

_____

How do you feel about how you were raised? Do you think your family gave you ample support, unconditional love, and validation? How has this affected your present relationships? _____

_____

How do you feel about the media attention devoted to gay and lesbian issues? Do you feel that it is important for us, as a society, to become more open and knowledgeable about gay and lesbian issues? _____

_____

Marie's Story

Marie, an Italian American, first came to the mental health clinic to be treated for depression when she was 15 and a sophomore in high school. The cause of her depression was identified as her mother's alcoholism. Marie's mother had divorced her father six years earlier, and Marie was living with her mother and older sister, Carla. Most of the work with Marie was focused on ridding her of the emotional responsibility she felt for her mother's binges and sister's immaturity.

After a few years, her mother went into recovery and her sister moved out of the house. Marie seemed better, but she still wasn't terribly happy. She had friends, but her friends seemed to be taking her mother's place. They were people who needed to be taken care of and nurtured. One was a pregnant teen and the other a gay male who was beaten and harassed at school because of his sexual orientation. Marie often complained that she didn't have any love relationships. She and her therapist talked about what Marie was looking for in a boyfriend and thought up ways for her to meet young men. The prom came and went with no date. Marie's therapy ended when she went away to college.

On her first winter vacation she stopped by the clinic and told her therapist that all the time she was in counseling she had been struggling with the dilemma of her sexual identity. Marie was a lesbian. "When I got to college," she said, " I took a deep breath and walked into the gay/lesbian student alliance meeting. I felt instantly accepted by my true peer group and got the support I needed so much."

Owning Our Own Feelings of Sexism

As trainers for the A World of Difference Institute of the ADL, we often have groups participate in an activity called *Concentric Circles*. The activity has individuals rotating as pairs, responding to questions and comments that get significantly more difficult as we go on. One of these questions is, "Share with your partner something you cannot do or were not allowed to do because of your gender." Participants are then asked not to use the "bathroom" thing as a way to cop out.

We particularly remember one instance when we were processing the activity. One gentleman responded, "You know, when you asked that question my first response was to think WHY WOULD I WANT TO DO ANYTHING LIKE A FEMALE?" He continued with "What got me is I have four daughters. How could I think such a thing.... I had no idea I was so sexist."

Continuum

Sexist Behavior →Recognition of Sexism →Protesting Sexism →Respecting Equality and Individuality

Hostility →Recognition of Difference →Supporting the Right to be Different →Open Communication on Issues of Sexual Orientation

Many of us recognize sexist behavior but continue to condone it in subtle ways by refusing to speak out against it. As we begin to develop our awareness of the ways that sexism infuses our language, thoughts, and everyday behavior, it's important to begin speaking up. Our words and actions can and will help generate a society that views everyone as equal, but individual.

Questions of sexual orientation often generate hostility and violence. At the risk of provoking these reactions, many of us prefer to remain silent or avoid examining our own biases. Consequently, many of our youth are raised with confused, often conflicting messages about their sexual identities and orientation. While we are not advocating confrontational behavior, we do feel that it is important to be vocal and stand up for the necessity of open discussion on questions of sexual orientation. Open discussion will encourage all of us to recognize our own biases and provide youth with environments that encourage learning and demystify much of their confusion.

Awareness

In order to build self-esteem in both girls and boys, we need to value gender differences and similarities.

Our culture presents powerful images to both boys and girls about how they are expected to behave. Discovering where the signals come from, in the media and through a range of role models (family, community, celebrities), and how these signals influence youth are critical steps toward untangling the messages. As facilitators, we need to make every effort to understand the messages and to be positive role models ourselves.

Verbal and non-verbal homophobia and heterosexist messages permeate the lives of youth, regardless of their individual sexual orientation. Creating a positive atmosphere under these conditions takes knowledge, persistence, and a willingness to talk about sexual orientation and identity.

Group Skills

Acknowledgment—Inequality and discrimination do exist. One of the first steps we can take is to recognize them when we see them.

Increased awareness—As we begin to acknowledge instances of inequality, our awareness naturally grows stronger. Awareness can be a great help in dispelling our fears and promoting increased sensitivity to gender issues as well as issues of sexual orientation.

De-escalation—Youth reflect the prevalent attitudes in our society and the messages they hear via the media and their families, caregivers, and educators. Open discussions about discrimination and sexual orientation will help them de-escalate many of their fears and encourage them to dispel the myths around these issues among their peers.

Support and validation—As fears are dispelled, your groups will learn to support and validate personal choice and freedom. At the same time, they will realize that they are earning the same treatment for themselves.

Activities

Bottoms Up

Activity Type:	De-Inhibitizer
Activity Level:	Moderate
Space:	A soft grassy field
Time: About	15 minutes
Group Size:	Any size
Prerequisite:	Requires some physical strength
Props	None

Opening

Let's get down and try to move our rear ends up!

Directions

Split your group into pairs and have each pair sit on the ground facing one another, with the bottoms of their feet against the bottoms of their partner's feet (sole sharing, we call it). Legs should be bent, feet held high, and posteriors fairly close to one another. Then, while putting all their weight on their arms, have them attempt to push against their partner's feet until both of their derrieres come off the ground. They will notice a tightening of the triceps muscles in their arms, considerable laughter, and not much vertical movement on the first couple of tries.

Diversity Skills

You might have so much laughter going on that there won't be a whole lot to talk about, but you can have the group discuss what effect, if any, their preconceived notions about gender, size, ability, etc. had on their ability to cooperate.

Processing

Ask if the size or strength of their partners made it easier or harder to lift their posteriors off the ground. What kind of assumptions did they make about strength and balance? Were they valid?

Red Baron Stretch

Activity Type:	Ice Breaker
Activity Level:	Low
Space:	Your meeting room or an outdoor spot
Time:	About 10 to 15 minutes
Group Size:	Any size
Prerequisite:	None
Props:	None

Opening

It's W.W. II and Snoopy's back fighting the Red Baron. The going's tough and they're all over the sky. Who's going to win, Snoopy or his archenemy?

Directions

Have the group pretend that each one of their hands is an airplane engaging in an aerial dogfight. The right hand is the Red Baron, the left hand, Snoopy. The planes can chase each other anywhere that body and arm movements allow, but they must keep their feet comfortably placed and stationary at all times. When you demonstrate, you might want to add the oral gunfire that sounds so natural to this exercise. To add a bit of cooperation to the dogfight, ask one person to be the Red Baron and another to be Snoopy, right hand to left hand, for example. All movements must be in slow motion so that the participants can stay in sync with one another.

Diversity Skills

Red Baron is good for just getting everyone a little loose, silly, and ready for a day of fun activities.

Processing

Again, there's not a whole lot of processing to this exercise. Don't push it if the group is feeling relaxed, but you might want to see if anyone has ever thought about which parts of their body feel more masculine or feminine as they stretch and move.

Yeah, But

Activity Type:	Trust Building
Activity Level:	Moderate
Space:	A gym or open field
Time:	About half an hour
Group Size:	Any size
Prerequisite:	We've said it before, and we'll probably say it again: trust is a fragile commodity and, once it's broken, it's hard to rebuild. Make sure you can count on your spotters to be responsible and do the activity without any unnecessary fooling around.
Props:	Blindfolds

Opening

You're on a mission to fight discrimination. But it isn't going to be easy. You never know what kind of preconceived ideas you might bump into!

Directions

Ask one member of the group to stand at one end of a basketball court with their back to the wall. Have the person assume the hands-up/palms-out-at-chest-height, protect-yourself position (bumpers-up). At this juncture, the individual is either blindfolded or has committed to keep their eyes closed. Ask the participant to jog SLOWLY toward the far wall at a steady, unchanging pace.

The remainder of the group is spread out in a flanking line with their backs to the wall that the blindfolded jogger is approaching. Their job is to stop the jogger before they run into the wall.

The results are impressive, and students generally choose to try it more than once. It's also a good, action-oriented preliminary to the *Trust Fall*.

Ask the spotters to be as quiet as possible in order to increase the commitment of the jogger.

Safety Note

Place a few spotters about three-quarters of the way down court on the sidelines to prevent wildly disoriented joggers from smacking into the bleachers or wall. Don't ignore this suggestion; it happens.

Pay close attention to each runner. If someone goes off course, and you think there is any possibility for a collision, yell STOP! Tell students that if you do this, they must stop immediately.

Diversity Skills

Yeah, But is a good trust-building exercise for any group anywhere and anytime.

Processing

- What were some of your fears or concerns while you were running?

- Did any of the fears that came up remind you of some of the fears you've had in the past? Do you want to share those experiences with the group?

- Did you feel sure that someone would be there to stop you from running straight into the wall?

- What would have helped you feel more comfortable?

- Did the spotters feel sure they could be there to protect the jogger?

- Did you have any concerns about your ability to stop the jogger because of your size or gender?

Trust Fall

Activity Type:	Trust Building
Activity Level:	Moderate
Space:	A clear, open space with enough room for falling bodies
Time:	Long enough for each member of the group who wants to have a try—anywhere from a half hour to two hours
Group Size:	Make sure you have at least ten to twelve able spotters for this activity.
Prerequisite:	Well, we're saying it again: trust is fragile. Make sure that your group is ready to engage in this activity and have all had practice with spotting skills in other activities, like *Trust Leans* and *Circle of Friends*. Review some of the earlier trust sequences that involve physical safety if you have any doubts whatsoever.
Props:	Something about five feet high that is sturdy and can be used to fall off of: a table or counter, for example.

Opening

Doing a *Trust Fall* means you will be taking a physical risk and entrusting your safety to the other members of the group. Sharing your concerns about sexual orientation and gender identity is risky, too. What makes you feel safe or unsafe when you share your emotions? If you're receiving someone else's concerns, how can you demonstrate your support?

Directions

You are going to ask one participant to stand on the table, stump, platform, or whatever object you are using to fall off of, and fall backward into the arms of the group. Again, there should be at least ten to twelve individuals standing on level ground to act as catchers.

Fallers should keep their arms close to the side of the body (hands crossed securely across the chest) and fall with the body held rigid; i.e., not bending at the waist or knees. If the falling person bends at the waist, it concentrates the force of the fall in one area (the derriere) and makes spotting much more difficult. Fallers should remove from their pockets all hard objects that may injure themselves or catchers. They also must

remove glasses, earrings, watches, pencils behind ears—anything that might do damage to either the faller or a catcher.

The catchers form two lines, standing facing one another, shoulder to shoulder, with hands extended, palms up, in an arms alternating pattern (like a zipper) to form a safe landing area. Do not grasp hands. Catchers should also remove all watches and wrist jewelry.

Before any fall occurs, practice the dialogue the group has used for *Trust Leans* until you feel they are comfortable with it.

Faller: "Are you ready to catch me?"

Catchers: "We're ready, _____ (insert catcher's name)."

Faller: "Falling."

Catchers: "Fall away."

Safety Note

This is an activity that requires a skilled facilitator with experience doing Trust activities. You should always place yourself in the line of catchers at about the place where the faller's head will land to ensure that an accidental drop does not injure the faller.

Flying elbows and misdirected falls—be sure that the faller is lined up to fall squarely into the catchers' arms. A badly angled fall can result in bumped heads, shoulders, etc. and diminished trust. Be certain that fallers are clear that they MUST keep their arms in at their sides or across their chests to prevent smacking a catcher with a flying elbow.

Don't let enthusiasm diminish attention to the task.

Reemphasize the catchers' responsibilities.

Ask participants to line up in different places as catchers so they can get a feel of what it's like to catch the head, shoulders, torso, and other parts of the body.

Diversity Skills

Trust Falls are an immediate physical exercise in building trust among the members of your group. They encourage discussion about any topic where trusting others is part of the learning process.

Processing

- What was this like for you as a faller or catcher?
- How do you perceive the trust level of this group?
- How is this group communicating with each other now?
- What would we need to do as a group if someone did not have a good experience?

Eye to Eye

Activity Type:	Trust Building
Activity Level:	Low
Space:	Your usual meeting room
Time:	About 20 minutes to half an hour
Group Size:	Any size
Prerequisite:	None
Props:	None

Opening

All of us may talk a good talk, but what about the nonverbal cues we give each other? Who decides when to make the next move?

Directions

Have the group stand up and ask everyone to pick a partner who somehow looks or seems different from themselves. Make sure everyone has found a partner and ask them to make eye contact with their partner. Then, ask them to move very slowly towards their partner without talking and without breaking eye contact until they've gotten as close as their personal space comfort zone allows. Let the group stand this way for a while before you tell them to relax.

Diversity Skills

Eye to Eye is a good trust-building activity for almost any subject.

Processing

■ How did you choose your partner?

■ What does your experience, background, cultural heritage say to you about sharing eye contact with someone?

■ Do you feel comfortable looking someone else in the eye? Why or why not?

■ How close did you let your partner get before you felt they were too close?

Nitro Crossing ■

Activity Type:	Group Initiative
Activity Level:	Moderate
Space:	An open space with a tree or sturdy pole that you can hang a swing rope from
Time:	30 to 45 minutes
Group Size:	10 or more
Prerequisite:	This activity requires a certain amount of physical coordination. Some members of the group may be intimidated by the idea of swinging on a rope.
Props:	Tin can, water, swing rope, two "trip wires"—this is usually an element on a low ropes course.

Opening

This bucket is full of nitro and in danger of exploding immediately and killing all the bystanders. It's your job to find a way to transport the bucket safely—without letting one drop spill—and get all the people over to the safety zone on the other side.

Directions

The object of this activity is to transport a group and a container—try a tin can—3/4 full of "nitro" (water) across an open area using a swing rope.

The rules are as follows:

Participants must swing over trip wires at the beginning and end of an open area without knocking either one off its support. If a trip wire is knocked off, the entire group must go back and start again. The trip wires are set up about 15–20 feet apart with the rope swing hanging down between them. The group's first challenge becomes retrieving the rope swing.

Don't tie any knots in the swing rope except for a large knot near the bottom. This knot can be held tightly between the legs to help members of the group support their weight.

The nitro must be transported in such a way that NO water is spilled. If any spillage takes place (one drop), the entire group must start over. The container must be topped off at the 3/4-full mark after each spill.

The swing rope must be obtained initially without stepping in the open area between the two trip wires.

The participants are allowed to use only themselves and their clothing to gain the swing rope.

Participants are not allowed to touch the ground while swinging between trip wires and must attempt the crossing again if they do so.

Safety Note

Spot the first few participants swinging across
until enough are over to spot the rest of the group.

Variation

You can do the nitro problem indoors by using a gymnasium climbing rope as the swing rope. Set up the "trip wires" using empty tennis ball cans as supports and a section of bamboo as the top cross piece. Fill the #10 nitro can with finely cut confetti to avoid a wet gym floor.

Diversity Skills

Nitro Crossing is a good activity to explore assumptions about people's physical abilities. It can also encourage discussion on any topic, according to how you process it.

Processing

- What kinds of stereotypes did you have about male and female abilities to complete this activity?

- Did any of these assumptions get shot down?

- Who did you look to, to be the leaders in this initiative and why do you think they were chosen?

- What encourages you to do things you didn't think you could do?

- What happens when you mess things up in your life? Who gives you support? How do you think others perceive you? What kind of feedback do you get from your family and friends?

Mine Field

Activity Type:	Group Initiative
Activity Level:	Moderate
Space:	An 8' wide by 30' long rectangle works well.
Time:	This activity takes anywhere from 30 minutes to an hour, depending on which variation you use and how challenging you want to make it for the group.
Group Size:	10–16 in pairs
Prerequisite:	As with any blindfolded activity, it's always a good idea to review the basic safety precautions: have participants keep their hands in the bumpers-up position and make sure the guides don't let their partners move too quickly. Ask if anyone needs or would feel more comfortable with extra support while they are blindfolded. Figure out what that support looks, feels, or sounds like. Let any students who feel uncomfortable with being blindfolded simply close their eyes—good place for a brief reminder of Challenge By Choice and your group's understanding of their Full Value Contract.
Props:	Tennis balls, fleece balls, rubber chickens, beach balls, squeeze toys, and any other soft obstacles you can use for setting up your obstacle course. Spot markers or rope to mark off the *Mine Field*. Enough blindfolds for

half the members of the group. Caution: if a person in your group is in a wheelchair, make sure the objects aren't too high, so that a chair can roll over them.

Opening

1. Say the wrong thing or don't listen to what someone is saying and the conversation can become similar to a mine field—you never know which next step might set off a mine. The objects in our physical *Mine Field* are obstacles that represent potentially sticky places in a conversation. Touching a *mine* means you've gone off track and hurt someone's feelings. It's important to clearly communicate your needs and ask other people what they need. But, since we are all human beings, stuff happens no matter what we do.

2. Make up your own fantasy about a dangerous journey full of adventures and challenges to be faced. The end could be a world where everyone is valued and listened to or a world where all our dreams come true. Getting there is the hard part, but the journey's full of adventure, too.

Directions

Ask the participants to help you spread out the tennis balls or whatever it is you've decided to use in a random pattern inside the area you've outlined on the ground. You can use more or fewer obstacles to increase or decrease the difficulty of getting from one end of the field to the other.

Have your group split into pairs and tell them that one person will be blindfolded to start.

The object is for the blindfolded participant to traverse the length of the obstacle enclosure. The sighted person will be the guide, but must stay outside of the enclosure and cannot touch their blindfolded partner. Only verbal cues are allowed. (Please see variations below for nonverbal cues.) If the blindfolded participant touches any obstacle, they must go back to the beginning and start again. Or you can have them count their touches and, when everyone has had a go, compare how they did. When all of the blindfolded players have had a chance, ask them to switch roles with their partners.

Challenge Levels

You can increase the challenge a number of different ways, depending on how your group is functioning. Have two blindfolded players go through holding hands or have all the blindfolded players go through at once. Either way, they'll learn a lot about careful movement and how to make their voices heard above the crowd (politely, of course). You could also try timing them and give a time penalty for each object touched. Another variation is to put three blindfolded players on either end of the *Mine Field* and have their guides lead them through. Which team reaches the end first and how did they develop their strategy, together or separately?

Variations

1. Before you start the activity, give each pair a pipe cleaner or some other object they can use to create a symbol. Use a variation of Opening 1, and describe the *Mine Field* as the area where all the problems exist that cause trouble at school, at camp, or where they live. Tell them that the pipe cleaner represents a support to help them through the problems. It might be a person, an object, a special skill, a place they go. Have them shape their pipe cleaner so they will recognize it in the *Mine Field* area.

   Have each pair place their support symbol somewhere in the area. Their goal is to retrieve their support without touching any of the other objects. As in the standard version of this game, one of the players is blindfolded and led verbally by a sighted partner.

2. Instead of verbal cues only, the pair establishes a set of tactile cues. In this scenario the guide can walk behind or beside the blindfolded person. The pair cannot hold hands or have any other continuous contact. Participants often devise signals like a quick tap on your right shoulder means shuffle to your right, etc. You can increase the challenge by penalizing guides who touch an object. Tactile cues can be used with Variation 1 as well.

3. Continuing with the theme of trying not to hurt other people's feelings, have each pair blow up a balloon and write down one of their biggest fears or despairs on it. Ask everyone to put their balloon somewhere in the *Mine Field*. The object is for the guides to help their blindfolded partners reach their balloons, pick them up, and carry them out. Once all the balloons are out of the *Mine Field*, you can have the group create a ceremony to solemnly burst them all.

Diversity Skills

People of all ages are fascinated with the notion of a journey that has many pitfalls and setbacks but can ultimately be completed. This activity has such a variety of uses that it can fit in at almost any stage of a group's development. Issues of trust and communication are so nicely woven into *Mine Field* that often participants are amazed to discover during the processing just how much they accomplished during their journey.

Processing

- How did you and your guide communicate? Did you feel as though your guide was taking care of you?

- What are some of the challenges to getting your point across in a conversation?

- What did you learn from this activity about getting support or asking for support?

- When you did the variation of the game, what were some of the problems you identified in the *Mine Field?*

- What did you identify as your support symbol? How does it help you in your daily lives?

- What did it feel like to depend on someone else to navigate your way through all the obstacles?

- Can you think of a time when you felt you were in an emotional pit—not knowing what emotions you were going stumble upon? What do you do when someone's emotions surprise you?

- How we each feel about our gender and sexual orientation can be pretty confusing sometimes. *The Mine Field* might even be a symbol of your own confusion, not someone else's. How did it feel to be walking through unknown territory?

- How did it feel to find your pipe cleaner or balloon?

- How did it feel to destroy your balloon?

The Mobile Ten-Person Pyramid

Activity Type:	Group Initiative
Activity Level:	Moderate to high
Space:	Outdoors or inside with enough room to move around
Time:	About 30 minutes
Group Size:	10 (If you have more, ask them to act as observers and spotters, then rotate students so everyone has a chance to participate.)
Prerequisite:	Trust-Building activities
Props:	If you are indoors, make sure that you have gym mats to protect knees, elbows, and noses.

Opening

Looks aren't always the best way to determine what someone can offer the group. Can you think of some of the times you've sized someone up and made assumptions about what they can or can't do?

Directions

The object of this activity is to build a ten-person pyramid that can

travel, or crawl, up to 25 feet. A world record was once set by a group of ten young adults who managed to travel the distance in 32.8 seconds. The old record was over 35.

When you present this activity, don't mention that the only way to do it is on their hands and knees. This will give them a chance to solve the problem on their own. The pyramid does have to be symmetrical and only a 4-3-2-1 sequence is acceptable.

Safety Note

Caution students that falling on the bottom people can hurt.
Be sure your group is showing a lot of trust and care for each other.
If not, **Do Not** do this activity.

Diversity Skills

Building allies, racial identity, physical and mental ability

Processing

■ What was your role in this activity?

■ If you spoke up about how to solve the problem, what encouraged you to share your ideas?

■ If you were afraid to offer any suggestions, what held you back?

■ Do you think your gender influenced the way you were treated during this activity? If not, why not? If so, why?

■ Who were your leaders and what did they do that gave them this role?

■ How was your frustration expressed?

■ How was encouragement expressed?

Finding Solutions

Activity Type:	Social Responsibility
Activity Level:	Low
Space:	Your usual meeting room
Time:	45 minutes to 1 hour
Group Size:	10–14
Prerequisite:	Trust activities, some time working together
Props:	Paper and pens

Opening

A woman was walking down the street in the middle of New York City and said to her friend, "I hear the song of a red-breasted sparrow!" Her friend said, "You've got to be kidding, not in the middle of the city." The first woman reached into her pocket and flung out some change into the air. Suddenly, everybody around her stopped what they were doing to listen. She looked at her friend and said, "See, I guess it just depends what you're listening for!"

Directions

We all know what it's like to feel different, to hear sparrows where everyone else hears traffic. Divide into groups of 3 or 4 people and give each person 5 index cards. Have each person write on a card a memory or experience where they felt very different and helpless because of their gender or feelings about sexual orientation. After time for reflection, have them share that experience in a small group. Then, ask them to share their cards and have each person write down solutions or ideas for different ways they think the other members of the group could have dealt with the problem. Let them keep sharing as long as they're comfortable.

Diversity Skills

You can approach a variety of subjects according to how you frame the activity. Have the group write their experience of feeling different because of their race, ethnicity, physical ability, class, background, looks, etc.

Processing

■ How did you know you were listened to and validated? What did you see and hear?

■ How can this be useful in your life?

Through the Looking Glass

Activity Type:	Social Responsibility
Activity Level:	Low
Space:	Your usual meeting room
Time:	Allow enough time for the group to have a good discussion on the questions. You'll probably need about an hour.
Group Size:	Enough to divide into a few groups of four people each
Prerequisite:	An atmosphere of trust and open discussion
Props:	None

Opening

How do you feel about being male or female? What are some of the messages we get from society about our gender? What do you hear and experience and how do you internalize those messages?

Directions

Divide into groups of 4 and answer the following questions in a round-robin fashion.

Describe what it feels like to be male or female and why you describe it the way you do.

Describe your earliest memories of realizing that boys and girls are different.

How have you experienced a sense of power or lack of power because of your gender?

How do you react when you think someone is responding negatively to you because of your gender or sexual orientation?

When the small groups have finished their discussion, ask everyone to get together and share what they've learned.

Diversity Skills

The questions you ask the group to discuss will determine the direction of this activity. Use it for any subject in the book if you want to encourage open discussion among the group about one or more of the topics presented here.

Processing

- What was comfortable?
- What was uncomfortable?
- What did you learn about yourself?
- What did you learn about others in your group?
- What were some of the reactions people described when they answered the last question in your small groups?
- What do you need from this group to help you come to terms with or understand more about your gender and/or sexual orientation?
- People in this country say that gender is not an issue. How would you respond to that statement based on your small-group discussion?
- How do males and females display their power?
- How comfortable do you feel discussing these questions?
- Why is this important?

Closing Activities

Passing the Magic Wand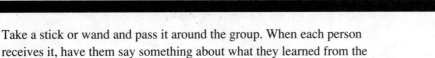

Take a stick or wand and pass it around the group. When each person receives it, have them say something about what they learned from the group that day.

Acknowledgment Mill

Give each person in the group a sheet of paper and ask them to jot down notes to themselves about three people who had an impact on them during the activities. When they're done, let them mill around and share their acknowledgments with those individuals. Before they go, ask them to stand in a circle and acknowledge the group.

Personal Journal Questions

What is frustrating for you about being a man or woman? What is rewarding?

How do you feel about some of the issues of sexual orientation that we discussed today? What was hard for you to share and hear?

Processing Questions

Can you name a feeling (mad, glad, sad, or scared) you had at any point in completing the activity? Where in your body did you feel it most?

❑ Is that feeling a common one in your life?

❑ Did you express that feeling to others? If not, what did you do with the feeling?

❑ Do you usually express feelings or suppress them?

❑ Would you like to feel differently in a similar situation? If so, how would you like to feel?

❑ How do you imagine others felt toward you at various times during the activity? Were these feelings expressed?

❑ What types of feelings are easiest to express? Most difficult?

❑ Do you find it difficult at times to be aware of some feelings? If so, which ones?

❑ Are some feelings not appropriate to express to the group? If so, which ones?

❑ Does expressing appropriate feelings help or hinder completing the initiative?

❑ Is it difficult for you to avoid judging others? Explain.

❑ Can you think of examples of when you judged others in the group today? When you didn't judge others?

❑ Can you think of specific examples of when the group cooperated in completing the activity? Explain.

❑ How did it feel to cooperate?

❑ How did cooperative behavior lead to successfully completing the activity?

❏ How are you different from some of the others in the group?

❏ How do these differences strengthen the group as a whole?

❏ What would this group be like if there were very few differences in people? How would you feel if this were so?

❏ What have you learned about trust, respect, acceptance, and cooperation as they relate to differences?

❏ Did you notice any differences in how girls versus boys reacted to the activity (for example, who talked more, who followed whom, who agreed with whom)?

❏ Did you find yourself responding to any stereotypes? What were they? How do you think you might handle the same situation in the future?

❏ What has changed for you as a result of participating in this activity? How do you think you'll perceive people who are different from you—blacks, whites, gays, or whoever is appropriate—as a result?

❏ How does this activity relate to the real-life experiences you are faced with at home, in school, in your neighborhood?

❏ What did it feel like to ask for help from someone you used to think of as a member of a group that wouldn't help or support you?

❏ Was there any kind of discrimination going on this activity? If so, what?

❏ What was the most difficult part of this activity as it relates to how you deal with people who are different from you?

❏ What was the easiest part of this activity as it relates to how you deal with people who are different from you?

❏ Did this activity challenge any of your beliefs?

❏ What are your feelings now?

❏ Is there anything in this activity you would do differently? Why?

❏ What are some of the things you think or feel as a result of this activity that we all have in common?

❏ Do you think there are more commonalties or differences between _____ and _____?

❏ What will you remember most about having participated in this activity?

12

Physical and Mental Ability

Societies have always been full of people with wide-ranging physical and mental abilities. The world has never been solely a place of Gandhis or Jackie Joyner-Kersees. But for centuries people with disabilities have often been viewed as unable, dependent, incapable of caring for themselves or contributing to their families and society. Some of the world's early cultures sacrificed children with disabilities to the gods. Equating a disability in one arena with inability in all areas is a misguided generalization. Individuals throughout history have proven the inaccuracy of this kind of stereotypical thinking—Beethoven, Mozart, Vincent Van Gogh, Franklin Delano Roosevelt, Stephen Hawking, Stevie Wonder… the list is endless.

As recently as the 1950s, it was still fairly typical for people to care privately for a family member with a disability—often going to great lengths to hide the disability or the person from their community. Medical advances, however, have greatly changed the spectrum of possibilities for people with disabilities. For example, in the 1950s a person with a spinal cord injury was likely to die. Today, doctors can stabilize and treat organ damage, enabling people with varied degrees of paralysis to live long, healthy lives as contributing members of our society. More and more premature babies survive, perhaps facing some complications, but invariably enjoying their childhood. Our population is living longer and longer, typically facing age-related disability along the way. People now survive cancer and live with birth defects and AIDS. The list goes on and on. The old stereotype that the hundreds of thousands of people in our country with disabilities lead less than full lives—are *unable* because they're *disabled,* dependent because they need different technological or personal support—has been and is continuously challenged.

It's important for us to keep in mind that while people with disabilities sometimes do need extra or different support from "able-bodied people," this does not make them incapable or less independent. In our modern world, technological advances from TDD to computers to wheelchairs have facilitated the increased presence of people with disabilities in society and the workplace. People with disabilities are more present because of their greater numbers, advancing technology, and, most importantly, their vocal and justified demand for civil rights.

The ADA

People with disabilities form the largest minority group in the United States and also the only minority group that could legally be discriminated against until July of 1990. The Americans with Disabilities Act (ADA), long-overdue civil rights legislation, is the result of years of hard work by people with disabilities and their allies. Many battles were fought along the way by diverse groups—parents who fought for the right to education for their developmentally delayed children, students at Gallaudet University who protested the selection of a nondeaf president, the highly visible civil disobedience of ADAPT (American Disabled for Accessible Public Transportation). In the ADA, the United States now has legislation that protects people with disabilities from discrimination.

Legislation alone, however, has not been enough to protect people with disabilities from the stigmatization and demeaning attitudes that still prevail. This despite the fact that there has been appreciable improvement in our understanding and acceptance of people with disabilities. Franklin Roosevelt hid his wheelchair from the public eye; today, Mac Cleland proudly wheels through the halls of the Senate (although not without having had to demand accessibility in our public halls). As recently as 30 years ago, many of the nation's children with Down syndrome were institutionalized. In the late '80s many Americans enjoyed the escapades of Corky (an actor with Down's syndrome who played an adolescent with Down syndrome) on the TV show *Life Goes On*.

An Individual Experience

As you and your group examine some of the social issues that people with disabilities face, it is important to understand that disabled people do not blur into one homogeneous group, but rather mirror society, rich in diversity and individual experiences. As with so many of the subjects we cover in this book, persons with disabilities are likely to share many common experiences. But do not interpret this to mean sameness of experience. Identity development for people with disabilities can also include issues of race, class, gender, and sexual orientation as well as the experience of their individual disability—hearing, vision, mobility, mental illness, etc.

In fact, many groups of people with disabilities have their own cultures—this though individuals within that broad culture may view their disability differently. Deaf Americans even have their own language, American Sign Language. Someone who was in a car accident last year and paralyzed from the waist down will most likely feel differently than someone who was born with cerebral palsy.

As we work with youth, it is essential to provide them with opportunities to promote understanding and diminish fear of people with disabilities. A three-year-old once told us, "We're all different, but we're all the same." Children have an innate ability to categorize without being rigid. As you work through the activities in this chapter, seek to create an environment that encourages your group to develop a better understanding of the different perspectives we all bring to our lives. Help them develop their ability to learn and grow through contact with role models from all walks of life.

Some Recurring Themes

Through our work over the years, we have noticed that several themes repeatedly surface when we work with groups around disability issues. These themes reflect the way individuals and society treat people with physical and mental disabilities. The following list, which is by no means exhaustive, attempts to provide you with a brief overview of some of these themes. Ideally, it will help you begin to process issues around disabilities with your group. Your understanding will expand and become deeper with your own and your group's experience.

> *Whether we voice our fears or not, they are real, they are communicated, and it requires a lot of self-reflection for us to confront them.*

We encourage you to treat this list as a tool to help you and your groups reflect more on the subject of disabilities. Brainstorm with your colleagues, group members, and people with disabilities and keep adding to this list as you go. As you work with groups to promote compassion and enlightenment, your knowledge and understanding will grow along with your group's. You will all be adding to your understanding of how individuals and society treat people with disabilities and helping the process of changing some of our most entrenched stereotypes.

Fear—most people are fearful of those with disabilities. It is a lot like the fear that surrounds people who are HIV positive. Let's face it, most of us are afraid of losing our physical abilities, of aging, of perhaps being in a wheelchair. Whether we voice our fears or not, they are real, they are communicated, and it requires a lot of self-reflection for us to confront them.

Caretaking—it is not uncommon to feel the need to take charge, to try to do everything for a person with a disability. Generally, this need to help and care for is couched as sympathy, but it can feel smothering and overpowering to the recipient of your good will. People with disabilities are, in most instances, fully independent. When people without disabilities insist on caretaking for those who have them, they are clearly communicating their belief that people with disabilities are unable to care for themselves.

Generalizing—we tend to generalize disability in one area to mean disability in all areas. Taken to extremes, we may assume that because someone is in a wheelchair, they're also mentally impaired, deaf, or generally incapable.

Assuming—a lot of times we simply assume that the life of a person with a disability is drudgery and not worth living. We tend to think that we could never bear to live our lives that way. We therefore pity people who actually lead happy lives.

Employment—people with disabilities are the most highly unemployed group in America. "Only one third of disabled people hold jobs. Seventy-nine percent of the rest say they can work and would like to work, according to a 1994 Harris poll, but they are prevented from doing so because, among other reasons, they face discrimination in hiring…" (Shapiro). This is due in part to the prevalent belief that if you have a disability, you can't work. In fact, most people with disabilities can work, in most cases with minor, if any, modifications to the physical work environment, schedules, and accepted work routine.

Separation—while the norms are slowly changing due to the Americans with Disabilities Act, children with disabilities are often educated and socialized separately. There are pros and cons to this, but it might be worth reflecting on whether or not this tendency is due to some of the attitudes and behaviors we have described in this list.

Inaccessibility—many public places still remain inaccessible to disabled people. Most people with disabilities find their own balance between asking for and getting needed assistance and acting independently. It's important to stress here that most people with disabilities are fully independent and should be treated that way.

Depersonalizing—as people with disabilities mature from teenager to adult, we often assume that the normal human process of maturing, with its attendant needs and crises, is not as important or disappears.

These beliefs manifest themselves in many different ways. Some of them seem quite obvious, the type of things we are constantly telling our children not to do, but these behaviors do not exclusively belong to children. What are they?

- Staring—many people stare, whether from lack of control or outright curiosity. It is human nature to be curious and seek understanding, but no one wants to be covertly or overtly inspected. If it is understanding you seek, approach that person and ask.

■ Ignorant remarks—"Are you deaf?" (when you are). "Are you drunk?" (when you're having trouble pumping gas at 9 AM). "I couldn't live if I were you." "You're so lucky you found someone to love you," etc.

■ Speaking slowly—we often act as though someone with a physical disability is mentally incapable of understanding as well. In fact, the vast majority of those with physical disabilities are quite capable of holding normal conversations. There is no need to treat a child, youth, or adult like an infant.

■ Decision making—we tend to make decisions for someone with a disability without consulting them. In group situations, it is not uncommon for members to consult everyone in the group except the person with the disability, even when the decisions under consideration apply directly and specifically to that person.

■ Exclusion—in groups, participants may make no effort to include the person with the disability in group processes.

■ Reticence—a lot of times we are afraid to ask a person about their disability. When we do ask, we mumble or act ashamed for the person. In most cases, people with disabilities will feel valued and in better control of the information about them if you ask directly about their disability and whether they might need any help.

■ Glorification—we tend to think of people with disabilities as somehow courageous or stronger willed than us. People with disabilities are just like everyone else, trying to be happy and fulfilled, making the best of their skills and talents.

Teaching Issues of Disability Through Activities

Not everyone can do everything. Most people, if their potential and actual contribution to the group is valued, will find a role in the activities. When you are doing activities that are intended to promote the discussion and understanding of disability issues, it is very important that you use universal activities. It would be counterproductive to the goals you have for your group to use an activity that is intrinsically exclusionary to teach inclusion. What is a universal activity? A universal activity is one that enables the active inclusion of all people with their varied abilities. Even if there are no people with disabilities in your group, do not use an activity that would not be accessible to discuss disability issues.

Generally speaking, most adventure activities are universal or can be modified to include all participants. If you have someone in your group with a hearing loss who reads lips, for example, you can adapt the activities to make sure that there is a visual cue to show where the conversation is going. Group members can toss a bean bag or a tennis ball as they speak. *It's Bean Great Hearing You* is an example of an activity that incorporates this bean bag toss, but you can use this for any activity. As you work with your group on this topic, you may want to make this simple adjustment to your day and center activity processing on how the bean bag changed the way group members communicated with one another. If there is someone in your group who tires easily, don't plan an entire day of running activities, but this doesn't mean you can't have one or two.

In our experience, it is better not to use blindfolds, earplugs, crutches, and/or a wheelchair to simulate what it feels like to have a disability. These experiences are too temporary and should not be used as a method of gaining insight or empathy into having a disability. It is much better to frame the use of temporary handicaps as a personal challenge and nothing more.

Following is a list of behaviors and techniques that will help you and your group learn how to include, rather than exclude, people with disabilities. As you work through these techniques, you may want to invite people with disabilities to join you for a day or a week and participate with your group in the activities and processing. We have found that this often helps groups gain a better understanding of the challenges people with disabilities face, as well as their potential for contributing new insights, learning, and enjoyment. Again, there are thousands of disabilities with millions of symptoms. We could never present a scenario for every situation that may come up for you and your group when facilitating these issues.

- The person is more important than the disability. Focus on the human being, not the disability.

- When you offer assistance, it is very important to ask and make sure that your assistance is wanted. By no means does this imply that you should not offer or should feel tentative about offering, simply that you respect the wishes of the person to whom you are offering assistance.

- For people in wheelchairs or who rely on any type of equipment, the equipment is an extension of their personal space. Do not lean on or use the chair without first getting permission.

- If you offer your arm to someone, make sure they want your help and then allow the person with the disability to take your arm. This way your arm provides guidance or leverage instead of acting as something that leads or feels to you like dragging.

- Talk to people in wheelchairs at their eye level. This is particularly important when you are having an extended conversation; it avoids a stiff neck for both of you.

- With someone who has a visual impairment, it is important to use verbal indications of where and how a conversation is traveling.

- Always tell someone with a visual impairment, in a normal tone of voice, when and where you are moving.

- If someone with a hearing impairment has a translator, allow some time for the translation to occur.

- Use a visual indicator for the movement of conversation with someone who has a hearing impairment and lip-reads. Show them with a gesture where the conversation is going or, if you have one handy, toss a bean bag or soft ball.

- Be patient, don't interrupt or finish sentences when you are talking to someone who has difficulty speaking.

- Use specific yardage or feet when you give directions to someone with a visual impairment.

Concluding Thoughts

Everyone has different strengths and weaknesses. Participants engaged in adventure activities will find roles in which they feel comfortable if the group actively values their potential contribution to the group.

Whether you are planning activities for groups with people with disabilities or a day of activities designed to promote discussion of disability issues, keep your activity sequences universal. Make sure that you plan a day with a majority of activities that enable the inclusion of everyone in the group.

Teach and model inclusion. If you have someone with a disability in your group, include that person in your planning process to the degree possible. Always ensure that participants with disabilities are comfortable before you begin the day. This is best done in private. Use this time as an opportunity to include the participant with disabilities in fine-tuning program plans, providing suggestions on how you and the group can give support or make the activities more accessible. If they are willing to share their observations with the group, encourage open discussion about the day's planning and encourage everyone to contribute. It will only increase their understanding of the issues.

Never assume knowledge or understanding of a person's physical condition. Ask, ask, and ask again. We cannot stress enough how important it is to ask questions if you are feeling uncertain about the best way to respond to a situation. But remember to keep your focus on the person, not on their disability. Asking questions shows that you are concerned, but more importantly, creates an atmosphere where the person with a disability participates in decisions about their welfare and is included and valued.

Worksheet

Take some time to think about the term, "temporarily disabled." What are some of your thoughts when you hear that term? _____

_____

_____

Do you, a family member, or close friend have a disability? What would you honestly like others to know about who you or they really are? _____

_____

_____

What skills do you think you can bring to your group for dealing with issues of ability? What skills do you think you are lacking? _____

_____

_____

Pick one disability—hearing-impaired, blind, paraplegic, etc.—and list some of the stereotypes you heard about people with that disability when you were growing up. Have any of those stereotypes been challenged? If so, what experiences made you change your mind. If not, why do you think you are holding on to some of your assumptions? _____

_____

_____

_____

A Job Interview

Jean walked to her job interview with confidence. Her walk may have looked pretty wobbly, but she felt OK. She felt confident. From what she understood of the job, she was well qualified. She got to the address the firm had given her and buzzed the door. Someone came to let her in. As they went through the front door, the young woman who let her in explained that the office was on the third floor, at the top of a steep and winding Victorian staircase.

Jean has a form of ataxia which has caused her peripheral nerves to degenerate and results in poor balance and coordination. Her confidence slipped a notch or two. It doesn't take much imagination to understand how daunting those two flights of twisting stairs, just prior to a job interview, seemed to her. With much clinging to the railing and a few stumbles, she made it to the top.

The interview lasted over an hour and seemed to go quite well. Within a week, they called her back for a second interview. Thankfully, they had moved to a new building with only one flight of stairs, straight up, railings on both sides. Jean felt good because apparently they had liked what she had to say, thought she spoke intelligently, and felt she was qualified and a contender for the position. Otherwise, why would they have called her back?

At the second interview, they asked her if she was drunk at the first interview. Jean attributed their question to her struggle up the stairs. She didn't think the question was based on the interview, and she answered, "No, why?"

"Well, one of our staff thought your breath smelled," they replied.

"Maybe I should have had some gum," said Jean, "but my struggle with the stairs was…" Her voice faltered as she sat there wondering why it was more comfortable for them to insult her personal hygiene than it was to talk about her stumbles on the stairs. Why did they have to lie to her when she was open to talking about her disability?

You Don't Know

Lisa once heard a young man with muscular dystrophy speak to his schoolmates as part of a panel discussion on prejudice and discrimination. He was the last panelist and as he rolled over in his wheelchair and a classmate brought the microphone to his mouth, he captured everyone's attention with his opening words. "You don't know how painful it is for me to go to lunch and start rolling toward a table and see how my classmates react. You avoid my eyes, make faces, and pretend that I'm not there so that I won't sit with you." You could have heard a pin drop in the audience of 600 students.

"It makes me so angry that you judge who I am when you see this body in a wheelchair," he continued. "You haven't even given me a chance. Some of you are afraid, some of you are disgusted by what you see, and some of you delight in making fun of me. I don't like it, and I refuse to accept your view of me. I am so much more and it is your loss for not knowing me. You are afraid of the unknown, but life is about the unknown and the journey to explore it. Don't be afraid to live and reach out to understand the unknown. It can give you so much joy and knowledge."

Continuum

Avoidance →Silence →Asking →Supporting

As the above vignette about the young man with muscular dystrophy so poignantly illustrates, many of us prefer to avoid looking at people with disabilities or including them in our daily lives. Often, when we do look, we stare or focus on the disability instead of the person. And, when we do recognize our behavior, we are afraid to ask questions, feeling that it might be perceived as inappropriate or too inquisitive.

Asking is the first step toward recognizing the person, not the disability, and through asking we begin to learn the ways we can give support.

Awareness

A disability in one area does not translate to an inability to contribute, participate, and share in other areas. None of us is capable of participating or contributing in every area of human endeavor. We all share weaknesses. What is important is that we recognize and applaud the strengths and abilities of all individuals.

Group Skills

Inclusion—this is the fundamental skill the activities in this book are designed to foster. Many able-bodied people feel embarrassed by people with disabilities, avoiding eye contact or not speaking directly to them. This chapter focuses on ways to engage everyone as active participants in the activities.

What does being able-bodied mean to you? Often, we take our physical abilities for granted or we assume that we couldn't bear to live our lives with a disability. Take the time to reflect on both of these themes with your group to help them gain more awareness of the assumptions we make.

Ask what kind of support is required. Able-bodied people tend to either avoid or take over when they sense that a person with a disability is having difficulty or struggling with a situation. Inclusion means appreciating that people with disabilities are capable and independent and will ask for help if and when they need it. This doesn't mean that you should not offer or should feel shy about offering your help, but it does mean that you should ask and make sure that your support is wanted.

Activities

It's Bean Great Hearing You

Activity Type:	Ice Breaker
Activity Level:	Low
Space:	Your usual meeting place
Time:	15 minutes
Group Size:	Any
Prerequisite:	None
Props:	A bean bag

Opening

This is a special bean bag that's been handed down from generation to generation in my family. We use it whenever we need to settle an argument or learn more about how someone is feeling or what we can do for them.

Directions

Have the group sit in a circle and explain to them that only the person holding the bean bag gets to speak. If someone wants to respond or add something to what has just been said, they have to make the "bean sign." This looks like a lower case "b" that's formed by making a circle with your index finger and thumb, with the other fingers pointing up. The speaker gets to decide who can speak next and passes the bean bag on to that person.

The person who receives the bean bag begins their turn by saying, "It's bean great hearing from you," and addresses the previous speaker by name.

You might want to begin this activity by introducing yourself first—with the help of your family bean bag heirloom, of course. Your introduction might go something like this: "Hi, I'm Lisa and I've been leading groups in adventure activities for the past two summers. This is the first time I've led a group that has people with disabilities and it would really help me a lot if you could tell me what you think you'll need from me and the other members of the group today. I sprained my ankle the other day, so I won't be able to do a lot of running around. You can support me by staying within hearing distance so that I don't have to do too much moving around to keep us together."

The person you hand the bean bag to begins with, "It's bean great hearing from you, Lisa," and goes on to tell the group their name and what they will need from the group.

Diversity Skills

This activity will help your participants get to know one another better at any time and any place.

Processing

- How did it feel to share your fears with the group?

- Was it hard to wait for the person to finish speaking before you got a chance to speak? Why?

- What about if you wanted the bean bag, but it didn't get passed to you? What did that feel like?

- Do you think you'll be able to support the other people in the group? Why or why not?

Killer

Activity Type:	De-Inhibitizer
Activity Level:	Low to moderate
Space:	Any
Time:	15 minutes
Group Size:	Any, but this activity is most effective with groups of ten or more players.
Prerequisite:	None
Props:	None

Opening

There's a *killer* loose among us and if we don't find out who it is, we're all going to die!

Directions

Explain to the group that you are going to select one of them as the "killer." (The easiest way to do this is to ask them all to close their eyes and then walk around them, touching one of them on top of the head to indicate their role.) To kill, the killer has to wink, not blink at someone. The person who receives the wink is dead and gets to act out their slow and agonizing death as loudly and elaborately as they want. Warn the victims that they MUST NOT die immediately after being killed. Tell them to give the killer 15 to 30 seconds to move away.

As the group saunters around the playing area, eyeing each other carefully, and someone thinks they know who the killer is, they shout, "I accuse!" The accuser has to be seconded by another player within ten seconds or else they are eliminated.

If there is a second, you say, "On the count of three, I want you both to point accusingly at the killer." If both people point at the same person, and they are right, the game is over. If they're wrong or they point at different people, they are eliminated. The game continues until the killer is caught or until everyone has been killed—no mean accomplishment!

Variations

If you have someone with a visual impairment in your group, this is a fun variation of the above. Everyone in the group has to go around whispering a compliment to each player they encounter. The only exception to this is the killer, who gets to whisper something along the lines of "Here comes the kiss of death," or "You're dead, friend."

Diversity Skills

Any subject

Processing

There's not a whole lot of subtlety to this game, but you might want to try asking what it felt like to be "the kiss of death" or how people figured out who the actual killer was. What gave them away in the end?

King Frog

Activity Type:	De-Inhibitizer
Activity Level:	Moderate
Space:	Any
Time:	30 minutes
Group Size:	8–12
Prerequisite:	None
Props:	None

Opening

Think of an animal that has always interested you and come up with a sign or a noise that represents that animal for you.

Directions

Have the group sit in a circle and ask everyone to introduce their sign. Include yourself in the introductions. You will be starting out as King Frog. Your challenge is to come up with as wacky a sign as possible to represent the King. We're still hoping that someone with a foot-long tongue will come along and start killing off flies, but until then a simple "ribbit" will do.

Encourage everyone to come up with expressive signs. When everyone has introduced their sign, go around once more to practice them. Tell the group that they must remember and be able to repeat everyone's sign.

When you feel that everyone is comfortable with the signs, announce that the group will begin to talk to each other using only the signs. Communication goes as follows: begin by making your King Frog sign, then the sign of someone else in the group. That person responds by making their own sign, then the sign of someone else, and so on.

After everyone is comfortable with this, announce that play will now begin. The object of the game is to climb the ladder to the King Frog seat. The lowest seat is to the Frog's left and so on around the circle. From now on, the signs the group created will remain with the seat where the activity begins. Make a mistake while communicating, and you must move to the lowest seat, with everyone else shifting one seat to the left and getting a new sign. Once play begins there should be no talking.

There are a few ways to make a mistake. Make the wrong sign, the wrong sequence, or a sign that doesn't exist, or don't respond when your sign is made, or don't respond quickly enough, and you must move to the bottom seat.

This game will start off slowly, but as everyone catches on, it can move quite quickly. Play as long as you have time for, and end it by crowning the person in the lowest seat as the King Frog for next time.

Variations

If there is someone in your group who has trouble with dexterity or coordination or for some other reason has trouble keeping up with an increase of pace, the game can be modified by allowing the recipient of the sign to count to two before sending a new sign.

You can increase the challenge by allowing people to add to the signs. For example, what was once only two thumps of the feet to represent a rabbit is now two thumps and a twitch of the nose. This can be added at timed intervals or at natural intervals in the game.

The signs can be purely visual, purely auditory, or a combination, depending on the needs of your group.

Diversity Skills

King Frog is a fun activity that works well with all groups. Encourage everyone to be as creative as possible and enjoy the resulting wackiness.

Processing

If you have used this activity specifically for disability issues, asking everyone to sign their animals without speaking, for example, have the group talk about how it felt to communicate with each other without words.

Boop

Activity Type:	Team Building/Trust/Ice Breaker
Activity Level:	Moderate to high
Space:	A large, open area cleared of chairs and other hazards (if you are outside, it helps if there's no wind)
Time:	10 to 15 minutes
Group Size:	Any
Prerequisite:	None
Props:	Blown-up balloons

Opening

Your balloon represents the spirit and feelings of another group member who is feeling down about him- or herself. Their tendency is to sink to the floor because they are so overwhelmed (demonstrating this is easy). Your task is to work together in different ways to lift the spirits of this person, and keep them up.

Directions

Split the large group up into small groups of three. You might end up with a couple of groups of four, depending on the numbers.

Ask the players in the small groups to join hands and give each group a balloon. Make sure that the groups are spread out enough to allow for some moving around.

The goal is for each group to keep their balloon in the air—off the ground—during the activity. They must keep their hands joined during the entire game. Give the groups a minute or so to practice. During this time let them use any part of their bodies to keep the balloon up.

After a short practice time, call out a body part. That's what each group must use to keep the balloon off the ground.

You'll want to change about every 10 to 15 seconds during the activity. For example, you could start with hands only (one of the easier ones), move to heads only after 15 seconds or so, then maybe elbows only, knees only, noses only, etc.

We like to move on to combinations after that, say head-hand-elbow. What this means is that a head shot must be followed by a hand shot, then an elbow shot and then back to a head shot, and so on. Have fun making up your own sequences, like nose-heel-shoulder.

Remind the groups that their hands must be joined at all times and that the balloons should never stop moving, even as you call out new body parts to use.

Options:

You can set a playing time before you start (like 3 minutes). If the group is in a competitive mood, you can have the groups keep track of how many times their balloons hit the ground and compare at the end. If they're not competitive, just play without counting floor touches.

A fun way to end the game is to tell the groups to do the next command for as long as possible to see who the *winners* are and then yell, "No body parts at all." How in the world do you do that? Ah…as in all of these activities there is a way. Only problem is they've got to figure it out before their balloon hits the ground. (One way we've seen people do this is to blow them up in the air with their mouths.)

Diversity Skills

Listening and communicating, validating feelings, group identities, individual identity, or any time you want to use a simple activity to help build trust among your participants.

Processing

- How did you discover a way to work together? Did you make a plan?

- What was it like to try to work together using different parts of your body? Could you sense what the next move should be?

- Did anyone have any physical problems that they had to consider while doing this activity?

- What role, if any, did someone's disability have in keeping the balloons off the floor?

- What issues did you have to consider in your plan; i.e., was everyone comfortable holding hands?

Coming and Going of the Rain ■

Activity Type:	Trust Building/Cooperative Skills/Ice Breaker
Activity Level:	Moderate
Space:	A secluded, quiet place
Time:	20 minutes
Group Size:	Any, up to 50
Prerequisite:	None
Props:	None

Opening

Do you know the feeling of relief from the heat that comes with a summer rainstorm? Think about the sounds a storm makes as it approaches and then blows away. We're going to try to experience the feeling together both physically and audibly, but I'm going to need all of you to cooperate as much as you can to make it happen.

Directions

Have your group make a circle and ask them to turn to the left or right; it doesn't matter which direction you choose, just make sure that everyone turns the same way. Tell them to close up the circle by sidestepping toward the center of the circle until they can easily touch the person's back in front of them.

Using the person in front of you, demonstrate the movements necessary to achieve the desired sounds as follows:

With your palms flat on the person's back (shoulders) in front of you, make a rotating movement with your hands to achieve a swishing sound (the increase of wind preceding a shower).

Change to a slapping motion with your fingertips on your partner's back (beginning raindrops).

Change to a heavier finger-slapping action (harder raindrops).

Return to the light slapping motions.

Return to the swishing sound.

STOP, and wait for all the sounds to cease.

When you begin the first motions, your partner passes along the motion to the person in front of them and so on until the motion is returned to you—you feel the person behind you rotating their hands on your back. Then, begin the first finger-slapping motions and so on until the end. Let your group figure out new methods of making these sounds if someone's disability inhibits using the above methods. (Please note, this activity is as much about movement as it is about sound, so it should not exclude someone whose hearing is impaired.)

Diversity Skills

This is an adventure classic—simple, but challenging. It will encourage your group to work together in a spirit of quiet cooperation.

Processing

- How did everyone cooperate?
- Was it hard to follow the movements as they changed?

Warp Speed

Activity Type:	Problem Solving/Group Initiative
Activity Level:	Moderate
Space:	Your usual meeting place or outdoors
Time:	20 minutes
Group Size:	Up to 15; fewer is better
Prerequisite:	Basic cooperative skills
Props:	A digital stopwatch and a fleece or Nerf ball

Opening

This activity breaks will require that we think "out of the box." We will have to think about the assumptions we make and try to solve the problem with as much creativity as possible.

Directions

We like this activity because the tossing at the beginning is frustrating for a group. But solutions to this problem usually do not require coordination.

Ask the group to form a circle and include yourself. Tell them you want to toss the ball around the circle until everyone has had it once, ending back at the first person. To make this go smoothly, have the group members who haven't had the ball yet hold their hands out in a catching position. Once they have received the ball, they put their hands down. Make sure that the ball is tossed across the circle—not to a person next to a tosser. Everyone needs to remember who they toss to and who tossed to them.

When this sequence is complete, ask the group to repeat it, only this time, have someone in the group be the official timer. If they have trouble remembering the order, give them a practice round before you introduce the clock.

Once you have an initial time established (usually about two seconds per participant), ask them to try to reduce that time by working together more closely as a team. Remember, the two basic rules are: 1) each person must touch the ball; and 2) in the order established. After a few more attempts, they should be able to get their time down through better cooperation and teamwork. Tell them you think they can reduce their score even more (by another five seconds perhaps).

Encourage the group to brainstorm, and then to try one idea at a time. They will be able to reduce their score even more. Don't be too strict with the rules; allow just about any idea the group feels comfortable with.

Here are some ideas they may come up with:

Rearrange the circle so that the person you toss to is next to you.

Arrange everyone's hands so that the ball has a ramp to travel down.

Eventually, they will most likely find a way to reduce their score to under five seconds. Congratulate the group on reaching *Warp Speed!*

Diversity Skills

Cooperation, problem solving, listening

Processing

- What were some of the ideas you had for moving the ball around the circle more quickly?

- What assumptions did you make about how you needed to solve the problem? What were some of the things wrong with these assumptions?

- What assumptions do you make about people with disabilities and what they can and cannot do?

■ Do you think you listened to everyone's ideas and tried them all? Why or why not?

■ How did you decide which ones to try?

■ Were there ideas that you didn't hear? Why?

■ How did you consider people's disabilities in the problem solving?

Pick and Choose

Activity Type:	Group Initiative/Problem Solving
Activity Level:	Moderate to high
Space:	A gym or open playing field
Time:	About 30 minutes
Group Size:	10 or more
Prerequisite:	Basic cooperative skills
Props:	Lots of used tennis balls and four or five wastebaskets or paper cores

Opening

There are very few areas in life where people can't find a way to contribute to a group goal or idea. Where do you fit in? How do you think you can make the biggest contribution?

Directions

The object of this activity is for your group to try to throw as many tennis balls as possible into the wastebaskets during a two-minute time period.

Place the wastebaskets at varying distances from your predesignated baseline. Each wastebasket has a different point value, with the closest scoring 1 point, the second 3 points, the third 5 points, and the furthest 9 points. The group competes against itself while trying to score the highest possible point total, either by shuffling thrower and retriever positions or making a decision about which wastebasket to target.

Give the group some time to decide who is going to throw and who is going to retrieve. The throwers must remain behind the baseline. The retrievers can stand anywhere they want to, but they are not allowed to physically assist the balls into the wastebaskets. Their job is simply to retrieve the missed shots and get the balls back to the throwers as quickly as possible. Once the clock starts, throwers and retrievers cannot exchange positions.

Play this game more than once so that you give the group a chance to change tactics and positions.

Diversity Skills

Again, whenever you want the group to work on cooperation, listening, and creative problem solving.

Processing

- How did you decide who would throw and who would receive?

- Did you consider abilities when you were searching for new strategies? Were some people more comfortable in certain roles?

- How were different abilities assets to the group's goals?

- Was anyone anxious about your own or other people's safety?

- Was anyone embarrassed?

- What do you think you contributed to the group in this activity?

- Were you comfortable with the way the group assigned roles?

- Did the group make any assumptions when assigning roles? What were they? Were these assumptions harmful?

Whale Watch

Activity Type:	Group Problem Solving Initiative
Activity Level:	Moderate to high
Space:	An open area where you can set up the *Whale Watch* platform
Time:	45 minutes to an hour
Group Size:	Any
Prerequisite:	Awareness of trust and physical safety issues
Props:	The *Whale Watch* is a low challenge course group problem solving initiative. It requires a pre-constructed tetter-totter-like platform. Contact Project Adventure at the toll-free number listed at the back of this book for information on how to have one of these platforms installed at your site.

Opening

The *Whale Watch* is the name of a famous ship that embarks regularly on adventure trips around the world. You're about to go on a trip around the world. The captain has entrusted you with the job of making sure that the boat doesn't run aground or hit any reefs.

Directions

The *Whale Watch* is a 8' x 13' platform balanced on a 6" x 6" fulcrum. When balanced, the beveled ends of the platform are approximately 12" from the ground. Kind of like a giant teeter-totter.

Split your group in half and position each half at opposite ends of the platform. Entering only from the ends, all of the group has to board the platform without allowing any ground touches on at least one side. (Your group may want to strategize first about how they are going to split themselves. In fact, we would urge giving your group this freedom if someone in your group uses a wheelchair or another device for mobility.) A ground touch means that you have hit a reef or run aground and have to go back to the *Whale Watch's* home port for repairs before embarking on a new journey. The journey is complete when the group manages to keep the platform balanced for at least ten seconds.

Diversity Skills

Whale Watch is, once again, one of those classic adventure activities that can fit into almost any stage of a group's development.

Processing

- How did you decide to enter the platform?

- Did you consider people's size, weight, abilities, or disabilities when you were working out how to enter and in what order?

- Did anyone's disability contribute to keeping the platform balanced. If so, how?

- Did everyone feel that they had a role in deciding how to enter the platform?

- Was anyone anxious about their own or other people's safety?

Lemons and Limes

Activity Type:	Social Responsibility
Activity Level:	Low
Space:	Your usual meeting room
Time:	30 to 45 minutes
Group Size:	Any
Prerequisite:	None
Props:	4 or 5 lemons that look as much alike as possible, 1 lime

Opening

Most of us feel like "outsiders" at some time or another. What does it feel like to you? How do you think other people might feel when they are excluded because they are "different" from the rest of the group?

Directions

Put all the lemons together in a pile on a desk in the middle of the group. Have the group brainstorm together and write down all the characteristics they can think of that are associated with lemons. Separate the large group into groups of 4 or 5 people and give each small group a lemon. Have them study their lemon and note down all its specific characteristics. Tell them they can't cut into the lemon or put any marks on it.

After they have studied their lemon, tell them to bring it up and put it back in the pile of lemons (bring an extra lemon to add to the pile). Ask them to send up a member of their group to identify their lemon. Make sure that the whole group agrees that this is their lemon and ask them to tell the group how they identified it. They will probably share its specific characteristics. If you've written down the general characteristics of lemons somewhere, you might want to add the specific characteristics of each lemon in separate columns for later comparison.

Next, ask the group to close their eyes. While their eyes are closed, place the lemons in a circle in the middle of the group. Ask them to open to their eyes and ask the following questions:

- What did they see when they first opened their eyes?

- What did they see after the first glance?

- How do they think the lemons are feeling?

Then, take one lemon and move it out of the circle.

- What do they think now?

- How is that single lemon feeling?

- How is the group of lemons feeling?

- What do you think they are they saying about each other?

Take another lemon from the group and put it with the single lemon.

- What is happening now?

Ask the group to close their eyes again. Take the lime you've been wondering what to do with until now and put it with the lemons in the circle.

- What do you see now?

- What do you think the lemons are feeling?

- What do you think the lime is feeling?

Place the lime outside the circle away from the lemons.

- What is happening?

Take a lemon and place it with the lime outside the circle.

- What do you think that lemon is doing with the lime?

- What does the lime think?

- What do the other lemons think?

- What kind of feelings do you think that single lemon with the lime has?

Variations

You place an ad for your lemon in the Personals section of a local newspaper and the lime shows up. What do the family, neighbors, and friends say? What do the lemon and lime say?

Diversity Skills

Lemons and Limes is a wonderful activity for encouraging groups to think about how it feels to be different from other people. Try it with any subject when your group is talking about this topic.

Processing

- Processing occurs throughout this activity. Try to note some of the prevalent themes as your group is engaged.

- How do you think this activity relates to what happens in your school environment?

- What are some the feelings involved in being different or excluded?

- What are some of the ways our behavior indicates how we feel about the people who seem to be different from us?

- What are some of the ways you can help people to feel included instead of excluded in the groups you encounter at school, at home, or in your neighborhood?

Mind, Body, and Soul

Activity Type:	Social Responsibility
Activity Level:	Low
Space:	Your usual meeting room
Time:	45 minutes to an hour
Group Size:	Any
Prerequisite:	This activity requires an environment of emotional safety and good communication skills.
Props:	Construction paper, crayons, scissors, and felt-tipped pens

Opening

Most of us make assumptions about people with disabilities that go unchallenged. Sometimes it's because we're afraid to ask questions and sometimes it's because we're afraid, period. Let's try to identify some of those assumptions and figure out what's wrong with them.

Directions

Ask everyone in the group to outline one of their hands (feet, a peer traces another's head, etc., whatever is appropriate for your group) on a piece of construction paper and then cut it out. Ask them to bring the hands to you and write down the following categories on the back of them: hearing impairment, visual impairment, physical disability, temporarily disabled, cerebral palsy, muscular dystrophy, etc. The number of categories you use will depend on the size of your group. Try to have at least three or four hands in each of the categories. Have each participant take a hand.

Ask the participants to find other people who belong to the same category and, once they've formed their groups, have them brainstorm a list of words, images, and stereotypes that they associate with the hand they've been given. When the lists are done, ask the groups to talk among themselves and share how they felt doing this activity. How did it feel to be associated with the "negative" images? With the "positive" ones?

Encourage participants to share their feelings and ask the other members of the group for help. What kind of support do they need from the other members of the group in order to cope with and process the emotions of anger, pain, or humiliation that may result from some of the words and images? Remember, the group's goal is to bring the dialogue associated with the images into the open and to find creative and positive ways of dealing with the "negative" associations. Does it help to let your anger out? Does it help knowing that someone else feels the same way? Will it help if someone else acts as your ally and stands by your side, ready to confront the images together with you? These are some of the questions you might want to ask the group as they do this activity.

Ask each of the smaller groups to share their feelings and solutions with the larger group.

Diversity Skills

You can frame this activity around any of the subjects in this book to help your group work on challenging the assumptions we make about people who are different from us.

Processing

This activity may take a long time to process. Remember to allow extra time, if necessary. When you process this activity, try to remain sensitive to the issues we've discussed earlier in this and other chapters.

- How did you feel doing this activity?

- What was the most challenging for you?

- What made you feel comfortable or uncomfortable in your small group?

- How did it feel to have one of the disabilities listed on the hands and see the images, words, and stereotypes in writing?

- If you don't have a disability, how did it feel to brainstorm information or be associated with a disability?

- What did you learn?

- Can you think of any ways that we consciously or unconsciously exclude people with disabilities because of some of the stereotypes we hold?

Closing Activities

Circle of Hands

Mix up the hands and arrange them in a circle on a big piece of paper. Have the group brainstorm a list inside the *Circle of Hands* of what people need from their group in order to help erase the negative images and stereotypes. Also list the strengths of the group and the qualities they have that will help them achieve this goal.

Passing the Magic Wand

Take a wand and pass it around the group. Invite the participant holding the wand to share a feeling regarding what happened in the group that day; what they learned from the group; what they are willing to give to the group; i.e., humor, support, leadership, risk taking, etc.; something they were unable to share before; or what they have gained from the group.

Making the Connection

Stand in a circle with a ball of yarn (preferably in exciting colors). Hold on to the end of the yarn and toss the ball across the circle to another participant. Before tossing, share with the group a feeling about the day, an insight you gained, or something you learned. The person who catches the ball of yarn does the same thing before tossing it on to someone else. Eventually, you'll get something that looks like a web connecting the group. This web may represent the support we give each other, or how we are all held together by the common bonds symbolized by the yarn. If one person drops their web corner because the group is not being supportive enough or because they are afraid, then the whole group is weakened.

Personal Journal Questions

What have you learned about people with disabilities? What do you think you can do to help erase some of the negative stereotypes and assumptions you've heard or learned from your friends and family?

If you have a disability, can you think of some special quality or strength that you would like everyone to know about?

Processing Questions

- ❏ Can anyone give an example of when you thought you communicated effectively with someone else in the group?

- ❏ How did you know that what you communicated was understood?

- ❏ Who didn't understand someone's attempt to communicate?

- ❏ What went wrong in the communication attempt?

- ❏ What could the communicator do differently next time to give a clearer message?

- ❏ What could the message receiver do differently next time to understand the message?

- ❏ Did you learn something about communication that will be helpful later? If so, what?

- ❏ Is it difficult for you to avoid judging others? Explain.

- ❏ Can you think of examples of when you judged others in the group today? When you didn't judge others?

- ❏ What were some advantages to you of not judging others?

- ❏ What were some advantages to others of your not judging them?

- ❏ How does judging and not judging others affect the completion of the activity?

- ❏ Were some behaviors of others easy not to judge and other behaviors difficult?

- ❏ How were group decisions made in completing the activity?

- ❏ Were you satisfied with the ways decisions were made? Explain.

❏ Did the group arrive at any decisions through group consensus? (Some didn't get their first choice, but they could live with the decision.)

❏ Were some decisions made by one or several individuals?

❏ Did everyone in the group express an opinion when a choice was available? If not, why not?

❏ What is the best way for this group to make decisions? Explain.

❏ Do you respond in similar ways in other groups?

❏ What did you like about how the group made decisions? What didn't you like?

❏ Did you find yourself responding to any stereotypes? What were they? How do you think you might respond to the same situation in the future?

❏ What have you learned about trust, respect, acceptance, and cooperation as they relate to differences?

❏ What has changed for you as a result of participating in this activity? How do you think you'll perceive people who are different from you—blacks, whites, gays or whoever is appropriate—as a result?

❏ Was anyone embarrassed, for themselves or someone else? Since able-bodied people would be embarrassed by moving in a clumsy, spastic, or uncoordinated way, we often assume that people with disabilities will feel similarly; they often don't.

❏ How did you feel about the length of time it took to complete the activity? Was it comfortable? Did anyone feel frustrated because it took too long? Did anyone feel rushed?

❏ Was anyone anxious about your own or other people's safety?

❏ How did you consider different abilities in your problem solving? (Include both thought processes and who did the considering—the person/people with the disabilities or everyone else or the whole group.)

❏ In the final solution, what abilities contributed to the problem or solution?

❏ Did anyone have physical or emotional problems that they had to consider when doing this activity? (A bad back, fear of heights, limited upper-body strength can all be disabilities.)

13

Class

· · · · · · · · · ·

Class background is often an undeclared reason for people discriminating against one another. Perhaps more than any of us would like to admit, the stereotypes we inherit from our families, peers, neighbors, and communities unconsciously govern our behaviors toward people from different economic and social backgrounds. The understanding of class in the United States is somewhat clouded by the unique history of our democratic government and ideals.

The notion of the American Dream derives from our Founding Fathers' commitment to egalitarian ideals and the principles of our constitution. Our social and political structure presupposes that this is a land of opportunity, open to everyone who is willing to work hard. We are in control of our personal destinies. The fundamental laws of our society guarantee upward mobility—the expectation that you will have more tomorrow than you do today—to everyone who perseveres. To a degree, this premise is true for all the citizens of the United States. A closer look, however, shows that while it may be possible through hard work to become richer tomorrow than we are today, the question must be asked whether money is all that's needed to gain access to the upper social classes that hold the reins of social, economic, and political power in our country.

Probably not. The architects of the our constitution gave power to white males who owned land. In other words, they gave voting rights to people within their own class, setting the stage for the historical conflict between social status and economic power. Colonial America was wracked by political, economic, religious, and racial conflict. The colonists fought with each other over land ownership, the right to govern the new society, and religious supremacy. They fought with the Native Americans for land during their westward expansion and eventually displaced them. Later, when slavery replaced the system of indentured servitude, they also faced the controversy of free versus slave labor.

In effect, as America evolved from a diverse group of colonies toward nationhood, there was "a profound tension between ideals of liberty and equality on one hand, and, on the other, the plunder of Indian land, the enslavement of African peoples, the exploitation of European-born workers, and the political and social inequality suffered by women" (Who Built America? American Social History Project). These contradictions, which shaped our American heritage, have prevented many different groups throughout various periods of our history from fully realizing the American Dream.

The American Revolution won our independence from the British government. This act simultaneously overthrew the British class system and its convenient, well-defined, inherited titles, ranks, and honors. Because our forefathers still clung to the control of economic and social power and shared according to social status, we have had to define new hierarchies that have never been institutionalized in our social or political structures. The result is that while we publicly embrace political and judicial equality, most of us still nurture a private, vertical system of class and social status that stems from our individual preconceptions about where "someone comes from." It's a contradiction in terms, because the structure of our social system implies that class differences do not exist or somehow don't matter. But we have also inherited a set of assumptions that assigns value to our hierarchical rank in the system. The American Dream says that as an immigrant nation, or "melting pot," anyone can move up or down the social ladder from one generation to another—the only criterion is your work ethic. Race, gender, and ethnicity supposedly have no impact on our ability to move up the ladder.

Defining Classes

How many classes are there in the United States? The simplest answer is that there are two—the rich and the poor, the employer and the employed, the haves and the have-nots. Most sociologists and the government, however, seem to favor the number of five: upper, upper middle, middle, lower middle, and lower. Paul Fussell, in his book *Class: A Guide Through the American Status System*, breaks it down even further into nine classes that range from top out-of-sight to bottom out-of-sight (below destitute). On each end of the spectrum there is a class that is out of sight, but the top out-of-sight class is invisible by choice, whereas the bottom out-of-sight group is unseen because we as a society make them invisible. Just think of how easily we ignore homeless people when we walk down the streets of a big city in the middle of winter.

Class, Social Status, and Classism

"A social class is a category of people similar in socioeconomic status when compared to other such categories in a stratified society. All societies larger than non-literate tribes are characterized by an unequal distribution of material goods, prestige or honor, and power over others. The formation of a hierarchy or pyramid of groups differentiated by their possession of greater and lesser amounts of these advantages constitutes the class structure of a society" (Grolier Multimedia Encyclopedia).

As a society, our country is confused about how to define class. Is it defined by the amount of money you do or don't have? Is it money combined with your education and the type of work you do? Or is class defined by taste, values, ideas, style, and behavior? Or does it just boil down to the fact that most people feel more comfortable with people from similar backgrounds or present positions? How do these factors impact access to power? How much of our access to power is based on social and political connections and how much on the basis of economic merit?

The most prevalent definition of class today derives from the work of the 20th-century German sociologist Max Weber and his followers. They believe that class is defined by the amount of money you have and the type of leverage it gives you. This means that status and power, primarily political and social, are equally inherent in a definition of class. The word status implies social prestige and how you relate to the larger world around you. There is also a political component—how much power do you have, and how much resistance do you have to getting pushed around?

"Max Weber recognized what he called 'status groups'—groups sharing a common style of life and valued collective identity—as being partially independent of classes based solely on economic position. Weber regarded the European aristocracy, surviving as a social and political force after it had lost its legal and economic privileges, as such a status group. The term has also been applied to ethnic groups in the United States and other societies where ethnicity is positively or negatively valued, and even to groups sharing a common cultural outlook rooted in educational experience" (Grolier Multimedia Encyclopedia).

Status groups have rituals, ceremonies, and symbols designed to reinforce and maintain the system and their position in it. Certain expectations—behavior, who you interact with and how, the friends you choose, the family you marry into—keep the system intact. Some of the rituals and symbols emphasize an unequal distribution of power. For example, the senior partner of a law firm may expect to be called "Mister" while he addresses his secretary by his first name.

Classism is defined as discrimination of others based on class or class background. Classism can and does move in all directions. Socially, this translates into a hierarchy of classes, each strata of which has very different manners and traditions that generally persist from birth to death. Our attitudes are learned and nurtured in childhood by the comments of friends and family. Most of us can say that we remember hearing things like, "Oh, they're from the other side of town," or, "They come from the wrong side of the tracks," or even, "Wow! You live there. That place is a mansion!" These thoughts and observations influence how we interact with each other; we feel either comfortable or uncomfortable because we know or don't know the unspoken rules and parameters in the different strata. Imagine going to a black-tie dinner with more silverware on the table than you know how to use. Are you enjoying the experience or worrying about which fork to use next? The same could be said of a backyard barbecue, where your fingers are the only cutlery required.

These examples serve to reinforce our notions that class background has a strong influence not only on how we interact with different groups, but also on how we perceive our ability to get ahead in life. Mr. Jones, the senior partner of our imaginary law firm, no doubt has a very different view of his potential than John, his secretary. On the other hand, John may feel supported and protected in an environment that makes Mr. Jones uncomfortable or uneasy. It is worth reflecting for a moment on the limits that our attitudes about class background put on our ability to interact with other people and build new relationships.

Class and Diversity

An examination of the issue of class and socioeconomic status through the lens of diversity turns up many indicators that it may be the most pervasive ingredient that defines how we see and judge each other. There is quite a bit of evidence that class is a determining factor in the divisions that persist within the realm of human diversity. Very few of us can contradict the assertion that the class one grows up in contributes to how we view the world and others. Many times, class barriers even serve to connect people of different racial, ethnic, gender, or physical and mental abilities within their confines. Most of us know at least a few people from diverse backgrounds or of differing abilities who we feel totally comfortable with despite the outward dissimilarities. If you take some time to think about it, perhaps there is a commonality—your socioeconomic class.

Unfortunately, a closer look through the lens of diversity turns up some anomalies and the edges of socioeconomic class borders grow hazy. Definitions of class refer not only to people of like backgrounds, but also can and do apply to gender and racial difference. The history of our labor unions is a good example of this. The labor unions came into existence to protect the rights of the poor working-class man, but as they grew, so did resistance and hostility towards including working-class people of different races and genders. As a result, separate labor unions were organized to address the concerns of African Americans and women. Socioeconomic class, political power, race, ethnicity, gender, and physical ability are all potential wedges for separatist behavior and attitudes.

In her book, *Assimilation Blues: Black Families in a White Community*, Beverly Daniel Tatum opens with the question: "What does it mean to be a middle class Black parent living, working, and raising children in the midst of a predominantly White Community? Does it mean opportunity, success, the American Dream realized, or is it rootlessness, isolation, and alienation?"

If we accept the notion that class is defined only by money, education, and professional status, why has it been so challenging for people of color to gain access to certain positions of prestige and power, particularly in American corporations? In his book, *The Rage of a Privileged Class*, Ellis Cose states that many of the black superachievers he interviewed felt that their "success not only came harder but almost invariably later and at a lower level than that for comparably credentialed whites." The black superachievers all went for MBAs at Harvard and Yale and did all the right things, but somehow success did not come together for them the way it did for their white peers. Few reported having mentors high in their organizations who took an interest in supporting their careers. While they are successful, they are not achieving the results they expected.

Even more than issues of race, it may simply be that the image of corporate leaders in the United States does not extend beyond heterosexual, white, and male. Gender, physical disabilities, and sexual orientation may all act as barriers to attaining insider status in the corporate and political power structures of our nation. Confronting the reality versus the myth of the American Dream can be disillusioning, a challenging experience for many people.

The tumultuous debate around affirmative action and what is fair highlights the struggle to gain access to economic and political power. Yes, we do live in a segregated society, and we are only being realistic when we acknowledge that access to educational and economic opportunities for women and people of color would not be the same today without affirmative action. But affirmative action policies have also generated an enormous amount of resentment because they have forced certain segments of our society to share their access to power, power that has a limited number of available positions both at school and in professional arenas. In *The Rage of a Privileged Class*, Ellis Cose shares a story illustrating some of the conflict and frustration that surround affirmative action. He talks about a young white man who was troubled by Supreme Court decisions in favor of affirmative action. "'How dare "unqualified minorities" demand preferential treatment? Why could they not compete like everyone else?'" he asks. Cose states, "When the young man paused to catch his breath, I took the occasion to observe that it seemed more than a bit hypocritical of him to rage on about preferential treatment. A person of modest intellect, he had gotten into Harvard largely on the basis of family connections. His first summer internship, with the White House, had been arranged by a family member. His second, with the World Bank, had been similarly arranged. Thanks to his nice internships and Harvard degree, he had been promised a coveted slot in a major company's executive training program. In short, he was already on his way to a distinguished career—a career made possible by preferential treatment."

Class and Educational Equality

In matters of educational equality, our courts have already begun to bar race as a determining factor. Texas has come up with an ingenious way to ensure that top achievers of all races are admitted to the state's public universities. The new law, signed by the governor in May of 1997, guarantees that all students whose grades are in the top ten percent of their graduating class will be automatically admitted to a public college or university in Texas. Once qualified graduates make their choices, public universities will fill the remaining slots through evaluation of academic performance, extracurricular activities, or other special abilities. "The smart thing about the Texas plan is that it focuses on equal opportunity based on individual academic performance at each school. What is striking about the Texas law is that it doesn't pretend that the public-school system itself supplies 'equal' education to all students. The very nature of how Americans pay for public schools ensures unequal opportunity" (Texas Has Found a Way to Level University Playing Field..."). The Texas law focuses on rewarding youth who do their best within the limits of their school systems. It guarantees that any high school student who tries hard enough will have the opportunity to go to college.

In Boston, the school system is currently waiting for a final court ruling on a suit filed by a white female student who was denied admission to one of its prestigious exam schools, Boston Latin, even though she scored higher than other students admitted under a racial quota policy. During this waiting period, the system is considering eliminating the racial quota policy and replacing it with one that admits children according to family income. The difficulty with implementing the new policy is the impact that the methods used for obtaining legal verification of income status will have on our right to privacy regarding income.

Access to opportunity—educational, political, professional, and economical—is the critical factor that will shape the future of affirmative action in our country. Current trends seem to favor incentives motivated by economical as opposed to racial factors. As many high school seniors and their parents know, colleges select their students not only on the basis of their academic records; they also try to mold their classes with a selection of students from different economic backgrounds, geographical origins, academic concentrations, and extracurricular activities. Race, gender, ethnicity, language, and physical ability should also be acknowledged as influential criteria in the selection process.

Concluding Thoughts

The central premise of the American Dream is that anyone, regardless of their background, can improve their lot through hard work. While it is possible for any and all of us to get richer through hard work, money is not the only prerequisite for achieving insider status in the groups that control the economic and political power of our nation. Many criteria apply, and one of these is social status or prestige.

Definitions of class include many different criteria. For some, money, and how much you do or don't have, defines the class you belong to. Education and professional status are more important for others. For still others, inherited tastes, values, and behavior take precedence over the other factors. Social status is an integral component of most of the assumptions we make about someone's class background.

Our attitudes and assumptions about class are formed early on and nurtured by the environment we grow up in. These attitudes and assumptions shape our view of the world and contribute to many of our opinions about human difference. Overcoming class barriers is an essential part of the struggle to eliminate discriminatory and judgmental behaviors.

Affirmative action has given opportunities to people of color and women that were traditionally reserved for those who were accorded preferential treatment because of their social connections. While affirmative action is by no means a perfect solution, it is worth evaluating how we accord special treatment to the different groups in our society.

Suggested Reading

Cose, Ellis. *The Rage of a Privileged Class*. New York: Harper Collins, 1993.

Fussell, Paul. *Class: A Guide Through the American Status System*. New York: Summit Books, 1983.

Steinberg, Stephen. *The Ethnic Myth: Race, Ethnicity, and Class in America*. Saddle Brook, NJ: American Book-Stratford Press, 1981.

Newman, Katherine. *Falling From Grace: The Experience of Downward Mobility in the American Middle Class*. New York: The Free Press, 1988.

Gutman, Herbert G. *Who Built America? Working People & The Nation's Economy, Politics, Culture and Society. (American Social History Project) Volume I*. New York: Pantheon Books, 1989.

Landry, Bart. *The New Black Middle Class*. Berkley: University of California Press, 1987.

Lapham, Lewis H. *Money and Class in America*. New York: Weidenfeld & Nicolson, 1988.

Marquez, Myriam. "Texas has found way to level university playing field without using race as factor." Originally published in Orlando Sentinel and republished in The Hartford Courant. Sunday, June 15, 1997.

Arnason, Wayne, and Cheryl Markoff Powers. *Life Issues for Teenagers (LIFT)*. Boston: Unitarian Universalist Association, 1985. Enables fifteen- to eighteen-year-olds to explore ethical, social and political issues that matter most to them.

Worksheet

List some of the ways you assign people to a certain class. These might include dress, accent, appearance, speech patterns, profession, how they eat, body language, etc. Why and how do you think these attributes affect your assumptions about where people come from?

Try your hand at some free associations with the words on the following list:

supper	....	dinner
cocktails	....	drinks
position	....	job
affluent	....	rich
gold chains	....	minimal jewelry
white collar	....	blue collar
Peter Pan collars	....	polyester
polo shirts	....	undershirt
baggy pants	....	khakis
pickup truck	....	Mercedes Benz

What are some of the assumptions you made as you went through the list? How do they relate to your thoughts on the first question? _____

_____

How do you think your own socioeconomic background has affected your ability to find a job and advance in your chosen career? What were some of the advantages? Disadvantages? _____

_____

Do you know anyone who has gotten a job through their connections? How did it make you feel? _____

_____

Can you think of someone close to you, a role model or someone in your family, who got ahead in life despite their background? What kind of abilities do you think they needed to achieve their goals? What do you think were some of the challenges they faced? Can you think of any advantages they had over other people? _____

_____

Disneyland

"Disneyland" is the nickname we gave our new neighborhood when we moved there. It's a well-kept, fairly integrated—8 families out of 55 come from diverse racial backgrounds—middle- to upper-middle-class part of a suburb in the hills of Connecticut. When we first moved in, one of our sons, Collin, became very friendly with Lance, a boy of the same age who lives down the hill in another subdivision. Lance has a brother of about the same age as my youngest son, and pretty soon all four of the boys were spending a lot of their free time together. The subdivision Lance's family lives in is full of huge, beautiful homes that seemed to be part of an entirely different realm from ours—a place for upper-class to really wealthy people.

One Saturday, Collin came home and asked, "Mom, can I spend the night at Lance's house?" Without thinking twice, I immediately replied, "No," a reaction that was entirely based on the ideas racing through my mind. They're really rich white people who live in a big house. Why do they want my son to spend the night? I wonder if he'll like the food? I don't want him to feel uncomfortable! Then I realized that I was making a snap judgment about a family I really didn't know. I was choosing my son's friends for him.

It took some courage, but I looked my son in the eye and admitted to him, "I just did something wrong. I passed judgment on Lance's family because they live in one of those big houses. Of course you can go." To this day, the brothers remain great friends and so are their parents.

Continuum

The American Dream →Distinguishing Between Myth and Reality →Creating True, Equal Opportunity

Many of us assume that the American Dream is accessible to everyone, even when confronted by evidence that some of us have an easier time getting ahead than others. It is important to recognize that many people are barred from the American Dream due to their class background. From there, we can begin to distinguish how class issues are often seen as other issues—racism, sexism, ethnic mistrust.

Awareness

Class issues are often an unspoken basis for discrimination. Many of us participate unconsciously in their perpetuation because of our inherited stereotypes about other classes and social groups. Learning about how class impacts our behaviors requires that we begin to recognize the stereotypes—"All rich people are snobs" or "All poor people are lazy," etc.—that we buy into without thinking. Define what class means to you and begin to recognize how your perceptions and class background affect your interaction with other people.

Group Skills

Acknowledge classism and how it affects our relationships.

Consciously recognize areas where our class background improves or impedes our ability to get ahead.

Create an internal checklist of how we personally use class boundaries to define the way we interact with other people.

Define and create possibilities for connecting beyond the limits we've established for ourselves.

Activities

■ Everybody's It

Activity Type:	Ice Breaker
Activity Level:	High
Space:	A grassy field is best for this game, but you can also mark off a section of the gym as a playing field.
Time:	About 15 minutes
Group Size:	Any
Prerequisite:	None
Props:	Four objects to establish the corners of the boundaries

Opening

The world has gone topsy-turvy and all of a sudden *Everybody's It!*

Directions

This activity has also been called "The World's Fastest Tag Game," and rightly so because everyone is literally IT. As in any tag game, if someone is IT, they chase someone else.

Set up your boundaries for the game and have the group spread out inside them. At your GO signal, everyone has to try to tag someone else. Whoever gets tagged first by someone else gets eliminated. Tell your participants to either sit down or put their hands on their heads to show that they are out. Whoever is lucky or skillful enough to make the tag keeps on going by trying to eliminate other players. The game continues until only one person is left, but don't let them rest on their laurels or congratulate themselves too hard; shout GO again and let the action renew itself.

Note: If the last few players are more cautious than confident, the game may drag as they try to avoid one another. To initiate action, announce that anyone who takes a backward step will be eliminated. The aggression is immediate.

Diversity Skills

Everybody's It is a great activity for helping groups make physical contact with one another in safe, trusting ways.

Processing

There's not a whole lot to process in this activity. You might just want to let everyone catch their breath.

Feelings Relay ■

Activity Type:	De-Inhibitizer
Activity Level:	Moderate
Space:	Your usual meeting room
Time:	20 minutes
Group Size:	Any
Prerequisite:	None
Props:	Index cards and felt-tipped pens. You can also purchase Feeling Marketplace cards from Project Adventure. Save the index cards from this activity for use in others, like *Body of Feeling*.

Opening

Have you ever been at a dinner party where there's more silverware on the table than you've ever seen in your life and sat there trying to guess which utensil you're supposed to use for what? When something like that happens, most of us are afraid to look foolish. Well, this is your chance to act goofy without worrying about what people are going to think.

Directions

Have the group sit down together and brainstorm a list of all the feelings they've ever had—from uncontrolled anger to hysterical laughter. Write each one on an index card and keep the pile next to you. Split the group in two. Have one person from each group pick a card from the pile. The person who took the card has to act-out that feeling to the group without speaking, and get them to guess what it is. Once they've guessed, the next person brings back the card and picks out another.

If no one in a group can guess what is on the card, let the actor exchange that card for another.

Diversity Skills

Feeling Relay is about communicating feelings in a fun, relaxed fashion. Try it any time and enjoy the silliness.

Processing

- How did it feel to act out the feeling or emotion?
- What did you notice?
- What did you learn about each other?
- What kinds of behaviors do you display when you feel certain emotions?
- Do you ever recognize people acting this way?

What Makes the World Go Round

Activity Type:	Trust Building/Problem Solving
Activity Level:	Low to moderate
Space:	Your usual meeting room
Time:	About half an hour
Group Size:	Any number over 4 or 5
Prerequisite:	None
Props:	You can make your own big puzzle out of cardboard or order a Diversity Puzzle from Project Adventure. Blindfolds.

Opening

A lot of times we get so caught up in what we think we have or don't have that we don't realize we're all in the same boat.

Directions

If you have more than 10 people in your group, divide it into 2 groups with 2 puzzles. Have the group choose 2 people to be their "guides." The two people need to be perceived as "different" from each other. In a few minutes, the rest of the group will be blindfolded and their task will be to put the puzzle together in a safe manner without talking or touching their guides. It's OK if they touch other members in their group, but they cannot talk.

The group which is to be blindfolded has 3 minutes to agree how they are going to communicate with each other nonverbally and how they are going to communicate with the guides without talking or touching them.

The guides should not be a part of the group discussion, but they can talk to each other to decide how they are going to communicate with their group without talking or touching.

Blindfold the group. Hand them the puzzle pieces. If you feel that your group may become quickly frustrated by this activity, you might want to impose a time limit before they begin, say three or five minutes.

After five minutes, which will be a long time for most groups, you may want to stop and process how everyone was feeling and then have the group go ahead and put the puzzle together with their eyes open. This will leave them with a positive experience and may encourage discussion about the need for open communication—keeping both eyes and ears open—in order to accomplish the task of making change happen.

Diversity Skills

This is a problem-solver that will fit in any time you're working on developing cooperation, trust, and team skills.

Processing

- How did it feel not to be able to see?
- How did it feel not to be able to talk?
- How did it feel not to be able to touch your guides?
- What was going on for the guides?
- How did you communicate with each other? What did you learn about communication?
- Did you notice any "status" differences between the guides and the puzzle makers?
- Was there collaboration between the guides and puzzle makers?
- What causes distrust among groups like these? Do you ever notice this at school?
- Did you learn anything new about trust, respect, and cooperation?
- Can you think of any ways to bring what you learned into your daily life?

Trust Pairs Walk

Activity Type:	Trust Building
Activity Level:	Moderate
Space:	A wooded area or outdoor space
Time:	About 45 minutes
Group Size:	8 or more
Prerequisite:	This activity can challenge the abilities of a group to take appropriate risks and to provide effective and safe leadership. Make sure your group has developed a high level of trust through the other trust-building activities.
Props:	Enough blindfolds for half the number of participants

Opening

You are about to embark on a journey through unfamiliar terrain, and surprises await you along the way. From here on in, you will be exploring the unknown.

Directions

Before starting this activity, set out a walking course that you feel comfortable with. There should be some obstacles (ups and downs, things to step over, things to go under, something to walk on top of, something small to climb up and/or down). But no obstacle should be included that will cause excessive risk to any participant. If you have any doubts when first setting a course, err on the side of caution until you observe how people manage the obstacles at hand. You may have to alter your course as you progress if the group is having too much trouble.

A wooded area seems best for this walk, but an appealing course can be created indoors. The best part about an outdoor trail with terrain unfamiliar to the participants is that it will create the impression of risk where little or no danger exists.

Lead the group to the area for the *Trust Walk*, stopping a short distance from where your trail begins. Brief the group at this point before taking them any further.

Working in pairs, one person will start blindfolded and one will be sighted, acting as guide. You can also ask players to close their eyes in a Challenge by Choice scenario. It is the sighted players' responsibility to keep their partners totally safe. The sighted guides must do whatever is necessary to prevent injury or discomfort to their partners. Guides must have physical contact with their partners at all times when they are moving, but they can position themselves any way they want in order to most effectively lead their partners safely through the course. A few examples of a guide's position are holding the partner's hand, putting one arm around the partner's waist, or walking in front with the partner's hands on their shoulders.

The guides should remember that they must be sensitive to their partner's emotional and psychological safety as well.

For most groups, we ask that the entire activity be accomplished in silence. The only breach of silence should be if there is a safety hazard or if any blindfolded partners begin to feel so uncomfortable that they want to stop. Be aware that some younger groups may need to verbally communicate in order to ensure safety.

Split your group into pairs. Ask for a volunteer from each pair to be blindfolded first. Give these students blindfolds and ask them to put them on. When everyone is ready, ask the guides to quietly go to their designated partners and put a hand on that person's shoulder. A hand on the shoulder assures the blindfolded students that someone is ready to guide them safely.

Explain that once they reach the halfway mark, you will signal to the guides to put their partners in an indicated safe place, then move away. The sightless partners will remove their blindfolds, hand them to someone who was previously a guide, then step away. Once the new group has put their blindfolds in place, the new set of guides will approach and place a hand on the shoulder of the individual they have chosen to guide—and the second half of the journey begins.

This technique adds a bit more uncertainty to the experience, since people will not know who their guide is to be. If this challenge seems too much, allow people to select their own guides.

Remind the leaders of the need to be responsible for their partners' safety. It might be helpful to offer an example of what that responsibility means.

Ask for any questions and if all the leaders are ready, tell the people that they need to follow as closely as possible in your footsteps. They should not deviate from your path to avoid obstacles. Pairs at the back of the line should follow the pair in front of them if they lose sight of your route.

Once you begin leading the group on the trail, WALK SLOWLY. Allow ample time for the pairs to negotiate the terrain and stop if necessary to prevent the pairs at the end of the line from dropping too far behind.

Move as quietly as you can and lead them through terrain that will challenge the guides and their partners.

If at any point you observe something that is unsafe and you fear someone may be injured, intervene immediately to spot, coach, or somehow assist the guide or blindfolded person.

When you reach the end, silently designate the safe area where the guides should leave their partners. Wait for everyone to finish and then ask the blindfolded people to remove their blindfolds.

Diversity Skills

Trust Pairs Walk can be a challenging activity for some groups, but it will work for almost any topic according to how you frame and process the way the pairs worked together. Be sure that your group is ready to physically take care of each other.

Processing

- What did it feel like being guided?

- What did it feel like being the guide?

- Were you frightened?

- What did your guide do to make you feel safe and comfortable?

- What, if any, communication took place between the guide and the partner?

- Have you ever experienced a situation where you felt "blinded"? What happened during this experience that might help you in a future situation where you feel lost or unsure about where you're going?

- Was there any difference between the first half of the journey and the second half? Did people experience it as being easier, harder, safer, more dangerous? Why?

- How did you establish a bond of trust between yourselves?

- Is there anything that you made you think you're not worthy to be a guide for other people? Worthy enough?

Field Wild Woosey

Activity Type:	Trust Building
Activity Level:	Moderately physical
Space:	Soft flooring, open area
Time:	20 minutes or so
Group Size:	Pairs
Prerequisite:	Some time working together
Props:	None. This is the field version of the low ropes course element *Wild Woosey*. (There is also a portable version available for purchase through Project Adventure.)

Opening

Learning to lean on each other can be difficult. It is even harder when we don't know a lot about the other person or we have made incorrect assumptions. In this activity, we're going to practice physically leaning on each other.

Directions

Keeping a stiff body, partners stand a short distance apart and grasp hands, leaning in toward each other for support.

After successfully holding that position for a specified number of seconds (goal time), have the pair increase the distance between themselves and try again.

After more than a few feet, spotters will be necessary on either side and underneath if the pair is really committed.

Have group members alternately choose someone they're comfortable with and someone they may not be so comfortable with.

Safety Note

Do not allow participants to interlock their fingers for a better grip. This locked position can cause excessive strain on their wrists if they begin to fall.

The only way students can achieve some distance between themselves is to commit to trusting that their partner will hold them up. Place one or two students under students going for a real lean. These spotters position themselves directly under the two leaning participants and bend at the waist with their hands on their knees. In this position, the spotters are prepared to take the weight of the leaning students if and when they achieve too much angle and fall forward.

Diversity Skills

Any, but be sure that your group has already spent some time together developing an atmosphere of safety and caring for one another.

Processing

- What does it take to succeed in this activity?
- How do these things relate to working together in real life?
- What concerns did you have when you saw who you were teamed with? Did your concerns end up being realistic?
- How did you communicate your concerns?
- What strengths (mental, emotional, physical) did your teammate bring to the activity?

Body of Feeling

Activity Type: Trust Building

Activity Level: Low

Space: Your usual meeting room

Time: About 45 minutes

Group Size: Any

Prerequisite: *Feeling Relay* activity, and the index cards used in it

Props: Large sheets of paper, marking pens, and yellow sticky pads

Opening

Your body is like a finely tuned machine. If you listen carefully, you can hear the gears grating when you don't shift smoothly. Let's try to find out what it is that makes the gears grind and see just what those feelings are trying to tell you.

Directions

Ask the group to go back and review their list of feelings from *Feeling Relay*. Discuss how we can isolate some of those feelings in our bodies. Get a volunteer to lie down on a large sheet of paper and have the group make an outline of the body on it. Give each person a yellow sticky pad and a marking pen. One at a time, say out loud the feelings that the group listed from *Feeling Relay*—anger, humiliation, joy, sadness, frustration, etc. As you say the feeling, have each person write it down with their name on one of the sticky sheets and then put it on the part of the body where they feel that emotion. You can stop at any time and process before you go on to the next feeling.

Put the outline up on the wall of your training room when the activity is done and refer back to it whenever some of these emotions come back into play for the group members. It can become a helpful visual aid during the rest of your work together.

Diversity Skills

This is a great activity for helping your group to identify, name, and understand emotions and their physical effects. It is important for young people to learn to express their emotions in a positive way as they explore their own issues with classism.

Processing

- What's easy about this?
- What's challenging?
- How in tune to your feelings are you?
- What's difficult or easy about identifying where you put your emotions?
- What kind of support do you need from the group to help you share your feelings?

Stepping Stones with a Twist

Activity Type:	Group Initiative
Activity Level:	Moderate to high
Space:	A good-sized room or outdoor space
Time:	Allow about an hour and a half for this activity.
Group Size:	10 or more
Prerequisite:	Good problem-solving skills
Props:	2 ropes for identifying the Take-Off (Point A) and Safe Zone (Point B), two-foot-square rug pads (one for each person), masking tape, one suitable safety or "rescue kit" to be carried along by group in the event of a catastrophe.

Opening

Explain to the group that they are on Planet Diversity—a marvelous world of beauty, peace, and fecundity. The people there want to spread their chromosomal bounty throughout the universe, so they are embarking on a space voyage to another world. To leave the planet they will need special life-support vehicles to carry them safely through space and shield their genetic treasure. Their life-support vehicles are the props. Any life-support system can support as many people as can stand on it.

Directions

The goal is to get from Point A to Point B without touching the ground in between. Give everyone a rug pad and have them write on a piece of masking tape what skill, resource, or experience they are bringing to help the group achieve its goal. Put the masking tape on the rug pad and ask everyone to share with the group what their rug represents. These rug pads will enable their group to cross to Point B. The group goal is to get everyone across. But before they begin, take away one rug pad—one of the skills will usually be repeated, so take away one of these doubles.

Anyone touching the ground in space; i.e., between the boundaries, must return to the home planet for decontamination and spiritual healing. Rescuing these travelers is recommended, since all people are expected to arrive safely at the new planet.

For a life-support vehicle/system to function, someone must be touching it at all times when it is in space to maintain the 98.6° temperature necessary to maintain DNA viability. If a life-support is untouched for even an instant, it ceases to function and is immediately removed from the activity. Example: A person tosses the support onto the ground, and then steps onto it. Because it left that person's grasp when it was tossed, it is lost forever. A correct use would be to place it on the ground and step onto it while maintaining contact.

Generally, life-support vehicles can only move in a forward direction. If you make this a rule, you may eliminate the possibility of a rescue should someone fall into space. Sometimes, only a few props are allowed to go in reverse, or props can only cross the universe one time. This rule attempts to prohibit the solution of having people "shuffle" across space using two props as skates and sending them back for another person to use. It's a creative solution, but individualistic; it doesn't require much teamwork or cooperation. It may, however, be a very effective technique for younger groups. Usually groups employ this method because they are stuck and can't think of anything else that will work. It's important for the group to pursue creative alternatives whenever possible, but on balance, it's probably better to limit the number of times props can cross the gap or prohibit them from going in reverse.

Be extremely watchful for untouched life-supports. People try to hide the fact that they make a mistake. Don't let an untouched prop remain in use unless the group really needs to succeed in order to keep morale up. Remind the group of the Full Value Contract and owning up to a mistake.

Setting boundaries: Generally, it makes sense to set the boundaries far enough apart so that the group will need to recycle some of their props in order to cross the gap. Step out the distance—one step for each person plus 5 more steps. This spacing requires the group to work together to use their props, using some of the materials twice to be successful.

Variation

Divide the group in half. Each group starts on a different planet—half at Point A and half at Point B. They must exchange places. Each group gets one fewer prop than people. Do not state it explicitly, but the groups may share their resources (props) if they choose to. The focus of the problem suddenly becomes one of identifying whether two different goals can be pursued simultaneously for a common good, or will the two groups operate independently and/or competitively.

Diversity Skills

This activity is a good opportunity for the group to learn how to communicate, cooperate, and compromise effectively with each other through trial-and-error participation in a problem-solving activity. It allows them to see what each of them brings to the process and how they validate each other.

Processing

- What was the first thing the group did to try to solve the problem? Did you plan? What was the plan?

- What roles did people take in planing? In completing the plan?

- What role did you take? Why? Did anyone feel pushed into a role?

- How do we place people into roles?

- How do we feel when we make mistakes? What do we do?

- Our resources help us get through life. A lot of times we limit ourselves by thinking that material resources are the only ones that count. We forget to look at our own inner resources or the resources that other people have to offer. How do you think you contributed to the challenge? Others?

Climbing the Wall ■

Activity Type:	Group Initiative
Activity Level:	High
Space:	This is a low challenge ropes course, problem solving initiative normally involving a pre-constructed wooden wall built outdoors.
Time:	45 minutes to an hour
Group Size:	8 or more
Prerequisite:	This activity is physically challenging and the less physically active members of the group may feel intimidated by it. Make sure that the group is working together well and respecting the Full Value Contract so that no one will feel left out or overwhelmed by this activity.
Props:	You will need a Project Adventure *Wall* for this activity. The *Wall* is a classic low ropes course element and is simply a 9–12-foot blank-faced wall with a platform built about 4 feet from the top on the back side for participants to stand on who make it over the top. There is a ladder, rope, or other means to descend from this platform. Contact Project Adventure for instructions on constructing your own *Wall* or having one built.

Opening

Do you need a good, swift kick in the seat of your "can'ts"? Well, this a chance to use others as resources to address your can'ts.

Directions

Using all its members, the group must get everyone up and over the *Wall*. The group may have three persons on the top of the wall, assisting a fourth person up and over. The sides of the wall and support trees or poles cannot be used. Articles of clothing are generally not used, but see Variations.

Facilitator's Responsibilities:

Check area for unsafe ground cover.

Inspect trees and support braces for soundness. Check wall surface for any deterioration.

Affix the descending rope behind the wall, or if it's a permanent attachment, check the rope for soundness.

Make sure that the top and face of the wall are smooth and free of splinters.

Make sure that no nails are protruding from the wall.

Check wall-related structures for soundness—platforms, braces, railings, support ropes, ladders.

Review spotting procedures, and remind the group of the importance of group spotting due to the height of the obstacle.

Secure a commitment from the group to pay particular attention to spotting the back side of the wall.

Stress the importance of spotting an individual throughout the entire task.

Stress proper lifting and support, especially when participants are standing on other participants' shoulders or are being lifted up to that position.

Gain a commitment from the group to pay particular attention to spotting the last two members, especially if they are to try a running and jumping attempt.

Do not allow the group to use belts, shoelaces, or other articles of clothing that might not support the heavier members of the group.

Participants' Responsibilities:

Agree to support everyone's effort and to spot each participant from the beginning of starting the wall, while on the top, and all the way down the back side.

Agree to have only three people on top of the wall and one in transition.

Agree to have an appropriate number of spotters on the front and back of the wall at all times with their focus being on spotting only.

Agree not to hang the next-to-last individual by the legs in order to reach the last member of the group.

Variations

If a group has difficulty with height or arm strength among the members, allow the rope to be used for the first and last two participants.

Immobilize an appendage to simulate a broken arm, leg, etc.

Attempt the task nonverbally.

Diversity Skills

The *Wall* is an excellent metaphor for the barriers to getting things accomplished that we face and construct in our lives. You can frame this activity as a metaphor for any situation.

Processing

- How were people's needs met?

- What was it like to have people there to support you?

- What happened to the group's needs?

- What parallels can you draw from your school concerns?

- How well did the group share their resources so that everyone could get over the wall?

The Rules of the Game ■

Activity Type:	Social Responsibility
Activity Level:	Moderate to high
Space:	Open playing field or gym
Time:	About 20 minutes, more if the group wants to keep going
Group Size:	15 or more
Prerequisite:	Trust activities
Props:	Lots and lots of tennis balls or similarly sized balls, a marking pen, and five hula hoops.

Opening

Access to information gives us power. How do you handle it when you can't get information? Does it discourage you or make you more determined?

Directions

Mark each ball with a large capital letter. Use the game Scrabble as a guide. This means you'll need more e's than c's, more a's than k's, only one z and x, and so on. Lay out the five hula hoops on the ground in the same pattern as the number five on a die; in other words, one in the center and four outside corner hoops. Put all the balls into the center loop. Place the corner hoops about 10 yards from each other. (The further apart you place them from each other, the more running will be involved.)

Divide the group into four smaller groups and have each one stand by one of the four corner hoops. On GO, one person from each group runs to the center hoop, picks up one ball, and returns to their home hoop. The picked-up ball must be immediately placed in the home hoop and cannot be protected from opposing players. As soon as the ball is deposited in the home hoop, any other player on another team (but only one) can take off to grab another ball from the center hoop, OR from any of the other hoops.

The point of all this scoping and scooping of balls is to get five balls that spell a word. A group can have more than five balls in the hoop, but five of them in combination must spell a word. The first team to do so wins. If you want to try it again, scoop up the balls and put them back in the center.

After you've gone through this activity once, tell them you're going to do it again the same way. Then hand each of the groups separate written instructions as follows:

Group 1: "Your job is to pick up any five letters in alphabetical order: a, b, c, d, e or any other combination."

Group 2: "Your job is to pick up five vowels."

Group 3: "Your job is to pick up five consonants."

Group 4: "You are the only group that is doing this activity the correct way. Follow my verbal instructions and make up words of five or more letters. When you see that the other groups are doing things differently, make fun of them, tease them, or ignore them altogether. Act superior, as if you know something they don't."

Use a stop sign or time-out signal at different moments during this activity to ask different participants to tell the group what kinds of emotions they are experiencing and what kinds of behaviors or reactions they think they are displaying.

Diversity Skills

All subjects

Processing

- How did it feel to be treated differently?

- What were some of your physical reactions? Emotional reactions?

- How did it feel to have different information than another group? Did it bother you at all?

- Where did you get the most support and validation?

- Do you ever feel you have a different set of instructions than others? Why do you think this is so?

- Do people from different classes have different "instructions" or goals? Why?

- How might these differing goals impact our ability to all get along?

- How does this game parallel what happens in your school or home life?

Islands of Life

Activity Type:	Social Responsibility
Activity Level:	Moderate
Space:	Open area with enough room for everyone to move around
Time:	40 minutes
Group Size:	12 or more
Prerequisite:	None
Props:	Ropes, balls, any stuff that can be tossed around to connect people

Opening

Is America really a land of equal opportunity? What can we do to level the playing field for everyone?

Directions

Have everyone line up side by side in a straight line. As they listen to the questions you read from the following list, tell them to move forward one step as an affirmative answer and backward one step as a negative answer.

After you've asked several questions, tell the people who are still standing more or less in a straight line to move together in a straight line shoulder to shoulder. Continue with the questions.

Stop whenever you want and ask the groups (islands) standing together to brainstorm ideas for building bridges between the groups to get them lined up equally. Let them use any of the props you have lying around.

Questions:

Did both of your parents graduate from college?

Do you like hockey?

Do you prefer basketball over hockey?

Have you ever had swimming lessons?

Is the newspaper read on a daily basis in your home?

Have you ever traveled outside the Untied States?

Is English your first language?

Do you live with both your parents?

Has your family been in this country for more than two generations?

Have you or anyone in your family ever used personal connections to get into school or to get a job?

Has your family started a fund for you to go to college?

Do you or have you ever gone to a private summer camp?

Does your family own a vacation home or time share?

Does your family go on regular vacations?

Do you consider yourself part of the dominant group in the United States?

Are you male?

Are you part of a group that made laws to exclude other racial and ethnic groups in this country?

Do you watch PBS or the Discovery channel often?

Do you have more than one personal computer at home?

Are you allowed to watch TV?

Have you ever had private music lessons?

Do you sing in a choir?

Do you have a piano at home?

Do you have a washer and dryer at home?

Do you go to the laundromat to wash your clothes?

Do you ride the bus to go to school?

Have you ever been on a subway?

Do you own a boom box?

Do you know what arros con pollo is?

Have you ever been through a rite of passage ceremony?

Have you ever been on an airplane?

Have you been on an airplane more than 5 times?

Do you iron your own clothes?

Do you live with more than one generation?

Diversity Skills

You can gear this activity to any subject according to the questions you ask the group.

Processing

- How did you feel about the questions that were asked?
- How did you feel about moving forward?
- How did it feel to move backward?
- What were some of the strategies you came up with to bring the groups together? How did you arrive at the solutions?

Closing Activity

Verbal Gift Giving

Have everyone pick one person in the group and state a positive attribute, characteristic, or trait that they uncovered about them during the day.

Personal Journal Questions

If you invited a homeless person to spend the night at your house, what would you find challenging? What would you be nervous about? What do you think the two of you would do or talk about?

Processing Questions

❏ Can you name a feeling (mad, glad, sad, or scared) you had at any point in completing the activity? Where in your body did you feel it most?

❏ Is that feeling a common one in your life?

❏ Did you express that feeling to others? If not, what did you do with the feeling?

❏ Do you usually express feelings or suppress them?

❏ Would you like to feel differently in a similar situation? If so, how would you like to feel?

❏ How do you imagine others felt toward you at various times during the activity? Were these feelings expressed?

❏ What types of feelings are easiest to express? Most difficult?

❏ Do you find it difficult to be aware of some feelings at times? If so, which ones?

❏ Are some feelings not appropriate to express to the group at times? If so, which ones?

❏ Does expressing appropriate feelings help or hinder completing the initiative?

❏ Is it difficult for you to avoid judging others? Explain.

❏ Can you think of examples of when you judged others in the group today? When you didn't judge others?

❏ What were some advantages to you of not judging others?

❏ What were some advantages to others of your not judging them?

❏ How does judging and not judging others affect the completion of the activity?

❏ Were some behaviors of others easy not to judge and other behaviors difficult?

❏ How were group decisions made in completing the activity?

❏ Were you satisfied with the ways decisions were made? Explain.

❏ Did the group arrive at any decisions through group consensus? (Some didn't get their first choice, but they could live with the decision.)

❏ Were some decisions made by one or several individuals?

❏ When a choice was available, did everyone in the group express an opinion? If not, why not?

❏ What is the best way for this group to make decisions? Explain.

❏ Do you respond in similar ways in other groups?

❏ What did you like about how the group made decisions? What didn't you like?

❏ Can you think of specific examples of when the group cooperated in completing the activity? Explain.

❏ How did it feel to cooperate?

❏ Do you cooperate in most things you do?

❏ How did you learn to cooperate?

❏ What are the rewards of cooperating?

❏ How did cooperative behavior lead to successfully completing the activity?

❏ How can you cooperate in other areas of your life?

❏ Did you think anyone was blocking the group from cooperating? Explain.

❏ Can you give examples of when you trusted someone in the group?

❏ Is it easier to trust some people more than others? Explain.

❏ Can you think of examples when trusting someone wasn't a good idea?

❏ How do you increase your level of trust for someone?

❏ On a scale of 1–10, rate how much trust you have in the group as a whole.
  Can you explain your rating?

❏ What did you do today that deserves the trust of others?

❏ How does the amount of fear you feel affect your trust of others?

❏ How are you different from some of the others in the group?

❏ How do these differences strengthen the group as a whole?

❏ What would this group be like if there were very few differences in people? How would you feel if this were so?

❏ How are you like some of the others in the group?

❏ Were these commonalities a help to the group in completing their task? Explain.

❏ Were these commonalities a hindrance to the group in completing their task? Explain.

❏ Do you think you have other things in common with some of the group members that you haven't found yet?

❏ How did this setting help you discover how you are similar to others?

❏ What have you learned about trust, respect, acceptance, and cooperation as they relate to differences?

❏ Did you find yourself responding to any stereotypes? What were they? How do you think you might respond to the same situation in the future?

❏ What has changed for you as a result of participating in this activity? How do you think you'll perceive people who are different from you—blacks, whites, gays, or whoever is appropriate—as a result?

❏ How does this activity relate to the real-life experiences you are faced with at home, in school, or in your neighborhood?

❏ What did it feel like to ask for help from someone you used to think of as the member of a group that wouldn't help or support you?

❏ Was there any kind of discrimination going on this activity? If so, what?

❏ What was the most difficult part of this activity as it relates to how you deal with people who are different from you?

❏   What was the easiest part of this activity as it relates to how you deal with people who are different from you?

❏   Did this activity challenge any of your beliefs?

❏   What are your feelings now?

❏   Is there anything in this activity you would do differently? Why?

❏   As a result of this activity, what are some of the things you think or feel that we all have in common?

❏   Do you think there are more commonalities or differences between _____ and _____?

❏   What will you remember most about having participated in this activity?

14

Prevention

· · · · · · · · · · · · · · · · · · ·

Over the years, in our combined experience as therapists, consultants and facilitators of diversity workshops for numerous organizations, we have come across many individuals suffering emotional pain—pain that is often debilitating and a direct result of prejudice and discrimination. The common denominator for all these people, regardless of the source of their pain—sexual orientation, physical disabilities, race, religion, gender, age, or ethnicity—is a life fraught with coping with the emotional repercussions. As we began to work together more, we started what has become a long series of discussions about how different people cope with discrimination and prejudice. If prejudicial thoughts and discriminatory acts are risk factors for some, then what are the protective factors that are in place for others? What is it that allows some people to cope in a manner that is not physically, emotionally, or spiritually damaging?

The more we talked about this, the more we began to think that if we could find ways to identify the protective factors people use and the skills needed to foster them, we could then help other individuals also learn to put them in place. We began this search by looking for both theoretical and experiential methods to teach people new ways of responding to prejudice and discrimination. New ways that might foster the kind of individual and group relationships that could become the seeds for positive change.

Many of those skills have already been reviewed in this workbook, but we would like to leave you here with some theoretical background on prevention theory and some program ideas that will help you keep getting the word out. The more we spread our knowledge and experience, the more diversity will become a positive concept that all of us embrace and welcome. It is our belief that we are all partners in the same struggle!

Prevention

Many people view William Lofquist as the "father of prevention theory." His view is that the common methods for dealing with problematic social behaviors—crime, delinquency, substance abuse, mental health problems, child abuse, violence, teen pregnancy, suicides, etc.—tend to be reactive as opposed to proactive. What this means is that instead of looking for and attempting to change the environmental factors contributing to unhealthy attitudes and behavior, our culture tends to focus on fixing the symptoms of problematic individual behavior. For example, a typical response to a teen suicide attempt would be to call in a counselor for individual problem solving. Often times, once the crisis has calmed and the youth appears to be coping more effectively, the intervention ends. Unfortunately, however, the risk factors in the youth's environment have not been dealt with and are probably still firmly in place. This is a reactive approach—we react to the symptoms.

But a suicide attempt is not an originating cause. We like to use the analogy of the smoke detector to describe this phenomenon. If the smoke detector in your house goes off, you probably wouldn't just pull the battery out—react—and then forget all about it. You'd go looking for a fire—proact—and once you found the source, you'd put it out. Too often, once a crisis subsides, we forget all about continuing to look for the fire that set off the smoke detector in the first place.

What is a proactive approach to prevention? A proactive approach looks at the existing norms around health and behavior and examines whether or not they are supporting or refuting the problematic behavior. Proactive "prevention is the active process of creating conditions and fostering personal attributes that promote the well-being of people." Instead of looking only at the individual, we must shift responsibility for the problems from the individual to the community. In the case of our attempted teen suicide, it doesn't mean that we should forego appropriate crisis intervention and treatment. It does mean that we should also look at the problem within the context of the broader conditions in which the youth lives.

Perhaps some of the issues that provoked the suicide attempt are common to many of the young adults in their school or community. If so, then an in-school program that provides problem-solving techniques for all students might be in order. And what about the parents? A proactive approach would include the parents in the solution as well. At this point, programs that include the community and promote healthy parent/child relationships are in order. A proactive approach to prevention should involve all members of the community in the solution because it is the most effective means of changing the fundamental norms and conditions that contributed to the suicide attempt. When we begin to work, not just with the individual, but also with changing the existing norms and environmental factors that surround the individual, we are looking for the fire, not just silencing the smoke detector.

In our opinion, learning how to search for the fire means that we must create a shift in the way our human services function. By human services, we mean anyone who works with people in an attempt to foster a process of positive change. Some of the characteristics of the reactive model, or paradigm, are as follows:

■ The focus is on delivering a service.

■ "Professional" individuals are responsible for affecting change.

■ Power is vested in agencies.

■ Professionals are the experts.

■ The decision-making process is closed or limited to professionals.

■ Linkage between agencies and professionals is limited to coordination and networking.

■ Community participation is limited to providing input and feedback.

■ Ethnic and cultural differences are made light of or ignored.

A healthier model might go as follows:

■ The focus is on community empowerment.

■ The community is the expert and responsible for affecting change.

■ The power to affect change resides in the community.

■ The decision-making process is inclusive.

■ Emphasis is placed on cooperation and collaboration.

■ The community is maximally involved at all levels.

■ Diversity—whether ethnic, racial, cultural, sexual, age, class, or ability related—is valued and regarded as a community asset.

As human service agents and prevention professionals, it is our responsibility to contribute actively to the process of engendering a paradigm shift from the old to the new in our schools and communities. If we continue to try to instill change without influencing the underlying organizational trends and environmental factors that contribute to the problems of our youth, the smoke detectors will continue to sound their alarms.

Risk and Protective Factors

Creating a shift from the old to a new paradigm of prevention is also an integral part of the process of creating communities that welcome and value human diversity. Proactive prevention should provide the framework for any educational program designed to teach the skills necessary for dealing with prejudicial or discriminatory attitudes. It is up to us to create programs that help individuals not only sharpen their own self-awareness, but also to improve their sense of self-esteem and self-worth. As you've probably learned through using this book, adventure learning techniques adapt wonderfully to this process, because they help groups create safe environments that facilitate discussion, compromise, and understanding around personal value.

We need to create these environments within our own communities. In order to achieve this goal, the emphasis of our work should be on eliminating the risk factors that contribute to the impact of prejudicial and discriminatory attitudes, while fostering the protective factors that shield individuals and communities from the effects of negative attitudes.

Risk factors are attitudes, beliefs, behaviors, situations, and actions that put individuals, groups, organizations, and communities at risk and create harmful or negative environments. Within the arena of human diversity, the major risk factors for our youth are engendered in their family, school, and peer groups and are signaled by some of the conditions we've listed below. Our list is not at all inclusive. We encourage you to add to it as you begin to identify other risk factors during your work with young adults.

Family

- Lack of clear behavioral expectations, particularly in regard to valuing and caring for others

- Insufficient monitoring of prejudicial thoughts and discriminatory acts

- Inadequate caring and affection

- Parental attitudes that foster prejudice and discrimination, including a history of prejudice and discrimination

School

- No clear, enforced policy regarding prejudicial and discriminatory attitudes and behavior

- Administrative and staff attitudes that foster prejudice and discrimination

■ Devaluing of individuals based on their race, ethnicity, age, gender, sexual orientation, class or religious beliefs. This includes both covert thinking and overt actions, such as class activities or the selection of important student leaders.

■ No commitment to change

Individual & Peer

■ Early discriminatory behavior

■ Alienation and rebelliousness

■ Susceptibility to peer influences

■ Favorable attitudes and friends who participate in prejudicial and discriminatory behavior

On the other end of the spectrum are the protective factors. These are the attitudes, beliefs, and actions that protect individuals, groups, organizations, and communities from the impacts of negative behavior. If you have used the activities in this book with a group of youth, you may have begun to recognize the development of some of these protective factors. You should also have begun to see how effective these protective factors can be in helping people turn the experience of human diversity into an enriching and rewarding opportunity for growth.

Protective Factors

■ Opportunities to contribute and be regarded as a resource

■ Positive, caring relationships with people who are different, whether it be in age, race, religion, gender, sexual orientation, class or whatever

■ A sense of humor

■ Healthy expectations and a positive outlook that includes all people

■ A strong sense of self-esteem and internal locus of control

■ Self-discipline

■ An environment that encourages the development of problem solving and critical thinking skills

■ Families that value diversity and consistently monitor and discourage prejudicial or discriminatory behaviors and attitudes

■ School, family, peer and community environments that actively promote and foster positive views of the full spectrum of diversity

Worksheet

How do you define prevention? _____

_____

_____

What are some of the biggest challenges you face when working with young people? _____

_____

_____

What are some of your greatest hopes for youth? _____

_____

_____

Where do you get your support? _____

_____

_____

How do you view the youth you work with? As resources, objects?

_____

_____

_____

What do you think were some of the risk factors in your environment when you were growing up? How do you think you overcame them? Where did your support come from? _____

_____

_____

The following vignettes are taken from the work that Project Adventure and the Community Prevention Partnership have done in the town of Brattleboro, Vermont. We feel that they are excellent examples of how the work of a few individuals can be felt throughout a community and generate widespread involvement. The Youth Offender's Workshop was an offshoot of a community policing training that Project Adventure and the Community Prevention Partnership organized for the Brattleboro Police Department. One of the officers, Sergeant Matt Nally, has become very involved in working with youth who are on probation or constantly coming up before the police for a variety of reasons—drug use, vandalism, delinquency, criminal behavior. The vignette that follows is his story of participation in an adventure-based workshop for paroled youth.

The Youth Offender's Workshop

The probationers program was for ten kids on parole. It was very positive. It was uplifting. It was productive. I [Sergeant Matt Nally, Police Department, Brattleboro, Vermont] wasn't the only one working with the kids. Dave Macmillan, one of Brattleboro's parole officers, and Kelly Brigham McMillan, from Project Adventure, were also there. The program lasted six weeks, and we met every Saturday for the whole day. I think I was able to get through to a couple of the kids during those six weeks. I also think we made a difference with those kids, and even though we might not have changed them totally, we got them started on thinking about other ways of getting through life.

It was uncomfortable at first, trying to get to know everybody's name, trying to do a Full Value Contract, and trying to get these kids involved with the work. No one wanted to volunteer to do anything. They didn't want to break down, and they didn't want to get into open dialogue.

The atmosphere was very difficult. These guys had their image; they were hiding behind it as if it was a shield or something. I can't explain it. It's like a kid going to the mall with his parents. He doesn't want to be seen with them. He's got that, 'I'm too cool to be here.' And I know that I made them especially uncomfortable because I had already dealt with most of them on the street.

After a meeting or two, the kids began to open up. We played a lot of games and I tried to be as open and the least threatening and the least intimidating as I could possibly be. And it worked. They started to open up. We had some issues with one of the kids who was smoking dope. He said it would be very difficult for him not to drink or get high from week to week. We worked out a compromise with him where he agreed not to get high or drink within 48 hours of our Saturday meetings. From Thursday night or Friday morning, he started to dry out and that worked. There were a few times when things got heated. A couple of times he threatened us, saying stuff like, 'Fine, if you don't like the way I am, I'll walk out now. I'm not going to continue with this stuff.' But he never did. We always managed to bring him back into the group and get him focused again on our goals.

There was a lot of growth between one of the guys and his Parole Officer, Dave. When we started, there was intimidation, fear, and a complete lack of communication and understanding between this one individual and his parole officer. When we were doing the workshop, though, we linked up with each other and shared a lot of our private thoughts. We did *The Being*, an activity where the group sets up the boundaries for the kind of environment they want to create by drawing the silhouette of a person on a big piece of paper. Inside the silhouette they write down the positive qualities they want the group to embody like respect, caring, listening and all those things that are a part of the Full Value Contract. Outside, they put all the negative things they don't want in the group like dissing, arguing, ignoring people's feelings, and all the other stuff we don't always have control over but that can hurt us when other people don't respond or listen to our needs. Well, by the time we had finished the activity and set up some strong, safe boundaries for the group's interaction, this guy moved over to his PO and said, 'Hey, listen Dave, there are times when I violate my probation, but I'm scared to death to be honest with you about it. I'm afraid something's going to happen and I'm going to get in trouble. But it's real difficult for me to lie to you, too.' It was so nice to see that relationship come around for the two of them.

One of the other kids, Dave, has pretty much straightened his stuff out. He's getting married this fall and invited me to the wedding. He and I still stay in touch. That never, never would have occurred if it wasn't for the course. He's been in some small time trouble, but nothing big. We never could have the relationship that we have now and it all goes back to what we did together. We've even talked about some of the things. I ask him if he's on schedule with what he planned to do. And he tells me the truth. His girlfriend got pregnant, had a baby and now they're planning on getting married. It's a good feeling. I know that in five years, if I look at this kid, really look at him, we can get back to what we once did together, what we once had. I'm convinced that would happen.

The entire program reinforced the idea for me that working one-on-one or with small groups of people, and treating people as individuals and maybe walking a mile in their shoes, help you understand when you deal with them out on the street again.

On the last day, we had a barbecue and they brought their girlfriends to it. What it really felt like that last day, it was like letting your kid walk out of the house for the first time to go over to his friend's house. There's a sign of independence there. These kids, there are two roads in front of them now. They can choose this path or that path. Before, they didn't know any better. They saw the cops as assholes. They saw the Parole Officer as who knows what? I can speak for the one kid; he saw him as a big monster that he was intimidated by and afraid of and who could squish them like a bug. Yet we were able to bring a personal touch along to the work without losing our professionalism. They all know that I'm still a cop, and if they're caught with dope on them, we have to deal with it. It's not like, 'I know Matt now, we can let this slide.' They know that and I think they respect that.

Talk N' Harmony

Talk N' Harmony is just one example of how the pieces of a community can come together. I couldn't state exactly when tension and frustration began building up in Harmony Parking Lot between kids who want to hang out, store owners who want a shopper-friendly downtown, police, and shoppers who wonder if they are safe. I do know that a few months ago, people started doing something about these frustrations. The Brattleboro Business Community, the police, CPP [The Community Prevention Partnership, a federally funded, Project Adventure sponsored community wide drug and alcohol abuse prevention organization], Office of Alcohol and Drug Abuse Prevention, Youth Services, the Recreation Department, 17 Flat Street [The Brattleboro, Vermont Teen Center], students from BUHS [Brattleboro Union High School], the Diversity Team and the Leadership Project, and young adults who spend time in the lot all found ways to connect to one another.

I wish I could name all the individuals who put a great deal of time into making the Talk N' Harmony dialogue happen, but there are too many to list. I will say it was a blast of see it happen: store owners talking with young people about how they spend their time, police officers in plain-clothes listening to rap music (I won't say they were all loving it), little kids running around and everyone hoping the rain would wait for us to finish (it almost did). We made connections. We know each other now, or know each other a little better. We have some ideas and some resources and a good deal of energy. We have a place and a time to meet again to see if we can make some stuff happen. I guess I feel like we already have a little 'harmony back in the lot.'

Denise Prescott, Reprinted from Prevention Connection, the Newsletter of the Community Prevention Partnership, June 1994.

Moving On

We realize that the information we've provided you in the previous two sections may seem overwhelming. Just when you thought you were finished with your program, here is a conclusion that offers you more information about how to move ahead with your group! Your group may or may not feel comfortable with continuing their work once the program is over, but then again, you may have generated so much enthusiasm that they'll be asking, "What next?" It's in this context that we provide some information on prevention theory as well as some ideas for activities, programs, and projects that will broaden the scope of the work you have been doing with your group. Some groups may want to include these projects as part of their program; others may feel that it's time to get their friends, family, or community involved in their learning once the program is over. Let the students decide how they want to incorporate the ideas from this chapter into their work. Your job is to support their enthusiasm to the best of your ability!

Remember that you most likely have a group of able and willing allies who just went on an adventure with you. They will probably become, if they are not already, your best resources for achieving these goals. You have a set of tools, and now the machine needs tuning up and rebuilding to make it work and improve on itself. We've provided the following list of ideas to help you continue your experience and plan some action around these issues in your environment.

For individuals:

Encourage the people you know and encounter to read books and articles by diverse authors and organize a discussion around the subjects they present. We've compiled a list of possible reading materials for you in Appendix IV.

Create an environment the encourages discussion and interaction. Get a group of your friends together and go to movies, art galleries, museums, festivals, and the theater.

Challenge people to buy and listen to music from other cultures.

Purchase magazines and publications that will familiarize you with issues that pertain to other cultures.

Talk to the people you know and meet about what you have gained and learned from experiencing this book.

When you hear prejudicial judgments and stereotypical remarks challenge them and encourage the speaker to examine where they came from.

Don't be afraid to engage in conversations that touch on the subjects covered in this book. It is okay to be uncomfortable. It's a learning experience.

Familiarize yourself with other religions by reading, attending services, and asking questions.

Reflect on some of the experiences you had as a young adult regarding some of the issues you know young adults are dealing with now. Interracial dating, interfaith marriages or dating, gay and lesbian relationships, sexual harassment and discrimination, name calling, how you feel now about going back to high school reunions, what dating was like for you in high school are just a few of the subjects.

Ask adults from diverse backgrounds to share their experiences with you.

Some Program Ideas

Organize a series of multi-cultural dinners. Have each course or each meal at a different house.

Consider developing a peer mediation program with your group. There are many curriculums available from your local youth services bureau. Incorporate a diversity component in the program.

Organize an art exhibition with a group of local young artists from diverse backgrounds. This could be a great fund-raiser.

Organize an open forum discussion between the local Board of Education or Town Council and your students concerning their experiences of diversity in the local community. This might be a way for you to ask for resources to deal with these issues.

Organize a small theater group to develop and perform skits about diversity issues for schools, religious, and civic organizations, and other community groups. Include a group discussion in your program, but be ready for some pretty tough processing of feelings and issues!

Contact your local cable network and public access channel and see if they are willing to help you develop special programming around diversity issues: Asian festivals, teen discussions about diversity, a teen/adult forum with community representatives such as the Mayor, etc.

Propose that your local newspaper provide a small, quarterly column written by teens about their experiences with diversity.

Contact the National Office of the Anti-Defamation League and request A World of Difference Training for your school or community. In particular, we recommend the *Names Can Really Hurt Us* video program. This is facilitated by A World of Difference trainers and a student panel. Once the video has been viewed by the audience, the students reflect upon their actual experiences recorded in the video. After, the trainers and students facilitate small, group discussions concerning the issues and problems raised by the program.

Encourage the teens you encounter to develop a critical eye concerning all types of media that produce stereotypical, discriminatory, and prejudicial images and words. They can take action against it! For example, have them write letters to the editor, contact the public relations department at TV and radio stations by letter, e-mail, or through an organized campaign to present your concerns. We've used an effective ruse before, and it's simple to do. Create a pre-printed adhesive message that outlines your viewpoint and return it on pre-paid postage magazine subscription cards. It costs them money and they DO get the message!

Develop discussion questions with the youth you come into regular contact with and ask them to share the questions with their parents.

Develop multi-generational and cross-cultural teams to help you fight these issues. Send them out with an organized program to train other groups. Use the activities in this book or purchase other Project Adventure books and create experiences that will challenge people to join you and spread the Experience of Diversity.

Further Reading

Lofquist, William. *Discovering the Meaning of Prevention: A Practical Approach to Positive Change*. Tucson, AZ: Associates for Youth Development. 1983

Appendix I

Defining Terms of Diversity

The list of terms we use to describe other people is practically infinite, and each of us ascribes to them different meaning. The following list represents all the terms we could think of to describe people. But instead of providing definitions for them, we'd like to you to come up with your own. Try to list the assumptions you make when you hear the terms as well. For example, what image does the term "blue collar" bring to mind? What kind of person hides behind the term? Describe that person.

Research any of the terms you are unfamiliar with. It is an interesting exercise to do this worksheet in a group. Have each person write out their definitions then put them all together and discuss them as a group. You may not have heard of all of the terms on the list and a group discussion may help you gain some insights into unfamiliar territories.

Identifying Descriptors of Diversity

Age	Learning styles	Bias
Class	Looks	Prejudice
Classism	Mannerisms	Discrimination
Communication styles	Mental ability	Glass ceiling
Country of origin	Physical ability	Privilege
Diversity	Race	Dominant culture
Ethnicity	Religion	Non-dominant culture
Gender	Sexual orientation	
Heterosexism	Oppression	

Race: Institutionalized Identifying Descriptors

Racism	European American	European
White	Bi-Racial	Puerto Rican
Latino	Multi-Racial	Multi-Cultural
African American	Asian-American	Chicano
Asian	Black	Indian
Pacific Islander	People of Color	Colored
Native American	Hispanic	Color-blind
Eskimo	Mexican	
Inuit	Mexican American	

Sexual Orientation: Identifying Descriptors

Heterosexual	Heterophobic	Transsexual
Homosexual	Transgender	Normal
Bisexual	Lesbian	Sexism
Homophobic	Gay	

Religion: Identifying Descriptors

Religious Freedom	Buddhist	Shinto
Catholic	Muslim	Zoroastrian
Protestant	Atheist	
Jewish	Agnostic	

Class: Identifying Descriptors

Rich	Community	Blue collar
Poor	Neighborhood	Pink collar
Wealthy	Hood	White collar
Middle Class	Ghetto	Rich
Lower Class	Gated community	Qualifications
Underclass	Owning class	Welfare
Upper Class	Working class	Power
WASP	Private property	Enfranchised
JAP	Public property	Disenfranchised
Privileged	Family	

Appendix II

Group Roles

compiled by Dr. H. L. (Lee) Gillis

There is no such thing as an unstructured group. Over the years, we have found that people will assume and take on a variety of roles as a group begins to form and progress through its development stages. Following is a list of some of the roles that students in your group may take on as well as some ideas for how you, as the facilitator, can best respond to students who fall within these guidelines.

Group facilitators may think that the only productive roles are those in which participants expresses their feelings and are given positive feedback from the group for doing so. There are however a variety of other roles participants experience—both productive and harmful—that are seen when groups spend intensive time together.

Productive Roles for Group Members

Information Seeker—This is a person who asks for clarification from the facilitator or another participant to help the point be better understood by other group members. A person in this role might also ask how a particular point under discussion relates to the overall group goal in order to keep the group focused on its task.

Opinion Seeker—In contrast to the information seeker, this person looks for the values involved in a particular statement and is not as concerned with the facts.

Initiator—A person in this role helps start the group discussion. The initiator also offers new ways of looking at an old problem or presents different ways the group might proceed in tackling a problem with which they are wrestling.

Interpreter—A student in this role will attempt to clarifying feelings expressed by other participants in the group. A participant in this role might also point out how other students' non-verbal behavior is inconsistent with what they are saying.

Supporter—This student models the acceptance of others' points of view through an expression of agreement or understanding.

Coordinator—In an attempt to coordinate the efforts of the group towards an overall goal, a coordinator pulls together points made by several different group members and notes their similarity or difference.

Energizer—This is the person who wants the group to make a decision, to do something, instead of talking an issue to death. In this role the member pushes for commitment and action.

Harmonizer—This is a role for someone who attempts to reconcile conflicts among members or relieve tension in the group through the use of appropriate humor or denial of conflict.

Unproductive Roles

These roles also exist in groups and present the greatest challenge for group facilitators. In counseling work, they are probably the primary reason many counselors prefer to work with individuals instead of accepting the more challenging work with groups.

Aggressor—A common role in which a participant attempts to deflate other group members by taking credit for contributions of others or by mocking others who shares their ideas.

If not properly dealt with immediately, this negative role can be reinforced by other students who are willing to join with the initial aggressor.

One strategy that can take away the power of an aggressor is to agree with them. Empathy expressed to this participant also can have some effect in lowering the amount of their aggression.

Should the aggression be focused toward another group member, the group leader must intervene if the group does not immediately do so. Depending upon how long the group has been together and how cohesive they are will influence how much verbal aggression they will tolerate.

Physical aggression is never allowed within a group setting. Follow the policies of your school or organization for dealing with any form of physical aggression, real or threatened.

Resister—The resister is someone who reacts negatively to nearly every idea brought out in a group. In this role the student might reject ideas for no rhyme or reason and may bring up old material that the group has dealt with and rejected.

The challenge for the facilitator is to find ways to avoid engaging the resister in a power struggle. The effort should be to utilize the resistance in having them buy into the program on some level.

Recognition Seeker—In an attempt to get attention this person will brag, boast or act in strange and unusual ways to draw the focus onto his or her concerns.

The group will usually handle this situation given enough time. Usually, as with other roles, the group will tolerate the action at first and then become very frustrated. Generally, a group will eventually confront consistent attention getting attempts by one member. Should the group not be able to deal with this type of person the facilitator can comment directly, privately if necessary to the person.

Be careful not to just avoid the recognition seeker as a way of punishing their attempts to seek attention. Call them on what they are doing and reinforce them when they are contributing appropriately to the group.

Comedian—Some humor is therapeutic when it breaks the tension or allows participants to laugh at themselves in a healthy way. The student in this negative role, however, uses humor as a defense by making a joke of everything.

Like other roles in this section, the group will usually deal with it over time. But negative humor, designed to put another person down or make fun of someone in a hurtful way should not be tolerated by the facilitator in the initial sessions. This is a good way to model right away what type of behavior is appropriate and what is not in this group.

Again, the person in this role may not be aware of what s/he is doing and some comment from you might be enough to stop it.

Also, their use of appropriate, tension-breaking positive humor should be reinforced.

Monopolizer—One of the most difficult group members for a group facilitator to deal with is the one who wants to talk all the time. Initially, it can often appears that this person is an initiator, but the facilitator soon becomes aware that this member's goal is simply to talk all the time.

While group members initially allow the monopolizer to talk so they will not have to deal with silence or talk themselves, they will eventually become irritated.

This is a role where the leader needs to intervene personally and actively in order not to threaten group norms and to help the group understand why one person would not be allowed to talk too much.

Initially, consider that the group has allowed itself to be monopolized and ask why they are willing to be so manipulated. Next, work directly with the monopolizer in an attempt to communicate that you want to hear more not less from them. The more you want to hear is depth, not constant jabbering to keep the group at arm's length.

This double approach—involving the group and dealing with the monopolizer— has been found to be the most productive stance a facilitator can take.

Silent Member—As challenging as a monopolizer or a resistant participant is the one who never speaks. There are many reasons for not talking such as fear, shame, resistance, shyness. There are also those who feel as if each utterance from their mouth must be perfect and, therefore, never say a word. Whatever the reason, the quiet, uninvolved member is a challenge.

The cause of the silence dictates the leader's response. Observation of the participant in other settings will offer some information as to why the person is silent in the group.

A helpful method of intervention is for the facilitator to comment on the silent participant's nonverbal behavior. What are gestures, facial expressions, or posture saying?

The leader can also have other group members comment on their reaction to the silent member's behavior.

If these methods are unsuccessful, check with this student periodically as a way of including them in the group process.

Victim/Help Rejecting Complainer—An attempt to elicit sympathy is the goal for this role. Statements designed to put oneself down through expressions of inadequacy or insecurities are observed in students in this role.

In addition, many who use this role also complain about how nothing ever goes their way while rejecting any and all offers at help. They are known as "yes-but" members because they agree with your suggestions, but tell you why it won't work for them.

Group members quickly tire of this person's behavior. They move from irritation to frustration and confusion as the participant constantly complains while rejecting any attempts at help.

Although a person in this role is asking for help, they do not actually want it, so the facilitator must be careful not to fall into the trap of giving it.

Also, avoid expressing frustration or resentment to this student as it just feeds the victim role. A better strategy is to help the student see how their problem is related to problems other group members are expressing. Efforts to get this individual to offer help to other members is another useful strategy.

After working with this person in group and, if it fits your style, you can share with this student their expressed attitude of "Why don't you …yes-but," as long as it can be shared in a playful and therapeutic spirit.

Expert—This is the *co-counselor* you don't want. The expert is often a student who has been in a similar group before. They are a "know-it-all" and want to show you and the group just how much they understand problems and concerns of others.

Again, the group will often handle this role by confronting the person with their action, but they will usually only do so after having tolerated the behavior for a while.

The facilitator has a choice of waiting for the group to act (usually the better course) or planning a course of action that asks the expert person for their help by being a "good group member."

Thus, you can ask the student to comment on what they are hearing from other group members, as a way of modeling the ability to reflect feelings, and then have the participant who initially spoke say whether the *expert* was correct or not.

Avoid power struggles with experts, since they are not worth the effort. Find ways to utilize the student's skills or wait for the group to confront them.

Diversity Group Roles

Compiled by Sharon Chappelle and Lisa Bigman as an addendum to the above list.

Discriminators—These are individuals who feel that the benefits developed for groups that have been traditionally discriminated against are, in fact, evidence of discriminatory attitudes toward their own group.

Try to organize your facilitation of the discussion around validating their feelings while creating a context that will provide them with a more in-depth understanding of the historical institutional and individual values that have condoned discrimination in this country. Try evaluating the emotions that surround power. "How do we use power and to what end?" To share it, deprive others of it, to control it, etc. Tread lightly, however, this person is most likely coming from a place of deep-seated anger and resentment.

Invalidators—These individuals are engaged in a contest of one-upmanship about discrimination and feel that their discriminatory experiences are equal to or greater than others in the group. As a result, they may inadvertently invalidate the experiences of other group members. What they mean to do is to connect and instead they offend.

Use your discussion time to validate their feelings and facilitate a group discussion that examines ways to connect with and support the individual.

Deniers—Deniers are individuals who, out of fear, ignorance or, unwillingness refuse to acknowledge their biases and prejudices. A typical statement might be, "when I look at _____ (an individual), I don't see _____ (fill in a qualifier based on race, religion, gender age, sexual orientation, or whatever), but a human being." Generally, this statement is meant as an affirmation of the person alluded to. But what this type of statement really does is to deny a piece of that person's identity. What happens is that the denier's ability to hear and celebrate who that person is has been shut down.

Facilitate a discussion that includes both individuals and that clarifies intentions, concerns, and feelings around this type of statement. When you make an assessment of how to negotiate this type of incident, try to keep the following in mind:

What is the tone or tenor of the entire group?

Will a discussion that involves all the members of the group improve group understanding or will it simply intimidate the individuals concerned with the statement?

How much time do you have to process the issue and how are you going to bring closure to the incident?

Would it be better for the group as a whole to have the individuals process the statement alone with you as their coach?

Process Avoiders—These individuals are generally threatened either by their perceptions, emotions, or a challenge to face their own beliefs, attitudes and feelings. Their body language is revelatory—crossed arms and legs—and they may appear very quiet or sullen. A typical statements from a process avoider is "I really don't have an opinion about that." Or, they will change the subject completely.

When faced with this student, the challenge is to confront them in a delicate and supportive fashion with the fact that their internal process has interrupted the group's processing of the matter at hand. It's very possible that the individual in question may not even be aware of what they are doing. It is only human for us to try to avoid pain. One way of dealing with this problem is to get feedback from the group on how they perceived the exchange, or the attempt to change the momentum and direction of the discussion.

Defenders—These individual are closely related to deniers; they are unable or unwilling to hear another point of view. They feel that their viewpoint is amply justifiable and, indeed, any other possible input may represent a threat to their conception of reality. Typical statements are "but, history supports…" or "I know what you are saying, but I know how it really is." The danger here is that if they do begin to accept another point of view, they may have difficulty holding on to their own long and deeply held beliefs. Then what? How do you replace a reality that has been shattered?

Tread very lightly because these individuals can totally disrupt your group's progress. Defenders are often quite vocal and may be verbalizing what some other members of the group are thinking, but are afraid to voice. If you attack their convictions, you may not only lose their support, but the support of some of the other group members as well. The key here is to offer support in every way possible. Not only do not challenge their views but communicate clearly that you hear them. Give them space to hold on to their viewpoint, but ask that they remain open to hearing what the other members of the group are saying.

Perceived Traitors—These individuals may strongly verbalize their support of and connection to one particular group. In doing so, they deny connection to and support of another group, the members of which may then view this individual as being a traitor to their origins. For example, you may have two individuals whose ethnic origins are Puerto Rican. When asked to choose whether they are white or a person of color, one chooses to identify himself as white and the other as a person of color. The other people of color may perceive this as a betrayal, while the whites aren't really sure.

Check on your own feelings about such issues issue before you jump in to process this type of situation. How do you feel?

This situation exemplifies the importance of supporting an individual's right to self-identify according to what makes them feel most comfortable and to their individual experiences. Stressing this fact and supporting the individual's right to self-identify will help others to keep the dialogue going.

Appendix III

Performing an Emotional Rescue

by H.L. "Lee" Gillis, Ph.D.

Lee Gillis serves as the Therapeutic Strand Manager for Project Adventure and also works with the direct service programs in the Covington, GA office as a consulting psychologist. In addition, he coordinates a Masters of Psychology program in Adventure Therapy at Georgia College in Milledgeville, GA.

I thought it was a car backfiring at first, but the second time I heard it, I was sure it was some 'good old boys' shooting guns on a Saturday afternoon. I wasn't worried that they would shoot into our group on the ropes course, as the sound was several miles away, but I was very aware that the workshop participant on the *Two Line Bridge* was quite affected by the sound. Larry (not his real name) became rigid and began to move so quickly that his belayer anxiously asked him to slow down. The scream that he let out when he reached the end of the element was not one of relief; it was a scream of terror. He quickly pulled himself together without verbally responding to the belayer or to me, the facilitator.

When he descended the element (in perfect form) and was safely on the ground, he unclipped his belay and walked 50 yards away from the group and sat down. He did not appear to be in any physical pain. His nonverbals communicated clearly that he wanted to be by himself. The workshop group and I struggled with how to balance our commitment to the Full Value Contract (FVC), respect what Larry needed, and ensure that he was OK (physically and emotionally).

When we had a *Go 'Round* following the activity and right before supper, Larry returned to the group but waived his turn to speak. I chose to respect this and not push him. When we processed the day's experience following dinner, he began to share his powerfully emotional story. He described an incident from 25 years earlier that had come back to him in vivid detail when he heard the two blasts from the gun earlier that day.

The group became involved in his story and tried to offer some solace as he wept. My mental health training was leading me to believe that Larry had had the kind of flashback associated with post traumatic stress disorder. I was concerned because he talked as though he was not 'in the moment, in the here and now' as the FVC challenges us to be; he spoke as if the trauma was happening all over again. He was also not, in my opinion, in a safe place as the FVC asks us to be.

My thinking was that many in the group, in their attempt to comfort Larry, were inadvertently keeping him in the traumatic scene of 25 years ago. I felt that such a tearful, emotional description was not healthy for Larry or for this group participating in a Project Adventure training: this was not a therapy group! Their questions and comments about what had happened were well meaning, but only served to keep him in the past. How could I facilitate an *emotional rescue* and help Larry come back to the group and back to the training experience for which he and the other group members had contracted? How could I facilitate this with the caring and compassion I felt for Larry?

Perhaps all of us in counseling, youth work, and Adventure programming have had a moment during a game, an initiative, or high ropes course activity when we felt the participant was 'somewhere else.' While we might not be able to put our finger on just where they were, we knew they were not 'in the group' at the moment. They may have appeared to be daydreaming or they may have been showing, like Larry, some signs of being emotionally impacted by events taking place around the activity. During the processing, we may or may not have become aware of just how the participant was affected by the activity.

What guidelines do we have as facilitators for conducting an emotional rescue when we have a feeling that the person needs to be brought back to the group in a safe and compassionate way? While reading this piece is in no way a substitute for training and experience, it does offer some points to consider in the field should an emotional rescue situation present itself to you. Much of the thinking in this article and some paraphrased dialogue comes from work I have done with my friend Martin Ringer, a consultant and group facilitator from Perth, Western Australia, whom I first met at an AEE (Association for Experiential Education) conference in 1992. The background for the concepts used in this article are contained in a past issue of the Journal of Experiential Education (JEE).

The JEE article examines several psychological depth levels that can aid facilitators in determining one dimension of where a group participant is at based on what he or she is saying. Questions the leader may ask (him or herself, not the group) are:

- How is the speaker involved in what they are saying?

- Who else is involved in what the participant is saying?

- To whom would the participant most likely share such information?

- How emotionally involved are they as they speak?.

The actual psychological depth levels will not be discussed here. For the purposes of this article, the reader should understand that many Adventure groups operate in a "current task" level when they discuss observations (facts) of what occurred in an Adventure activity with their group. When a group member speaks of how he or she felt about interactions (among group members) during the activity, he or she is thought to be at the deeper level of 'encounter'. When conversation begins to involve persons not in the current group; e.g., family, friends or co-workers, or events from the past; e.g., recollections or even 're- covered memories', the group member is thought to be speaking at much deeper psychological levels—levels that are more appropriately dealt with in counsel- ing or psychotherapy groups.

When a group member makes a statement that is deeper than the level of emotional or psychological depth than is appropriate for that situation, it is vital that the person's statement is empathetically acknowledged and the con- versation is compassionately returned to the level at which the group has ar- ranged to work. In the illustrated case of a workshop situation, the negotiated level was for training, not for a counseling experience. The contract was to work at the current task and encounter levels, but not to work at levels deeper than that.

There are at least two types of problems that can arise in the process of ac- knowledging and moving back to the agreed level. The first type of problem is that the leader's empathic response may lead a participant or the whole group into further discussion at a deeper level. The second is that the leader—perhaps out of fear or out of a lack of knowing what to do—'cuts off', or worse yet, ignores the participant for fear of deepening the level in the whole group. There is a need for a fine balance.

As a general rule, a leader or facilitator's first response to a statement from a participant that is deeper than the agreed upon level needs to acknowledge how the participant is feeling at that moment. Later, responses can link the group member back to the contracted level. As the leader, I asked myself several questions as Larry was speaking about his past trauma experience. I used my own answers to assist me in navigating through a tricky situation that involved multiple psychological levels.

How is the speaker involved in this? Additional questions here are: "Are they talking about him/herself, or are they talking about other people?" "In what capacity are they talking about themselves?"

In the case illustrated, Larry was totally involved in what he was saying. His experience of personally witnessing multiple deaths was the subject of the con- versation. Evidence gathered by applying the question "How is the speaker involved...", suggested that Larry was re-experiencing himself at a very deep level of emotion.

Who else is involved in this person's world as she/he speaks? This question enables the facilitator to hypothesize about the intensity and importance of the relationships underlying the subject that the participant is speaking about. If the topic of conversation is about persons with whom the speaker has strong emotional ties, such as immediate family members, the conversation will be much deeper than if the topic of conversation is about a person with whom they have no special attachment. In Larry's case, he was recalling vivid memories of people whose tragic deaths he had witnessed. He was in the company of group members with whom he had strong ties when the deaths occurred. He and the group members were deeply impacted as they were responsible for the accidental deaths occurring.

How much emotional arousal are they likely to feel? Larry became quite distressed. He cried out in the group and sobbed as he told his story. The question "How much emotion is the participant likely to feel?" is a very subjective question, one that depends heavily on the leader's own perception of the significance of different emotions and different events. Most of the time, unless a group member chooses to share, we as facilitators of Adventure activities in training situations do not have as much background about participants' emotional vulnerabilities as we do about their physical limitations. This is as it should be in a training situation out of respect for an individual's privacy and confidentiality. Project Adventure's work in direct service of adjudicated youth or others engaged in clearly therapeutic work presents a different story altogether. In this latter situation, we usually have more information about past trauma and past behavior because we are conducting a therapeutic program.

With whom would they normally talk about this? This query establishes the level of privacy normally required for a given topic. Once again, there is wide variation among people and cultures as to who normally talks about what to whom, but this criterion at least gives us a basis from which to work. The context is important. Close friends talking one to one about their intimate relationships may not be 'psychotherapy', but the same people talking about the same topic in the context of a therapeutic group are more likely to be viewed as operating at a level deeper than where the group has contracted to go. Larry did not talk in the whole group about early history, but his reaction indicated clearly to group participants that he was distressed. His sharing of the traumatic event of the past was not inappropriate given his earlier reaction. It was the group's exploration of that past event during the training workshop that I felt violated the contract.

My response to Larry came from experience, training, and a working knowledge of the concept of managing psychological depth (since I was in the process of co-authoring the article with Martin Ringer at the time of the workshop with Larry). Such knowledge was not visible to Larry or the other group participants, yet it perhaps kept the whole group from the potentially turning a training experience into a counseling or psychotherapy group. Such a move towards counseling or psychotherapy in this training group would have been most unethical and unprofessional. The group had contracted for training, not therapy. I had a professional responsibility to operate within that contract.

Even when very familiar with the management of psychological depth, a leader cannot be expected to keep the diagnostic questions noted above in her/his mind at all times. High levels of competence in managing psychological depth require sound personal and professional functioning on the part of the group leader, including good self-management skills, sound psychological health, well developed intuition, and creativity. The first cue that a group member is beginning to operate at a deeper level than the contract calls for may be little more than an intuitive sense of unease on the part of the leader. The astute group leader pays attention to this unease and uses it as a cue to assess where the group is operating and where they might be headed.

The internal awareness of unease or external awareness that something is not right and acknowledging the participant's perspective with a statement that communicates accurate empathy for how they are feeling at that moment is the first step in an emotional rescue. I told Larry that what I observed from him suggested he was in pain as a result of his memory associated with the deaths he had witnessed 25 years ago and for which he felt responsible. He acknowledged that this was accurate. My next step was to try, with compassion, to move Larry from that scene of long ago (however vivid) back to the current group. I used present tense language to express my observations of him during the workshop when he was helping others. I made statements trying to link the experiences and feelings I witnessed from other group members to things I had observed Larry do with them earlier that day and earlier in the workshop.

Group members began to speak to Larry about their experience of him in the present tense. Larry began to regain his composure and the focus of the discussion was brought back to the appropriate subject of reviewing the workshop day and how members felt about their experience of the various activities that day. This was not a callous move on my part, but an compassionate attempt to keep Larry and the group from delving into areas that could not be resolved during a short training, areas of personal experience at a too intense and emotional level for the training experience. In other contexts; e.g., a residential treatment center, and with a more clearly defined contract for therapy, I would have proceeded differently.

What was needed with Larry was some way to contain the conversation at an appropriate level. The emotional rescue strategy worked here. I did check with Larry several times after that group experience to see if he was doing OK. He and I discussed his desire to get involved (again in his case) with a support group once he returned home. These responses were appropriate as a follow-up to the emotional rescue: stabilization, monitoring, and linking with some continued help.

Such rescues might be avoided when group facilitators are clear with group members about the level of interaction and encounter expected during debriefs. Such a discussion is not a fail safe as I had had an extensive conversation with this training group about the difference in training and therapy and the appropriate boundaries for the workshop.

'Things' can happen during any Adventure experience that the leader cannot predict or control. I could not control the gun blast taking place several miles away that Saturday afternoon. I could control the level of briefing and frontloading I did with the group so as to not imply that we would discuss elements of their lives that involved experiences other than were appropriate to their training. Still, as Forrest Gump noted, "it happens". When 'it' did, the strategy of acknowledging where the participant, Larry, was at that moment and helping him move, with the group's, back to an appropriate level, was a useful one in rescuing him and the group from going into deeper psychological levels.

This article originally appeared in *Zip Lines,*
a journal for the field of Adventure and experiential education
published quarterly by Project Adventure, Inc.

Appendix IV

Resource List

In this section, we've listed some of the books, videos, foundations and associations that we've uncovered over the years. The list is by no means exhaustive, and we're sure that you'll find many of your own resources to add to it. Please also check the references listed in each chapter for specific topics.

Books, Educational and Theoretical

Acuna, Rudy. O*ccupied America: A History of Chicanos*. New York: Harper Collins, 1988.

Anderson, Charles H. White Protestant Americans: From National Origins to Religious Groups. Englewood Cliffs, NJ: Prentice-Hall, 1970.

Anderson, Glenn, and Cynthia Grace. "The Black Deaf Adolescent: A Diverse and Underserved Population" *The Volta Review, 93:4* Washington, D.C: The Alexander Graham Bell Association for the Deaf, 1991

Archdeacon, Thomas J. *Becoming American: An Ethnic History*. New York: The Free Press, 1983.

Bailyn, Bernard. *Voyagers to the West: A Passage in the Peopling of America on the Eve of the Revolution*. New York: Vintage Books, 1988.

Baker-Miller, J. *Toward a New Psychology of Women*. Boston: Beacon Press, 1986. Author redefines women's experience and its social/political reflection.

Banks, J. A. *Teaching Strategies for Ethnic Studies*. Boston: Allyn and Bacon, 1991. Major Reference for teaching ethnic studies from kindergarten through high school.

Bell, Derrick. *Faces at the Bottom of the Well: The Permanence of Racism*. New York: Basic Book, Inc., 1992. "Racism is so ingrained that no matter what Blacks do they are doomed to fail as long as ...whites do not see their own well being threatened by the status quo."

Bergin, Victoria. *Special Education Needs in Bilingual Programs*. Rosslyn, VA: National Clearinghouse for Bilingual Education, 1980.

Blank, Renee, and Sandra Slipp. *Voices of Diversity: Real People Talk about Problems and Solutions in a Workplace Where Everyone Is Not Alike*. New York: American Management Association, 1994. Stories about people's experiences in the workplace along with some practical problem solving methods for managing diversity in the workplace.

Blauner, Robert. *Racial Oppression in America.* San Francisco: Harper & Row, 1972. A good overall look at racial oppresssion in America—Black, Latino, Asian, Native American.

Chan, Sucheng. *Asian Americans, An Interpretive History.* Twayne, 1991.

Cheeseboro, James W. *Gay Speak: Gay Male and Lesbian Communications.* Pilgrim Press,1981.

Coles, Robert, and Jon Erickson. *The Middle Americans: Proud and Uncertain.* Boston: Little, Brown & Co., 1971.

Comer, James P. MD, and Alvin F. Poussaint. *Black Child Care, How to Bring up a Healthy Black Child in America: A Guide to Emotional and Psychological Developement* . New York: Simon & Schuster, 1975. A developmental look at issues faced by African American children that also includes insights and methods for dealing constructively with some of the problems they face.

Creighton, Allan, and Paul Kivel. *Helping Teens Stop Violence: A Practical Guide for Counselors, Educators,and Parents.* Emeryville, CA: Hunter House, 1992. A student curriculum guide for helping highschool students as well as other populations deal with oppression and violence.

Cose, Ellis. *The Rage of a Privileged Class.* New York: Harper Collins, 1993.

Dana, Daniel. *Managing Differences: How to Build Better Relationships at Work and Home.* Wolcott, CT: MTI Publications, 1988. Reviews comunication skills necessary to address interpersonal and organizational conflict.

Dickens, Floyd, Jr., and Jacqueline Dickens. *The Black Manager: Making It in the Corporate World.* New York: AMACOM, American Management Association, 1982. This book is the culmination of a lengthy study about how successful black managers coped, survived, and made it in the white corporate world.

Duvall, Lynn. *Respecting Our Differences; A Guide to Getting Along in a Changing World.* Minneapolis: Free Spirit Publishing, 1994.

Erickson, Charlotte. *Invisible Immigrants: The Adaptation of English and Scottish Immigrants in NineteenthCentury America.* New York: Weidenfeld & Nicholson, 1972.

Feldstein, Stanley, and Lawrence Costello (eds.). *The Ordeal of Assimilation.* New York: Anchor Books. 1974.

Ford, Clyde W. *We CAN All Get Along: 50 Steps You Can take to Help End Racism.* New York: Dell Publishing, 1994. Steps that individuals and communities can take to heal injustice and pain of racism.

Fraser, Steven (Editor). *The Bell Curve Wars: Race, Intelligence and the Future of America.* New York: Basic Books, 1995.

Franklin John Hope, and Alfred A. Moss. *From Slavery to Freedom, A History of Negro Americans.* New York: Alfred A. Knopf, 1988. A historical look at the African-American experience in America.

Fussell, Paul. *Class: A Guide Through the American Status System.* New York: Summit Books, 1983.

Gauld, Joseph W. *Character First: The Hyde School Difference.* San Francisco: Institute of Contemporary Studies. Through the use of five "values" — courage, integrity, leadership, curiosity, concern—the Hyde Leadership schools have developed a model for the next millenium where our increasingly diverse global society will find ways to acknowledge, validate and relate to one another.

Gilligan, Carol. *In a Different Voice: Psychological Theory and Women's Development.* Cambridge: Harvard University Press, 1993. "The most insightful book on women, men and the differences between them."

Ginsburg, Herbert. *The Myth of the Deprived Child: Poor Children's Intellect and Education.* Englewood Cliffs, NJ: Prentice-Hall, Inc., 1972. Describes the impact of social economics upon children and their education.

Golab, Caroline. *Immigrant Destinations.* Temple, NC: Temple University Press, 1977.

Greeley, Andrew. *Ethnicity: A Preliminary Reconnaissance.* New York: John Wiley & Sons, 1974.

Haskin,Jim, Hugh F. Butts, MD. *"Don" say no mo' wid yo' mouf dan yo' back kin stan", The Psychology of Black Language.* New York: Barnes & Noble Books, 1973. An interesting discussion about the use of "Black language"

Hacker, Andrew. *Two Nations: Black and White, Separate, Hostile. Unequal.* New York: Charles Scribner and Sons, 1992. Reviews the author's understanding of the role and meaning of the major two races in America today. Discusses how our nation is moving towards two societies, black and white, separate and unequal.

Hansen, Marcus Lee. *The Atlantic Migration, 1607–1860: A History of the Continuing Settlement of the United States.* Cambridge: Harvard University Press, 1940.

Hansen, Marcus Lee. *The Immigrants in American History.* New York: Harpertorch Books, 1940.

Herberg, Will. *Protestant-Catholic-Jew.* Chicago: University of Chicago Press, 1983.

Higham, John. *Strangers in the Land: Patterns of American Nativism.* New York: Atheneum Paperbacks, 1963.

Hill, Linda. *Overcoming Difficulties: Using Multicultural Literature.* Huntington Beach, CA: Teacher Created Materials, Inc., 1994. Activity resource book for primary grades based in literature.

Howe, Irving. *World of Our Fathers.* Schocken Books, 1989.

Jamieson, David, and Julie O'Mara. *Managing Workforce 2000: Gaining the Diversity Advantage.* San Francisco: Jossey-Bass Publishers, 1991.

Johnson, D.W. *Reaching Out: Interpersonal Effectiveness and Self-Actualization.* Boston: Allyn and Bacon, 1993. Theoretical analysis with practical activities for middle and high school students.

Johnson, D.W., and F. P Johnson. *Joining Together: Group Theory and Group Skills.* Englewood Cliffs, NJ: Prentice Hall, 1991.

Jones, Maldwyn Allen. *American Immigration.* Chicago: University of Chicago Press, 1960.

Katz, William Loren. *A History of Multicultural America: Minorities Today.* Austin, TX: Steck Vaughn Publishers, 1993.

Kennedy, Eugene, and Sara C. Charles, M.D. *On Becoming a Counselor: A Basic Guide for Nonprofessional Counselors.* New York: The Continuum Publishing Company, 1990. Provides professional and non-professional counselors with the essential tools needed to respond to counseling concerns with compassion and intelligence.

Kennedy, John E. *A Nation of Immigrants.* San Francisco: Harper & Row, 1964.

Kephart, William M. *Extraordinary Groups: The Sodology of Unconventional Life-Styles.* New York: St. Martin's Press, 1987.

Kivel, Paul. *Men's Work: How to Stop the Violence That Tears Our Lives Apart.* New York: Ballantine Books, 1992. Excellent resource that explores methods for ending male violence.

Kivel, Paul. *Uprooting Racism: How White People Can Work for Racial Justice.* Philadelphia: New Society Publishers, 1996.

Kochman, Thomas. *Black and White Styles in Conflict.* Chicago: University of Chicago Press, Chicago, 1981.

Gutman, Herbert G. *Who Built America? Working People & The Nation's Economy, Politics, Culture and Society.* Vol. 1. American Social History Project. New York: Pantheon Books, 1989.

KunJufu, Jawanza. *Developing Positive Self-Images & Discipline in Black Children.* Chicago: African American Images, 1984.

KunJufu, Jawanza. *To Be Popular or Smart: The Black Peer Group.* Chicago: African-American Images, 1988. This is a good book for adults working in the field of education. A discussion of the difficulties children of African descent face when confronted with the notions that "white equals smart."

Landry, Bart. *The New Black Middle Class.* Berkeley: University of California Press, 1987.

Lapham, Lewis H. *Money and Class in America.* New York: Weidenfeld & Nicholson, 1988.

Loden, Marilyn, and Judy B. Rosener. *Workforce America! Managing Employee Diversity as a Vital Resource.* New York: Irwin Professional Publishing, 1991. Excellent analysis and explanation of what diversity is and what it means to all of us. Also provides insights into how to manage diversity and create positive results.

Loewen, James W. *Lies My Teacher Told Me: Everything Your American History Textbook Got Wrong.* New York: The New York Press, 1995. Honest research of multiethnic histories.

Maldonado, Lionel, and Joan Moore, (eds.). *Urban Ethnicity in the United States.* Sage Publications, 1985.

Marcus, Eric. *Is It A Choice? Answers to 300 of the Most Frequently Asked Questions about Gays and Lesbians.* New York: Harper Collins Publishers, 1993.

Mazer, Anne. (Editor) *Going Where I'm Coming From: Memoirs of American Youth.* New York: Persea Books, Inc., 1995. Fourteen autobiographical narratives of growing up with two cultures

Mizell, Linda. *Think About Racism.* New York: Walker and Company, 1992.

Montague, Ashley. *Man's Most Dangerous Myth: The Fallacy of Race* (4th Edition). Ohio: World Publishing Company, 1965.

Nadler, Reldan S., and John L. Luckner. *Processing the Adventure Experience: Theory and Practice.* Dubuque, IA: Kendall/Hunt Publishing Company, 1992. Theory and practical techniques for immediate application.

Neidle, Cecyle S. *America's Immigrant Women.* Twayne Publishers, 1975.

Newman, Katherine. *Falling From Grace: The Experience of Downward Mobility in the American Middle Class.* New York: The Free Press, 1988.

O'Brine, David J., and Stephen S. Fidget. *The Japanese American Experience.* Bloomington: Indiana University Press, 1991.

Orenstein, Peggy, the and American Association of University Women. *School Girls: Young Women, Self-Esteem and the Confidence Gap.* New York: Anchor Books, 1994

Parr, Susan. *Homophobia; A Weapon of Sexism,* Little Rock, Ark: Susan Parr, The Women's Project, 1988. Little book about the effect of homophobia and sexism in personal/organizational lives.

Pascoe, Elaine. *Issues in American History: Racial Prejudice.* New York: Franklin Watts, 1985. A review of the history of racial prejudice in this country.

Pipher, Mary. *Reviving Ophelia: Saving the Selves of Adolescent Girls.* New York: G.P. Putnam and Sons, 1994.

Rodgers, Carl. *Personal Power.* New York: Delacorte Press, 1977.

Russell, K., M. Wilson, and R. Hall. *Color Complex: The Politics of Skin Color Among African Americans.* Orlando: Harcourt Brace Jovanovich Publishers, 1992. Demonstrates an "insightful examination of color prejudices...and how deeply white racism continues to intrude on black psyche and behavior."

Schaef, Anne Wilson. *Women's Reality: An Emerging Female System in a White Male Society.* San Francisco: Harper & Row, 1981. A surprising look at gender discrimination issues.

Schoel, J., D. Prouty, and P. Radcliffe. *Islands of Healing: A Guide to Adventure Based Counseling.* Hamilton, MA: Project Adventure, Inc., 1988.

Seller, Maxine. *They Seek America: A History of Ethnic Life in the United States.* J.S. Ozer, 1988.

SoIomon, Barbara Miller. *Ancestors and Immigrants, and Changing New England Tradition.* Cambridge: Harvard University Press, 1956.

Steinberg, Stephen. *The Ethnic Myth: Race, Ethnicity, and Class in America.* Saddle Brook, NJ: American Book-Stratford Press, 1981.

Sussman, Harris. *How Diversity Works.* Cambridge, MA: Workaways Press, 1995.

Tatum, Beverly Daniel. *Assimilation Blues: Black Families in a White Community.* Northampton, MA: Hazel-Maxwell Publishing, 1987. An interesting look at African American middle class issues as they relate to those who live in predominantly white communities.

Terkel, Studs. *Race: How Blacks and Whites Think and Feel About the American Obession.* New York: The New Press, 1992. A collection of essays that reflect how blacks and whites feel about race in America today.

Thomas, R. Roosevelt Jr. *Beyond Race and Gender: Unleashing the Power of Your Total Work Force by Managing Diversity.* New York: Amerian Management Association, 1991. Looks at the total realm of diversity issues.

Ward, Collen A. *Altered States of Consciousness and Mental Health: A Cross Cultural Perspective.* Sage Publications, 1989. Cross cultural views of insane/healing aspects of altered states.

Ward, David. *Cities and Immigrants: A Geography of Change in Nineteenth-Century America.* Oxford: Oxford University Press, 1971.

Weatherford, Jack. *Indian Givers: How the Indians of the Americas Transformed the World.* New York: Fawcett Columbine, 1988. Resource about the influence of Native American culture on the world.

Weisberger, Bernard A. *The American People.* New York: American Heritage. 1971.

West, Come. *Race Matters.* New York: Vintage Books, 1994.

Books: Fiction and Non Fiction for Youth and Adults

Anaga, Rudolfo A. *Bless Me, Ultimo*. Tonatiuli - Quinto Sol International, 1972. Non-fiction. Story of a Latino youth. Grades 8 and up.

Angelou, Maya. *I Know Why the Caged Bird Sings*. New York: Random House, 1970. Non-fiction. Recommended for grades 7 and up.

Ashabranner, Brent. *Children of the Maya: A Guatemalan Indian Odyssey*. New York: G.P. Putnam & Sons, 1986. Non-fiction. Grades 9 and up.

Augenbraum, Harold, and Lian Stevens (editors*). Growing Up Latino: Memories & Stories*. Boston: Houghton Miffin Co., 1993. A compilation of memoirs about growing up Latino in the United States.

Bode, Janet. *New Kids on the Block: Oral History of Immigrant Teens*. New York: Franklin Watts Inc.,1989. Non-fiction. Stories of Asian American youth. For grades 7 and up.

Brimmer, Larry Dane. *A Migrant Family*. Lamer, 1992. Non-fiction. Grades 5 through 8.

Brooks, Bruce. *The Moves Make the Man*. New York: Harper Collins, 1984. Fiction. The story of an African American youth. Recommended reading for grades 7 through 12.

Brown, Dee. *Bury My Heart at Wounded Knee: An Indian History of the American West*. Orlando: Holt, Rinehard & Winston, 1971. Non-fiction. Grades 9 and up.

Brownstone, David. *The Chinese-American Heritage*. New York: Facts on File, 1988. Non-fiction. For grades 7 and up..

Cisneros, Sandra. *The House on Mango Street*. Arte Publico. 1984. Fiction. Grades 12 and up.

Cosby, Bill, *Childhood*. New York: G.P. Putnam & Sons, 1991. A full funny, enlightening look at childhood.

Dorris, Michael. *Morning Girl*. New York: Hyperion, 1992. Non-fiction. Grades 5 through 9.

Dorris, Michael. *A Yellow Raft in Blue Water*. Orlando: Holt, Rinehard & Winston, 1987. Non-fiction. Grades 9 and up.

Erdrich, Louise. *Love Medicine, The Beet Queen and Tracks*. . Orlando: Holt, Rinehard & Winston, 1984. Non-fiction. Grades 9 through 12.

Greenberg, Joanne. *I Never Promised You a Rose Garden*. NAL, 1964. Fiction. Grades 7 through 12.

Greene, Bette. *Summer of My German Soldier*. New York: Dial Books for Young Readers, 1973. Fiction. Grades 10 and up.

Hill, Kirkpatrick. *Toughboy and Sister*. Macmillan/Margaret K. McElderry, 1990. Fiction. Grades 4 and up.

Huynh, Quang Nhuong. *The Land I Lost: Adventures of a Boy in Vietnam*. New York: Harper Books,1982. Non-fiction. The story of a Vietnamese youth. For grades 5 and up.

Kotowitz, Alex. *There Are No Children Here: The Story of Two Boys Growing Up in the Other America*. New York: Doubleday & Sons, 1991. Non fiction, grades 7 and up.

Miller, Arthur. *Incident at Vichy*. New York: Penguin, USA, 1965. Non-fiction. Grades 7 and up.

Morrison, Toni. *Beloved*. New York: Alfred A. Knopf, 1987. Fiction. Recommended for grades 10 and up.

Myers, Walter Dean. *Scorpions*. New York: Harper Collins, 1988. Fiction. Recommended for grades 10 and up.

Ng, Fac Mgenne. *Bone*. New York: Hyperion Books. 1993. Fiction. A story of Asian American youth. For grades 7 and up.

Oates, Stephen. *Let the Trumpet Sound: The Life of Martin Luther King*. NAL, 1982. Non-fiction. A biography of Martin Luther King.

Perera, Hilda. *KiKi: A Cuban Boy's Adventures in America*. Translated by Warren Humpton & Hilda Gonzalez. Pickering Press, 1992. Non-fiction. Grades 8 and up.

Richter, Conrad. *A Light in the Forest*. New York: Alfred A. Knopf, 1953. Fiction. Grades 7 and up.

Sanders, Dori. *Clover*. New York: Algonquin Press, 1990. Fiction. Recommended for grades 8 and up.

Tan, Amy. *The Joy Luck Club*. New York: G.P. Putnam's Sons, 1989. Fiction. Best-selling novel about Chinese American women and their mothers. For grades 5 and up.

Taylor, Mildred. *Roll of Thunder, Hear My Cry*. New York: Bantam Books. 1976. Fiction.

Wolff, Virginia Euwer. *The Mozart Season*. . Orlando: Holt, Rinehard & Winston, 1991. Fiction. Grades 5 through 9.

Wright Edelman. Marian. *The Measure of Our Success A Letter to My Children & Yours*. New York: Harper Collins, 1992. A wonderful evaluation of how our country views and treats our children. The book's center piece is a letter to her sons with "twenty-five Lessons of Life.

X, Malcolm and Haley, Alex. *The Autobiography of Malcolm X*. New York: Ballantine Books, 1965. Non-fiction.

Other Multicultural Resources

Alternative Videos
837 Exposition Avenue
Dallas, TX 75226
(214) 823-6030

African-American Culture & Arts Network, Inc.
2090 Adam Clayton Powell Blvd.
New York, NY 10031
(212) 749-4408
(800) 439-6262

Afro-American History and Cultures Exhibit
Anacostia Neighborhood Museum
Smithsonian Institution
1921 Fort Place, SE
Washington, DC 20020
(202) 287-3306

National Museum of African Art
Smithsonian Institution
950 Independence Avenue, SW
Washington, DC 20560
(202) 357-4600

American Visions
Visions Foundation, Inc.
Carter G. Woodson House
1538 Ninth Street, NW
Washington, DC 20001
(202) 462-1779

Association for the Study of Afro-American Life & History
140 12th Street, NW
Washington, DC 20005
(202) 667-2822

DuSable Museum
57th and Cottage Grove
Chicago, IL 60637
(312) 947-0600

Midwest Desegregation Center
401 Bluemont Hall
Kansas State Uniyersity
Manhattan, KS 66506
(913) 532-6408

Museum of Afro-American History
P.O. Box 5
Boston, MA02119
(617) 742-1852

Schomburg Center for Research in Black Culture
515 Malcolm X Boulevard
New York, NY 10037
(212) 491-2200

Studio Museum in Harlem
144 West 125th Street
New York, NY 10027
(212) 864-4500

Arthur M. Sadder Gallery
1050 Independence Avenue, SW
Washington, DC 20560
(202) 357-1300

Asia Sodety
725 Park Avenue
New York, NY 10021
(212) 288-6400

Asian and Pacific American Chamber
of Commerce
1112 Carper Street
McLean, VA 22101
(202) 659-4037

Asian and Pacific Island Curricular Materials and Professional Development Materials Evaluation, Dissemination and Assessment Center
California State University at Los Angeles
5151 State University Drive
Los Angeles, CA 90032

Bureau of East Asia and Pacific Affairs
Department of State Public Affairs
Room 5310, 2201 C Street, NW
Washington, DC 20520
(202) 647-2538

Japan Society
333 E. 47th Street
New York,NY 10017
(212) 832-1155

Korean Information Service
14134 22nd Street, NW
Washington, DC 20037
(202) 296-4256

Library of Congress
Asian Division
Washington, DC 20540
(202) 287-5420

Oriental Library
University of California at Los Angeles
Room 21617, Research Library
Los Angeles, CA 90014

Pacific Asia Museum
46 N. Los Robles
Pasadena, CA 91101
(818) 449-2742

The East-West Center
1777 East-West Road
Honolulu, HI 96848
(808) 944-7204

**American Academy of Arts
and Letters**
633 West 155th Street
New York, NY 10032
(212) 368-5900

Center for Inter-American Relations
680 Park Avenue
New York, NY10021
(212) 249-8950

Central America in the Classroom
Network of Educators on Central
America
1118 22nd Street, NW
Washington, DC 20037
(202) 429-0137

**Council on Hemispheric Affairs
(COHA)**
1900 L Street, NW, Suite 201
Washington, DC 20036
(202) 775-0216

Hispanic Magazine
Hispanic Publishing Corporation
11 Massachusetts Avenue, NW
Suite 410
Washington, DC 20001

Hispanic Sodety
613 West 155th Street
New York, NY 10032
(212) 690-0743

**Information Services on Latin
America (ISLA)**
4641 9thStreet
Oakland, CA 94612
(415) 835-0678

Library of Congress
Hispanic Division
Room 239E
Washington, DC 20540
(202) 287-5420

Museo del Barrio
1230 5th Avenue
New York, NY 10629
(212)831-7272

Washington Office on Latin America
110 Maryland Avenue, NE
Washington, DC 20002
(202) 544-8045

Alaska Native Arts and Crafts Center of Fairbanks, Alaska
1603 College Road
Fairbanks, AK 99701
(907) 456-2323

American Indian Archaeological Institute
Curtis Road 1 Off Route 199
P. O. Box 260
Washington, DC 06793
(203) 868-0518

American Indian Community House
404 Lafayette Street
New York, NY 10003
(212) 598-0100

Center of the American Indian
2100 Northeast 52nd Street
Kirkpatrick Center
Oklahoma City, OK 73111
(405) 427-5461

Cherokee National Museum (Heritage Center)
P.O. Box 515
Tahlequah, OK 74464
(918) 456-6007

Chickasaw Council House Museum
Court House Square, P.O. Box 717
Tishomingo, OK 73460
(405) 371-3351

Choctaw Council House Historical Museum
Route 1, Box 105-3A
Tuskohoma, OK. 74574
(918) 569-4465

Creek Council House and Museum
Town Square
Okmulgee, OK 74447
(918) 756-2324

Eight Northern Pueblo Indian Artisans Guild
P.O. Box 1079
San Juan Pueblo, NM 87566
(505) 852-4283

Field Museum of Natural History
Roosevelt Road at Lake Shore Dr.
Chicago, IL 60505
(312) 922-9410

The Five Civilized Tribes Museum
Agency Hill, Honor Heights Drive
Muskogee, OK 74401
(918) 683-1701

Indian Pueblo Cultural Center, Inc.
2401 12thStreet,NW
Albuquerque, NM 87102
(505) 843-7270 or 843-7271

Iroquois Indian Museum
Box 158, N. Main Street, Dep~ DB
Schoharie, NY 12157
(518) 295-8553

Kiowa Tribal Museum
RO. Box 369
Carnegie, OK 73015
(405) 654-2300

Makali Cultural and Research Center
P.O. Box 95
Neah Bay, WA 98357
(206) 645-2711

Mescalero Apache Cultural Center
P.O. Box 175
Mescalero, NM 88340
(505) 671-4495

Mound City Group National Monument
16062 State Route 104
Chilicothe, OH 45601
(614) 774-1125

Museum of the American Indian
Heye Foundation
155th Street and Broadway
New York, NY 10032
(212) 283-2420

Museum of the Cherokee Indian
US Highway 441 North
P.O. Box 770-A
Cherokee, NC 28719
(704) 497-3481

Museum of Indian Heritage
6040 De Long Road
Eagle Creek Park
Indianapolis, IN 46254
(317) 293-4488

Museum of Native American Culture
East 200 Cataldo Street
Spokane, WA 99220
(509) 326-4550

Museum of the Plains Indians and Craft Center
P.O. Box 400
Browning, MT 59417
(406) 338-2230

Navajo Tribal Museum
Box 308, Highway 264
Wmdow R6ck, AZ 86515
(602) 871-6673 or 6675

Osage Tribal Museum
Osage Agency Campus
Grandview Avenue
Pawhuska, OK 74056
(918) 287-2495, ext. 280

Pueblo Grande Museum
4619 East Washington Street
Phoenix, AZ 85034
(602) 275-3452

Seminole Nation Museum
P.O.Box 1532
524 South Wewoka Avenue
Wewoka, OK 74884
(405) 257-5580

Seneca-Iroquois National Museum
RO. Box 442, Broad St. Extension
Salamanca, NY 14779
(716) 945-1738

Sioux Indian Museum
Box 1504
Rapid City, SD 57709
(605) 348-0557 or 8834

Society for American Indian Studies and Research
RO. Box 443
Hurst, IX 76053
(817)~281-3784

Southeast Alaska Indian Culture Center
RO. Box 944
Sitka,AK 99835
(907) 747-6281

Southwestern Association on Indian Affairs, Inc.
La Fonda Hotel
Santa Fe, NM 87501
(505) 983-5220

United Indians of All Tribes Foundation
Daybreak Star Arts Center
Discovery Park
P.O. Box 99253
Seattle, WA 98199
(206) 285-4425

Robert H. Lowie Museum of Anthropology
University of California
103 Kroeber Hall
Berkeley, CA 94720
(415) 642-3681

Wheelwright Museum of the American Indian
704 Camino Lejo
P.O.~Box 5153
Santa Fe, NM 87502
(505) 982-4636

Claudia's Caravan
P.O.Box 1582
Alameda, CA 94501
(501) 521-7871

Baldi Institute for Ethnic Studies
18 S.7th Street
Philadelphia, PA 19106
(215) 925-8292

Appalachia Educational Laboratory
ERIC Clearinghouse for Rural and Small Schools
P.O. Box 1348
Charleston, WV 25325
(800) 624-9120

CHIME/National Center for Immigrant Students
100 Boylston Street, #737
Boston, MA 02116
(800) 441-7192
(617) 357-8507

Ethnic Materials Information Exchange Task Force
68–78 Bell Boulevard
Bayside,NY 11364
(212) 229-1510 or 520-7194

Immigration History Society
690 Cedar Street
St. Paul, MN 55101

Information Center on Children's Cultures
331 East 38th Street
New York, NY 10016
(212) 686-5522

Multicultural Review
Greenwood Publishing Group
88 Post Road West
P.O. Box 5007
Westport, CT 06881-5007

National Association of Bilingual Education
810 1st Street, NE, 3rd Floor
Washington, DC 20002
(202) 898-1829

National Geographic Traveler
P.O. Box 37054
Washington, DC 20036
(202) 828-5485

Society for Ethnomusicology
Box 2984
Ann Arbor,MI 15106
(313) 663-1947

Southwest Educational Development Laboratory
211 East 7th Street
Austin, TX 78701
(512) 4Y6-6861

Videos

The Songs Are Free
1991. Mystic Fire Video. 58 min.
$29.95.
Grades: 10–12.

Black Americans of Achievement
1992. Library Video Company.
12 Titles (each 30 minutes), $39.95 each
Grades: 9–2.

Family Gathering
1989. PBS Video. 60 min. $59.95.
Grades:10–12.

American Eyes
1990. The Media Guild. 30 min.
$345.00.
Grades: 8–12.

Victor
1989. Ban Films. 25 min. $420.00.
Grades:5–7.

Chicano Park
1989. The Cinema Guild. 60 min.
$350.00.
Grades:9–12.

Molly S. Pilgrim
1985. Phoenix BFA. 24 min. $325.00.
Grades:10–12.

Broken Treaties
1989. Coronel 33 minutes. $250.00.
Grades: 7–12.

Words on a Page
1986. Beacon. 28 minutes. $149.00.
Grades: 5–8.

Internet Sites Relevant to Cultural Diversity

African Studies Web

(http://www. African.upenn.edu/African - Studies/AS.html)

Asian American Resources

(http://yuggoth.ces.cwru.edu/yamauchi/ar.html)

Chicano-Latino Net

(gopher://Iatino, sscnet.ucIa.edu/1)

Diversity—University of Maryland, College Park

(http://www.inform.und.edu/EdRes/Topic/Diversity)

Ethnic Heritage Council

(http://www.eskimo.com/-millerd/ehc)

Inter-Tribal Network for Native Americans

(gopher://cns.csns.com:70/11/News%20%2Olnformation/itn)

Latin American Network Information Center

(gopher://lanic.utexas.edU:7O/1)

Links to Indian In formation

(http://www.fcaglp.unlp.edu.ar/-spaoli/india/india2.html)

Multicultural Alliance

(http://branson.org/mca/index.html)

National Center for Research on Cultural Diversity and Second Language Learning

(http//lzzyx. Ucsc.edu/Cntr/cntr/html)

The Pluribus Unum Gopher

(gopher://pluribus.tc.columbia.edu/)

Appendix V

Activity Index

Ice Breakers

De-Inhibitizers

Trust Building

Group Initiative/Problem Solving

Social Responsibility

Project Adventure
Services and Publications

Services

Project Adventure, Inc. is a national, non-profit corporation dedicated to helping schools, youth groups, camps, corporations, counseling groups, physical education programs and others implement Project Adventure ideas. Characterized by an atmosphere that is fun, supportive and challenging, Project Adventure programs use non-competitive games, group problem-solving Initiatives and ropes course events as the principal activities to help individuals reach their goals; to improve self-esteem, to develop strategies that enhance decision making, and to learn to respect differences within a group. Toward these ends, the following services are available:

Project Adventure Workshops

Through a network of national certified trainers, Project Adventure conducts workshops for teachers, counselors, youth workers, and other professionals who work with people. These workshops are given in various sections of the country. Separate workshops are offered in Project Adventure Games and Initiatives, Challenge Ropes Course Skills, Counseling Theory and Techniques for Adventure Based Programs, and Interdisciplinary Academic Curriculum.

Challenge Course Design and Installation

Project Adventure has been designing and installing ropes courses (a series of individual and group challenge elements situated indoors in a gymnasium or outdoors in trees) since 1971. PA Staff can travel to your site and design/install a course appropriate for your needs and budget.

Equipment Sales

A catalog service of hard-to-find props, materials and tools used in adventure programs and the installation and use of Challenge Ropes Courses.

Corporate Programs

Management workshops for business people and professionals. These workshops are designed for increasing efficiency of team members in the workplace. The trust, communication, and risk-taking ability learned in these programs translate into a more cohesive and productive team at work.

Program Accreditation

The Accreditation process is an outside review of a program by PA staff. Programs that undertake the accreditation process are seeking outside evaluation with regard to quality and safety. The term accreditation means "formal written confirmation." Programs seeking confirmation are looking to ensure that they are within the current standards of safety and risk management. This assurance may be useful for making changes in program equipment and/or design, and in providing information on program quality to third parties such as administrators, insurance companies and the public.

Publications

If you would like to obtain additional copies of this book, an order form is provided on the next page. Project Adventure also publishes many books in related areas. Described below are some of our best sellers, which can be ordered on the same form. Call or write to Project Adventure for a complete publications list.

■ QuickSilver

Adventure Games, Initiative Problems, Trust Activities and a Guide to Effective Leadership

This latest offering from cooperative games master Karl Rohnke contains over 150 new games, problem solving initiatives, ice breakers, variations on old standards, trust, closures and more. There is also a section on leadership with co-author, Steve Butler, in which they impart many of the *secrets* that they use when leading and designing programs.

by Karl Rohnke and Steve Butler

■ Cowstails and Cobras II

Karl Rohnke's classic guide to games, Initiative problems and Adventure activities. Offering a thorough treatment of Project Adventure's philosophy and approach to group activities, *Cowstails II* provides both the experienced practitioner and the novice with a unique and valuable resource.

By Karl Rohnke

■ Silver Bullets

More Initiative problems, Adventure games and trust activities from Karl Rohnke: 165 great games and activities that require few, if any, props. Use this as a companion to *Cowstails and Cobras II* or a stand alone guide to invigorate your program.

By Karl Rohnke

■ Youth Leadership In Action

All too often young people have little access to the resources necessary to improve their skills and develop their leadership potential. *Youth Leadership In Action* addresses this need by providing a guide for youth leaders to implement experiential, cooperative activities and techniques into their programs.

But the most striking and unique feature of this book is that it was written by a group of youth leaders. This group of eight leaders have taken 54 of Project Adventure's most popular Adventure games and activities and rewritten the instructions and rules in the way *they* present and play them. They also give a brief history of Project Adventure, present their own definition of Adventure, and explain some of PA's basic concepts and techniques — Full Value Contract, Challenge By Choice, debriefing, sequencing, etc. They also provide a section on effective leadership and how to start several types of programs.

Edited by Steve Fortier

■ Islands of Healing
A Guide to Adventure Based Counseling

Long a standard in the field, *Islands* presents a comprehensive discussion of this rapidly growing counseling approach. Started in 1974, ABC is an innovative, community-based, group counseling model that uses cooperative games, Initiative problem solving, low and high Challenge Ropes Course elements, and other Adventure activities. The book contains extensive " how-to" information on group selection, training, goal setting, sequencing, and leading and debriefing activities. Also included are explorations of model ABC programs at several representative sites — junior and senior high schools, a psychiatric hospital, and court referred programs.

By Jim Schoel, Dick Prouty, and Paul Radcliffe